Introduction to Organic Laboratory Techniques:

A Small Scale Approach
Chem 315 | 318

George Mason University

Donald L. Pavia | Gary M. Lampman | George S. Kriz | Randall G. Engel

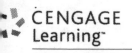
CENGAGE
Learning

Australia • Brazil • Japan • Korea • Mexico • Singapore • Spain • United Kingdom • United States

CENGAGE
Learning™

Introduction to Organic Laboratory Techniques: A Small Scale Approach, Chem 315 | 318, George Mason University

A Small Scale Approach to Organic Laboratory Techniques, 3rd Edition
Donald L. Pavia | Gary M. Lampman | George S. Kriz | Randall G. Engel

© 2011 Cengage Learning. All rights reserved.

Executive Editors:
Maureen Staudt
Michael Stranz

Senior Project Development Manager:
Linda deStefano

Marketing Specialist:
Courtney Sheldon

Senior Production/Manufacturing Manager:
Donna M. Brown

PreMedia Manager:
Joel Brennecke

Sr. Rights Acquisition Account Manager:
Todd Osborne

Cover Image:
Getty Images*

*Unless otherwise noted, all cover images used by Custom Solutions, a part of Cengage Learning, have been supplied courtesy of Getty Images with the exception of the Earthview cover image, which has been supplied by the National Aeronautics and Space Administration (NASA).

For product information and technology assistance, contact us at
Cengage Learning Customer & Sales Support, 1-800-354-9706

For permission to use material from this text or product,
submit all requests online at **cengage.com/permissions**
Further permissions questions can be emailed to
permissionrequest@cengage.com

This book contains select works from existing Cengage Learning resources and was produced by Cengage Learning Custom Solutions for collegiate use. As such, those adopting and/or contributing to this work are responsible for editorial content accuracy, continuity and completeness.

Compilation © 2010 Cengage Learning
ISBN-13: 978-1-111-40114-6

ISBN-10: 1-111-40114-4

Cengage Learning
5191 Natorp Boulevard
Mason, Ohio 45040
USA
Cengage Learning is a leading provider of customized learning solutions with office locations around the globe, including Singapore, the United Kingdom, Australia, Mexico, Brazil, and Japan. Locate your local office at:
international.cengage.com/region.

Cengage Learning products are represented in Canada by Nelson Education, Ltd.
For your lifelong learning solutions, visit **www.cengage.com/custom.**
Visit our corporate website at **www.cengage.com.**

Printed in the United States of America

This book is dedicated to our organic
chemistry laboratory students.

Preface

STATEMENT OF MISSION AND PURPOSE IN REVISING THE TEXTBOOK

The purpose of this lab book is to teach students the techniques of organic chemistry. We desire to share our love of the organic chemistry lab and the joy it brings us with our students! In this edition, we have provided many new, up-to-date experiments that will demonstrate how organic chemistry is evolving. For example, new experiments involving nanotechnology and biofuels are included in this book. We have also selected several new experiments based on Nobel Prize awards, such as using organometallic catalysts for synthesis (Sonogashira coupling using a palladium catalyst and Ring-Opening-Metathesis polymerization using a Grubbs catalyst). Several new Green Chemistry experiments are also included, and the "green" aspects of experiments from our previous book have been improved. We think that you will be enthusiastic about this new edition. Many of the new experiments will not be found in other laboratory manuals, but we have been careful to retain all of the standard reactions and techniques, such as the Friedel-Crafts reaction, aldol condensation, Grignard synthesis, and basic experiments designed to teach crystallization, chromatography, and distillation.

SCALE IN THE ORGANIC LABORATORY

When we set out to write the first edition of *Introduction to Organic Laboratory Techniques: A Small-Scale Approach*, we initially envisioned it as a "fourth edition" of our successful "macroscale" organic laboratory textbook. During this period, we had gained experience with microscale techniques in the organic laboratory through the development of experiments for the microscale versions of our laboratory textbook. That experience taught us that students *can* learn to do careful work in the organic laboratory on a small scale. Since there are many advantages to working on a smaller scale, we recast our "macroscale" textbook as a **small-scale** approach to the laboratory. Working on a smaller scale greatly reduces cost since fewer chemicals are required and less waste is generated. There are also significant safety benefits due to the release of fewer hazardous fumes into the laboratory and a decreased chance of fires or explosions.

In the traditional macroscale approach, the chemical quantities used are on the order of 5–100 grams. In our version of the macroscale approach, called **small-scale**, the experiments use smaller amounts of chemicals (1–10 grams) and employ ℑ 19/22 standard tapered glassware. The microscale approach is described in another one of our textbooks, entitled *Introduction to Organic Laboratory Techniques: A Microscale Approach, Fourth Edition*. The experiments in the microscale book use very small amounts of chemicals (0.050–1.000 g) and ℑ 14/10 standard tapered glassware.

v

MAJOR FEATURES OF THE TEXTBOOK THAT WILL BENEFIT THE STUDENT

Organic chemistry significantly impacts our lives in the real world. Organic chemistry plays a major role in industry, medicine, and consumer products. Composite plastics are being increasingly used in cars and airplanes to decrease weight while increasing strength. Biodiesel is a hot topic today as we try to find ways to reduce our need for petroleum and replace it with materials that are renewable. Sustainability is the key word here. We need to replace the resources that we consume.

A number of experiments are linked together to create multistep syntheses. The advantage of this approach is that you will be doing something different from your neighbor in the laboratory. Wouldn't you like to be carrying out an experiment that is not the same as your neighbor's? Maybe you will be synthesizing a new compound that hasn't been reported in the chemical literature! You and your fellow students will not all be doing the same reaction on the same compounds: for example, some of you will be carrying out the chalcone reaction, others green epoxidation, and still others cyclopropanation of the resulting chalcones.

NEW TO THIS EDITION

Since the second edition of our small-scale textbook appeared in 2005, new developments have emerged in the teaching of organic chemistry in the laboratory. This third edition includes many new experiments that reflect these new developments. This edition also includes significant updating of the essays and chapters on techniques.

New experiments added for this edition include:

Experiment 1	Solubility: Part F Nanotechnology Demonstration
Experiment 25	Biodiesel
Experiment 26	Ethanol from Corn
Experiment 29	Reduction of Ketones Using Carrot Extract
Experiment 34	Aqueous-Based Organozinc Reactions
Experiment 35	Sonogashira Coupling of Iodoaromatic Compounds with Alkynes
Experiment 36	Grubbs-Catalyzed Metathesis of Eugenol with cis-1,4-Butenediol
Experiment 38	A Green Enantioselective Aldol Condensation Reaction
Experiment 40	Preparation of Triarylpyridines
Experiment 48	Synthesis of a Polymer Using Grubbs' Catalyst
Experiment 50	Diels-Alder Reaction with Anthracene-9-methanol
Experiment 58	Competing Nucleophiles in S_N1 and S_N2 Reactions: Investigations Using 2-Pentanol and 3-Pentanol
Experiment 64	Green Epoxidation of Chalcones
Experiment 65	Cyclopropanation of Chalcones

We have also included a new essay on biofuels. Substantial revisions were made to the *Petroleum and Fossil Fuels* essay, and other essays have been updated as well.

We have made a number of improvements in this edition that significantly enhance safety in the laboratory. We have also added several new experiments that incorporate the principles of Green Chemistry. The Green Chemistry experiments decrease the need for hazardous waste disposal, leading to reduced contamination of the environment. Other experiments have been modified to reduce their use of hazardous solvents. In our view, it is most timely that students begin to think about how to conduct chemical experiments in a more environmentally benign manner. Many other experiments have been modified to improve their reliability and safety.

For the qualitative analysis experiment (Experiment 55), we have added a new optional test that can be used in place of the traditional chromic acid test. This new test is safer and does not require contact with hazardous chromium compounds. In keeping with the Green Chemistry approach, we have suggested an alternative way of approaching qualitative organic analysis. This approach makes extensive use of spectroscopy to solve the structure of organic unknowns. In this approach, some of the traditional tests have been retained, but the main emphasis is on using spectroscopy. In this way, we have also attempted to show students how to solve structures in a more modern way, similar to that used in a research laboratory. The added advantage to this approach is that waste is considerably reduced. The tables of unknowns for the qualitative analysis experiment (Experiment 55 and Appendix 1) have been greatly expanded.

New techniques have also been introduced in this edition. Two Green Chemistry experiments involve techniques such as solid phase extraction and the use of a microwave reaction system. Chiral gas chromatography has been included in the analysis of the products obtained in two experiments. A size-exclusion-chromatography column has been added to an HPLC unit to obtain molecular weights of polymers. A new method of obtaining boiling points using a temperature probe with a Vernier LabPro interface, laptop computer, and temperature probe has also been introduced.

Many of the chapters on techniques have been updated. New problems have been added to the chapters on infrared and NMR spectroscopy (Techniques 25, 26, and 27). Many of the old 60 MHz NMR spectra have been replaced by more modern 300 MHz spectra. As in previous editions, the techniques chapters include both microscale and macroscale methods.

CUSTOMIZED OPTIONS

Because we realize that the traditional, comprehensive laboratory textbook may not fit every classroom's needs or every student's budget, we offer the opportunity to create personalized course materials. This book can be purchased in customized formats that may exclude unneeded experiments, include your local materials, and, if desired, incorporate additional content from other Cengage Learning, Brooks/Cole products. For more information on custom possibilities, visit **www.signaturelabs.com** or contact your local Cengage Learning, Brooks/Cole representative. You can find contact information for your representative by visiting **www.cengagelearning.com** and using the "Find Your Rep" link at the top of the page.

SUPPORTING RESOURCES

Premium Companion Website with Pre-Lab Technique Video Exercises

The new, optional, premium companion website offers videos illustrating the steps required to *assemble an apparatus* or *carry out a technique* used in this book. These exercises can be viewed *prior* to going to the laboratory so students can visualize the set-ups in addition to reading the technique description. Techniques with videos available are indicated with an asterisk in the Required Reading list at the start of each experiment and by a margin note at the beginning of the technique. The lab videos feature questions that can be assigned to students prior to attending lab, to ensure that they are prepared. An access card for the website may be bundled with a new book, or students can purchase Instant Access at **www.cengagebrain.com** with ISBN 0495911003.

Instructor's Manual

We would like to call your attention to the Instructor's Manual that accompanies our textbook and which is available as a digital download to qualified instructors. The manual contains complete instructions for the preparation of reagents and equipment for each experiment, as well as answers to each of the questions in this textbook. In some cases, additional optional experiments are included. Other comments that should prove helpful to the instructor include the estimated time to complete each experiment—and notes regarding special equipment or reagent handling.

We strongly recommend that instructors obtain a copy of this manual by visiting **www.cengage.com/chemistry/pavia** and following the instructions at the Faculty Companion site. You may also contact your local Cengage Learning, Brooks/Cole representative for assistance. Contact information for your representative is available at **www.cengagelearning.com** through the "Find Your Rep" link at the top of the page.

Digital Files of Text Art

New for this edition, select text art will be available for download of digital files from the Faculty Companion website for this textbook by visiting www.cengage.com/chemistry/pavia. These files can be used to prepare PowerPoint sets, overhead transparencies, and other lab documents.

ACKNOWLEDGMENTS

We owe our sincere thanks to the many colleagues who have used our textbooks and who have offered their suggestions for changes and improvements to our laboratory procedures or discussions. Although we cannot mention everyone who has made important contributions, we must make special mention of Albert Burns (North Seattle Community College), Charles Wandler (Western Washington University), Emily Borda (Western Washington University), and Frank Deering (North Seattle Community College), Gregory O'Neil (Western Washington University), James Vyvyan (Western Washington University), Jeff Covey (North Seattle Community College), Kalyn Owens (North Seattle CommunityCollege), Nadine Fattaleh (Clark College), Timothy Clark (Western Washington University), Tracy Furutani (North Seattle Community College).

In preparing this new edition, we have also attempted to incorporate the many improvements and suggestions that have been forwarded to us by the many instructors who have been using our materials over the past several years.

We thank all who contributed, with special thanks to our Executive Editor, Lisa Lockwood; Senior Development Editor, Peter McGahey; Assistant Editor, Elizabeth Woods; Senior Content Project Manager, Matthew Ballantyne; Media Editor,

Stephanie VanCamp; Marketing Manager, Nicole Hamm; Pre-Production Editor at Pre-Press PMG; and Rebecca Heider, who filled in admirably during Peter McGahey's paternity leave.

We are especially grateful to the students and friends who have volunteered to participate in the development of experiments or who offered their help and criticism. We thank Gretchen Bartleson, Greta Bowen, Heather Brogan, Gail Butler, Sara Champoux, Danielle Conrardy, Natalia DeKalb, Courtney Engles, Erin Gilmore, Heather Hanson, Katie Holmstrom, Peter Lechner, Matt Lockett, Lisa Mammoser, Brian Michel, Sherri Phillips, Sean Rumberger, Sian Thornton, and Tuan Truong.

Finally, we wish to thank our families and special friends, especially Neva-Jean Pavia, Marian Lampman, Carolyn Kriz, and Karin Granstrom, for their encouragement, support, and patience.

Donald L. Pavia   (pavia@chem.wwu.edu)
Gary M. Lampman   (lampman@chem.wwu.edu)
George S. Kriz   (George.Kriz@wwu.edu)
Randall G. Engel   (rengel@sccd.ctc.edu)

November 2009

How To Use This Book

OVERALL STRUCTURE OF THE BOOK

This textbook is divided into two major sections (see Table of Contents). The first section, which includes Part One through Part Five, contains all of the experiments in this book. The second major section includes only Part Six and contains all of the important techniques that you will use in performing the experiments in this book. Interspersed among the experiments in Part One through Part Three are a series of essays. The essays provide a context for many of the experiments and often relate the experiments to real-world applications. When your instructor assigns an experiment, he or she will often assign an essay and/or several techniques chapters along with the experiment. Before you come to lab, you should read through these. In addition, it is likely that you will need to prepare some sections in your laboratory notebook (see Technique 3) before you come to the lab.

STRUCTURE OF THE EXPERIMENTS

In this section, we discuss how each experiment is organized in the textbook. To follow this discussion, you may want to refer to a specific experiment, such as Experiment 11.

Multiple-Parts Experiments

Some experiments, such as Experiment 11, are divided into two or more individual parts that are designated by the experiment number and the letters A, B, etc. In some experiments, for example Experiment 11, each part is a separate, but related experiment, and you will most likely perform only one part. In Experiment 11, you would do Experiment 11A (Isolation of Caffeine from Tea Leaves) or Experiment 11B (Isolation of Caffeine from a Tea Bag). In other experiments, for example Experiment 32, the various parts can be linked together to form a multi-step synthesis. In a few experiments, for example Experiment 20, the last part describes how you should analyze your final product.

Featured Topics and Techniques Lists

Directly under the title of each experiment (see Experiment 11), a list of topics appears. These topics may explain what kind of experiment it is, such as isolation of a natural product or Green Chemistry. The topics may also include major techniques that are required to perform the experiment, such as crystallization or extraction.

Required Reading

In the introduction to each experiment, there will be a section labeled Required Reading. Within this section, some of the required readings are labeled **Review** and some are labeled **New**. You should always read the chapters listed in the **New** section. Sometimes it will also be helpful to do the readings in the **Review** section.

Special Instructions

You should always read this section since it may include instructions that are essential to the success of the experiment.

Suggested Waste Disposal

This very important section gives instructions on how to dispose of the waste generated in the experiment. Often your instructor will provide you with additional instructions on how to handle the waste.

Notes to Instructor

It will usually not be necessary to read this section. This section provides special instructions for the instructor that will help to make the experiment successful.

Procedure

This section provides detailed instructions on how to carry out the experiments. Within the procedure, there will be many references to the techniques chapters, which you may need to consult in order to perform an experiment.

Report

In some experiments, specific suggestions for what should be included in the laboratory report will be given. Your instructor may refer to these instructions or may have other instructions that you should follow.

Questions

At the end of most experiments will be a list of questions related to the experiment. It is likely that your instructor will assign at least some of these questions, along with the laboratory report.

Contents

APPENDICES

INDEX

Experiments & Essays

ESSAY

Esters—Flavors and Fragrances

Esters are a class of compounds widely distributed in nature. They have the general formula

$$R - \overset{\displaystyle O}{\overset{\displaystyle \|}{C}} - OR'$$

The simple esters tend to have pleasant odors. In many but not all cases, the characteristic flavors and fragrances of flowers and fruits are due to compounds with the ester functional group. An exception is the case of the essential oils. The **organoleptic** qualities (odors and flavors) of fruits and flowers may often be due to a single ester, but more often, the flavor or the aroma is due to a complex mixture in which a single ester predominates. Some common flavor principles are listed in Table 1. Food and beverage manufacturers are familiar with these esters and often

TABLE 1 Ester Flavors and Fragrances

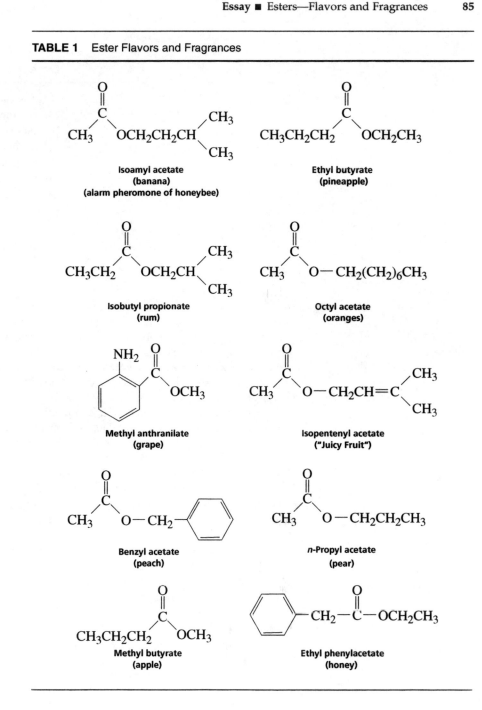

Isoamyl acetate
(banana)
(alarm pheromone of honeybee)

Ethyl butyrate
(pineapple)

Isobutyl propionate
(rum)

Octyl acetate
(oranges)

Methyl anthranilate
(grape)

Isopentenyl acetate
("Juicy Fruit")

Benzyl acetate
(peach)

n-Propyl acetate
(pear)

Methyl butyrate
(apple)

Ethyl phenylacetate
(honey)

TABLE 2 Artificial Pineapple Flavor

Pure Compounds	%	Essential Oils	%
Allyl caproate	5	Oil of sweet birch	1
Isoamyl acetate	3	Oil of spruce	2
Isoamyl isovalerate	3	Balsam Peru	4
Ethyl acetate	15	Volatile mustard oil	1
Ethyl butyrate	22	Oil of cognac	5
Terpinyl propionate	3	Concentrated orange oil	4
Ethyl crotonate	5	Distilled oil of lime	2
Caproic acid	8		19
Butyric acid	12		
Acetic acid	5		
	81		

use them as additives to spruce up the flavor or odor of a dessert or beverage. Many times, such flavors or odors do not even have a natural basis, as is the case with the "juicy fruit" principle, isopentenyl acetate. An instant pudding that has the flavor of rum may never have seen its alcoholic namesake; this flavor can be duplicated by the proper admixture, along with other minor components, of ethyl formate and isobutyl propionate. The natural flavor and odor are not exactly duplicated, but most people can be fooled. Often, only a professional taster, a trained person with a high degree of gustatory perception, can tell the difference.

A single compound is rarely used in good-quality imitation flavoring agents. A formula for an imitation pineapple flavor that might fool an expert is listed in Table 2. The formula includes 10 esters and carboxylic acids that can easily be synthesized in the laboratory. The remaining seven oils are isolated from natural sources.

Flavor is a combination of taste, sensation, and odor transmitted by receptors in the mouth (taste buds) and nose (olfactory receptors). The stereochemical theory of odor is discussed in the essay that precedes Experiment 15. The four basic tastes (sweet, sour, salty, and bitter) are perceived in specific areas of the tongue. The sides of the tongue perceive sour and salty tastes, the tip is most sensitive to sweet tastes, and the back of the tongue detects bitter tastes. The perception of flavor, however, is not so simple. If it were, it would require only the formulation of various combinations of four basic substances—a bitter substance (a base), a sour substance (an acid), a salty substance (sodium chloride), and a sweet substance (sugar)—to duplicate any flavor! In fact, we cannot duplicate flavors in this way. Humans possess about 9,000 taste buds. The combined response of these taste buds is what allows perception of a particular flavor.

Although the "fruity" tastes and odors of esters are pleasant, they are seldom used in perfumes or scents that are applied to the body. The reason for this is chemical. The ester group is not as stable under perspiration as the ingredients of the more expensive essential-oil perfumes. The latter are usually hydrocarbons (terpenes), ketones, and ethers extracted from natural sources. Esters, however, are used only for the cheapest toilet waters, because on contact with sweat they undergo hydrolysis, giving organic acids. These acids, unlike their precursor esters, generally do not have a pleasant odor.

$$R-\overset{\overset{\textstyle O}{\|}}{C}-OR' + H_2O \longrightarrow R-\overset{\overset{\textstyle O}{\|}}{C}-OH + R'OH$$

Butyric acid, for instance, has a strong odor like that of rancid butter (of which it is an ingredient) and is a component of what we normally call body odor. It is this substance that makes foul-smelling humans so easy for an animal to detect when downwind of them. It is also of great help to the bloodhound, which is trained to follow small traces of this odor.

Ethyl butyrate and methyl butyrate, however, which are the *esters* of butyric acid, smell like pineapple and apple, respectively.

A sweet, fruity odor also has the disadvantage of possibly attracting fruit flies and other insects in search of food. Isoamyl acetate, the familiar solvent called banana oil, is particularly interesting. It is identical to a component of the alarm **pheromone** of the honeybee. Pheromone is the name applied to a chemical secreted by an organism that evokes a specific response in another member of the same species. This kind of communication is common among insects who otherwise lack means of exchanging information. When a honeybee worker stings an intruder, an alarm pheromone, composed partly of isoamyl acetate, is secreted along with the sting venom. This chemical causes aggressive attack on the intruder by other bees, who swarm around the intruder. Obviously, it wouldn't be wise to wear a perfume compounded of isoamyl acetate near a beehive. Pheromones are discussed in more detail in the essay preceding Experiment 45.

REFERENCES

Bauer, K.; Garbe, D. *Common Fragrance and Flavor Materials;* VCH Publishers: Weinheim, 1985.

The Givaudan Index; Givaudan-Delawanna: New York, 1949. (Gives specifications of synthetics and isolates for perfumery.)

Gould, R. F., Ed. *Flavor Chemistry, Advances in Chemistry Series* 56; American Chemical Society: Washington, DC, 1966.

Layman, P. L. Flavors and Fragrances Industry Taking on New Look. *Chem. Eng. News* **1987,** (Jul 20), 35.

Moyler, D. Natural Ingredients for Flavours and Fragrances. *Chem. Ind.* **1991,** (Jan 7), 11.

Rasmussen, P. W. Qualitative Analysis by Gas Chromatography—G.C. versus the Nose in Formulation of Artificial Fruit Flavors. *J. Chem. Educ.* **1984,** 61 (Jan), 62.

Shreve, R. N.; Brink, J. *Chemical Process Industries,* 4th ed.; McGraw-Hill: New York, 1977.

Welsh, F. W.; Williams, R. E. Lipase Mediated Production of Flavor and Fragrance Esters from Fusel Oil. *J. Food Sci.* **1989,** 54 (Nov/Dec), 1565.

12   E X P E R I M E N T   1 2

Isopentyl Acetate (Banana Oil)

Esterification

Heating under reflux

Separatory funnel

Extraction

Simple distillation

In this experiment, you will prepare an ester, isopentyl acetate. This ester is often referred to as banana oil, because it has the familiar odor of this fruit.

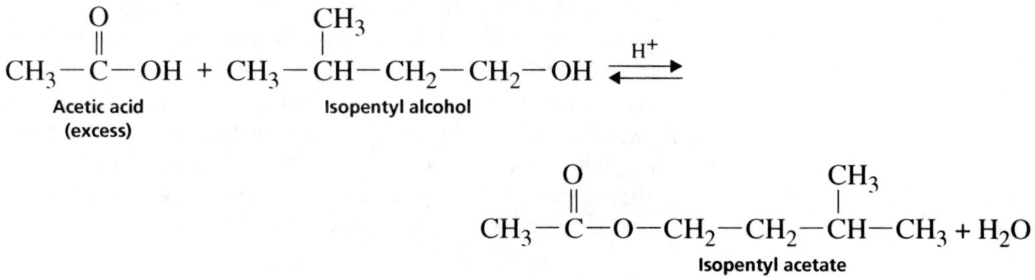

$$CH_3-\overset{\overset{\displaystyle O}{\|}}{C}-OH + CH_3-\overset{\overset{\displaystyle CH_3}{|}}{CH}-CH_2-CH_2-OH \underset{}{\overset{H^+}{\rightleftharpoons}}$$

Acetic acid   Isopentyl alcohol
(excess)

$$CH_3-\overset{\overset{\displaystyle O}{\|}}{C}-O-CH_2-CH_2-\overset{\overset{\displaystyle CH_3}{|}}{CH}-CH_3 + H_2O$$

Isopentyl acetate

Isopentyl acetate is prepared by the direct esterification of acetic acid with isopentyl alcohol. Because the equilibrium does not favor the formation of the ester, it must be shifted to the right, in favor of the product, by using an excess of one of the starting materials. Acetic acid is used in excess because it is less expensive than isopentyl alcohol and more easily removed from the reaction mixture.

In the isolation procedure, much of the excess acetic acid and the remaining isopentyl alcohol are removed by extraction with sodium bicarbonate and water. After drying with anhydrous sodium sulfate, the ester is purified by distillation. The purity of the liquid product is analyzed by determining the infrared spectrum.

REQUIRED READING

Sign in at www
.cengage.com to access
Pre-Lab Video Exercises
for techniques marked
with an asterisk.

Review:	Techniques 5 and 6	
New:	*Technique 7	Reaction Methods
	*Technique 12	Extractions, Separations, and Drying Agents
	Technique 13	Physical Constants of Liquids, Part A. Boiling Points and Thermometer Correction
	*Technique 14	Simple Distillation
	Essay	Esters—Flavors and Fragrances

If performing the optional infrared spectroscopy, also read

Technique 25,   Part A

SPECIAL INSTRUCTIONS

Be careful when dispensing sulfuric and glacial acetic acids. They are very corrosive and will attack your skin if you make contact with them. If you get one of these acids on your skin, wash the affected area with copious quantities of running water for 10–15 minutes.

Because a 1-hour reflux is required, you should start the experiment at the very beginning of the laboratory period. During the reflux period, you may perform other experimental work.

SUGGESTED WASTE DISPOSAL

Any aqueous solutions should be placed in a container specially designated for dilute aqueous waste. Place any excess ester in the nonhalogenated organic waste container.

NOTES TO THE INSTRUCTOR

This experiment has been carried out successfully using Dowex 50X2-100 ion exchange resin instead of the sulfuric acid.

PROCEDURE

Apparatus. Assemble a reflux apparatus, using a 25-mL round-bottom flask and a water-cooled condenser (refer to Technique 7, Figure 7.6,). Use a heating mantle to heat. In order to control vapors, place a drying tube packed with calcium chloride on top of the condenser.

Reaction Mixture. Weigh (tare) an empty 10-mL graduated cylinder and record its weight. Place approximately 5.0 mL of isopentyl alcohol in the graduated cylinder and reweigh it to determine the weight of alcohol. Disconnect the roundbottom flask from the reflux apparatus and transfer the alcohol into it. Do not clean or wash the graduated cylinder. Using the same graduated cylinder, measure approximately 7.0 mL of glacial acetic acid ($MW = 60.1$, $d = 1.06$ g/mL) and add it to the alcohol already in the flask. Using a calibrated Pasteur pipet, add 1 mL of concentrated sulfuric acid, mixing *immediately* (with swirling), to the reaction mixture contained in the flask. Add a corundum boiling stone and reconnect the flask. Do not use a calcium carbonate (marble) boiling stone because it will dissolve in the acidic medium.

Reflux. Start water circulating in the condenser and bring the mixture to a boil. Continue heating under reflux for 60–75 minutes. Then disconnect or remove the heating source and allow the mixture to cool to room temperature.

Extractions. Disassemble the apparatus and transfer the reaction mixture to a separatory funnel (125-mL) placed in a ring that is attached to a ring stand. Be sure that the stopcock is closed and, using a funnel, pour the mixture into the top of the separatory funnel. Also be careful to avoid transferring the boiling stone, or you will need to remove it after the transfer. Add 10 mL of water, stopper the funnel, and mix the phases by careful shaking and venting (see Technique 12, Section 12.4, and Figure 12.6). Allow the phases to separate and then unstopper the funnel and drain the lower aqueous layer through the stopcock into a beaker or other suitable container. Next, extract the organic layer with 5 mL of 5% aqueous sodium bicarbonate just as you did previously with water. Extract the organic layer once again, this time with 5 mL of saturated aqueous sodium chloride.

Drying. Transfer the crude ester to a clean, dry 25-mL Erlenmeyer flask and add approximately 1.0 g of anhydrous granular sodium sulfate. Cork the mixture and allow it to stand for 10–15 minutes while you prepare the apparatus for distillation. If the mixture does not appear dry (the drying agent clumps and does not "flow," the solution is cloudy, or drops of water are obvious), transfer the ester to a new clean, dry 25-mL Erlenmeyer flask and add a new 0.5-g portion of anhydrous sodium sulfate to complete the drying.

Distillation. Assemble a distillation apparatus using your smallest roundbottom flask to distill from (see Technique 14, Figure 14.1). Use a heating mantle to heat. Preweigh (tare) and use another small round-bottom flask, or an Erlenmeyer flask, to collect the product. Immerse the collection flask in a beaker of ice to ensure condensation and to reduce odors. You should look up the boiling point of your expected product in a handbook so you will know what to anticipate. Continue distillation until only one or two drops of liquid remain in the distilling flask. Record the observed boiling point range in your notebook.

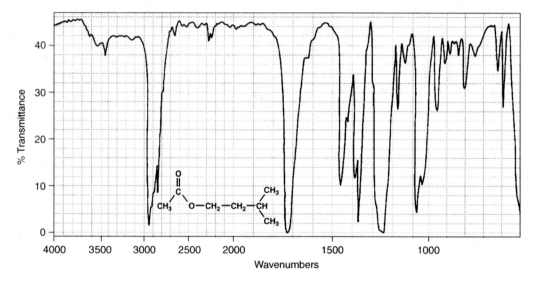

Yield Determination. Weigh the product and calculate the percentage yield of the ester. If your instructor requests it, determine the boiling point using one of the methods described in Technique 13, Sections 13.2 and 13.3.

Spectroscopy. If your instructor requests it, obtain an infrared spectrum using salt plates (see Technique 25, Section 25.2). Compare your spectrum with the one reproduced in the text. Interpret the spectrum and include it in your report to the instructor. You may also be required to determine and interpret the proton and carbon-13 NMR spectra (see Technique 26, Part A and Technique 27, Section 27.1). Submit your sample in a properly labeled vial with your report.

QUESTIONS

1. One method of favoring the formation of an ester is to add excess acetic acid. Suggest another method, involving the right-hand side of the equation, that will favor the formation of the ester.

2. Why is the mixture extracted with sodium bicarbonate? Give an equation and explain its relevance.

3. Why are gas bubbles observed when the sodium bicarbonate is added?

4. Which starting material is the limiting reagent in this procedure? Which reagent is used in excess? How great is the molar excess (how many times greater)?

5. Outline a separation scheme for isolating pure isopentyl acetate from the reaction mixture.

6. Interpret the principal absorption bands in the infrared spectrum of isopentyl acetate or, if you did not determine the infrared spectrum of your ester, do this for the spectrum of isopentyl acetate shown in the previous figure. (Technique 25 may be of some help.)

7. Write a mechanism for the acid-catalyzed esterification of acetic acid with isopentyl alcohol.

8. Why is glacial acetic acid designated as "glacial"? (*Hint:* Consult a handbook of physical properties.)

21   **EXPERIMENT 21**

Synthesis of n-Butyl Bromide and t-Pentyl Chloride

Synthesis of alkyl halides

Extraction

Simple distillation

The synthesis of two alkyl halides from alcohols is the basis for these experiments. In the first experiment, a primary alkyl halide *n*-butyl bromide is prepared as shown in equation 1.

$CH_3\text{-}CH_2\text{-}CH_2\text{-}CH_2\text{-}OH + NaBr + H_2SO_4 \longrightarrow$
  ***n*-Butyl alcohol**

$CH_3\text{-}CH_2\text{-}CH_2\text{-}CH_2\text{-}Br + NaHSO_4 + H_2O$ [1]
  ***n*-Butyl bromide**

In the second experiment, a tertiary alkyl halide *t*-pentyl chloride is prepared as shown in equation 2.

$$CH_3-CH_2-\overset{\overset{\displaystyle CH_3}{|}}{\underset{\underset{\displaystyle OH}{|}}{C}}-CH_3 + HCl \longrightarrow CH_3-CH_2-\overset{\overset{\displaystyle CH_3}{|}}{\underset{\underset{\displaystyle Cl}{|}}{C}}-CH_3 + H_2O \qquad [2]$$

t-Pentyl alcohol   **t-Pentyl chloride**

These reactions provide an interesting contrast in mechanisms. The *n*-butyl bromide synthesis proceeds by an S_N2 mechanism, while *t*-pentyl chloride is prepared by an S_N1 reaction.

n-BUTYL BROMIDE

The primary alkyl halide *n*-butyl bromide can be prepared easily by allowing *n*-butyl alcohol to react with sodium bromide and sulfuric acid by equation 1. The sodium bromide reacts with sulfuric acid to produce hydrobromic acid.

$$2 \text{ NaBr} + H_2SO_4 \longrightarrow 2 \text{ HBr} + Na_2SO_4$$

Excess sulfuric acid serves to shift the equilibrium and thus to speed the reaction by producing a higher concentration of hydrobromic acid. The sulfuric acid also protonates the hydroxyl group of *n*-butyl alcohol so that water is displaced rather than the hydroxide ion OH^-. The acid also protonates the water as it is produced in the reaction and deactivates it as a nucleophile. Deactivation of water keeps the alkyl halide from being converted back to the alcohol by nucleophilic attack of water. The reaction of the primary substrate proceeds via an S_N2 mechanism.

$$CH_3-CH_2-CH_2-CH_2-O-H + H^+ \xrightarrow{\text{fast}} CH_3-CH_2-CH_2-CH_2-\overset{+}{O}-H$$
$$\underset{\displaystyle H}{|}$$

$$CH_3-CH_2-CH_2-CH_2-\overset{+}{\underset{\underset{\displaystyle H}{|}}{O}}-H + Br^- \xrightarrow[S_N2]{\text{slow}} CH_3-CH_2-CH_2-CH_2-Br + H_2O$$

During the isolation of the *n*-butyl bromide, the crude product is washed with sulfuric acid, water, and sodium bicarbonate to remove any remaining acid or *n*-butyl alcohol.

t-PENTYL CHLORIDE

The tertiary alkyl halide can be prepared by allowing *t*-pentyl alcohol to react with concentrated hydrochloric acid according to equation 2. The reaction is accomplished simply by shaking the two reagents in a separatory funnel. As the reaction proceeds, the insoluble alkyl halide product forms an upper phase. The reaction of the tertiary substrate occurs via an S_N1 mechanism.

$$CH_3-CH_2-\overset{\overset{\displaystyle CH_3}{|}}{\underset{\underset{\displaystyle OH}{|}}{C}}-CH_3 + H^+ \xrightarrow{\text{fast}} CH_3-CH_2-\overset{\overset{\displaystyle CH_3}{|}}{\underset{\underset{\displaystyle \overset{+}{O}}{|}}{C}}-CH_3$$
$$\underset{\underset{\displaystyle H \qquad H}{}}{}$$

$$CH_3-CH_2-\overset{\overset{\displaystyle CH_3}{|}}{\underset{\underset{\displaystyle \overset{+}{O}}{|}}{C}}-CH_3 \xrightarrow{\text{slow}} CH_3-CH_2-\overset{\overset{\displaystyle CH_3}{|}}{\underset{}{\overset{+}{C}}}-CH_3 + H_2O$$
$$\underset{\underset{\displaystyle H \qquad H}{}}{}$$

$$CH_3-CH_2-\overset{\overset{\displaystyle CH_3}{|}}{\underset{}{\overset{+}{C}}}-CH_3 + Cl^- \xrightarrow{\text{fast}} CH_3-CH_2-\overset{\overset{\displaystyle CH_3}{|}}{\underset{\underset{\displaystyle Cl}{|}}{C}}-CH_3$$

A small amount of alkene, 2-methyl-2-butene, is produced as a by-product in this reaction. If sulfuric acid had been used as it was for *n*-butyl bromide, a much larger amount of this alkene would have been produced.

REQUIRED READING

Review: Techniques 5, 6, 7, 12, and 14

SPECIAL INSTRUCTIONS

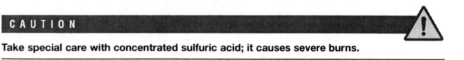

CAUTION

Take special care with concentrated sulfuric acid; it causes severe burns.

As your instructor indicates, perform either the *n*-butyl bromide or the *t*-pentyl chloride procedure, or both.

SUGGESTED WASTE DISPOSAL

Dispose of all aqueous solutions produced in this experiment in the container marked for the disposal of aqueous waste. If your instructor asks you to dispose of your alkyl halide product, dispose of it in the container marked for the disposal of alkyl halides. Note that your instructor may have specific instructions for the disposal of wastes that differ from the instructions given here.

22   EXPERIMENT 22

4-Methylcyclohexene

Preparation of an alkene

Dehydration of an alcohol

Distillation

Bromine and permanganate tests for unsaturation

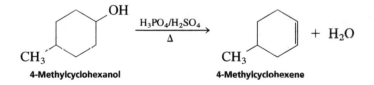

4-Methylcyclohexanol   4-Methylcyclohexene

Alcohol dehydration is an acid-catalyzed reaction performed by strong, concentrated mineral acids such as sulfuric and phosphoric acids. The acid protonates the alcoholic hydroxyl group, permitting it to dissociate as water. Loss of a proton from the intermediate (elimination) brings about an alkene. Because sulfuric acid often causes extensive charring in this reaction, phosphoric acid, which is comparatively free of this problem, is a better choice. In order to make the reaction proceed faster, however, you will also use a minimal amount of sulfuric acid.

The equilibrium that attends this reaction will be shifted in favor of the product by distilling it from the reaction mixture as it is formed. The 4-methylcyclohexene (bp 101–102°C) will codistill with the water that is also formed. By continuously removing the products, you can obtain a high yield of 4-methylcyclohexene. Because the starting material, 4-methylcyclohexanol, also has a somewhat low boiling point (bp 171–173°C), the distillation must be done carefully so that the alcohol does not also distill.

Unavoidably, a small amount of phosphoric acid codistills with the product. It is removed by washing the distillate mixture with a saturated sodium chloride solution. This step also partially removes the water from the 4-methylcyclohexene layer; the drying process will be completed by allowing the product to stand over anhydrous sodium sulfate.

Compounds containing double bonds react with a bromine solution (red) to decolorize it. Similarly, they react with a solution of potassium permanganate (purple) to discharge its color and produce a brown precipitate (MnO_2). These reactions are often used as qualitative tests to determine the presence of a double bond in an organic molecule (see Experiment 55C). Both tests will be performed on the 4-methylcyclohexene formed in this experiment.

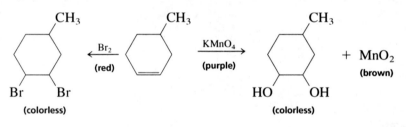

REQUIRED READING

Sign in at www .cengage.com to access Pre-Lab Video Exercises for techniques marked with an asterisk.

Review:	Techniques 5 and 6	
	*Technique 12	Extractions, Separations, and Drying Agents, Sections 12.7, 12.8, and 12.9
New:	*Technique 14	Simple Distillation

If performing the optional infrared spectroscopy, also read

Technique 25   Infrared Spectroscopy

SPECIAL INSTRUCTIONS

Phosphoric and sulfuric acids are very corrosive. Do not allow either acid to touch your skin.

SUGGESTED WASTE DISPOSAL

Dispose of aqueous wastes by pouring them into the container designated for aqueous wastes. Residues that remain after the first distillation may also be placed in the aqueous waste container. Discard the solutions that remain after the bromine test for unsaturation in an organic waste container designated for the disposal of *halogenated* wastes. The solutions that remain after the potassium permanganate test should be discarded into a waste container specifically marked for the disposal of potassium permanganate waste.

PROCEDURE

Apparatus Assembly. Place 7.5 mL of 4-methylcyclohexanol (*MW* = 114.2) in a tared 50-mL round-bottom flask and reweigh the flask to determine an accurate weight for the alcohol. Add 2.0 mL of 85% phosphoric acid and 30 drops (0.40 mL) of concentrated sulfuric acid to the flask. Mix the liquids thoroughly using a glass stirring rod and add a boiling stone. Assemble a distillation apparatus as shown in Technique 14, Figure 14.1 (omit the condenser), using a 25-mL flask as a receiver. Immerse the receiving flask in an ice-water bath to minimize the possibility that 4-methylcyclohexene vapors will escape into the laboratory.

Dehydration. Start circulating the cooling water in the condenser and heat the mixture with a heating mantle until the product begins to distill and collect in the receiver. The heating should be regulated so that the distillation requires about 30 minutes. Too rapid distillation leads to incomplete reaction and isolation of the starting material, 4-methylcyclohexanol. Continue the distillation until no more liquid is collected. The distillate contains 4-methylcyclohexene as well as water.

Isolation and Drying of the Product. Transfer the distillate to a centrifuge tube with the aid of 1 or 2 mL of saturated sodium chloride solution. Allow the layers to separate and remove the bottom aqueous layer with a Pasteur pipet (discard it). Using a dry Pasteur pipet, transfer the organic layer remaining in the centrifuge tube to an Erlenmeyer flask containing a small amount of granular anhydrous sodium sulfate. Place a stopper in the flask and set it aside for 10−15 minutes to remove the last traces of water. During this time, wash and dry the distillation apparatus, using small amounts of acetone and an air stream to aid the drying process.

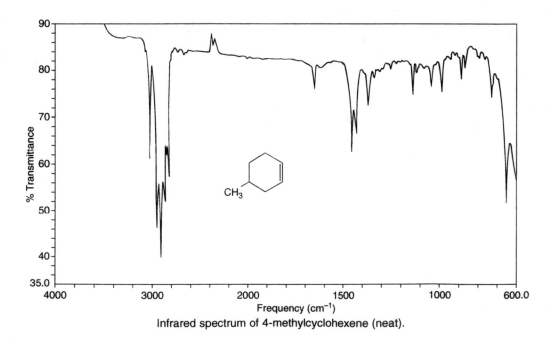

Infrared spectrum of 4-methylcyclohexene (neat).

Distillation. Transfer as much of the dried liquid as possible to the clean, dry 50-mL round-bottom flask, being careful to leave as much of the solid drying agent behind as possible. Add a boiling stone to the flask and assemble the distillation apparatus as before, using a *preweighed* 25-mL receiving flask. Because 4-methylcyclohexene is so volatile, you will recover more product if you cool the receiver in an ice-water bath. Using a heating mantle, distill the 4-methylcyclohexene, collecting the material that boils over the range 100°C–105°C. Record your observed boiling-point range in your notebook. There will be little or no forerun, and very little liquid will remain in the distilling flask at the end of the distillation. Reweigh the receiving flask to determine how much 4-methylcyclohexene you prepared. Calculate the percentage yield of 4-methylcyclohexene ($MW = 96.2$).

Spectroscopy. If your instructor requests it, obtain the infrared spectrum of 4-methylcyclohexene (see Technique 25, Section 25.2, or 25.3). Because 4-methylcyclohexene is so volatile, you must work quickly to obtain a good spectrum using sodium chloride plates. Compare the spectrum with the one shown in this experiment. After performing the following tests, submit your sample, along with the report, to the instructor.[1]

UNSATURATION TESTS

Place 4–5 drops of 4-methylcyclohexanol in each of two small test tubes. In each of another pair of small test tubes, place 4–5 drops of the 4-methylcyclohexene you prepared. Do not confuse the test tubes. Take one test tube from each group and add a solution of bromine in carbon tetrachloride or methylene chloride, drop by drop, to the contents of the test tube until the red color is no longer discharged. Record the result in each case, including the number of drops required. Test the remaining two test tubes in a similar fashion with a solution of potassium permanganate. Because aqueous potassium permanganate is not miscible with organic compounds, you will have to add about 0.3 mL of 1,2-dimethoxyethane to each test tube before making the test. Record your results and explain them.

QUESTIONS

1. Outline a mechanism for the dehydration of 4-methylcyclohexanol catalyzed by phosphoric acid.
2. What major alkene product is produced by the dehydration of the following alcohols?
   a. Cyclohexanol
   b. 1-Methylcyclohexanol
   c. 2-Methylcyclohexanol
   d. 2,2-Dimethylcyclohexanol
   e. 1,2-Cyclohexanediol (*Hint:* Consider keto-enol tautomerism.)

---

[1]The product of the distillation may also be analyzed by gas chromatography. We have found that when using gas chromatography–mass spectrometry to analyze the products of this reaction, it is possible to observe the presence of isomeric methylcyclohexenes. These isomers arise from rearrangement reactions that occur during the dehydration.

3. Compare and interpret the infrared spectra of 4-methylcyclohexene and 4-methylcyclohexanol.

4. Identify the C — H out-of-plane bending vibrations in the infrared spectrum of 4-methylcyclohexene. What structural information can be obtained from these bands?

5. In this experiment, 1–2 mL of saturated sodium chloride is used to transfer the crude product after the initial distillation. Why is saturated sodium chloride, rather than pure water, used for this procedure?

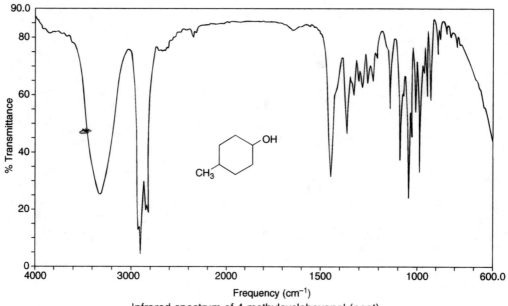

Infrared spectrum of 4-methylcyclohexanol (neat).

ESSAY

Biofuels

In recent years there has been an increasing interest in **biofuels,** fuels that are produced from biological materials such as corn or vegetable oil. These sources of biofuels are considered to be renewable because they can be produced in relatively short time. On the other hand, **fossil fuels** are formed by the slow decay of marine animal and plant organisms that lived millions of years ago. Fossil fuels, which include petroleum, natural gas, and coal, are considered to be nonrenewable.

The increased emphasis on biofuels is due primarily to the increasing cost and demand for liquid fuels such as gasoline and diesel, and our desire to be less dependent on foreign oil. In addition to increased demand, the higher cost of petroleum may be related to the peak oil theory, discussed in the essay on petroleum and fossil fuels. According to this theory, the amount of petroleum in the earth is finite;

and at some point, the total amount of petroleum produced each year will begin to decrease. Many experts believe that we have either already reached the peak in oil production, or we will reach it within a few years.

In addition to biofuels, the use of many other types of alternative energy sources has been increasing in recent years. Alternative energy sources such as solar, wind, and geothermal are used primarily to produce electricity, and they cannot replace liquid fuels such as gasoline and diesel. As long as we continue to depend on automobiles and other vehicles with the current engine technology, we will need to produce more liquid fuels. Because of this, the demand to produce more biofuels is very great. In this essay, we will focus on the biofuels ethanol and biodiesel.

Ethanol

The knowledge of how to produce ethanol from grains has been around for many centuries (see the essay "Ethanol and Fermentation Chemistry" that precedes Experiment 16). Until recently, most of the ethanol produced by fermentation was used mainly in alcoholic beverages. In 1978, Congress passed the National Energy Act, which encouraged the use of fuels such as Gasohol, a blend of gasoline with at least 10% ethanol produced from renewable resources. Ethanol can be produced by the fermentation of sugars such as sucrose, which is found in sugar cane or beets. In this country, it is more common to use corn kernels as the feedstock to produce Ethanol. Corn contains starch, a polymer of glucose that must first be broken down into glucose units. This is usually accomplished by adding a mixture of enzymes that catalyze the hydrolysis of starch into glucose. Other enzymes are then added to promote the fermentation of glucose into ethanol:

$$C_6H_{12}O_6 \xrightarrow{\text{Enzymes}} 2CH_3CH_2OH + 2CO_2$$

Glucose   **Ethanol**

After fermentation, fractional distillation is used to separate the Ethanol from the fermentation mixture. In Experiment 26, you will produce and isolate ethanol from frozen corn kernels.

The use of corn to produce ethanol as a biofuels has been strongly encouraged in the United States. Government subsidies have resulted in a higher production of corn in the Midwest, and many new ethanol refineries have also been built. However, it is now clear that use of Ethanol as a biofuel has some significant drawbacks. First, as more corn is planted and used for fuel production, less corn and other crops are available as a source of food. This has led to food shortages and higher prices, which is especially hard on people who are already struggling to get enough food. Second, it now appears that the total amount of energy expended to grow corn and to produce ethanol is almost as much as the amount of energy released by burning the ethanol. Third, recent studies have indicated that growing corn to produce ethanol for use as a fuel results in the production of more greenhouse gases than the use of similar amounts of fossil fuels. Therefore, the use of corn ethanol may actually increase global warming compared to fossil fuels. In spite of these drawbacks, given that so much investment in corn ethanol has already been made, it is still likely that corn will continue to be a source of ethanol in this country for some time to come.

One alternative to corn ethanol is **cellulosic ethanol**. Sources of cellulose that can be used to produce ethanol include fast-growing grasses such as switchgrass, agricultural waste such as corn stalks, and waste wood from the milling of lumber.

Like starch, cellulose is a polymer of glucose, but the structure is slightly different than starch and it is much more difficult to break down. Cellulose can be broken down by acid or base treatment at high temperature and by hydrolysis reactions with enzymes. Once the cellulose is broken down into glucose, it can be fermented to produce ethanol, just like with corn starch. Cellulosic ethanol addresses some of the drawbacks for corn ethanol mentioned in the previous paragraph. Many of the sources of cellulosic ethanol can be grown on non-arable land that would not normally be used to produce food. It also appears that the overall energy production is more favorable than corn ethanol. Finally, the contribution to greenhouse gases is not so great. However, because of the difficulty of breaking down cellulose, there is not yet a commercial plant in operation that produces cellulosic ethanol.

Evaluating biofuels in terms of contribution to global warming is difficult to do. Initially, it was believed that all biofuels produced less greenhouse gases than fossil fuels. This is because carbon dioxide is absorbed by the plants as they grow, which helps to offset the carbon dioxide that is released when the biofuels is burned. However, recent studies suggest that the situation is more complicated. In order to grow the crops required to make biofuels and to replace the food crops that are now used to make biofuels, it is often necessary to destroy forestland. Forests are much more effective than farmland at absorbing carbon dioxide from the air. When the loss of forests is also factored in, it appears that ethanol production from corn or even other sources such as switchgrass may contribute more to the greenhouse effect than burning fossil fuels.

Another option for producing ethanol exists that may have advantages over both of the methods described above. This newer option involves the conversion of carbon-containing matter into **syngas**. Almost any material that contains carbon, such as municipal waste, old tires, or agricultural waste, can be used. The feedstock is gasified into a mixture of carbon monoxide and hydrogen, which is known as syngas. Syngas can then be catalytically converted into ethanol. This process is much more efficient energetically than the methods described above and its also created less greenhouse gases, especially when the feedstock is some kind of waste material. Furthermore, these feedstocks do not compete with food crops.

Biodiesel

Another biofuel that is widely used in the United States is **biodiesel**. Biodiesel is produced from fats or oils in a based-catalyzed transesterification reaction:

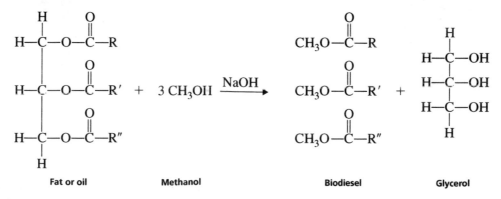

| Fat or oil | Methanol | | Biodiesel | Glycerol |

Because the R groups may have different numbers of carbons and double bonds, biodiesel is a mixture of different molecules, all of which are methyl esters of fatty acids. Most of the R groups have between 12–18 carbons arranged in straight chains. Any kind of vegetable oil can be used to make biodiesel, but the most common ones used are the oils from soybean, canola, and palm. In Experiment 25, biodiesel is made from coconut oil and other vegetable oils.

Biodiesel has similar properties to the diesel fuel that is produced from petroleum, and it can be burned in any vehicle with a diesel engine or in furnaces that burn diesel fuel. It should be noted that vegetable oil can also be burned as a fuel, but because the viscosity of vegetable oil is somewhat greater than diesel fuel, engines must be modified in order to burn vegetable oil.

How does biodiesel compare with ethanol? Like corn ethanol, growing the vegetables required to produce the oil feedstock results in diverting farmland from growing food to producing fuels. In fact, this is more of a problem with biodiesel because more land is required to produce an equivalent amount of fuel compared to corn ethanol. The net energy produced by biodiesel is greater than for corn ethanol, but less than for cellulosic ethanol. Finally, it appears that the production of biodiesel, like ethanol, produces more greenhouse gases than fossil fuels, again because forested land must be destroyed in order to grow the vegetables required to produce biodiesel.

Some alternative approaches for making biodiesel exist that could address some of these issues. Algae can produce oils that can be used to make biodiesel. Algae can be grown in ponds or even waste water and does not require the use of farmland. The algae oil can be converted into biodiesel in the same way that vegetable oil is converted. Recently, a different chemical method for making biodiesel from vegetable oil has been developed. This method utilizes a sulfated zirconia catalyst that is placed in a column, similar to column chromatography. As the mixture of oil and alcohol is passed through the column at high temperature and pressure, biodiesel is produced and elutes from the bottom of the column. The process is much more efficient than the current methods used to produce biodiesel. An interesting side story related to this process is that the original idea for this method was based on the work that a student completed for his undergraduate research project in chemistry!

Because of the importance of liquid fuels in this country, fuels other than ethanol and biodiesel are also being researched. There is also considerable interest in the use of plug-in electrical cars that would not require any liquid fuels. If the electrical energy used to charge the batteries in electric cars comes from renewable sources of electricity such as wind, solar, or geothermal, then the need for liquid fuels could be greatly decreased.

In 2007, the United States consumed a combined total of about 7.5 billion gallons of ethanol and biodiesel. By comparison, about 140 billion gallons of gasoline and 40 billion gallons of diesel fuel were consumed. Therefore, biofuels presently represent a small percentage of our total fuel consumption. Recently, Congress passed a bill requiring 36 billion gallons of biofuel to be produced yearly by 2022. Even if this goal is met, it is likely that we will still primarily rely on both fossil fuels and biofuel for the foreseeable future.

REFERENCE

Biello, D. Grass Makes Better Ethanol than Corn Does. *Sci. Am.* [Online] **2008,** (Jan).
Dale, B. E.; Pimentel, D. Point/Counterpoint: The costs of Biofuels. *Chem. Eng. News* **2007,** *85* (Dec 17), 12.

Fargione, J.; Hill, J.; Tilman, D.; Polasky, S.; Hawthorne, P. Land Clearing and Biofuel Carbon Debt. *Science* **2008,** *319* (Feb 29), 1235.

Grunwald, M. The Clean Energy Scam. *Time* **2008,** *171* (Apr 7), 40.

Heywood, J. B. Fueling our Transportation Future. *Sci. Am.* **2006,** *295* (Sep), 60.

Kammen, D. M. The Rise of Renewable Energy. *Sci. Am.* **2006,** *295* (Sep), 84.

Kram, J. W. Minnesota Scientists Create New Biodiesel Manufacturing Process. *Biodiesel Magazine,* (Apr 7, 2008).

Searchinger, T. Use of U.S. Croplands, for Biofuels Increases Greenhouse Gases Through Emissions from Land-Use Change. *Science* **2008,** *319* (Feb 29), 1238–1248.

25   EXPERIMENT 25

Biodiesel [1]

In this experiment, you will prepare biodiesel from a vegetable oil in a base-catalyzed transesterification reaction:

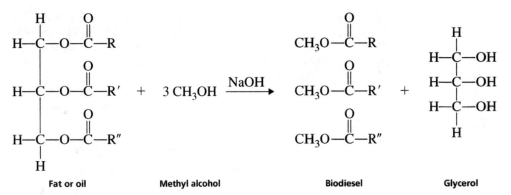

Fat or oil   **Methyl alcohol**   **Biodiesel**   **Glycerol**

The first step in the mechanism for this synthesis is an acid-base reaction between sodium hydroxide and methyl alcohol:

$$NaOH + CH_3OH \longrightarrow Na^+ \ OCH_3^- + H_2O$$
Sodium methoxide

Methoxide ion is a strong nucleophile that now attacks the three carbonyl groups in the vegetable oil molecule. In the last step, glycerol and biodiesel are produced.

[1]This experiment is based on a similar experiment developed by John Thompson, Lane Community College, Eugene, Oregon. It is posted on Greener Educational Materials (GEMs), an interactive database on green chemistry that is found on the University of Oregon green chemistry website (http://greenchem.uoregon.edu/).

Because the R groups may have different numbers of carbons and they may be saturated (no double bonds) or may have one or two double bonds, biodiesel is a mixture of different molecules—all of which are methyl esters of fatty acids that made up the original vegetable oil. Most of the R groups have between 10–18 carbons that are arranged in straight chains.

When the reaction is complete, the mixture is cooled and then centrifuged in order to separate the layers more completely. Since some unreacted methyl alcohol will be dissolved in the biodiesel layer, this layer is heated in an open container to remove all the methyl alcohol. The remaining liquid should be pure biodiesel.

When biodiesel is burned as a fuel, the following reaction occurs:

$$\overset{\displaystyle O}{\underset{\displaystyle \|}{}}$$

$$CH_3O\text{-}C\text{-}(CH_2)_{15}CH_3 + 26\ O_2 \longrightarrow 18\ CO_2 + 18\ H_2O_{15} + energy$$
One possible
biodiesel molecule

Burning biodiesel will produce a specific amount of energy, which can be measured using a bomb calorimeter. By combusting a specific weight of your biodiesel and measuring the temperature increase of the calorimeter, you can calculate the heat of combustion of biodiesel.

In Experiment 25A, coconut oil is converted into biodiesel, and other oils are converted into biodiesel in Experiment 25B. In Experiment 25C, the biodiesel is analyzed by infrared spectroscopy, NMR spectroscopy, and gas chromatography-mass spectrometry (GC-MS). The heat of combustion of biodiesel can also be determined in Experiment 25C.

REQUIRED READING

New: Technique 22   Gas Chromatography, Section 22.13

Technique 25   Infrared Spectroscopy

Technique 26   Nuclear Magnetic Resonance Spectroscopy

Essays: Biofuels

Fats and Oils

SUGGESTED WASTE DISPOSAL

Discard the glycerol layer and leftover biodiesel into the container for the disposal of nonhalogenated organic waste.

NOTES TO THE INSTRUCTOR

We have found this experiment to be a good way to introduce infrared spectroscopy, NMR spectroscopy, and GC-MS. It is helpful to place the bottle containing the coconut oil into a beaker of warm water to keep the oil in the liquid state.

25A   EXPERIMENT 25A

Biodiesel from Coconut Oil

PROCEDURE

Prepare a warm water bath in 250-mL beaker. Use about 50 mL of water and heat the water to 55-60°C on a hot plate. (Do not let the temperature exceed 60° during the reaction on a hot plate period.) Weigh a 25-mL round-bottom flask. Add 10 mL of coconut oil to the flask and reweigh to get the weight of the oil. (Note: The coconut oil must be heated slightly in order to convert it to a liquid that can be measured in a graduated cylinder. It may also be advisable to warm the graduated cylinder.) Transfer 2.0 mL of sodium hydroxide dissolved in methyl alcohol solution to the flask.[2] (Note: Swirl the sodium hydroxide mixture before taking the 2-mL portion to make sure that the mixture is homogenous.) Place a magnetic stir bar in the round-bottom flask and attach the flask to a water condenser. (You do not need to run water through the water-condenser.) Clamp the condenser so that the round-bottom flask is close to the bottom of the beaker. Turn on the magnetic stirrer to the highest level possible (this may not be the highest setting on the stirrer if the stir bar does not spin smoothly at high speeds). Stir for 30 minutes.

Transfer all of the liquid in the flask to a 15-mL plastic centrifuge tube with a cap and let it set for about 15 minutes. The mixture should separate into two layers: the larger top layer is biodiesel and the lower layer is mainly glycerol. To separate the layers more completely, place the tube in a centrifuge and spin for about 5 minutes (don't forget to counterbalance the centrifuge). If the layers have not separated completely after centrifugation, continue to centrifuge for another 5–10 minutes at a higher speed.

Using a Pasteur pipet, carefully remove the top layer of biodiesel and transfer this layer to a preweighed 50-mL beaker. You should leave behind a little of the biodiesel layer to make sure you don't contaminate it with the bottom layer.

Place the beaker on a hot plate and insert a thermometer into the biodiesel, holding the thermometer in place with a clamp. Heat the biodiesel to about 70°C for 15–20 minutes to remove all the methyl alcohol. When the biodiesel has cooled to room temperature, weigh the beaker and liquid and calculate the weight of biodiesel produced. Record the appearance of the biodiesel.

To analyze your biodiesel, proceed to Experiment 25C.

---

[2]Note to instructor: Dry sodium hydroxide pellets overnight in an oven at 100°C. After grinding the dried sodium hydroxide with a mortar and pestle, add 0.875 g of this to an Erlenmeyer flask containing 50 mL of highly pure methanol. Place a magnetic stir bar in the flask and stir until all of the sodium hydroxide has dissolved. The mixture will be slightly cloudy.

EXPERIMENT 25B

Biodiesel from Other Oils

Follow the procedure in Experiment 25A (Biodiesel from Coconut Oil), except use a different oil than coconut. Any of the oils listed at the bottom of Table 2 in the essay "Fats and Oils" than precedes Experiment 23 can be used. It will not be necessary to heat the oil when measuring out the 10 mL of oil, as all of these oils are liquids at room temperature.

To analyze your biodiesel, proceed to Experiment 25C.

EXPERIMENT 25C

Analysis of Biodiesel

Spectroscopy. Obtain an infrared spectrum using salt plates (see Technique 25, Section 25.2). Determine the proton NMR spectrum using 3–4 drops of your biodiesel in 0.7 mL of deuterated chloroform. Since biodiesel consists of a mixture of different molecules, it is not helpful to perform an integration of the area under the peaks. Compare the NMR spectrum of biodiesel to the spectrum of vegetable oil shown here. Finally, analyze your sample using gas chromatography-mass spectrometry (GC-MS). Your instructor will provide you with instructions on how to do this.

Calorimetry (optional). Determine the heat of combustion (in kjoules/gram) of your biodiesel. Your instructor will provide instructions on how to use the bomb calorimeter and how to perform the calculations.

REPORT

Calculate the percent yield of biodiesel. This is difficult to do in the normal way based on moles because the vegetable oil and biodiesel molecules have variable composition. Therefore, you can base this calculation on the weight of oil used and the weight of biodiesel produced.

Analyze the infrared spectrum by identifying the principal absorption bands. Look for peaks in the spectrum that may indicate possible contamination from methanol, glycerol, or free fatty acids. Indicate any impurities found in your biodiesel bases on the infrared spectrum.

Analyze the NMR spectrum by comparing it to the NMR spectrum of vegetable oil with some of the signals labeled that is shown below. Look for evidence in the NMR spectrum for contamination by methanol, free fatty acids, or the original vegetable oil. Indicate any impurities found based on the NMR spectrum.

The library search contained in the software for the GC-MS instrument will give you a list of components detected in your sample, as well as the retention time and relative area (percentage) for each component. The results will also list possible substances that the computer has tried to match against the mass spectrum of each component. This list—often called a "hit list"—will include the name of each possible compound, its Chemical Abstracts Registry number (CAS number), and a "quality" ("confidence") measure expressed as a percentage. The "quality" parameter estimates how closely the mass spectrum of the substance on the "hit list" fits the observed spectrum of that component in the gas chromatogram. The components that you identify from the GC-MS will be the methyl esters of the fatty acids that were initially part of the vegetable oil molecule. From the GC-MS data, you can determine the fatty acid composition (by percentages) in the original vegetable oil. Make a table of the main fatty acid components and the relative percentages. Compare this with the fatty acid composition given for this oil in Table 2 in the essay "Fats and Oils" that precedes Experiment 23. Is the fatty acid composition the same, and how do the relative percentages compare?

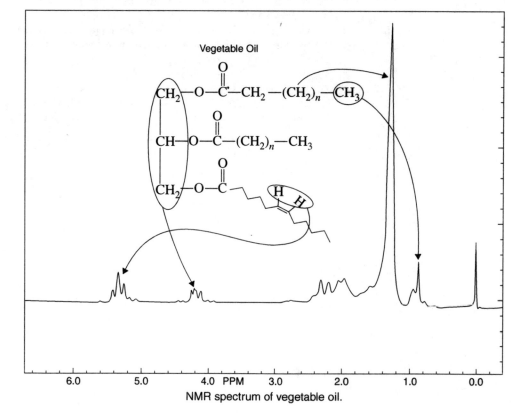

NMR spectrum of vegetable oil.

If you performed the experiment with the bomb calorimeter, list the data and calculate the heat of combustion for biodiesel in kj/g. The heat of combustion for heptane, a component of gasoline, is 45 kj/g. How do they compare? If you also determined the heat of combustion of ethanol in Experiment 26 (Ethanol from Corn), you should compare the heats of combustion for biodiesel and ethanol.

QUESTIONS

1. Write a complete reaction mechanism for this based-catalyzed transesterification reaction. Rather than starting with a complete oil molecule, give the mechanism for the reaction between the following ester and methanol in the presence of NaOH.

$$CH_3CH_2\overset{\overset{\displaystyle O}{\parallel}}{C}OCH_2CH_3 + CH_3OH \xrightarrow{\text{NaOH}} CH_3CH_2\overset{\overset{\displaystyle O}{\parallel}}{C}OCH_3 + CH_3CH_2OH$$

2. If you calculated the heat of combustion of biodiesel and ethanol using bomb calorimeter, answer the following questions:
   a. Compare the heat of combustion of biodiesel with heptane. Why does heptane have a larger heat of combustion? The heat of combustion of heptane is 45 kj/g. (*Hint:* In answering this question, it may be helpful to compare the molecular formulas of biodiesel and heptane).
   b. If you also determined the heat of combustion of ethanol, compare the heats of combustion of biodiesel and ethanol. Why does biodiesel have a larger heat of combustion than ethanol?

3. One argument for using biodiesel rather than gasoline is that the net amount of carbon dioxide released into the atmosphere from combusting biodiesel is sometimes claimed to be zero (or near zero). How can this argument be made, given that the combustion of biodiesel also releases carbon dioxide?

4. When the reaction for making biodiesel occurs, two layers are formed: biodiesel and glycerol. In which layer will most of each of the following substances be found? If a substance will be found to a large extent in both layers, you should indicate this.

$$CH_3OH \qquad OCH_3^- \qquad H_2O \qquad Na^+ \qquad OH^-$$

ESSAY

Green Chemistry

The economic prosperity of the United States demands that it continue to have a robust chemical industry. In this age of environmental consciousness, however, we can no longer afford to allow the type of industry that has been characteristic of past practices to continue operating as it always has. There is a real need to develop an environmentally benign, or "green," technology. Chemists must not only create new products, but also design the chemical syntheses in a way that carefully considers their environmental ramifications.

Beginning with the first Earth Day celebration in 1970, scientists and the general public began to understand that the earth is a closed system in which the consumption of resources and indiscriminate disposal of waste materials are certain to bring about profound and long-lasting effects on the worldwide environment. Over the past decade, interest has begun to grow in an initiative known as *green chemistry*.

Green Chemistry may be defined as the invention, design, and application of chemical products and processes to reduce or eliminate the use and generation of hazardous substances. Practitioners of green chemistry strive to protect the environment by cleaning up toxic waste sites and by inventing new chemical methods that do not pollute and that minimize the consumption of energy and natural resources. Guidelines for developing green chemistry technologies are summarized in the "Twelve Principles of Green Chemistry" shown in the table.

THE TWELVE PRINCIPLES OF GREEN CHEMISTRY

---

1. It is better to prevent waste than to treat or clean up waste after it is formed.
2. Synthetic methods should be designed to maximize the incorporation of all materials used in the process into the final product.
3. Wherever practicable, synthetic methodologies should be designed to use and generate substances that possess little or no toxicity to human health and the environment.
4. Chemical products should be designed to preserve efficacy of function while reducing toxicity.
5. The use of auxiliary substances (solvents, separation agents, etc.) should be made unnecessary whenever possible and innocuous when used.

6. Energy requirements should be recognized for their environmental and economic impacts and should be minimized. Synthetic methods should be conducted at ambient temperature and pressure.

7. A raw material or feedstock should be renewable rather than depleting whenever technically and economically practicable.

8. Unnecessary privatization (blocking group, protection/deprotection, temporary modification of physical/chemical processes) should be avoided whenever possible.

9. Catalytic reagents (as selective as possible) are superior to stoichiometric reagents.

10. Chemical products should be designed so that at end of their function they do not persist in the environment and do break down into innocuous degradation products.

11. Analytical methodologies need to be further developed to allow for real-time, in-process monitoring and control before the formation of hazardous substances.

12. Substances and the form of a substance used in a chemical process should be chosen to minimize the potential for chemical accidents, including releases, explosions, and fires.

Source: P. T. Anastas and J. C. Warner, *Green Chemistry: Theory and Practice.* New York: Oxford University Press, 1998. Reprinted by permission of the publisher.

The green chemistry program was begun shortly after the passage of the Pollution Prevention Act of 1990 and is the central focus of the Environmental Prevention Agency's Design for the Environment Program. As a stimulus for research in the area of reducing the impact of chemical industry on the environment, the Presidential Green Chemistry Challenge Award was begun in 1995. The theme of the Green Chemistry Challenge is "Chemistry is not the problem; it's the solution." Since 1995, award winners have been responsible for the elimination of more than 460 million pounds of hazardous chemicals and have saved more than 440 million gallons of water and 26 million barrels of oil.

Winners of the Green Chemistry Challenge Award have developed foam fire retardants that do not use halons (compounds containing fluorine, chlorine, or bromine), cleaning agents that do not use tetrachloroethylene, methods that facilitate the recycling of polyethylene terephthalate soft-drink bottles, a method of synthesizing ibuprofen that minimizes the use of solvents and the generation of wastes, and a formulation that promotes the efficient release of ammonia from urea-based fertilizers. This latter contribution allows a more environmentally friendly means of applying fertilizers without the need for tilling or disturbing (and losing) precious topsoil.

Green syntheses of the future will require making choices about reactants, solvents, and reaction conditions that are designed to reduce resource consumption and waste production. We need to think about performing a synthesis in a way that will not consume excessive amounts of resources (and thus use less energy and be more economical), that will not produce excessive amounts of toxic or harmful by-products, and that will require milder reaction conditions.

The application of green-chemistry principles in an organic synthesis begins with the selection of the starting materials, called **feedstock**. Most organic compounds used as feedstock are derived from petroleum, a nonrenewable resource (see essay "Petroleum and Fossil Fuels" that preceeds Experiment 24). A green approach is to replace these petrochemicals with chemicals derived from biological sources such as trees, corn, or soybeans. Not only is this approach more sustainable, but the refining of organic compounds from these plant-derived materials, sometimes called **biomass**, is also less polluting than the refining process for petrochemicals. Many pharmaceuticals, plastics, agricultural chemicals, and even transportation fuels can now be produced from chemicals derived from biomass. A good example of this is adipic acid, an organic chemical widely used in the production of nylon and lubricants. Adipic acid can be produced from benzene, a toxic petrochemical, or from glucose, which is found in plant sources.

Industrial processes are being designed that are based on the concept of **atom economy**. Atom economy means that close attention is paid to the design of chemical reactions so that all or most of the atoms that are starting materials in the process are converted into molecules of the desired product rather than into wasted by-products. Atom economy in the industrial world is the equivalent of ensuring that a chemical reaction proceeds with a high percentage yield in a classroom laboratory experiment.

The atom economy for a reaction can be calculated using the following equation:

$$\text{Percent atom economy} = \frac{\text{Molecular weight of desired product}}{\text{Molecular weights of all rectants}} \times 100\%$$

For example, consider the reaction for the synthesis of aspirin (Experiment 8, "Acetylsalicylic Acid"):

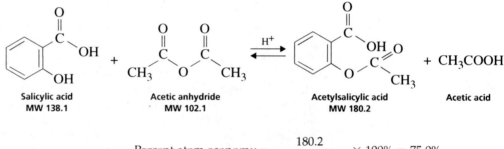

| Salicylic acid MW 138.1 | Acetic anhydride MW 102.1 | Acetylsalicylic acid MW 180.2 | Acetic acid |

$$\text{Percent atom economy} = \frac{180.2}{138.1 + 102.1} \times 100\% = 75.0\%$$

This calculation assumes the complete conversion of reactants into product and 100% recovery of the product, which is not possible. Furthermore, the calculation does not take into account that often an excess of one reactant is used to drive the reaction to completion. In this reaction, acetic anhydride is used in large excess to ensure the production of more acetylsalicylic acid. Nonetheless, the atom economy calculation is a good way to compare different possible pathways to a given product.

To illustrate the benefits of atom economy, consider the synthesis of ibuprofen, mentioned earlier, that won the Presidential Green Chemistry Challenge Award in 1997. In the former process, developed in the 1960s, only 40% of the reactant atoms were incorporated into the desired ibuprofen product; the remaining 60% of the reactant atoms found their way into unwanted by-products or wastes that required disposal. The new method requires fewer reaction steps and recovers 77% of the reactant atoms in the desired product. This "green" process eliminates millions of pounds of waste chemical by-products every year, and it reduces by millions of pounds the amount of reactants needed to prepare this widely used analgesic.

Another green chemistry approach is to select safer reagents that are used to carry out the synthesis of a given organic compound. In one example of this, milder or less toxic oxidizing reagents may be selected to carry out a conversion that is normally done in a less green way. For example, sodium hypochlorite (bleach) can be used in some oxidation reactions instead of the highly toxic dichromate/sulfuric acid mixture. In some reactions, it is possible to use biological reagents, such as enzymes, to carry out a transformation. Another approach in green chemistry is to use a reagent that can promote the formation of a given product in less time and with greater yield. Finally, some reagents, especially catalysts, can be recovered at the end of the reaction period and recycled for use again in the same conversion.

Many solvents used in traditional organic syntheses are highly toxic. The green chemistry approach to the selection of solvents has resulted in several strategies. One method that has been developed is to use supercritical carbon dioxide as a solvent. Supercritical carbon dioxide is formed under conditions of high pressure in which the gas and liquid phases of carbon dioxide combine to a single-phase compressible fluid that becomes an environmentally benign solvent (temperature 31°C; pressure 7280 kpa, or 72 atmospheres). Supercritical CO_2 has remarkable properties. It behaves as a material whose properties are intermediate between those of a solid and those of a liquid. The properties can be controlled by manipulating temperature and pressure. Supercritical CO_2 is environmentally benign because of its low toxicity and easy recyclability. Carbon dioxide is not added to the atmosphere; rather, it is removed from the atmosphere for use in chemical processes. It is used as a medium to carry out a large number of reactions that would otherwise have many negative environmental consequences. It is even possible to perform stereoselective synthesis in supercritical CO_2.

Some reactions can be carried out in ordinary water, the most green solvent possible. Recently, there has been much success in using near-critical water at higher temperatures where water behaves more like an organic solvent. Two of the award winners of the 2004 Green Chemistry Award, Charles Eckert and Charles Liotta, have advanced our understanding of supercritical CO_2 and near-critical water as solvents. One example of their work takes advantage of the dissociation of water that takes place under near-critical conditions, leading to a high concentration of hydronium and hydroxide ions. These ions can serve as self-neutralizing catalysts, and they can replace catalysts that must normally be added to the reaction mixture. Eckert and Liotta were able to run Friedel-Crafts reactions (Experiment 60, "Friedel-Crafts Acylation") in near-critical water without the need for the acid catalyst $AICI_3$, which is normally used in large amounts in these reactions.

Research has also focused on **ionic liquids**, salts that are liquid at room temperature and do not evaporate. Ionic liquids are excellent solvents for many materials, and they can be recycled. An example of an ionic liquid is

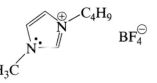

Even though many of the ionic liquids are expensive, their high initial cost is mitigated because, through recycling, they are not consumed or discarded. In addition, product recovery is often easier than with traditional solvents. In the past five years, many new ionic liquids have been developed with a broad range of properties. By selecting the appropriate ionic liquid, it is now possible to carry out many types of organic reactions in these solvents. In some reactions, a well-designed ionic solvent can lead to better yields under milder conditions than is possible with traditional solvents. Recently, researchers have developed ionic liquids made from artificial "sweeteners" that are nontoxic and extend even further the concept of green chemistry.

It is possible in some organic syntheses to completely eliminate the need for any solvent! Some reactions that are traditionally carried out in solvents can be carried out either in the solid or gas phases without the presence of any solvent.

Another approach to making organic chemistry greener involves the way in which a reaction is carried out, rather than in the selection of starting material, reagents, or solvents. Microwave technology (see Technique 7, Section 7) can be used in some reactions to provide the heat energy required to make the transformation go to completion. With microwave technology, reactions can take place with less toxic reagents, in a shorter time, and with fewer side reactions—all goals of green chemistry. Microwave technology has also been used to create supercritical water that behaves more like an organic solvent and could replace more toxic solvents in carrying out organic reactions.

Another green approach involving technology is the use of solid-phase extraction (SPE) columns (see Technique 12, Section 12.14). Using SPE columns, extractions such as removing caffeine from tea can be carried out more quickly and with less toxic solvents. In other applications, SPE columns can be used to carry out the synthesis of organic compounds more efficiently with less use of toxic reagents.

Industry has discovered that environmental stewardship makes good economic sense, and there is a renewed interest in cleaning up manufacturing processes and products. In spite of the continuing adversarial nature of relations between industry and environmentalists, companies are discovering that preventing pollution in the first place, using less energy, and developing atom-economic methods makes as much sense as spending less money on raw materials or capturing a greater share of the market for their product. Although U.S. chemical industries are by no means near their stated goal of reducing the emission of toxic substances to zero or near-zero levels, significant progress is being made.

The teaching of the principles of green chemistry is beginning to find its way into the classroom. In this textbook, we have attempted to improve the green qualities of some of the experiments and have added several green experiments. The following table lists the experiments in this textbook that have a significant green component, along with the primary aspect of the experiment that makes it green.

Experiment	Green Aspect
Exp. 24, "Gas Chromatographic Analysis of Gasolines"	Discussion of pollution-controlling additives
Exp. 25, "Biodiesel"	Transportation fuel using recycled materials
Exp. 26, "Ethanol from Corn"	Transportation fuel made from renewable resources
Exp. 27, "Chiral Reduction of Ethyl Acetoacetate"	Biological reagent, baker's yeast
Exp. 28, "Nitration of Aromatic Compounds Using a Recyclable Catalyst"	Use of a recyclable catalyst to increase reaction efficiency
Exp. 29, "Reduction of Ketones Using Carrot Extract"	Biological reagent
Exp. 30, "An Oxidation-Reduction Scheme: Borneol, Camphor, Isoborneol"	Less-toxic oxidizing agents
Exp. 34, "Aqueous-Based Organozinc Reactions"	Water used as the solvent
Exp. 35, "Sonogashira Coupling of Iodoaromatic Compounds with Alkynes"	Use of a recyclable catalyst to increase reaction efficiency

Experiment	Green Aspect
Exp. 36, "Grubb's-Catalyzed Matathesis of Eugenol with *cis*-1,4-Butenediol"	Use of a recyclable catalyst to increase reaction efficiency
Exp. 38, "A Green Enantioselective Aldol Condensation Reaction"	Use of less-toxic reagents
Exp. 40, "Preparation of Triarylpyridines"	Solvent-less reaction
Exp. 41, "1,4-Dipheny1-1,3-butadiene"	Solvent-less reaction
Exp. 48, "Synthesis of a New Polymer Using Grubb's Catalyst"	Use of a recyclable catalyst to increase reaction efficiency
Exp. 50, "Diels-Alder Reaction with Anthracene-9-methanol"	Water used as the solvent
Exp. 64, "Green Epoxidation of Chalcones"	Use of a less-toxic reagents
Exp. 65, "Cyclopropanation of Chalcones"	Use of a less-toxic reagents

In addition, Experiment 55 (Identification of Unknowns) offers a "green" alternative procedure. This procedure avoids the use of toxic chemicals for classification tests and substitutes the use of spectroscopy, which does not require any chemical reagents (except a small amount of organic solvent).

Certainly, enormous challenges remain. Generations of new scientists must be taught that it is important to consider the environmental impact of any new methods that are introduced. Industry and business leaders must learn to appreciate that adopting an atom-economic approach to the development of chemical processes makes good long-term economic sense and is a responsible means of conducting business. Political leaders must also develop an understanding of what the benefits of a green technology can be and why it is responsible to encourage such initiatives.

REFERENCES

Amato, I. Green Chemistry Proves It Pays companies to Find New Ways to Show That Preventing Pollution Makes More Sense Than Cleaning Up Afterward. *Fortune* [Online], Jul 24, 2000. www.fortune.com/fortune/articles/0.15114.368198.00.html

Freemantle, M. Ionic Liquids in Organic Synthesis. *Chem. Eng. News* **2004,** *82* (Nov 8), 44.

Jacoby, M. Making Olefins from Soybeans. *Chem. Eng. News* **2005,** *83* (Jan 3), 10.

Mark, V. Riding the Microwave. *Chem. Eng. News* **2004,** *82* (Dec 13), 14.

Matlack, A. Some Recent Trends and Problems in Green Chemistry. *Green Chem.* 2003 (Feb), G7 G11.

Mullin, R. Sustainable Specialties. *Chem. Eng. News* **2004,** *82* (Nov 8), 29.

Oakes, R. S.; Clifford, A. A.; Bartle, K. D.; Pett, M. T.; Rayner, C. M. Sulfur Oxidation in Supercritical Corbon Dioxide: Dramatic Pressure Dependent Enhancement of Diastereo-selectivity for Sulfoxidation of Cysteine Derivatives. *Chem. Comm.* **1999,** 247–248.

Ritter, S. K. Green Innovations. *Chem. Eng. News* **2004,** *82* (Jul 12), 25.

33   EXPERIMENT 33

Triphenylmethanol and Benzoic Acid

Grignard reaction

Extraction

Crystallization

In this experiment, you will prepare a Grignard reagent or organomagnesium reagent. The reagent is phenylmagnesium bromide.

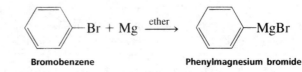

Bromobenzene   **Phenylmagnesium bromide**

This reagent will be converted to a tertiary alcohol or a carboxylic acid, depending on the experiment selected.

EXPERIMENT 33A

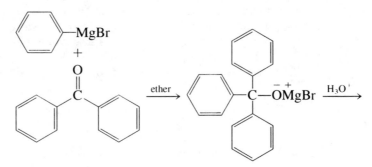

Benzophenone

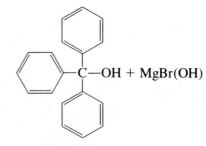

Triphenylmethanol

EXPERIMENT 33B

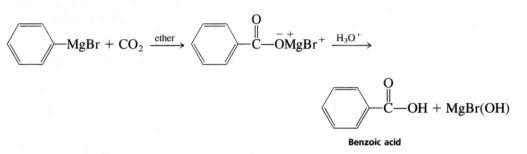

Benzoic acid

The alkyl portion of the Grignard reagent behaves as if it had the characteristics of a **carbanion**. We may write the structure of the reagent as a partially ionic compound:

$$\overset{\delta-}{R} \cdots \overset{\delta+}{MgX}$$

This partially bonded carbanion is a Lewis base. It reacts with strong acids, as you would expect, to give an alkane.

$$\overset{\delta-}{R} \cdots \overset{\delta+}{MgX} + HX \longrightarrow R - H + MgX_2$$

Any compound with a suitably acidic hydrogen will donate a proton to destroy the reagent. Water, alcohols, terminal acetylenes, phenols, and carboxylic acids are all acidic enough to bring about this reaction.

The Grignard reagent also functions as a good nucleophile in nucleophilic addition reactions of the carbonyl group. The carbonyl group has an electrophilic character at its carbon atom (due to resonance), and a good nucleophile seeks out this center for addition.

$$\left[\begin{array}{c} \ddot{O} \\ \| \\ C \end{array} \longleftrightarrow \begin{array}{c} :\ddot{O}:^- \\ | \\ C \\ + \end{array} \right] \qquad \overset{\delta+}{C} = \overset{\delta-}{\ddot{O}}$$

The magnesium salts produced form a complex with the addition product, an alkoxide salt. In the second step of the reaction, these must be hydrolyzed (protonated) by addition of dilute aqueous acid.

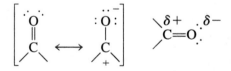

Step 1   Step 2

The Grignard reaction is used synthetically to prepare secondary alcohols from aldehydes and tertiary alcohols from ketones. The Grignard reagent will react with esters twice to give tertiary alcohols. Synthetically, it can also be allowed to react with carbon dioxide to give carboxylic acids and with oxygen to give hydroperoxides.

$$RMgX + O{=}C{=}O \longrightarrow R-\overset{\overset{\displaystyle O}{\|}}{C}-OMgX \xrightarrow[H_2O]{HX} R-\overset{\overset{\displaystyle O}{\|}}{C}-OH$$

Carboxylic acid

$$RMgX + O_2 \longrightarrow ROOMgX \xrightarrow[H_2O]{HX} ROOH$$

Hydroperoxide

Because the Grignard reagent reacts with water, carbon dioxide, and oxygen, it must be protected from air and moisture when it is used. The apparatus in which the reaction is to be conducted must be scrupulously dry (recall that 18 mL of H_2O is 1 mole), and the solvent must be free of water or anhydrous. During the reaction, the flask must be protected by a calcium chloride drying tube. Oxygen should also be excluded. In practice, this can be done by allowing the solvent ether to reflux. This blanket of solvent vapor keeps air from the surface of the reaction mixture.

In the experiment described here, the principal impurity is **biphenyl**, which is formed by a heat- or light-catalyzed coupling reaction of the Grignard reagent and unreacted bromobenzene. A high reaction temperature favors the formation of this product. Biphenyl is highly soluble in petroleum ether, and it is easily separated from triphenylmethanol. Biphenyl can be separated from benzoic acid by extraction.

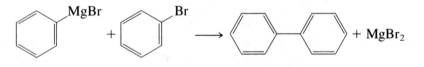

REQUIRED READING

Sign in at www
.cengage.com to access
Pre-Lab Video Exercises
for techniques marked
with an asterisk.

Review: *Technique 8   Filtration, Section 8.3

*Technique 11   Crystallization: Purification of Solids, Section 11.3

*Technique 12   Extractions, Separations, and Drying Agents,
                Sections 12.4, 12.5, 12.8, and 12.10

Technique 25   Infrared Spectroscopy, Section 25.5

SPECIAL INSTRUCTIONS

This experiment must be conducted in one laboratory period, either to the point after which benzophenone is added (Experiment 33A) or to the point after which the Grignard reagent is poured over dry ice (Experiment 33B). The Grignard reagent cannot be stored; you must react it before stopping. This experiment uses diethyl ether, which is extremely flammable. Be certain that no open flames are in your vicinity when you are using ether.

During this experiment, you will need to use *anhydrous* diethyl ether, which is usually contained in metal cans with a screw cap. You are instructed in the experiment to transfer a small portion of this solvent to a stoppered Erlenmeyer flask. Be certain to minimize exposure to atmospheric water during this transfer. Always recap the ether container after use. Do not use solvent-grade ether, because it may contain some water.

All students will prepare the same Grignard reagent, phenylmagnesium bromide. If your instructor requests it, you should then proceed to either Experiment 33A (triphenylmethanol) or Experiment 33B (benzoic acid) when your reagent is ready.

SUGGESTED WASTE DISPOSAL

All aqueous solutions should be placed in a container designated for aqueous waste. Be sure to decant these solutions away from any magnesium chips before placing them in the waste container. The unreacted magnesium chips that you separate should be placed in a solid waste container designated for that purpose. Place all ether solutions in the container for nonhalogenated liquid wastes. Likewise, the mother liquor from the crystallization, using isopropyl alcohol (Experiment 33A), should also be placed in the container for nonhalogenated liquid wastes.

NOTES TO THE INSTRUCTOR

Whenever possible, you should require that your class wash and dry the necessary glassware *the period before this experiment is scheduled*. It is not a good idea to use glassware that has been washed earlier in the same period, even if it has been dried in the oven. When drying, be certain that no Teflon stopcocks, plastic stoppers, or plastic clips are placed in the oven.

PROCEDURE

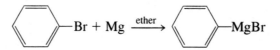

PREPARATION OF THE GRIGNARD REAGENT: PHENYLMAGNESIUM BROMIDE

Glassware.   The following glassware is used:

100-mL round-bottom flask	Claisen head
125-mL separatory funnel	water-jacketed condenser
CaCl$_2$ drying tubes (2)	50-mL Erlenmeyer flasks (2)
10-mL graduated cylinder	

Preparation of Glassware. If necessary, dry all the pieces of *glassware* (no plastic parts), given in the list, in an oven at 110°C for at least 30 minutes. This step can be omitted if your glassware is clean and has been unused in your drawer for at least two to three days. Otherwise, all glassware used in your Grignard reaction must be scrupulously dried. Surprisingly, large amounts of water adhere to the walls of glassware, even when it is apparently dry. Glassware washed and dried the same day, if it is to be used, can still cause problems in starting a Grignard reaction.

Apparatus. Add a clean, dry stirring bar to the 100-mL round-bottom flask, and assemble the apparatus as shown in the figure. Place drying tubes (filled with fresh calcium chloride) on both the separatory funnel and on the top of the condenser. A stirring hot plate will be used to stir and heat the reaction.[1] Make sure that the apparatus can be moved up and down easily on the ring stand. Movement up and down relative to the hot plate will be used to control the amount of heat applied to the reaction.

CAUTION ⚠

Do not place any plasticware, plastic connectors, or Teflon stoppers in the oven, as they may melt, burn, or soften. Check with your instructor if in doubt.

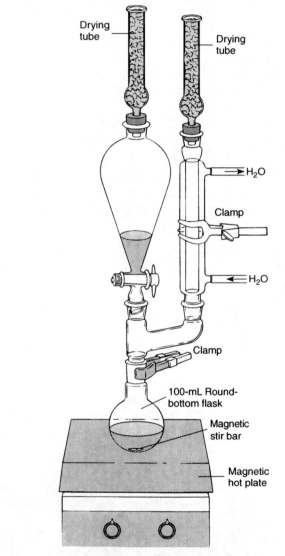

Apparatus for Grignard reactions.

_____

[1]A steam bath or steam cone may be used, but you will probably have to forgo any stirring and use a boiling stone instead of a spin bar. A heating mantle could be used to heat the reaction. With a heating mantle, it is probably best to clamp the apparatus securely and to support the heating mantle under the reaction flask with wooden blocks that can be added or removed. When the blocks are removed, the heating mantle can be lowered away from the flask.

Formation of the Grignard Reagent. Using smooth paper or a small beaker, weigh about 0.5 g of magnesium turnings ($AW = 24.3$) and place them in the 100-mL round-bottom flask. Using a preweighed 10-mL graduated cylinder, measure approximately 2.1 mL of bromobenzene ($MW = 157.0$), and reweigh the cylinder to determine the exact mass of the bromobenzene. Transfer the bromobenzene to a stoppered 50-mL Erlenmeyer flask. Without cleaning the graduated cylinder, measure a 10-mL portion of anhydrous ether and transfer it to the same 50-mL Erlenmeyer flask containing the bromobenzene. Mix the solution (swirl) and then, using a dry, disposable Pasteur pipet, transfer about half of it into the round-bottom flask containing the magnesium turnings. Add the remainder of the solution to the 125-mL separatory funnel. Then add an additional 7.0 mL of anhydrous ether to the bromobenzene solution in the separatory funnel. At this point, make sure all joints are sealed and that the drying tubes are in place.

Position the apparatus just above the hot plate, and stir the mixture *gently* to avoid throwing the magnesium out of the solution and onto the side of the flask. You should begin to notice the evolution of bubbles from the surface of the metal, which signals that the reaction is starting. It will probably be necessary to heat the mixture, using your hot plate, to start the reaction. The hot plate should be adjusted to its lowest setting. Because ether has a low boiling point (35°C), it should be sufficient to heat the reaction by placing the round-bottom flask just above the hot plate. Once the ether is boiling, check to see if the bubbling action continues after the apparatus is lifted above the hot plate. If the reaction continues to bubble without heating, the magnesium is reacting. You may have to repeat the heating several times to successfully start the reaction. After you have made several attempts at heating, the reaction should start, but if you are still experiencing difficulty, proceed to the next paragraph.

Optional Steps. You may need to employ one or more of the following procedures if heating fails to start the reaction. If you are experiencing difficulty, remove the separatory funnel. Place a long, *dry*, glass stirring rod into the flask, and gently twist the stirring rod to crush the magnesium against the glass surface. *Be careful not to poke a hole in the bottom of the flask; do this gently!* Reattach the separatory funnel and heat the mixture again. Repeat the crushing procedure several times, if necessary, to start the reaction. If the crushing procedure fails to start the reaction, then add one small crystal of iodine to the flask. Again, heat the mixture *gently.* The most drastic action, other than starting the experiment over again, is to prepare a small sample of the Grignard reagent *externally* in a test tube. When this external reaction starts, add it to the main reaction mixture. This "booster shot" will react with any water that is present in the mixture and allow the reaction to get started.

Completing the Grignard Preparation. When the reaction has started, you should observe the formation of a brownish-gray, cloudy solution. Add the remaining solution of bromobenzene slowly over a period of 5 minutes at a rate that keeps the solution boiling gently. If the boiling stops, add more bromobenzene. It may be necessary to heat the mixture occasionally with the hot plate during the addition. If the reaction becomes too vigorous, slow the addition of the bromobenzene solution, and raise the apparatus higher above the hot plate. Ideally, the mixture will boil without the application of external heat. *It is important that you heat the mixture if the reflux slows or stops.* As the reaction proceeds, you should observe the gradual disintegration of the magnesium metal. When all the bromobenzene has been added, place an additional 1.0 mL of *anhydrous* ether in the separatory funnel to rinse it and add it to the reaction mixture. Remove the separatory funnel after making this addition, and replace it with a stopper. Heat the solution under gentle reflux until most of the remaining magnesium dissolves (don't worry about a few small pieces). This should require about 15 minutes. Note the level of the solution in the flask. You should add additional anhydrous ether to replace any that is lost during the reflux period. During this reflux period, you can prepare any solution needed for Experiment 33A or Experiment 33B. When the reflux is complete, allow the mixture to cool to room temperature. As your instructor designates, go on to either Experiment 33A or Experiment 33B.

EXPERIMENT 33B

Benzoic Acid

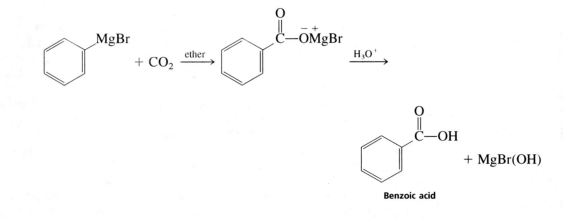

Benzoic acid

PROCEDURE

Addition of Dry Ice. When the phenylmagnesium bromide solution has cooled to room temperature, pour it as quickly as possible onto 10 g of crushed dry ice contained in a 250-mL beaker. The dry ice should be weighed as quickly as possible to avoid contact with atmospheric moisture. It need not be weighed precisely. Rinse the flask, in which the phenylmagnesium bromide was prepared, with 2 mL of anhydrous ether and add it to the beaker.

> **CAUTION**
>
> Exercise caution in handling dry ice. Contact with the skin can cause severe frostbite. Always use gloves or tongs. The dry ice is best crushed by wrapping large pieces in a clean, dry towel and striking them with a hammer or a wooden block. It should be used as soon as possible after crushing it to avoid contact with atmospheric water.

Cover the reaction mixture with a watch glass, and allow it to stand until the excess dry ice has completely sublimed. The Grignard addition compound will appear as a viscous, glassy mass.

Hydrolysis. Hydrolyze the Grignard adduct by slowly adding approximately 8 mL of 6 M hydrochloric acid to the beaker and stirring the mixture with a glass rod or spatula. Any remaining magnesium chips will react with the acid to evolve hydrogen. At this point, you should have two distinct liquid phases in the beaker. If you have solid present (other than magnesium), try adding a little more ether. If the solid is insoluble in ether, try adding a little more 6 *M* hydrochloric acid solution or water. Benzoic acid is soluble in ether, and inorganic compounds (MgX_2) are soluble in the aqueous acid solution. Transfer the liquid phases to an Erlenmeyer flask, leaving behind any residual magnesium. Add more ether to the beaker to rinse it, and add this additional ether to the Erlenmeyer flask. You may stop here. Stopper the flask with a cork, and continue with the experiment during the next laboratory period.

Isolation of the Product. If you stored your product and the ether layer evaporated, add several milliliters of ether. If the solids do not dissolve on stirring or if no water layer is apparent, try adding some water. Transfer your mixture to a 125-mL separatory funnel. If some material remains undissolved or if there are three layers, add more ether and hydrochloric acid to the separatory funnel, stopper it, shake it, and allow the layers to separate. Continue adding small portions of ether and hydrochloric acid to the separatory funnel, and shake it until everything dissolves. After the layers have separated, remove the lower aqueous layer. The aqueous phase contains inorganic salts and may be discarded. The ether layer contains the product benzoic acid and the by-product biphenyl. Add 5.0 mL of 5% sodium hydroxide solution, restopper the funnel, and shake it. Allow the layers to separate, *remove the lower aqueous layer, and save this layer in a beaker.* This extraction removes benzoic acid from the ether layer by converting it to the water-soluble sodium benzoate. The by-product biphenyl stays in the ether layer along with some remaining benzoic acid. Again, shake the remaining ether phase in the separatory funnel with a second 5.0-mL portion of 5% sodium hydroxide, and transfer the lower aqueous layer into the beaker with the first extract. Repeat the extraction process with a third portion (5.0 mL) of 5% sodium hydroxide, and save the aqueous layer as before. Discard the ether layer, which contains the biphenyl impurity, into the waste container designated for nonhalogenated organic wastes.

Heat the combined basic extracts while stirring on a hot plate (100°C–120°C) for about 5 minutes to remove any ether that may be dissolved in this aqueous phase. Ether is soluble in water to the extent of 7%. During this heating period, you may observe slight bubbling, but the volume of liquid *will not* decrease substantially. Unless the ether is removed before the benzoic acid is precipitated, the product may appear as a waxy solid instead of crystals.

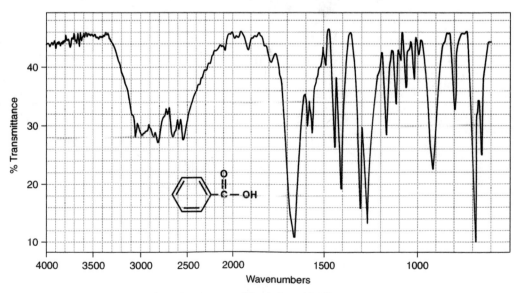

Infrared spectrum of benzoic acid, KBr.

Cool the alkaline solution, and precipitate the benzoic acid by adding 10.0 mL of 6.0 *M* hydrochloric acid while stirring. Cool the mixture in an ice bath. Collect the solid by vacuum filtration on a Büchner funnel (see Technique 8, Section 8.3 and Figure 8.5). The transfer may be aided and the solid washed with several small portions of cold water. Allow the crystals to dry thoroughly at room temperature at least overnight. Weigh the solid, and calculate the percentage yield of benzoic acid (*MW* = 122.1).

Crystallization. Crystallize your product from hot water, using a Büchner funnel to collect the product by vacuum filtration (see Technique 11, Section 11.3 and Figure 11.4). Step 2 in Figure 11.4 (removal of insoluble impurities) should not be required in this crystallization. Set the crystals aside to air-dry at room temperature before determining the melting point of the purified benzoic acid (literature value, 122°C) and the recovered yield in grams.[3] Submit your product to your instructor in a properly labeled vial.

Spectroscopy. If your instructor requests it, determine the infrared spectrum of the purified material in a KBr pellet (see Technique 25, Section 25.5). Your instructor may assign certain tests on the product you prepared. These tests are described in the Instructor's Manual.

QUESTIONS

1. Benzene is often produced as a side product during Grignard reactions using phenylmagnesium bromide. How can its formation be explained? Give a balanced equation for its formation.

2. Write a balanced equation for the reaction of benzoic acid with hydroxide ion. Why is it necessary to extract the ether layer with sodium hydroxide?

3. Interpret the principal peaks in the infrared spectrum of either triphenylmethanol or benzoic acid, depending on the procedure used in this experiment.

4. Outline a separation scheme for isolating either triphenylmethanol or benzoic acid from the reaction mixture, depending on the procedure used in this experiment.

5. Provide methods for preparing the following compounds by the Grignard method:

(a)

(c)

(b)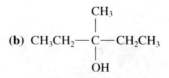

(d)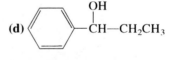

---

[3]If necessary, the crystals may be dried in a low temperature (ca. 50°C) oven for a short period of time. Be warned that benzoic acid sublimes, and heating it for a long time at elevated temperatures could result in loss of your product.

QUESTIONS

1. Using resonance structures, show why the amino group is activating. Consider an attack by the electrophile E^+ at the *para* position.

2. For the substituent in this experiment that was found to be least activating, explain why bromination took place at the position on the ring indicated by the experimental results.

3. What other experimental techniques (including spectroscopy) might be used to identify the products in this experiment?

| 43 | **EXPERIMENT 43** |

Nitration of Methyl Benzoate

Aromatic substitution

Crystallization

The nitration of methyl benzoate to prepare methyl *m*-nitrobenzoate is an example of an electrophilic aromatic substitution reaction, in which a proton of the aromatic ring is replaced by a nitro group:

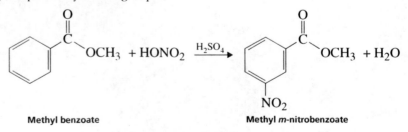

Methyl benzoate   Methyl *m*-nitrobenzoate

Many such aromatic substitution reactions are known to occur when an aromatic substrate is allowed to react with a suitable electrophilic reagent, and many other groups besides nitro may be introduced into the ring.

You may recall that alkenes (which are electron-rich due to an excess of electrons in the π system) can react with an electrophilic reagent. The intermediate formed is electron-deficient. It reacts with the nucleophile to complete the reaction. The overall sequence is called **electrophilic addition**. Addition of HX to cyclohexene is an example.

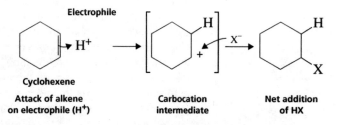

| Attack of alkene on electrophile (H⁺) | Carbocation intermediate | Net addition of HX |

Aromatic compounds are not fundamentally different from cyclohexene. They can also react with electrophiles. However, because of resonance in the ring, the electrons of the π system are generally less available for addition reactions because an addition would mean the loss of the stabilization that resonance provides. In practice, this means that aromatic compounds react only with *powerfully electrophilic reagents,* usually at somewhat elevated temperatures.

Benzene, for example, can be nitrated at 50°C with a mixture of concentrated nitric and sulfuric acids; the electrophile is NO_2^+ (nitronium ion), whose formation is promoted by action of the concentrated sulfuric acid on nitric acid:

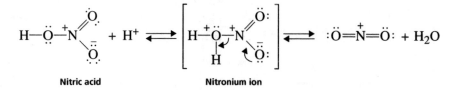

Nitric acid   **Nitronium ion**

The nitronium ion thus formed is sufficiently electrophilic to add to the benzene ring, *temporarily* interrupting ring resonance:

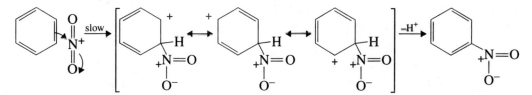

The intermediate first formed is somewhat stabilized by resonance and does not rapidly undergo reaction with a nucleophile; in this behavior, it is different from the unstabilized carbocation formed from cyclohexene plus an electrophile. In fact, aromaticity can be restored to the ring if *elimination* occurs instead. (Recall that elimination is often a reaction of carbocations.) Removal of a proton, probably by HSO_4^-, from the sp^3-ring carbon *restores the aromatic system* and yields a net *substitution* wherein a hydrogen has been replaced by a nitro group. Many similar reactions are known, and they are called **electrophilic aromatic substitution reactions**.

The substitution of a nitro group for a ring hydrogen occurs with methyl benzoate in the same way it does with benzene. In principle, one might expect that any hydrogen on the ring could be replaced by a nitro group. However, for reasons beyond our scope here (see your lecture textbook), the carbomethoxy group directs the aromatic substitution preferentially to those positions that are *meta* to it. As a result, methyl *m*-nitrobenzoate is the principal product formed. In addition, one might expect the nitration to occur more than once on the ring. However, both the carbomethoxy group and the nitro group that has just been attached to the ring *deactivate* the ring against further substitution. Consequently, the formation of a methyl dinitrobenzoate product is much less favorable than the formation of the mononitration product.

Although the products described previously are the principal ones formed in the reaction, it is possible to obtain as impurities in the reaction small amounts of the ortho and para isomers of methyl *m*-nitrobenzoate and of the dinitration products. These side products are removed when the desired product is washed with methanol and purified by crystallization.

Water has a retarding effect on the nitration because it interferes with the nitric acid–sulfuric acid equilibria that form the nitronium ions. The smaller the amount of water present, the more active the nitrating mixture. Also, the reactivity of the nitrating mixture can be controlled by varying the amount of sulfuric acid used. This acid must protonate nitric acid, which is a *weak* base, and the larger the amount of acid available, the more numerous the protonated species (and hence NO_2^+) in the solution. Water interferes because it is a stronger base than H_2SO_4 or HNO_3. Temperature is also a factor in determining the extent of nitration. The higher the temperature, the greater will be the amounts of dinitration products formed in the reaction.

Experiment 28 illustrates a Green Chemistry alternative to the nitration of aromatic hydrocarbons. In this version, a recyclable catalyst (ytterbium triflate) is used to generate the nitronium ion. The catalyst is recovered at the end of the experiment.

REQUIRED READING

Sign in at www
.cengage.com to access
Pre-Lab Video Exercises
for techniques marked
with an asterisk.

Review: *Techniques 11   Crystallization: Purification of Solids

Technique 25   Infrared Spectroscopy, Sections 25.4 and 25.5

SPECIAL INSTRUCTIONS

It is important that the temperature of the reaction mixture be maintained at or below 15°C. Nitric acid and sulfuric acid, especially when mixed, are very corrosive substances. Be careful not to get these acids on your skin. If you do get some of these acids on your skin, flush the affected area liberally with water.

SUGGESTED WASTE DISPOSAL

All aqueous solutions should be placed in a container specially designated for aqueous wastes. Place the methanol used to recrystallize the methyl nitrobenzoate in the container designated for nonhalogenated organic waste.

PROCEDURE

In a 100-mL beaker, cool 6 mL of concentrated sulfuric acid to about 0°C and add 3.05 g of methyl benzoate. Using an ice–salt bath (see Technique 6, Section 6.9), cool the mixture to 0°C or below and very slowly add, using a Pasteur pipet, a cool mixture of 2 mL of concentrated sulfuric acid and 2 mL of concentrated nitric acid. During the addition of the acids, stir the mixture continuously and maintain the temperature of the reaction below 15°C. If the mixture rises above this temperature, the formation of by-product increases rapidly, bringing about a decrease in the yield of the desired product.

After you have added all of the acid, warm the mixture to room temperature. After 15 minutes, pour the acid mixture over 25 g of crushed ice in a 150-mL beaker. After the ice has melted, isolate the product by vacuum filtration through a Büchner funnel and wash it with two 12-mL portions of cold water and then with two 5-mL portions of ice-cold methanol. Weigh the product and recrystallize it from an equal weight of methanol (see Technique 11, Section 11.3). The melting point of the recrystallized product should be 78°C. Obtain the infrared spectrum using the dry-film method (see Technique 25, Section 25.4) or as a KBr pellet (see Technique 25, Section 25.5). Compare your infrared spectrum with the one reproduced here. Calculate the percentage yield and submit the product to the instructor in a labeled vial.

Molecular Modeling (Optional)

If you are working alone, complete Part A. If you have a partner, one of you should complete Part A and the other complete Part B. If you work with a partner, you should combine results at the end of the experiment.

Part A. Nitration of Methyl Benzoate

In this exercise, you will try to explain the observed outcome of the nitration of methyl benzoate. The major product of this reaction is methyl *m*-nitrobenzoate, where the nitro group has been added to the *meta* position of the ring. The rate-determining step of this reaction is the attack of the nitronium ion on the benzene ring. Three different benzenium ion intermediates (*ortho*, *meta*, and *para*) are possible:

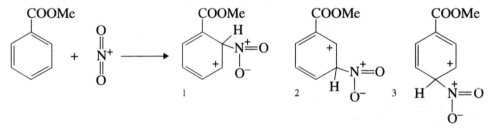

You will calculate the heats of formation for these intermediates to determine which of the three has the lowest energy. Assume that the activation energies are similar to the energies of the intermediates themselves. This is an application of the Hammond Postulate, which states that the activation energy leading to an intermediate of higher energy will be higher than the activation energy leading to an intermediate of lower energy, and vice versa. Although there are prominent exceptions, this postulate is generally true.

Make models of each of the three benzenium ion intermediates (separately) and calculate their heats of formation using an AM1-level calculation with geometry optimization. Don't forget to specify a positive charge when you submit the calculation. What do you conclude?

Now take a piece of paper and draw the resonance structures that are possible for each intermediate. Do not worry about structures involving the nitro group; consider only where the charge in the ring may be delocalized. Also note the polarity of the carbonyl group by placing a δ+ symbol on the carbon and a δ− symbol on the oxygen. What do you conclude from your resonance analysis?

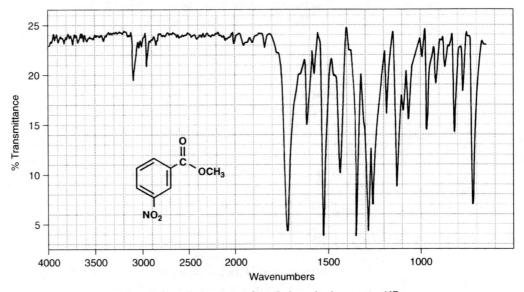

Infrared spectrum of methyl *m*-nitrobenzoate, KBr.

Part B. Nitration of Anisole

For this computation, you will analyze the three benzenium ions formed from anisole (methoxybenzene) and the nitronium ion (see Part A). Calculate the heats of formation using AM1-level calculations with geometry optimization. Don't forget to specify a positive charge. What do you conclude for anisole? How do the results compare to those for methyl benzoate?

Now take a piece of paper and draw the resonance structures that are possible for each intermediate. Do not worry about structures involving the nitro group; consider only where the charge in the ring may be delocalized. Do not forget that the electrons on the oxygen can participate in the resonance. What do you conclude from your resonance analysis?

QUESTIONS

1. Why is methyl *m*-nitrobenzoate formed in this reaction instead of the *ortho* or *para* isomers?

2. Why does the amount of the dinitration increase at high temperatures?

3. Why is it important to add the nitric acid–sulfuric acid mixture slowly over a 15-minute period?

4. Interpret the infrared spectrum of methyl *m*-nitrobenzoate.

5. Indicate the product formed on nitration of each of the following compounds: benzene, toluene, chlorobenzene, and benzoic acid.

55   EXPERIMENT 55

Identification of Unknowns

Qualitative organic analysis, the identification and characterization of unknown compounds, is an important part of organic chemistry. Every chemist must learn the appropriate methods for establishing the identity of a compound. In this experiment, you will be issued an unknown compound and will be asked to identify it through chemical and spectroscopic methods. Your instructor may give you a general unknown or a specific unknown. With a **general unknown**, you must first determine the class of compound to which the unknown belongs, that is, identify its main functional group; then you must determine the specific compound in that class that corresponds to the unknown. With a **specific unknown**, you will know the class of compound (ketone, alcohol, amine, and so on) in advance, and it will be necessary to determine only whatever specific member of that class was issued to you as an unknown. This experiment is designed so that the instructor can issue several general unknowns or as many as six successive specific unknowns, each having a different main functional group.

Although there are millions of organic compounds that an organic chemist might be called on to identify, the scope of this experiment is necessarily limited. In this textbook, about 500 compounds are included in the tables of possible unknowns given for the experiment (see Appendix 1). Your instructor may wish to expand the list of possible unknowns, however. In such a case, you will have to consult more extensive tables, such as those found in the work compiled by Rappoport (see References). In addition, the experiment is restricted to include only seven important functional groups:

Aldehydes	Amines
Ketones	Alcohols
Carboxylic acids	Esters
Phenols	

Even though this list of functional groups omits some of the important types of compounds (alkyl halides, alkenes, alkynes, aromatics, ethers, amides, mercaptans, nitriles, acid chlorides, acid anhydrides, nitro compounds, and so on), the methods introduced here can be applied equally well to other classes of compounds. The list is sufficiently broad to illustrate all the principles involved in identifying an unknown compound.

In addition, although many of the functional groups listed as being excluded will not appear as the major functional group in a compound, several of them will frequently appear as secondary, or subsidiary, functional groups. Three examples of this are presented here.

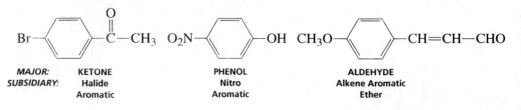

MAJOR:	KETONE	PHENOL	ALDEHYDE
SUBSIDIARY:	Halide	Nitro	Alkene Aromatic
	Aromatic	Aromatic	Ether

The groups included that have subsidiary status are

—Cl	Chloro	—NO_2	Nitro	C=C	Double Bond
—Br	Bromo	—C≡N	Cyano	C≡C	Triple Bond
—I	Iodo	—OR	Alkoxy	⬡	Aromatic

The experiment presents all of the chief chemical and spectroscopic methods of determining the main functional groups, and it includes methods for verifying the presence of the subsidiary functional groups as well. It will usually not be necessary to determine the presence of the subsidiary functional groups to identify the unknown compound correctly. Every piece of information helps the identification, however, and if these groups can be detected easily, you should not hesitate to determine them. Finally, complex bifunctional compounds are generally avoided in this experiment; only a few are included.

How to Proceed—Option 1

Fortunately, we can detail a fairly straightforward procedure for determining all of the necessary pieces of information. This procedure consists of the following steps:

Part One: Chemical Classification

1. Preliminary classification by physical state, color, and odor
2. Melting-point or boiling-point determination; other physical data
3. Purification, if necessary
4. Determination of solubility behavior in water and in acids and bases
5. Simple preliminary tests: Beilstein, ignition (combustion)
6. Application of relevant chemical classification tests
7. Inspection of tables for possible structure(s) of unknown; elimination of unlikely compounds

Part Two: Spectroscopy

8. Determination of infrared and NMR spectra

Part Three: Optional Procedures

9. Elemental analysis, if necessary
10. Preparation of derivatives, if required
11. Confirmation of identity

Each of these steps is discussed briefly starting on page 449.

Green Chemistry Method: How to Proceed—Option 2

At the option of your instructor, another approach may be taken in determining the structure of unknowns in the organic laboratory. This approach makes minimal use of classification tests but retains the solubility tests as the main way of determining functional groups and spectroscopy as a way of determining the detailed structure of an unknown. Elimination of classification tests described in Part One, number 6, tremendously reduces the waste generated in the laboratory. It also eliminates the use of many of the toxic and potentially dangerous reagents that are a standard part of the traditional classification tests. This approach is, therefore, a "Green" approach to solving structures of organic compounds.

Although classification tests can be useful in determining the identity of an unknown compound, spectroscopic methods have become the principal means by which an organic chemist identifies unknown substances. The technology and instrumentation available has almost obviated the need for classification tests, because valuable information can be discovered simply by obtaining infrared and NMR spectra. Option 2 relies heavily on the spectroscopic results; if acetone-d_6 or DMSO-d_6 are used as NMR spectroscopy solvents, this becomes a more environmentally sound approach.

The ability to use IR and NMR spectroscopy and evaluate spectra inherently requires a logical sequence of steps in the identification of an unknown. By relying on these techniques, students learn the techniques and higher-order thinking skills that they would be required to know and use for a career in chemistry. This approach more closely simulates the types of structure-proof methods that one would find in a modern research or industrial laboratory. Students can still learn how to go through the logical steps used in the classification tests by practicing these methods in a more environmentally friendly scenario through the use of computer simulations.

The procedure for determining the structure of a compound using the environmentally friendly approach is fairly straightforward and consists of the following steps:

Part One: Chemical Classification

1. Preliminary classification by physical state, color, and odor
2. Melting point or boiling point determination; other physical data
3. Purification, if necessary
4. Determination of solubility behavior in water and in acids and bases
5. Simple preliminary tests: Beilstein, ignition (combustion)
6. Inspection of tables for possible structure(s) of unknowns

Part Two: Spectroscopy

7. Determination of infrared and NMR (proton and ^{13}C, if available) spectra
8. Confirmation of structure

In many cases, the type of compound and functional group should be discovered after completing Part One. Spectroscopy (Part Two) will be used *principally* to confirm the structural assignment and to provide further information toward identifying the unknown. Your instructor may not allow you to obtain spectroscopic information (infrared or NMR) until you have completed Part One. Show your test results to your instructor for approval. Once this part has been completed, you should have narrowed the list of possible compounds to a few likely candidates, *all containing the same functional group*. In other words, you should have determined the principal functional group. You *must* obtain approval from the instructor to perform spectroscopy.

The functional groups that may be included in the unknowns are listed on the first page of this experiment. Tables of possible compounds are listed in the Appendix 1 of this book.

1. PRELIMINARY CLASSIFICATION

Note the physical characteristics of the unknown, including its color, odor, and physical state (liquid, solid, crystalline form). Many compounds have characteristic colors or odors, or they crystallize with a specific crystal structure. This information can often be found in a handbook and can be checked later. Compounds with a high degree of conjugation are frequently yellow to red. Amines often have a fishlike odor. Esters have a pleasant fruity or floral odor. Acids have a sharp and pungent odor. A part of the training of every good chemist includes cultivating the ability to recognize familiar or typical odors. As a note of caution, many compounds have distinctly unpleasant or nauseating odors. Some have corrosive vapors. Sniff any unknown substance with the greatest caution. As a first step, open the container, hold it away from you, and using your hand, carefully waft the vapors toward your nose. If you get past this stage, a closer inspection will be possible.

2. MELTING-POINT OR BOILING-POINT DETERMINATION

The single most useful piece of information to have for an unknown compound is its melting point or boiling point. Either piece of data will drastically limit the compounds that are possible. The electric melting-point apparatus gives a rapid and accurate measurement (see Technique 9, Sections 9.5 and 9.7). To save time, you can often determine two separate melting points. The first determination can be made rapidly to get an approximate value. Then you can determine the second melting point more carefully. Because some of the unknown solids contain traces of impurities, you may find that your observed melting point is lower than the values found in the tables in Appendix 1. This is especially true for low-melting compounds (<50°C). For these low-melting compounds, it is a good idea to look at compounds in the tables in Appendix 1 that have melting points above your observed melting-point range. The same advice may apply to other solid compounds issued to you as unknowns.

The boiling point is easily obtained by a simple distillation of the unknown (see Technique 14, Section 14.3) by reflux (see Technique 13, Section 13.2), by a microboiling-point determination (see Technique 13, Section 13.2), or by Vernier LabPro interface method (see Technique 13, Section 13.5). The simple distillation has the advantage in that it also purifies the compound. The smallest distilling flask available should be used if a simple distillation is performed, and you should be sure that the thermometer bulb is fully immersed in the vapor of the distilling liquid. The liquid should be distilled rapidly to determine an accurate boiling-point value. The microboiling-point method requires the least amount of unknown, but the refluxing method is more reliable and requires much less liquid than that required for distillation.

When inspecting the tables of unknowns in Appendix 1, you may find that the observed boiling point that you determined is lower than the value for the corresponding compound listed in the tables. This is especially true for compounds boiling above 200°C. It is less likely, but not impossible, that the observed boiling point of your unknown will be higher than the value given in the table. Thus, your strategy should be to look for boiling points of compounds in the tables that are nearly equal to or above the value you obtained, within a range of about ±5°C. For high-boiling liquid compounds (>200°C), you may need to apply a thermometer correction (see Technique 13, Section 13.3).

3. PURIFICATION

If the melting point of a solid has a wide range (about 5°C), the solid should be recrystallized and the melting point redetermined.

If a liquid was highly colored before distillation, if it yielded a wide boiling-point range, or if the temperature did not hold constant during the distillation, it should be redistilled to determine a new temperature range. A reduced-pressure distillation is in order for high-boiling liquids or for those that show any sign of decomposition on heating.

Occasionally, column chromatography may be necessary to purify solids that have large amounts of impurities and do not yield satisfactory results on crystallization.

Acidic or basic impurities that contaminate a neutral compound may often be removed by dissolving the compound in a low-boiling solvent, such as CH_2Cl_2 or ether, and extracting with 5% $NaHCO_3$ or 5% HCl, respectively. Conversely, acidic or basic compounds can be purified by dissolving them in 5% $NaHCO_3$ or 5% HCl, respectively, and extracting them with a low-boiling organic solvent to remove impurities. After the aqueous solution has been neutralized, the desired compound can be recovered by extraction.

4. SOLUBILITY BEHAVIOR

Tests on solubility are described fully in Experiment 55A. They are extremely important. Determine the solubility of small amounts of the unknown in water, 5% HCl, 5% $NaHCO_3$, 5% NaOH, concentrated H_2SO_4, and organic solvents. This information reveals whether a compound is an acid, a base, or a neutral substance. The sulfuric acid test reveals whether a neutral compound has a functional group that contains an oxygen, a nitrogen, or a sulfur atom that can be protonated. This information allows you to eliminate or to choose various functional-group possibilities. The solubility tests must be made on *all* unknowns.

5. PRELIMINARY TESTS

The two combustion tests, the Beilstein test (Experiment 55B) and the ignition test (Experiment 55C), can be performed easily and quickly, and they often give valuable information. It is recommended that they be performed on all unknowns.

6. CHEMICAL CLASSIFICATION TESTS

The solubility tests usually suggest or eliminate several possible functional groups. The chemical classification tests listed in Experiments 55D to 55I allow you to distinguish among the possible choices. Choose only those tests that the solubility tests suggest might be meaningful. Time will be wasted performing unnecessary tests. There is no substitute for a firsthand, thorough knowledge of these tests. Study each of the sections carefully until you understand the significance of each test. Also, it is essential to actually try the tests on *known* substances. In this way, it will be easier to recognize a positive test. Appropriate test compounds are listed for many of the tests. When you are performing a test that is new to you, it is always good practice to run the test separately on both a known substance and the unknown *at the same time*. This practice lets you compare results directly.

Do not perform the chemical tests either haphazardly or in a methodical, comprehensive sequence. Instead, use the tests selectively. Solubility tests automatically eliminate the need for some of the chemical tests. Each successive test will either eliminate the need for another test or dictate its use. You should also examine the tables of unknowns in Appendix 1 carefully. The boiling point or the melting point of the unknown may eliminate the need for many of the tests. For instance, the possible compounds may simply not include one with a double bond. *Efficiency* is the key word here. Do not waste time performing nonsensical or unnecessary tests. Many possibilities can be eliminated on the basis of logic alone.

How you proceed with the following steps may be limited by your instructor's wishes. Many instructors may restrict your access to infrared and NMR spectra until you have narrowed your choices to a few compounds, *all within the same class*. Others may have you determine these data routinely. Some instructors may want students to perform elemental analysis on all unknowns; others may restrict it to only the most essential situations. Again, some instructors may require derivatives as a final confirmation of the compound's identity; others may not wish to use them at all.

7. INSPECTION OF TABLES FOR POSSIBLE STRUCTURES

Once the melting or boiling point, the solubilities, and the main chemical classification tests have been made, you should be able to identify the class of compound (aldehyde, ketone, and so on). At this stage, with the melting point or boiling point as a guide, you can compile a list of possible compounds from one of the appropriate tables in Appendix 1. It is very important to draw out the structures of compounds that fit the solubility, classification tests, and melting point or boiling point that were determined. If necessary, you can look up the structures in the *CRC Handbook, The Merck Index,* or the *Aldrich Handbook*. Remember that the boiling point or melting point recorded in the table may be higher than what you obtained in the laboratory (see Section 2 above).

The short list that you developed by inspection of the tables in Appendix 1 and the structures drawn should suggest that some additional tests may be needed to distinguish among the possibilities. For instance, one compound may be a methyl ketone, and the other may not. The iodoform test is called for to distinguish the two possibilities. The tests for the subsidiary functional groups may also be required. These tests are described in Experiments 55B and 55C. These tests should also be studied carefully; there is no substitute for firsthand knowledge about these tests.

8. SPECTROSCOPY

Spectroscopy is probably the most powerful and modern tool available to the chemist for determining the structure of an unknown compound. It is often possible to determine the structure through spectroscopy alone. On the other hand, there are also situations for which spectroscopy may not be of much help, and the traditional methods must be relied on. For this reason, you should not use spectroscopy to the exclusion of the more traditional tests but rather as a confirmation of those results. Nevertheless, the main functional groups and their immediate environmental features can be determined quickly and accurately with spectroscopy.

9. ELEMENTAL ANALYSIS

Elemental analysis—which allows you to determine the presence of nitrogen, sulfur, or a specific halogen atom (Cl, Br, I) in a compound—is often useful; however, other information may render these tests unnecessary. A compound identified as an amine by solubility tests obviously contains nitrogen. Many nitrogen-containing groups (for instance, nitro groups) can be identified by infrared spectroscopy. Finally, it is not usually necessary to identify a specific halogen. The simple information that the compound contains a halogen (any halogen) may be enough information to distinguish between two compounds. A simple Beilstein test provides this information.

10. DERIVATIVES

One of the principal tests for the correct identification of an unknown compound is to convert the compound by a chemical reaction to another known compound. This second compound is called a **derivative**. The best derivatives are solid compounds, because the melting point of a solid provides an accurate and reliable identification of most compounds. Solids are also easily purified through crystallization. The derivative provides a way of distinguishing two otherwise very similar compounds. Usually, they will have derivatives (both prepared by the same reaction) that have different melting points. Tables of unknowns and derivatives are listed in Appendix 1. Procedures for preparing derivatives are given in Appendix 2.

11. CONFIRMATION OF IDENTITY

A rigid and final test for identifying an unknown can be made if an "authentic" sample of the compound is available for comparison. One can compare infrared and NMR spectra of the unknown compound with the spectra of the known compound. If the spectra match, peak for peak, then the identity is probably certain. Other physical and chemical properties can also be compared. If the compound is a solid, a convenient test is the mixture melting point (see Technique 9, Section 9.4). Thin-layer or gas-chromatographic comparisons may also be useful. For thin-layer analysis, however, it may be necessary to experiment with several different development solvents to reach a satisfactory conclusion about the identity of the substance in question.

Although we cannot be complete in this experiment in terms of the functional groups covered or the tests described, the experiment should provide a good introduction to the methods and the techniques chemists use to identify unknown compounds. Textbooks that cover the subject more thoroughly are listed in the References. You are encouraged to consult these for more information, including specific methods and classification tests.

REFERENCES

Comprehensive Textbooks

Cheronis, N. D.; Entrikin, J. B. *Identification of Organic Compounds*; Wiley-Interscience: New York, 1963.

Pasto, D. J.; Johnson, C. R. *Laboratory Text for Organic Chemistry*; Prentice-Hall: Englewood Cliffs, NJ, 1979.

Shriner, R. L.; Hermann, C. K. F.; Morrill, T. C.; Curtin, D. Y.; Fuson, R. C. *The Systematic Identification of Organic Compounds*, 8th ed.; Wiley: New York, 2003.

Spectroscopy

Bellamy, L. J. *The Infra-red Spectra of Complex Molecules*, 3rd ed.; Methuen: New York, 1975.

Colthup, N. B.; Daly, L. H.; Wiberly, S. E. *Introduction to Infrared and Raman Spectroscopy*, 3rd ed.; Academic Press: San Diego, CA, 1990.

Lin-Vien, D.; Colthup, N. B.; Fateley, W. B.; Grasselli, J. G. *The Handbook of Infrared and Raman Characteristic Frequencies of Organic Molecules*; Academic Press: San Diego, CA, 1991.

Nakanishi, K. *Infrared Absorption Spectroscopy*, 2nd ed.; Holden-Day: San Francisco, 1977.

Pavia, D. L.; Lampman, G. M.; Kriz, G. S.; Vyryan, J. R. *Introduction to Spectroscopy: A Guide for Students of Organic Chemistry*, 4th ed.; Brooks/Cole: Belmont, CA, 2009.

Silverstein, R. M.; Webster, F. X.; Kiemle. *Spectrometric Identification of Organic Compounds*, 7th ed.; Wiley: New York, 2004.

Extensive Tables of Compounds and Derivatives

Rappoport, Z., Ed. *Handbook of Tables for Organic Compound Identification*, 3rd ed.; CRC Press: Boca Raton, FL, 1967.

55A   EXPERIMENT 55A

Solubility Tests

Solubility tests should be performed on *every unknown*. They are extremely important in determining the nature of the main functional group of the unknown compound. The tests are very simple and require only small amounts of the unknown. In addition, solubility tests reveal whether the compound is a strong base (amine), a weak acid (phenol), a strong acid (carboxylic acid), or a neutral substance (aldehyde, ketone, alcohol, ester). The common solvents used to determine solubility types are

5% HCl	Concentrated H_2SO_4
5% $NaHCO_3$	Water
5% NaOH	Organic solvents

The solubility chart given in the next page indicates solvents in which compounds containing the various functional groups are likely to dissolve. The summary charts in Experiments 55D through 55I repeat this information for each functional group included in this experiment. In this section, the correct procedure for determining whether a compound is soluble in a test solvent is given. Also given is a series of explanations detailing the reasons that compounds having specific functional groups are soluble only in specific solvents. This is accomplished by indicating the type of chemistry or the type of chemical interaction that is possible in each solvent.

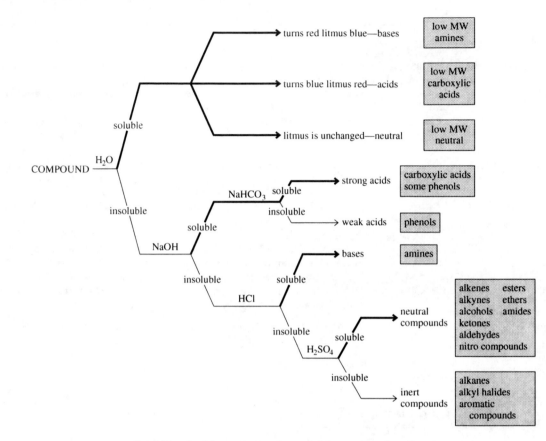

Solubility chart for compounds containing various functional groups.

SUGGESTED WASTE DISPOSAL

Dispose of all aqueous solutions in the container designated for aqueous waste. Any remaining organic compounds must be disposed of in the appropriate organic waste container.

SOLUBILITY TESTS

Procedure. Place about 2 mL of the solvent in a small test tube. Add *1 drop* of an unknown liquid from a Pasteur pipet or a few crystals of an unknown solid using the end of a spatula directly into the solvent. Gently tap the test tube with your finger to ensure mixing, and then observe whether any mixing lines appear in the solution. The disappearance of the liquid or solid or the appearance of the mixing lines indicates that solution is taking place. Add several more drops of the liquid or a few more crystals of the solid to determine the extent of the compound's solubility. A common mistake in determining the solubility of a compound is testing with a quantity of the unknown too large to dissolve in the chosen solvent. Use only small amounts of the unknown. It may take several minutes to dissolve solids. Compounds in the form of large crystals need more time to dissolve than powders or very small crystals. In some cases, it is helpful to use a mortar and pestle to pulverize a compound with large crystals. Sometimes, gentle heating helps, but strong heating is discouraged as it often leads to reaction. When colored compounds dissolve, the solution often assumes the color.

Using the preceding procedure, determine the solubility of the unknown in each of the following solvents: water, 5% HCl, 5% $NaHCO_3$, 5% NaOH, and concentrated H_2SO_4. With sulfuric acid, a color change may be observed rather than solution. A color change should be regarded as a positive solubility test. Unknown solids that do not dissolve in any of the test solvents may be inorganic substances. To eliminate this possibility, determine the solubility of the unknown in several organic solvents, such as ether. If the compound is organic, a solvent that will dissolve it can usually be found.

If a compound is found to dissolve in water, the pH of the aqueous solution should be estimated with pH paper or litmus. Compounds soluble in water are usually soluble in *all* the aqueous solvents. If a compound is only slightly soluble in water, it may be *more* soluble in another aqueous solvent. For instance, carboxylic acid may be only slightly soluble in water but very much soluble in dilute base. It often will not be necessary to determine the solubility of the unknown in every solvent.

Test Compounds. Five solubility unknowns can be found on the supply shelf. The five unknowns include a base, a weak acid, a strong acid, a neutral substance with an oxygen-containing functional group, and a neutral substance that is inert. Using solubility tests, distinguish these unknowns by type. Verify your answer with the instructor. A general discussion of solubility behavior is provided in Technique 10, Section 10.2.

Discussion

Solubility in Water

Compounds that contain four or fewer carbons and also contain oxygen, nitrogen, or sulfur are often soluble in water. Almost any functional group containing these elements will lead to water solubility for low–molecular weight (C_4) compounds. Compounds having five or six carbons and any of those elements are often insoluble in water or have borderline solubility. Branching of the alkyl chain in a compound lowers the intermolecular forces between its molecules. This is usually reflected in a lowered boiling point or melting point and a greater solubility in water for the branched compound than for the corresponding straight-chain compound. This occurs simply because the molecules of the branched compound are more easily separated from one another. Thus, *t*-butyl alcohol would be expected to be more soluble in water than *n*-butyl alcohol.

When the ratio of the oxygen, nitrogen, or sulfur atoms in a compound to the carbon atoms is increased, the solubility of that compound in water often increases. This is due to the increased number of polar functional groups. Thus, 1,5-pentanediol would be expected to be more soluble in water than 1-pentanol.

As the size of the alkyl chain of a compound is increased beyond about four carbons, the influence of a polar functional group is diminished, and the water solubility begins to decrease. A few examples of these generalizations are given here.

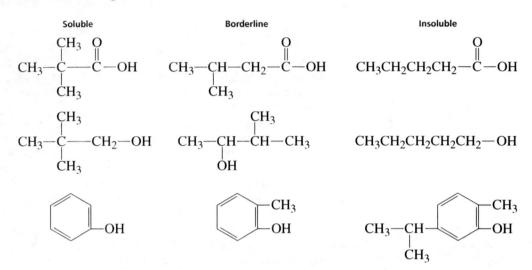

| Soluble | Borderline | Insoluble |

Solubility in 5% HCl

The possibility of an amine should be considered immediately if a compound is soluble in dilute acid (5% HCl). Aliphatic amines (RNH_2, R_2NH, R_3N) are basic compounds that readily dissolve in acid because they form hydrochloride salts that are soluble in the aqueous medium:

$$R—\overset{..}{N}H_2 + HCl \rightarrow R—NH_3^+ + Cl^-$$

The substitution of an aromatic (benzene) ring Ar for an alkyl group R reduces the basicity of an amine somewhat, but the amine will still protonate, and it will still generally be soluble in dilute acid. The reduction in basicity in an aromatic amine is due to the resonance delocalization of the unshared electrons on the amino nitrogen of the free base. The delocalization is lost on protonation, a problem that does not exist for aliphatic amines. The substitution of two or three aromatic rings on an amine nitrogen reduces the basicity of the amine even further. Diaryl and triaryl amines do not dissolve in dilute HCl because they do not protonate easily. Thus, Ar_2NH and Ar_3N are insoluble in dilute acid. Some amines of very high molecular weight, such as tribromoaniline ($MW=330$), may also be insoluble in dilute acid.

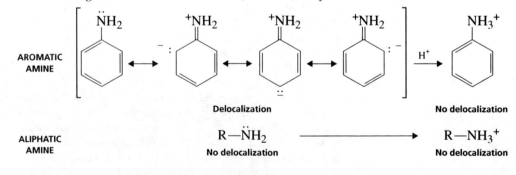

Solubility in 5% NaHCO₃ and 5% NaOH

Compounds that dissolve in sodium bicarbonate, a weak base, are strong acids. Compounds that dissolve in sodium hydroxide, a strong base, may be either strong or weak acids. Thus, one can distinguish weak and strong acids by determining their solubility in both strong

(NaOH) and weak (NaHCO$_3$) base. The classification of some functional groups as either weak or strong acids is given in the table below.

In this experiment, carboxylic acids (pK_a ~ 5) are generally indicated when a compound is soluble in both bases, and phenols (pK_a ~ 10) are indicated when it is soluble in NaOH only.

Compounds dissolve in base because they form sodium salts that are soluble in the aqueous medium. The salts of some high-molecular-weight compounds are not soluble, however, and precipitate. The salts of the long-chain carboxylic acids, such as myristic acid C$_{14}$, palmitic acid C$_{16}$, and stearic acid C$_{18}$, which form soaps, belong to this category. Some phenols also produce insoluble sodium salts, and often these are colored due to resonance in the anion.

Strong Acids (Soluble in Both NaOH and NaHCO$_3$)		Weak Acids (Soluble in NaOH but Not in NaHCO$_3$)	

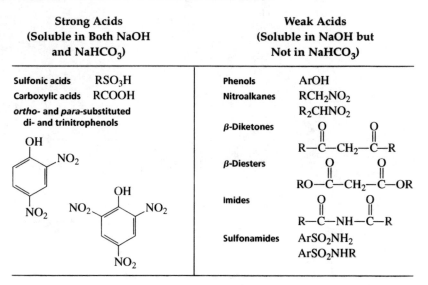

Sulfonic acids	RSO$_3$H	Phenols	ArOH
Carboxylic acids	RCOOH	Nitroalkanes	RCH$_2$NO$_2$
ortho- and *para*-substituted di- and trinitrophenols			R$_2$CHNO$_2$
		β-Diketones	
		β-Diesters	
		Imides	
		Sulfonamides	ArSO$_2$NH$_2$
			ArSO$_2$NHR

Both phenols and carboxylic acids produce resonance-stabilized conjugate bases. Thus, bases of appropriate strength may easily remove their acidic protons to form the sodium salts.

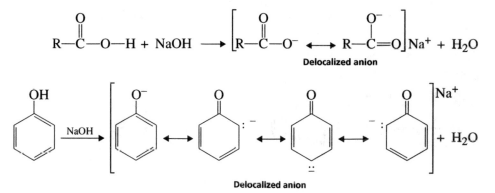

In phenols, substitution of nitro groups in the *ortho* and *para* positions of the ring increases acidity. Nitro groups in these positions provide additional delocalization in the conjugate anion. Phenols that have two or three nitro groups in the *ortho* and *para* positions often dissolve in *both* sodium hydroxide and sodium bicarbonate solutions.

Solubility in Concentrated Sulfuric Acid

Many compounds are soluble in cold, concentrated sulfuric acid. Of the compounds included in this experiment, alcohols, ketones, aldehydes, and esters belong to this category. These compounds are described as being "neutral." Other compounds that also dissolve include alkenes, alkynes, ethers, nitroaromatics, and amides. Because several different kinds of compounds are soluble in sulfuric acid, further chemical tests and spectroscopy will be needed to differentiate among them.

Compounds that are soluble in concentrated sulfuric acid but not in dilute acid are extremely weak bases. Almost any compound containing a nitrogen, an oxygen, or a sulfur atom can be protonated in concentrated sulfuric acid. The ions produced are soluble in the medium.

$$R\text{—}\overset{..}{\underset{..}{O}}\text{—}H + H_2SO_4 \longrightarrow R\text{—}\overset{+}{\underset{|}{O}}\text{—}H + HSO_4^- \longrightarrow R^+ + H_2O + HSO_4^-$$
$$\hspace{6.5cm} H$$

$$\overset{\displaystyle :O:}{\underset{\displaystyle \|}{R\text{—}C\text{—}R}} + H_2SO_4 \longrightarrow \overset{\displaystyle +\overset{..}{O}\text{—}H}{\underset{\displaystyle \|}{R\text{—}C\text{—}R}} + HSO_4^-$$

$$\overset{\displaystyle :O:}{\underset{\displaystyle \|}{R\text{—}C\text{—}OR}} + H_2SO_4 \longrightarrow \overset{\displaystyle +\overset{..}{O}\text{—}H}{\underset{\displaystyle \|}{R\text{—}C\text{—}OR}} + HSO_4^-$$

$$\underset{R}{\overset{R}{\diagup}}C{=}C\underset{R}{\overset{R}{\diagdown}} + H_2SO_4 \longrightarrow \overset{\displaystyle R \quad R}{\underset{\displaystyle H}{R\text{—}C\text{—}\overset{+}{C}\text{—}R}} + HSO_4^-$$

Inert Compounds

Compounds not soluble in concentrated sulfuric acid or any of the other solvents are said to be **inert**. Compounds not soluble in concentrated sulfuric acid include the alkanes, the most simple aromatics, and the alkyl halides. Some examples of inert compounds are hexane, benzene, chlorobenzene, chlorohexane, and toluene.

55B   EXPERIMENT 55B

Tests for the Elements (N, S, X)

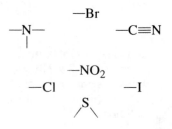

Except for amines (Experiment 55G), which are easily detected by their solubility behavior, all compounds issued in this experiment will contain heteroelements (N, S, Cl, Br, or I) only as *secondary* functional groups. These will be subsidiary to some other important functional group. Thus, no alkyl or aryl halides, nitro compounds, thiols, or thioethers will be issued. However, some of the unknowns may contain a halogen or a nitro group. Less frequently, they may contain a sulfur atom or a cyano group.

Consider as an example *p*-bromobenzaldehyde, an **aldehyde** that contains bromine as a ring substituent. The identification of this compound would hinge on whether the investigator could identify it as an aldehyde. It could probably be identified *without* proving the existence of bromine in the molecule. That information, however, could make the identification easier. In this experiment, methods are given for identifying the presence of a halogen or a nitro group in an unknown compound. Also given is a general method (sodium fusion) for detecting the principal heteroelements that may exist in organic molecules.

Classification tests

Halides	Nitro Groups	N, S, X (Cl, Br, I)
Beilstein test	Ferrous hydroxide	Sodium fusion
Silver nitrate		
Sodium iodide/acetone		

SUGGESTED WASTE DISPOSAL

Dispose of all solutions containing silver into a waste container designated for this purpose. Any other aqueous solutions should be disposed of in the container designated for aqueous waste. Any remaining organic compounds must be disposed of in the appropriate organic waste container under the hood. This is particularly true of any solution containing benzyl bromide, which is a lachrymator.

TESTS FOR A HALIDE

Beilstein Test

Procedure. Adjust the air and gas mixture so that the flame of a Bunsen burner or microburner is blue. Bend the end of a piece of copper wire so that a small closed loop is created. Heat the loop end of the wire in the flame until it glows brightly. After the wire has cooled, dip the wire directly into a sample of the unknown. If the unknown is a solid and won't adhere to the copper wire, place a small amount of the substance on a watch glass, wet the copper wire in distilled water, and place the wire into the sample on the watch glass. The solid should adhere to the wire. Again heat the wire in the Bunsen burner flame. The compound will first burn. After the burning, a green flame will be produced if a halogen is present. You should hold the wire in the flame either just above the tip of the flame or at its outside edge near the bottom of the flame. You will need to experiment to find the best position to hold the copper wire to obtain the best result.

Test Compounds. Try this test on bromobenzene and benzoic acid.

Discussion

Halogens can be detected easily and reliably by the Beilstein test. It is the simplest method for determining the presence of a halogen, but it does not differentiate among chlorine, bromine, and iodine, any one of which will give a positive test. However, when the identity of the unknown has been narrowed to two choices, of which one has a halogen and one does not, the Beilstein test will often be enough to distinguish between the two.

A positive Beilstein test results from the production of a volatile copper halide when an organic halide is heated with copper oxide. The copper halide imparts a blue-green color to the flame.

This test can be very sensitive to small amounts of halide impurities in some compounds. Therefore, use caution in interpreting the results of the test if you obtain only a weak color.

Silver Nitrate Test

Procedure. Add 1 drop of a liquid or 5 drops of a concentrated ethanolic solution of the unknown solid to 2 mL of a 2% ethanolic silver nitrate solution. If no reaction is observed after 5 minutes at room temperature, heat the solution in a hot water bath at about 100°C, and note whether a precipitate forms. If a precipitate forms, add 2 drops of 5% nitric acid, and note whether the precipitate dissolves. Carboxylic acids give a false test by precipitating in silver nitrate, but they dissolve when nitric acid is added. Silver halides, in contrast, do not dissolve in nitric acid.

Test Compounds. Apply this test to benzyl bromide (α-bromotoluene) and bromobenzene. Discard all waste reagents in a suitable waste container in the hood because benzyl bromide is a lachrymator.

Discussion

This test depends on the formation of a white or off-white precipitate of silver halide when silver nitrate is allowed to react with a sufficiently reactive halide.

$$RX + Ag^+NO_3^- \rightarrow \underset{\text{Precipitate}}{AgX} + R^+NO_3^- \xrightarrow{CH_3CH_2OH} R\text{-}O\text{-}CH_2CH_3$$

The test does not distinguish among chlorides, bromides, and iodides but does distinguish **labile** (reactive) halides from halides that are unreactive. Halides substituted on an aromatic ring will not usually give a positive silver nitrate test; however, alkyl halides of many types will give a positive test.

The most reactive compounds are those able to form stable carbocations in solution and those equipped with good leaving groups (X = I, Br, Cl). Benzyl, allyl, and tertiary halides react immediately with silver nitrate. Secondary and primary halides do not react at room temperature but react readily when heated. Aryl and vinyl halides do not react at all, even at elevated temperatures. This pattern of reactivity fits the stability order for various carbocations quite well. Compounds that produce stable carbocations react at higher rates than those that do not.

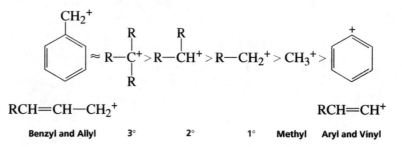

$$RCH\!=\!CH\!-\!CH_2{}^+ \qquad\qquad\qquad\qquad RCH\!=\!CH^+$$

| **Benzyl and Allyl** | **3°** | **2°** | **1°** | **Methyl** | **Aryl and Vinyl** |

The fast reaction of benzylic and allylic halides is a result of the resonance stabilization that is available to the intermediate carbocations formed. Tertiary halides are more reactive than secondary halides, which are in turn more reactive than primary or methyl halides because alkyl substituents are able to stabilize the intermediate carbocations by an electron-releasing effect. The methyl carbocations have no alkyl groups and are the least stable of all carbocations mentioned thus far. Vinyl and aryl carbocations are extremely unstable because the charge is localized on an sp^2-hybridized carbon (double-bond carbon) rather than one that is sp^3-hybridized.

Sodium Iodide in Acetone

Procedure. This test is described in Experiment 19.

Test Compounds. Apply this test to benzyl bromide (α-bromotoluene), bromobenzene, and 2-chloro-2-methylpropane (*tert*-butyl chloride).

DETECTION OF NITRO GROUPS

Although nitro compounds will not be issued as distinct unknowns, many of the unknowns may have a nitro group as a secondary functional group. The presence of a nitro group, and hence nitrogen, in an unknown compound is determined most easily by infrared spectroscopy. However, many nitro compounds give a positive result in the following test. Unfortunately, functional groups other than the nitro group may also give a positive result. You should interpret the results of this test with caution.

Ferrous Hydroxide Test

Procedure. Place 1.5 mL of freshly prepared 5% aqueous ferrous ammonium sulfate in a small test tube, and add about 10 mg of a solid or 5 drops of a liquid compound. Mix the solution well, and then add first 1 drop of 2 M sulfuric acid and then 1 mL of 2 M potassium hydroxide in methanol. Stopper the test tube and shake it vigorously. A positive test is indicated by the formation of a red-brown precipitate, usually within 1 minute.

Test Compound. Apply this test to 2-nitrotoluene.

Discussion

Most nitro compounds oxidize ferrous hydroxide to ferric hydroxide, which is a red-brown solid. A precipitate indicates a positive test.

$$R\!-\!NO_2 + 4H_2O + 6Fe(OH)_2 \longrightarrow R\!-\!NH_2 + 6Fe(OH)_3$$

Infrared Spectroscopy

The nitro group gives two strong bands near 1560 cm^{-1} and 1350 cm^{-1}. See Technique 25 for details.

DETECTION OF A CYANO GROUP

Although nitriles will not be given as unknowns in this experiment, the cyano group may be a subsidiary functional group whose presence or absence is important to the final identification of an unknown compound. The cyano group can be hydrolyzed in a strong base by heating vigorously to give carboxylic acid and ammonia gas:

$$R\text{—}C\equiv N + 2\,H_2O \xrightarrow[\Delta]{NaOH} R\text{—}COOH + NH_3$$

The ammonia gas can be detected by its odor or by using moist pH paper. However, this method is somewhat difficult, and the presence of a nitrile group is confirmed most easily by infrared spectroscopy. No other functional groups (except some C≡C) absorb in the same region of the spectrum as C≡N.

Infrared Spectroscopy

C≡N stretch is a sharp band of medium intensity near 2250 cm^{-1}. See Technique 25 for details.

Sodium Fusion Tests (Detection of N, S, And X) (Optional)

When an organic compound containing nitrogen, sulfur, or halide atoms is fused with sodium metal, there is a reductive decomposition of the compound, which converts these atoms to the sodium salts of the inorganic ions CN^-, S^{2-}, and X^-.

$$[N, S, X] \xrightarrow[\Delta]{Na} NaCN, Na_2S, NaX$$

When the fusion mixture is dissolved in distilled water, the cyanide, sulfide, and halide ions can be detected by standard qualitative inorganic tests.

> **CAUTION**
>
> Always remember to manipulate the sodium metal with a knife or a forceps. Do not touch it with your fingers. Keep sodium away from water. Destroy all waste sodium with 1-butanol or ethanol. Wear safety glasses.

PREPARATION OF STOCK SOLUTION

General Method

Procedure. Using a forceps and a knife, take some sodium from the storage container, cut a small piece about the size of a small pea (3 mm on a side), and dry it on a paper towel. Place this small piece of sodium in a clean, dry, small test tube (10 mm × 75 mm). Clamp the test tube to a ring stand, and heat the bottom of the tube with a microburner until the sodium melts and its metallic vapor can be seen to rise about a third of the way up the tube.

The bottom of the tube will probably have a dull red glow. Remove the burner and *immediately* drop the sample directly into the tube. Use about 10 mg of a solid placed on the end of a spatula or 2–3 drops of a liquid. Be sure to drop the sample directly down the center of the tube so that it touches the hot sodium metal and does not adhere to the side of the test tube. If the fusion is successful, there will usually be a flash or a small explosion. If the reaction is not successful, heat the tube to red heat for a few seconds to ensure complete reaction.

Allow the test tube to cool to room temperature, and then carefully add 10 drops of methanol, a drop at a time, to the fusion mixture. Using a spatula or a long glass rod, reach into the test tube and stir the mixture to ensure complete reaction of any excess sodium metal. The fusion will have destroyed the test tube for other uses. Thus, the easiest way to recover the fusion mixture is to crush the test tube into a small beaker containing 5–10 mL of *distilled* water. The tube is easily crushed if it is placed in the angle of a clamp holder. Tighten the clamp until the tube is securely held near its bottom and then—standing back from the beaker and holding the clamp at its opposite end—continue tightening the clamp until the test tube breaks and the pieces fall into the beaker. Stir the solution well, heat until it boils, and then filter it by gravity through a fluted filter (see Technique 8, Figure 8.3). Portions of this solution will be used in the tests to detect nitrogen, sulfur, and the halogens.

Alternative Method

Procedure. With some volatile liquids, the previous method will not work. The compounds volatilize before they reach the sodium vapors. For such compounds, place 4 or 5 drops of the pure liquid in a clean, dry test tube, clamp it, and cautiously add the small piece of sodium metal. If there is any reaction, wait until it subsides. Then heat the test tube to red heat, and continue according to the instructions in the second paragraph of the preceding procedure.

Nitrogen Test

Procedure. Using pH paper and a 10% sodium hydroxide solution, adjust the pH of about 1 mL of the stock solution to pH 13. Add 2 drops of saturated ferrous ammonium sulfate solution and 2 drops of 30% potassium fluoride solution. Boil the solution for about 30 seconds. Then acidify the hot solution by adding 30% sulfuric acid dropwise until the iron hydroxides dissolve. Avoid using excess acid. If nitrogen is present, a dark blue (not green) precipitate of Prussian blue $NaFe_2(CN)_6$ will form, or the solution will assume a dark blue color.

Reagents. Dissolve 5 g of ferrous ammonium sulfate in 100 mL of water. Dissolve 30 g of potassium fluoride in 100 mL of water.

Sulfur Test

Procedure. Acidify about 1 mL of the test solution with acetic acid, and add a few drops of a 1% lead acetate solution. The presence of sulfur is indicated by a black precipitate of lead sulfide (PbS).

CAUTION ⚠

Many compounds of lead(II) are suspected carcinogens (see Technique 1, Section 1.4) and should be handled with care. Avoid contact.

Halide Tests

Procedure. Cyanide and sulfide ions interfere with the test for halides. If such ions are present, they must be removed. To accomplish this, acidify the solution with dilute nitric acid and boil it for about 2 minutes. This will drive off any HCN or H_2S that is formed. When the solution cools, add a few drops of a 5% silver nitrate solution. A *voluminous* precipitate indicates a halide. A faint turbidity *does not* mean a positive test. Silver chloride is white. Silver bromide is off-white. Silver iodide is yellow. Silver chloride will readily dissolve in concentrated ammonium hydroxide, whereas silver bromide is only slightly soluble.

Differentiation of Chloride, Bromide, and Iodide

Procedure. Acidify 2 mL of the test solution with 10% sulfuric acid, and boil it for about 2 minutes. Cool the solution and add about 0.5 mL of methylene chloride. Add a few drops of chlorine water or 2–4 mg of calcium hypochlorite.[1] Check to be sure that the solution is still acidic. Then stopper the tube, shake it vigorously, and set it aside to allow the layers to separate. An orange to brown color in the methylene chloride layer indicates bromine. Violet indicates iodine. No color or a *light* yellow indicates chlorine.

 EXPERIMENT 55C

Tests for Unsaturation

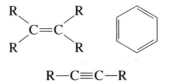

$$R-C\equiv C-R$$

The unknowns to be issued for this experiment have neither a double bond nor a triple bond as their *only* functional group. Hence, simple alkenes and alkynes can be ruled out as possible compounds. Some of the unknowns may have a double or a triple bond, however, *in addition to* another more important functional group. The tests described allow you to determine the presence of a double bond or a triple bond (unsaturation) in such compounds.

Classification tests

Unsaturation	Aromaticity
Bromine–methylene chloride	Ignition test
Potassium permanganate	

_____

[1]Clorox, the commercial bleach, is a permissible substitute for chlorine water, as is any other brand of bleach, provided that it is based on sodium hypochlorite.

SUGGESTED WASTE DISPOSAL

Test reagents that contain bromine should be discarded into a special waste container designated for this purpose. Methylene chloride must be placed in the organic waste container designated for the disposal of halogenated organic wastes. Dispose of all other aqueous solutions in the container designated for aqueous waste. Any remaining organic compounds must be disposed of in the appropriate organic waste container.

TEST FOR SIMPLE MULTIPLE BONDS

Bromine in Methylene Chloride

Procedure. Dissolve 50 mg of the unknown solid or 4 drops of the unknown liquid in 1 mL of methylene chloride (dichloromethane) or in 1,2-dimethoxyethane. Add a 2% (by volume) solution of bromine in methylene chloride, dropwise, with shaking. If you find that the red color remains after adding 1 or 2 drops of the bromine solution, the test is negative. If the red color disappears, continue adding the bromine in methylene chloride until the red bromine color remains. The test is positive if more than 5 drops of the bromine solution were added, with discharge of the red color of bromine. If the red color disappears, try adding more drops of the bromine solution to see how many drops are necessary before the red color persists. Usually, many drops of the bromine solution will be decolorized when an isolated double bond is present. Hydrogen bromide should not be evolved. If hydrogen bromide gas is evolved, you will note a "fog" when you blow across the mouth of the test tube. The HBr can also be detected by a moistened piece of litmus or pH paper. If hydrogen bromide is evolved, the reaction is a **substitution reaction** (see following discussion) and not an **addition reaction**, and a double or triple bond is probably not present.

Reagent. The classic method for running this test is to use bromine dissolved in carbon tetrachloride. Because of the toxic nature of this solvent, methylene chloride has been substituted for carbon tetrachloride. The instructor must prepare this reagent because of the danger associated with the very toxic bromine vapor. Be sure to work in an efficient fume hood. Dissolve 2 mL of bromine in 100 mL of methylene chloride (dichloromethane). The solvent will undergo a light-induced, free-radical substitution producing hydrogen bromide over a period of time. After about 1 week, the color of the 2% solution of bromine in methylene chloride fades noticeably, and the odor of the HBr can be detected in the reagent. Although the decolorization tests still work satisfactorily, the presence of HBr makes it difficult to distinguish between addition and substitution reactions. A freshly prepared solution of bromine in methylene chloride must be used to make this distinction. Deterioration of the reagent can be forestalled by storing it in a brown glass bottle.

Test Compounds. Try this test with cyclohexene, cyclohexane, toluene, and acetone.

Discussion

A successful test depends on the addition of bromine, a red liquid, to a double or a triple bond to give a colorless dibromide:

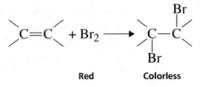

Red   Colorless

Not all double bonds react with the bromine solution. Only those that are electron-rich are sufficiently reactive nucleophiles to initiate the reaction. A double bond that is substituted by electron-withdrawing groups often fails to react or reacts slowly. Fumaric acid is an example of a compound that fails to give the reaction.

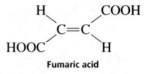

Fumaric acid

Aromatic compounds either do not react with the bromine reagent, or they react by **substitution**. Only the aromatic rings that have activating groups as substituents (—OH, —OR, or —NR$_2$) give the substitution reaction.

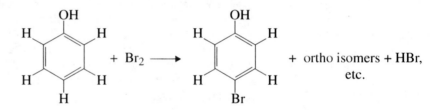

Some ketones and aldehydes react with bromine to give a **substitution product**, but this reaction is slow except for ketones that have a high enol content. When substitution occurs, not only is the bromine color discharged, but hydrogen bromide gas is also evolved.

Potassium Permanganate (Baeyer Test)

Procedure. Dissolve 25 mg of the unknown solid or 2 drops of the unknown liquid in 2 mL of 95% ethanol (1,2-dimethoxyethane may also be used). Slowly add a 1% aqueous solution (weight/volume) of potassium permanganate, drop by drop while shaking, to the unknown. In a positive test, the purple color of the reagent is discharged, and a brown precipitate of manganese dioxide forms, usually within 1 minute. If alcohol was the solvent, the solution should not be allowed to stand for more than 5 minutes, because oxidation of the alcohol will begin slowly. Because permanganate solutions undergo some decomposition to manganese dioxide on standing, any small amount of precipitate should be interpreted with caution.

Test Compounds. Try this test on cyclohexene and toluene.

Discussion

This test is positive for double and triple bonds but not for aromatic rings. It depends on the conversion of the purple ion MnO$_4^-$ to a brown precipitate of MnO$_2$ following the oxidation of an unsaturated compound.

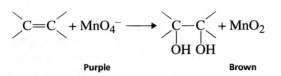

Purple   Brown

Other easily oxidized compounds also give a positive test with potassium permanganate solution. These substances include aldehydes, some alcohols, phenols, and aromatic amines. If you suspect that any of these functional groups is present, you should interpret the test with caution.

Spectroscopy

Infrared

Double Bonds (C=C)

C=C stretch usually occurs near 1680–1620 cm^{-1}. Symmetrical alkenes may have no absorption.

C—H stretch of vinyl hydrogens occurs > 3000 cm^{-1}, but usually not higher than 3150 cm^{-1}.

C—H out-of-plane bending occurs near 1000–700 cm^{-1}.

Triple Bonds (C≡C)

C≡C stretch usually occurs near 2250–2100 cm^{-1}. The peak is usually sharp. Symmetrical alkynes show no absorption.

C—H stretch of terminal acetylenes occurs near 3310–3200 cm^{-1}.

See Technique 25 for details.

Nuclear Magnetic Resonance

Vinyl hydrogens have resonance near 5–7 ppm and have coupling values as follows: J_{trans} = 11–18 Hz, J_{cis} = 6–15 Hz, $J_{geminal}$ = 0–5 Hz. Allylic hydrogens have resonance near 2 ppm. Acetylenic hydrogens have resonance near 2.8–3.0 ppm. See Technique 26 for details on proton NMR. Carbon NMR is described in Technique 27.

TESTS FOR AROMATICITY

None of the unknowns to be issued for this experiment will be simple aromatic hydrocarbons. All aromatic compounds will have a principal functional group as a part of their structure. Nevertheless, in many cases it will be useful to be able to recognize the presence of an aromatic ring. Although infrared and nuclear magnetic spectroscopy provide the most reliable methods of determining aromatic compounds, often they can be detected by a simple ignition test.

Ignition Test

Procedure. Working in a hood, place a small amount of the compound on a spatula and place it in the flame of a Bunsen burner. Observe whether a sooty flame results. Compounds giving the sooty yellow flame have a high degree of unsaturation and may be aromatic. This test should be interpreted with care because some nonaromatic compounds may produce soot. If in doubt, use spectroscopy to more reliably determine the presence or absence of an aromatic ring.

Test Compounds. Try this test with ethyl benzoate and benzoin.

Discussion

The presence of an aromatic ring will usually lead to the production of a sooty yellow flame in this test. In addition, halogenated alkanes and high–molecular weight aliphatic compounds may produce a sooty yellow flame. Aromatic compounds with high oxygen content may burn cleaner and produce less soot even though the compound contains an aromatic ring.

This is actually a test to determine the ratio of carbon to hydrogen, and oxygen in an unknown substance. If the carbon-to-hydrogen ratio is high and if little or no oxygen is present, you will observe a sooty flame. For instance, acetylene, C_2H_2 (a gas), will burn with a sooty flame unless mixed with oxygen. When the carbon-to-hydrogen ratio is nearly equal to one, you will be very likely to see a sooty flame.

Spectroscopy

Infrared

$C\!=\!C$ aromatic-ring double bonds appear in the 1600–1450 cm^{-1} region. There are often four sharp absorptions that occur in pairs near 1600 cm^{-1} and 1450 cm^{-1}, which are characteristic of an aromatic ring.

Special ring absorptions: There are often weak ring absorptions around 2000–1600 cm^{-1}. These are frequently obscured, but when they can be observed, the relative shapes and numbers of these peaks can often be used to ascertain the type of ring substitution.

$=\!C\!-\!H$ stretch, aromatic ring: The aromatic $C\!-\!H$ stretch always occurs at a higher frequency than 3000 cm^{-1}.

$=\!C\!-\!H$ out-of-plane bending peaks appear in the region 900–690 cm^{-1}. The number and position of these peaks can be used to determine the substitution pattern of the ring.

See Technique 25 for details.

Nuclear Magnetic Resonance

Hydrogens attached to an aromatic ring usually have resonance near 7 ppm. Monosubstituted rings not substituted by anisotropic or electronegative groups often give a single resonance for all of the ring hydrogens. Monosubstituted rings with anisotropic or electronegative groups usually have the aromatic resonances split into two groups integrating either 3:2 or 2:3. A nonsymmetric, *para*-disubstituted ring has a characteristic four-peak splitting pattern (see Technique 26). Carbon NMR is described in Technique 27.

55D   EXPERIMENT 55D

Aldehydes and Ketones

Compounds containing the carbonyl functional group $\overset{\diagdown}{\underset{\diagup}{C}}=O$, where it has only hydrogen atoms or alkyl groups as substituents, are called aldehydes, RCHO, or ketones, RCOR'. The chemistry of these compounds is primarily due to the chemistry of the carbonyl functional groups. These compounds are identified by the distinctive reactions of the carbonyl function.

Solubility Characteristics	Classification Tests	
HCl NaHCO₃ NaOH H₂SO₄ Ether	**Aldehydes and ketones**	
(−) (−) (−) (+) (+)	2,4-Dinitrophenylhydrazine	
Water: $< C_5$ and some $C_6(+)$	**Aldehydes only**	**Methyl ketones**
$\qquad > C_5(-)$	Tollens reagent	Iodoform test
	Chromic acid	
	Compounds with high enol content	
	Ferric chloride test	

SUGGESTED WASTE DISPOSAL

Solutions containing 2,4-dinitrophenylhydrazine or derivatives formed from it should be placed in a waste container designated for these compounds. Any solution containing chromium must be disposed of in a waste container specifically identified for the disposal of chromium wastes. Dispose of all solutions containing silver by acidifying them with 5% hydrochloric acid and then placing them in a waste container designated for this purpose. Dispose of all other aqueous solutions in the container designated for aqueous waste. Any remaining organic compounds must be disposed of in the appropriate organic waste container.

CLASSIFICATION TESTS

Most aldehydes and ketones give a solid, yellow to red precipitate when mixed with 2,4-dinitrophenylhydrazine. However, only aldehydes will reduce chromium(VI) or silver(I). By this difference in behavior, you can differentiate between aldehydes and ketones.

2, 4- Dinitrophenylhydrazine

Procedure. Place 1 drop of the liquid unknown in a small test tube and add 1 mL of the 2,4-dinitrophenylhydrazine reagent. If the unknown is a solid, dissolve about 10 mg (estimate) in a minimum amount of 95% ethanol or di(ethylene glycol) diethyl ether before adding the reagent. Shake the mixture vigorously. Most aldehydes and ketones will give a yellow to red precipitate immediately. However, some compounds will require up to 15 minutes, or even *gentle* heating, to give a precipitate. A precipitate indicates a positive test.

Test Compounds. Try this test on cyclohexanone, benzaldehyde, and benzophenone.

Reagent. Dissolve 3.0 g of 2,4-dinitrophenylhydrazine in 15 mL of concentrated sulfuric acid. In a beaker, slowly add, with mixing, 23 mL of water until the solid dissolves. Add 75 mL of 95% ethanol to the warm solution, while stirring. After thorough mixing, filter the solution if any solid remains. This reagent needs to be prepared fresh each time.

Discussion

Most aldehydes and ketones give a precipitate, but esters generally do not give this result. Thus, an ester usually can be eliminated by this test. The color of the 2,4-dinitrophenylhydrazone (precipitate) formed is often a guide to the amount of conjugation in the original aldehyde or ketone. Unconjugated ketones, such as cyclohexanone, give yellow precipitates, whereas conjugated ketones, such as benzophenone, give orange to red precipitates. Compounds that are highly conjugated give red precipitates. However, the 2,4-dinitrophenylhydrazine reagent is itself orange-red, and the color of any precipitate must be judged cautiously. Occasionally, compounds that are either strongly basic or strongly acidic precipitate the unreacted reagent.

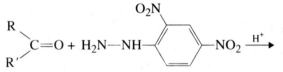

Aldehyde
or ketone   2,4-Dinitrophenylhydrazine

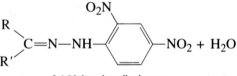

2,4-Dinitrophenylhydrazone

Some allylic and benzylic alcohols give this test result because the reagent can oxidize them to aldehydes and ketones, which subsequently react. Some alcohols may be contaminated with carbonyl impurities, either as a result of their method of synthesis (reduction) or as a result of their becoming air-oxidized. A precipitate formed from small amounts of impurity in the solution will be formed in small amounts. With some caution, a test that gives only a slight amount of precipitate can usually be ignored. The infrared spectrum of the compound should establish its identity and identify any impurities present.

Tollens Test

Procedure. The reagent must be prepared immediately before use. To prepare the reagent, mix 1 mL of Tollens solution A with 1 mL of Tollens solution B. A precipitate of silver oxide will form. Add enough dilute (10%) ammonia solution (dropwise) to the mixture to dissolve the silver oxide *just barely*. The reagent so prepared can be used immediately for the following test.

Dissolve 1 drop of a liquid aldehyde or 10 mg (approximate) of a solid aldehyde in the minimum amount of di(ethylene glycol) diethyl ether. Add this solution, a little at a time, to the 2–3 mL of reagent contained in a small test tube. Shake the solution well. If a mirror of silver is deposited on the inner walls of the test tube, the test is positive. In some cases, it may be necessary to warm the test tube in a warm water bath.

Test Compounds. Try the test on benzaldehyde, butanal (butyraldehyde), and cyclohexanone.

CAUTION

The reagent should be prepared immediately before use and all residues disposed of immediately after use. Dispose of any residues by acidifying them with 5% hydrochloric acid and then placing them in a waste container designated for this purpose. On standing, the reagent tends to form silver fulminate, a *very explosive* substance. Solutions containing the mixed Tollens reagent should never be stored.

Reagents. *Solution A:* Dissolve 3.0 g of silver nitrate in 30 mL of water. *Solution B:* Prepare a 10% sodium hydroxide solution.

Discussion

Most aldehydes reduce ammoniacal silver nitrate solution to give a precipitate of silver metal. The aldehyde is oxidized to a carboxylic acid:

$$RCHO + 2\ Ag(NH_3)_2OH \longrightarrow 2\ Ag + RCOO^-NH_4^+ + H_2O + NH_3$$

Ordinary ketones do not give a positive result in this test. The test should be used only if it has already been shown that the unknown compound is either an aldehyde or a ketone.

Chromic Acid Test: Alternative Test

CAUTION

Many chromium (VI) compounds are suspected carcinogens. If you would like to run this test, talk to your instructor first. Most often, the Tollens test will easily distinguish between aldehydes and ketones, and you should do that test first. If you run the chromic acid test, be sure to wear gloves to avoid contact with this reagent.

Procedure. Dissolve 1 drop of a liquid or 10 mg (approximate) of a solid aldehyde in 1 mL of *reagent-grade* acetone. Add several drops of the chromic acid reagent, a drop at a time, while shaking the mixture. A positive test is indicated by a green precipitate and a loss of the orange color in the reagent. With aliphatic aldehydes, RCHO, the solution turns cloudy within 5 seconds, and a precipitate appears within 30 seconds. With aromatic aldehydes, ArCHO, it generally takes 30–120 seconds for a precipitate to form, but with some it may take even longer. In some cases, however, you may find that some of the original orange color may remain, together with a green or brown precipitate. This should be interpreted as a positive test. In a negative test, a nongreen precipitate may form in an orange solution.

In performing this test, make sure that the acetone used for the solvent does not give a positive test with the reagent. Add several drops of the chromic acid reagent to a few drops of the reagent acetone contained in a small test tube. Allow this mixture to stand for 3–5 minutes. If no reaction has occurred by this time, the acetone is pure enough to use as a solvent for the test. If a positive test resulted, try another bottle of acetone.

Test Compounds. Try the test on benzaldehyde, butanal (butyraldehyde), and cyclohexanone.

Reagent. Dissolve 20 g of chromium trioxide (CrO_3) in 60 mL of cold water in a beaker. With stirring, slowly and carefully add 20 mL of concentrated sulfuric acid to the solution. This reagent should be prepared fresh each time.

Discussion

This test has as its basis on the fact that aldehydes are easily oxidized to the corresponding carboxylic acid by chromic acid. The green precipitate is due to chromous sulfate.

$$2\ CrO_3 + 2\ H_2O \xrightleftharpoons{H^+} 2\ H_2CrO_4 \xrightleftharpoons{H^+} H_2Cr_2O_7 + H_2O$$

$$\underset{\text{Orange}}{3\ RCHO + H_2Cr_2O_7 + 3\ H_2SO_4} \longrightarrow 3\ RCOOH + \underset{\text{Green}}{Cr_2(SO_4)_3 + 4\ H_2O}$$

Primary and secondary alcohols are also oxidized by this reagent (see Experiment 55H). Therefore, this test is not useful in identifying aldehydes *unless* a positive identification of the carbonyl group has already been made. Aldehydes give a 2,4-dinitrophenylhydrazine test result, whereas alcohols do not.

There are numerous other tests used to detect the aldehyde functional group. Most are based on an easily detectable oxidation of the aldehyde to a carboxylic acid. The most common tests are the Tollens, Fehling's, and Benedict's tests. Only the Tollens test is described in this book. The Tollens test is often more reliable than the chromic acid test for aldehydes.

Iodoform Test

Procedure. Prepare a 60–70°C water bath in a beaker. Using a Pasteur pipet, add 6 drops of a liquid unknown to a 15-mm x 100-mm or 15-mm x 125-mm test tube. Alternatively, 0.06 g of the unknown solid may be used. Dissolve the unknown liquid or solid compound in 2 mL of 1,2-dimethoxyethane. Add 2 mL of 10% aqueous sodium hydroxide solution, and place the test tube in the hot-water bath. Next add 4 mL of iodine–potassium iodide solution in 1-mL portions to the test tube. *Cork* the test tube and shake it after adding each portion of iodine reagent. Heat the mixture in the hot-water bath for about 5 minutes, shaking the test tube occasionally. It is likely that some or all of the dark color of the iodine reagent will be discharged.

If the dark color of the iodine reagent is still apparent following heating, add 10% sodium hydroxide solution until the dark color of the iodine reagent has been discharged. Shake the mixture in the test tube (corked) during the addition of sodium hydroxide. Care need not be taken to avoid adding excess sodium hydroxide.

After the dark iodine color of the solution has been discharged, fill the test tube with water to within 2 cm of the top. Cork the test tube and shake it vigorously. Allow the tube to stand for at least 15 minutes at room temperature. The appearance of a pale yellow precipitate of iodoform, CHI_3, constitutes a positive test, indicating that the unknown is a methyl ketone or a compound that is easily oxidized to a methyl ketone, such as a 2-alkanol. Other ketones will also decolorize the iodine solution, but they will not give a precipitate of iodoform *unless* there is an impurity of a methyl ketone present in the unknown.

The yellow precipitate usually settles out slowly onto the bottom of the test tube. Sometimes, the yellow color of iodoform is masked by a dark substance. If this is the case, cork the test tube and shake it vigorously. If the dark color persists, add more sodium hydroxide solution, and shake the test tube again. Then allow the tube to stand for at least 15 minutes. If there is some doubt as to whether the solid is iodoform, collect the precipitate on a Hirsch funnel and dry it. Iodoform melts at 119–121°C.

You may find on some occasions that methyl ketone gives only a yellow coloration to the solution rather than a distinct yellow precipitate. You should be cautious about drawing any conclusions from this result. Therefore, you should depend on proton NMR to confirm the presence of a methyl group attached directly to a carbonyl group (singlet at about 2 ppm).

Test Compounds. Try the test on 2-heptanone, 4-heptanone (dipropyl ketone), and 2-pentanol.

Reagents. The iodine reagent is prepared by dissolving 20 g of potassium iodide and 10 g of iodine in 100 mL of water. The aqueous sodium hydroxide solution is prepared by dissolving 10 g of sodium hydroxide in 100 mL of water.

Discussion

The basis of this test is the ability of certain compounds to form a precipitate of iodoform when treated with a basic solution of iodine. Methyl ketones are the most common types of compounds that give a positive result in this test. However, acetaldehyde, CH_3CHO, and alcohols with the hydroxyl group at the 2-position of the chain also give a precipitate of iodoform. 2-Alkanols of the type described are easily oxidized to methyl ketones under the conditions of the reaction. The other product of the reaction, besides iodoform, is the sodium or potassium salt of a carboxylic acid.

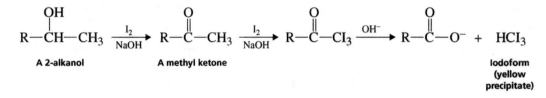

Ferric Chloride Test

Procedure. Some aldehydes and ketones, those that have a high **enol content**, give a positive ferric chloride test, as described for phenols in Experiment 55F.

Spectroscopy

Infrared

The carbonyl group is usually one of the strongest-absorbing groups in the infrared spectrum, with a very broad range: 1800–1650 cm^{-1}. The aldehyde functional group has *very characteristic* C—H stretch absorptions: two sharp peaks that lie *far outside* the usual region for —C—H, =C—H or ≡C—H.

Aldehydes

C=O stretch at approximately
1725 cm^{-1} is normal.
1725–1685 cm^{-1}.*

C—H stretch (aldehyde–CHO)
has two weak bands at about
2750 cm^{-1} and 2850 cm^{-1}.

Ketones

C=O stretch at approximately
1715 cm^{-1} is normal.
1780–1665 cm^{-1}.*

See Technique 25 for details.

Nuclear Magnetic Resonance

Hydrogens alpha to a carbonyl group have resonance in the region between 2 ppm
and 3 ppm. The hydrogen of an aldehyde group has a characteristic resonance
between 9 ppm and 10 ppm. In aldehydes, there is coupling between the aldehyde
hydrogen and any alpha hydrogens (J = 1–3 Hz).

See Technique 26 for details on proton NMR. Carbon NMR is described in
Technique 27.

Derivatives

The most common derivatives of aldehydes and ketones are 2,4-dinitrophenyl-
hydrazones, oximes, and semicarbazones. Procedures for preparing these derivatives are given in Appendix 2.

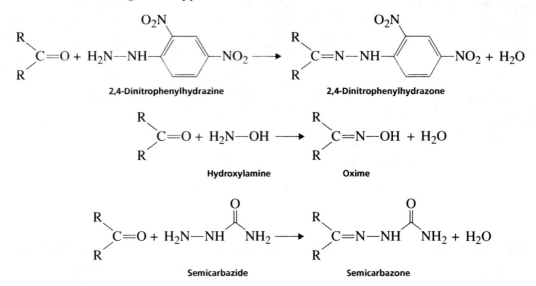

***Conjugation** moves the absorption to lower frequencies. **Ring strain** (cyclic ketones) moves the
absorption to higher frequencies.

55H **EXPERIMENT 55H**

Alcohols

Alcohols are neutral compounds. The only other classes of neutral compounds used in this experiment are the aldehydes, ketones, and esters. Alcohols and esters usually do not give a positive 2,4-dinitrophenylhydrazine test; aldehydes and ketones do. Esters do not react with Ce(IV) or acetyl chloride or with Lucas reagent, as alcohols do, and they are easily distinguished from alcohols on this basis. Primary and secondary alcohols are easily oxidized; esters and tertiary alcohols are not. A combination of the Lucas test and the chromic acid test will differentiate among primary, secondary, and tertiary alcohols.

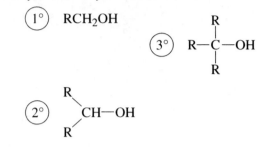

Solubility Characteristics					Classification Tests
HCl	NaHCO$_3$	NaOH	H$_2$SO$_4$	Ether	Cerium(IV) test
(−)	(−)	(−)	(+)	(+)	Acetyl chloride
Water: < C$_6$(+)					Lucas test
> C$_6$(−)					Chromic acid test
					Iodoform test

SUGGESTED WASTE DISPOSAL

Any solution containing chromium must be disposed of by placing it in a waste container specifically identified for the disposal of chromium wastes. Dispose of all other aqueous solutions in the container designated for aqueous waste. Any remaining organic compounds must be disposed of in the appropriate organic waste container.

CLASSIFICATION TESTS

Cerium (IV) Test

Procedure for Water-Soluble or Partially Soluble Compounds. Add 3 mL of water to 0.5 mL of Cerium(IV) reagent in a test tube. Gently shake the solution to thoroughly mix it, and then add 4 drops of the compound to be tested. Gently shake the mixture and look for an immediate color change from a yellow-orange solution to a red-orange or deep red color indicating the presence of an —OH group in an alcohol or phenol. Phenol forms a dark-brown precipitate.

Test Compounds. Try this test on 1-butanol, 2-pentanol, 2-methyl-2-butanol, phenol, butanal, cyclohexanone, and ethyl acetate.

Procedure for Water-Insoluble Compounds. Add 3 mL of 1,2-dimethoxyethane to 0.5 mL of Cerium(IV) reagent in a dry test tube. Gently shake the solution to thoroughly mix it, and then add 4 drops of a liquid compound to be tested. If you have a solid, you can directly add a few milligrams of the solid to the solution. Enough will dissolve to test if an —OH group is present. Gently shake the mixture, and look for an *immediate color change* from a yellow-orange solution to a reddish-brown color indicating the presence of an alcohol or phenol.

Test Compounds. Try this test 1-octanol, β-naphthol (2-naphthol), and benzoic acid.

Reagent. Prepare 2 M nitric acid solution by diluting 12.8 mL of concentrated nitric acid with 100 mL of water. Dissolve 8 g of ceric ammonium nitrate $[Ce(NH_4)_2(NO_3)_6]$ in 20 mL of the dilute nitric acid solution.

Discussion

Primary, secondary, and tertiary alcohols and phenols form 1:1 colored complexes with Ce(IV) and are an excellent way to detect hydroxyl groups. However, this is limited to compounds with no more than 10 carbon atoms. Unfortunately, the test cannot distinguish between primary, secondary, and tertiary alcohols. The Lucast test or chromium oxide test will have to be used for this purpose. Esters, ketones, carboxylic acids, and simple aldehydes do not change the color of the reagent and give a negative test with the Ce(IV) reagent. Thus, esters and other neutral compounds can be distinguished from alcohols by this test. Amines produce a flocculent white precipitate with the reagent. Cerium solutions can oxidize alcohols, but this usually occurs when the solution is heated or when the alcohol is in contact with the reagent for long periods.

Acetyl Chloride

Procedure. Cautiously add about 5–10 drops of acetyl chloride, drop by drop, to about 0.25 mL of the liquid alcohol contained in a small test tube. Evolution of heat and hydrogen chloride gas indicates a positive reaction. Check for the evolution of HCl with a piece of wet blue litmus paper. Hydrogen chloride will turn the litmus paper red. Adding water will sometimes precipitate the acetate.

Test Compounds. Try this test with 1-butanol.

Discussion

Acid chlorides react with alcohols to form esters. Acetyl chloride forms acetate esters.

$$CH_3-\overset{\displaystyle O}{\overset{\displaystyle \|}{C}}-Cl + ROH \longrightarrow CH_3-\overset{\displaystyle O}{\overset{\displaystyle \|}{C}}-O-R + HCl$$

Usually, the reaction is exothermic, and the heat evolved is easily detected. Phenols react with acid chlorides somewhat as alcohols do. Hence, phenols should be eliminated as possibilities before this test is attempted. Amines also react with acetyl chloride to evolve heat (see Experiment 55G). This test does not work well with solid alcohols.

Lucas Test

Procedure. Place 2 mL of Lucas reagent in a small test tube, and add 3–4 drops of the alcohol. Stopper the test tube and shake it vigorously. Tertiary (3°), benzylic, and allylic alcohols give an immediate cloudiness in the solution as the insoluble alkyl halide separates from the aqueous solution. After a short time, the immiscible alkyl halide may form a separate layer. Secondary (2°) alcohols produce a cloudiness after 2–5 minutes. Primary (1°) alcohols dissolve in the reagent to give a clear solution (no cloudiness). Some secondary alcohols may have to be heated slightly to encourage reaction with the reagent.

NOTE: This test works only for alcohols that are soluble in the reagent. This often means that alcohols with more than six carbon atoms cannot be tested.

Test Compounds. Try this test with 1-butanol (*n*-butyl alcohol), 2-butanol (*sec*-butyl alcohol), and 2-methyl-2-proponal (*t*-butyl alcohol).

Reagent. Cool 10 mL of concentrated hydrochloric acid in a beaker, using an ice bath. While still cooling and while stirring, dissolve 16 g of anhydrous zinc chloride in the acid.

This test depends on the appearance of an alkyl chloride as an insoluble second layer when an alcohol is treated with a mixture of hydrochloric acid and zinc chloride (Lucas reagent):

$$R—OH + HCl \xrightarrow{ZnCl_2} R—Cl + H_2O$$

Primary alcohols do not react at room temperature; therefore, the alcohol is seen simply to dissolve. Secondary alcohols react slowly, whereas tertiary, benzylic, and allylic alcohols react instantly. These relative reactivities are explained on the same basis as the silver nitrate reaction, which is discussed in Experiment 55B. Primary carbocations are unstable and do not form under the conditions of this test; hence, no results are observed for primary alcohols.

$$R—\overset{\overset{\displaystyle R}{|}}{\underset{\underset{\displaystyle R}{|}}{C}}—OH + ZnCl_2 \longrightarrow R—\overset{\overset{\displaystyle R}{|}}{\underset{\underset{\displaystyle R}{|}}{C}}—\overset{\delta^+}{O}\cdots\overset{\delta^-}{ZnCl_2} \longrightarrow \left[R—\overset{\overset{\displaystyle R}{|}}{\underset{\underset{\displaystyle R}{|}}{C^+}}\right]\xrightarrow{Cl^-} R—\overset{\overset{\displaystyle R}{|}}{\underset{\underset{\displaystyle R}{|}}{C}}—Cl$$

The Lucas test does not work well with solid alcohols or liquid alcohols containing six or more carbon atoms.

Chromic Acid Test: Alternative Test

CAUTION ⚠

Many chromium(VI) compounds are suspected carcinogens. If you would like to run this test, talk to your instructor first. The Lucas test will distinguish between 1°, 2°, and 3° alcohols, and you should do that test first. If you run the chromic acid test, be sure to wear gloves to avoid contact with this reagent.

Procedure. Dissolve 1 drop of a liquid or about 10 mg of a solid alcohol in 1 mL of *reagent-grade* acetone. Add 1 drop of the chromic acid reagent, and note the result that occurs within 2 seconds. A positive test for a primary or a secondary alcohol is the appearance of a blue-green color. Tertiary alcohols do not produce the test result within 2 seconds, and the solution remains orange. To make sure that the acetone solvent is pure and does not give a positive test result, add 1 drop of chromic acid to 1 mL of acetone that does not have an unknown dissolved in it. The orange color of the reagent should persist for *at least* 3 seconds. If it does not, a new bottle of acetone should be used.

Test Compounds. Try this test with 1-butanol (*n*-butyl alcohol), 2-butanol (*sec*-butyl alcohol), and 2-methyl-2-propanol (*t*-butyl alcohol).

Reagent. Dissolve 20 g of chromium trioxide (CrO_3) in 60 mL of cold water in a beaker. Add a magnetic stir bar to the solution. With stirring, slowly and carefully add 20 mL of concentrated sulfuric acid to the solution. This reagent should be prepared fresh each term.

Discussion

This test is based on the reduction of chromium(VI), which is orange, to chromium(III), which is green, when an alcohol is oxidized by the reagent. A change in color of the reagent from orange to green represents a positive test. Primary alcohols are oxidized by the reagent to carboxylic acids; secondary alcohols are oxidized to ketones.

$$2\ CrO_3 + 2\ H_2O \xrightarrow{H^+} 2\ H_2CrO_4 \xrightarrow{H^+} H_2Cr_2O_7 + H_2O$$

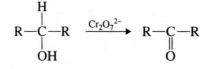

Primary alcohols

Secondary alcohols

Although primary alcohols are first oxidized to aldehydes, the aldehydes are further oxidized to carboxylic acids. The ability of chromic acid to oxidize aldehydes but not ketones is taken advantage of in a test that uses chromic acid to distinguish between aldehydes and ketones (see Experiment 55D). Secondary alcohols are oxidized to ketones, but no further. Tertiary alcohols are not oxidized at all by the reagent; hence, this test can be used to distinguish primary and secondary alcohols from tertiary alcohols. Unlike the Lucas test, this test can be used with all alcohols regardless of molecular weight and solubility.

Iodoform Test

Alcohols with the hydroxyl group at the 2-position of the chain give a positive iodoform test. See the discussion in Experiment 55D.

Spectroscopy

Infrared

O—H stretch. A medium to strong, and usually broad, absorption comes in the region 3600–3200 cm^{-1}. In dilute solutions or with little hydrogen bonding, there is a sharp absorption near 3600 cm^{-1}. In more concentrated solutions, or with considerable hydrogen bonding, there is a broad absorption near 3400 cm^{-1}. Sometimes both bands appear.

C—O stretch. There is a strong absorption in the region 1200–1500 cm^{-1}. Primary alcohols absorb nearer 1050 cm^{-1}; tertiary alcohols and phenols absorb nearer 1200 cm^{-1}. Secondary alcohols absorb in the middle of this range.

See Technique 25 for details.

Nuclear Magnetic Resonance

The hydroxyl resonance is extremely concentration-dependent, but it is usually found between 1 ppm and 5 ppm. Under normal conditions, the hydroxyl proton does not couple with protons on adjacent carbon atoms.

See Technique 26 for details. Carbon NMR is described in Technique 27.

Derivatives

The most common derivatives for alcohols are the 3,5-dinitrobenzoate esters and the phenylurethanes. Occasionally, the α-naphthylurethanes (Experiment 55F) are also prepared, but these latter derivatives are more often used for phenols.

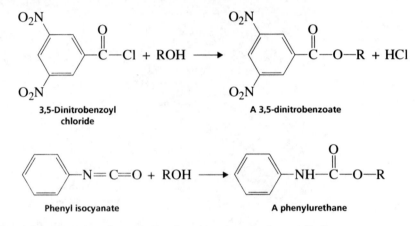

3,5-Dinitrobenzoyl
chloride

A 3,5-dinitrobenzoate

Phenyl isocyanate

A phenylurethane

Procedures for preparing these derivatives are given in Appendix 2.

PART 6

The Techniques

1   **TECHNIQUE 1**

Laboratory Safety

In any laboratory course, familiarity with the fundamentals of laboratory safety is critical. Any chemistry laboratory, particularly an organic chemistry laboratory, can be a dangerous place in which to work. Understanding potential hazards will serve you well in minimizing that danger. It is ultimately your responsibility, along with your laboratory instructor's, to make sure that all laboratory work is carried out in a safe manner.

1.1 Safety Guidelines

It is vital that you take necessary precautions in the organic chemistry laboratory. Your laboratory instructor will advise you of specific rules for the laboratory in which you work. The following list of safety guidelines should be observed in all organic chemistry laboratories.

A. Eye Safety

Always Wear Approved Safety Glasses or Goggles. It is essential to wear eye protection whenever you are in the laboratory. Even if you are not actually carrying out an experiment, a person near you might have an accident that could endanger your eyes. Even dishwashing can be hazardous. We know of cases in which a person has been cleaning glassware—only to have an undetected piece of reactive material explode, throwing fragments into the person's eyes. To avoid such accidents, wear your safety glasses or goggles at all times.

Learn the Location of Eyewash Facilities. If there are eyewash fountains in your laboratory, determine which one is nearest to you before you start to work. If any chemical enters your eyes, go immediately to the eyewash fountain and flush your eyes and face with large amounts of water. If an eyewash fountain is not available, the laboratory will usually have at least one sink fitted with a piece of flexible hose. When the water is turned on, this hose can be aimed upward, and the water can be directed into the face, working much as an eyewash fountain does. To avoid damaging the eyes, the water flow rate should not be set too high, and the water temperature should be slightly warm.

B. Fires

Use Care with Open Flames in the Laboratory. Because an organic chemistry laboratory course deals with flammable organic solvents, the danger of fire is frequently present. Because of this danger, DO NOT SMOKE IN THE LABORATORY. Furthermore, use extreme caution when you light matches or use any open flame. Always check to see whether your neighbors on either side, across the bench, and behind you are using flammable solvents. If so, either wait or move to a safe location, such as a fume hood, to use your open flame. Many flammable organic substances are the source of dense vapors that can travel for some distance down a bench. These vapors present a fire danger, and you should be careful, as the source of those vapors may be far away from you. Do not use the bench sinks to dispose of flammable solvents. If your bench has a trough running along it, pour only *water* (no flammable solvents!) into it. The troughs and sinks are designed to carry water—not flammable materials—from the condenser hoses and aspirators.

Learn the Location of Fire Extinguishers, Fire Showers, and Fire Blankets. For your own protection in case of a fire, you should immediately determine the location of the nearest fire extinguisher, fire shower, and fire blanket. You should learn how to operate these safety devices, particularly the fire extinguisher. Your instructor can demonstrate this.

If there is a fire, the best advice is to get away from it and let the instructor or laboratory assistant take care of it. DON'T PANIC! Time spent thinking before acting is never wasted. If it is a small fire in a container, it can usually be extinguished quickly by placing a wire-gauze screen with a ceramic fiber center or, possibly, a watch glass over the mouth of the container. It is good practice to have a wire screen or watch glass handy whenever you are using a flame. If this method does not extinguish the fire and if help from an experienced person is not readily available, then extinguish the fire yourself with a fire extinguisher.

Should your clothing catch on fire, DO NOT RUN. Walk *purposefully* toward the fire shower station or the nearest fire blanket. Running will fan the flames and intensify them.

C. Organic Solvents: Their Hazards

Avoid Contact with Organic Solvents. It is essential to remember that most organic solvents are flammable and will burn if they are exposed to an open flame or a match. Remember also that on repeated or excessive exposure, some organic solvents may be toxic, carcinogenic (cancer causing), or both. For example, many chlorocarbon solvents, when accumulated in the body, result in liver deterioration similar to cirrhosis caused by excessive use of ethanol. The body does not easily rid itself of chlorocarbons nor does it detoxify them; they build up over time and may cause future illness. Some chlorocarbons are also suspected of being carcinogens. MINIMIZE YOUR EXPOSURE. Long-term exposure to benzene may cause a form of leukemia. Do not sniff benzene and avoid spilling it on yourself. Many other solvents, such as chloroform and ether, are good anesthetics and will put you to sleep if you breathe too much of them. They subsequently cause nausea. Many of these solvents have a synergistic effect with ethanol, meaning that they enhance its effect. Pyridine causes temporary impotence. In other words, organic solvents are just as dangerous as corrosive chemicals, such as sulfuric acid, but manifest their hazardous nature in other, more subtle ways.

If you are pregnant, you may want to consider taking this course at a later time. Some exposure to organic fumes is inevitable, and any possible risk to an unborn baby should be avoided.

Minimize any direct exposure to solvents and treat them with respect. The laboratory room should be well ventilated. Normal cautious handling of solvents should not result in any health problems. If you are trying to evaporate a solution in an open container, you must do the evaporation in the hood. Excess solvents should be discarded in a container specifically intended for waste solvents, rather than down the drain at the laboratory bench.

A sensible precaution is to wear gloves when working with solvents. Gloves made from polyethylene are inexpensive and provide good protection.

The disadvantage of polyethylene gloves is that they are slippery. Disposable surgical gloves provide a better grip on glassware and other equipment, but they do not offer as much protection as polyethylene gloves. Nitrile gloves offer better protection.

Do Not Breathe Solvent Vapors. In checking the odor of a substance, be careful not to inhale very much of the material. The technique for smelling flowers is not advisable here; you could inhale dangerous amounts of the compound. Rather, a technique for smelling minute amounts of a substance should be used. Pass a stopper or spatula moistened with the substance (if it is a liquid) under your nose. Or hold the substance away from you and waft the vapors toward you with your hand. But *never* hold your nose over the container and inhale deeply!

The hazards associated with organic solvents you are likely to encounter in the organic laboratory are discussed in detail in Section 1.3. If you use proper safety precautions, your exposure to harmful organic vapors will be minimized and should present no health risks.

Safe Transportation of Chemicals. When transporting chemicals from one location to another, particularly from one room to another, it is always best to use some form of **secondary containment**. This means that the bottle or flask is carried inside another, larger container. This outer container serves to contain the contents of the inner vessel in case a leak or breakage should occur. Scientific suppliers offer a variety of chemical-resistant carriers for this purpose.

D. Waste Disposal

Do Not Place Any Liquid or Solid Waste in Sinks; Use Appropriate Waste Containers. Many substances are toxic, flammable, and difficult to degrade; it is neither legal nor advisable to dispose of organic solvents or other liquid or solid reagents by pouring them down the sink.

The correct disposal method for wastes is to put them in appropriately labeled waste containers. These containers should be placed in the hoods in the laboratory. The waste containers will be disposed of safely by qualified persons using approved protocols.

Specific guidelines for disposing of waste will be determined by the people in charge of your particular laboratory and by local regulations. Two alternative systems for handling waste disposal are presented here. For each experiment that you are assigned, you will be instructed to dispose of all wastes according to the system that is in operation in your laboratory.

In one model of waste collection, a separate waste container for each experiment is placed in the laboratory. In some cases, more than one container, each labeled according to the type of waste that is anticipated, is set out. The containers will be labeled with a list that details each substance that is present in the container. In this model, it is common practice to use separate waste containers for aqueous solutions, organic halogenated solvents, and other organic nonhalogenated materials. At the end of the laboratory class period, the waste containers are transported to a central hazardous materials storage location. These wastes may be later consolidated and poured into large drums for shipping. Complete labeling, detailing each chemical contained in the waste, is required at each stage of this waste-handling process, even when the waste is consolidated into drums.

In a second model of waste collection, you will be instructed to dispose of all wastes in one of the following ways:

Nonhazardous solids. Nonhazardous solids such as paper and cork can be placed in an ordinary wastebasket.

Broken glassware. Broken glassware should be put into a container specifically designated for broken glassware.

Organic solids. Solid products that are not turned in or any other organic solids should be disposed of in the container designated for organic solids.

Inorganic solids. Solids such as alumina and silica gel should be put in a container specifically designated for them.

Nonhalogenated organic solvents. Organic solvents such as diethyl ether, hexane, and toluene, or any solvent that does not contain a halogen atom, should be disposed of in the container designated for nonhalogenated organic solvents.

Halogenated solvents. Methylene chloride (dichloromethane), chloroform, and carbon tetrachloride are examples of common halogenated organic solvents. Dispose of all halogenated solvents in the container designated for them.

Strong inorganic acids and bases. Strong acids such as hydrochloric, sulfuric, and nitric acid will be collected in specially marked containers. Strong bases such as sodium hydroxide and potassium hydroxide will also be collected in specially designated containers.

Aqueous solutions. Aqueous solutions will be collected in a specially marked waste container. It is not necessary to separate each type of aqueous solution (unless the solution contains heavy metals); rather, unless otherwise instructed, you may combine all aqueous solutions into the same waste container. Although many types of solutions (aqueous sodium bicarbonate, aqueous sodium chloride, and so on) may seem innocuous and it may seem that their disposal down the sink drain is not likely to cause harm, many communities are becoming increasingly restrictive about what substances they will permit to enter municipal sewage-treatment systems. In light of this trend toward greater caution, it is important to develop good laboratory habits regarding the disposal of *all* chemicals.

Heavy metals. Many heavy metal ions such as mercury and chromium are highly toxic and should be disposed of in specifically designated waste containers.

Whichever method is used, the waste containers must eventually be labeled with a complete list of each substance that is present in the waste. Individual waste containers are collected, and their contents are consolidated and placed into drums for transport to the waste-disposal site. Even these drums must bear labels that detail each of the substances contained in the waste.

In either waste-handling method, certain principles will always apply:

- Aqueous solutions should not be mixed with organic liquids.
- Concentrated acids should be stored in separate containers; certainly they must *never* be allowed to come into contact with organic waste.
- Organic materials that contain halogen atoms (fluorine, chlorine, bromine, or iodine) should be stored in separate containers from those used to store materials that do not contain halogen atoms.

In each experiment in this textbook, we have suggested a method of collecting and storing wastes. Your instructor may opt to use another method for collecting wastes.

E. Use of Flames

Even though organic solvents are frequently flammable (for example, hexane, diethyl ether, methanol, acetone, and petroleum ether), there are certain laboratory procedures for which a flame must be used. Most often, these procedures involve an aqueous solution. In fact, as a general rule, use a flame to heat only aqueous solutions. Heating methods that do not use a flame are discussed in detail in Technique 6. Most organic solvents boil below 100°C, and an aluminum block, heating mantle, sand bath, or water bath may be used to heat these solvents safely. Common organic solvents are listed in Technique 10, Table 10.3. Solvents marked in the table with boldface type will burn. Diethyl ether, pentane, and hexane are especially dangerous, because in combination with the correct amount of air, they may explode.

Some common-sense rules apply to using a flame in the presence of flammable solvents. Again, we stress that you should check to see whether anyone in your vicinity is using flammable solvents before you ignite any open flame. If someone is using a flammable solvent, move to a safer location before you light your flame. Your laboratory should have an area set aside for using a burner to prepare micropipets or other pieces of glassware.

The drainage troughs or sinks should never be used to dispose of flammable organic solvents. They will vaporize if they are low boiling and may encounter a flame farther down the bench on their way to the sink.

F. Inadvertently Mixed Chemicals

To avoid unnecessary hazards of fire and explosion, never pour any reagent back into a stock bottle. There is always the chance that you may accidentally pour back some foreign substance that will react explosively with the chemical in the stock bottle. Of course, by pouring reagents back into the stock bottles, you may also introduce impurities that could spoil the experiment for the person using the stock reagent after you. Pouring reagents back into bottles is not only a dangerous practice, but an inconsiderate one. Thus, you should not take more chemicals than you need.

G. Unauthorized Experiments

Never undertake any unauthorized experiments. The risk of an accident is high, particularly if the experiment has not been completely checked to reduce hazards. Never work alone in the laboratory. The laboratory instructor or supervisor must always be present.

H. Food in the Laboratory

Because all chemicals are potentially toxic, avoid accidentally ingesting any toxic substance; therefore, never eat or drink any food while in the laboratory. There is always the possibility that whatever you are eating or drinking may become contaminated with a potentially hazardous material.

I. Clothing

Always wear closed shoes in the laboratory; open-toed shoes or sandals offer inadequate protection against spilled chemicals or broken glass. Do not wear your best clothing in the laboratory because some chemicals can make holes in or permanent stains on your clothing. To protect yourself and your clothing, it is advisable to wear a full-length laboratory apron or coat.

When working with chemicals that are very toxic, wear some type of gloves. Disposable gloves are inexpensive, offer good protection, provide acceptable "feel," and can be bought in many departmental stockrooms and college bookstores. Disposable latex surgical or polyethylene gloves are the least expensive type of glove; they are satisfactory when working with inorganic reagents and solutions. Better protection is afforded by disposable nitrile gloves. This type of glove provides good protection against organic chemicals and solvents. Heavier nitrile gloves are also available.

Finally, hair that is shoulder length or longer should be tied back. This precaution is especially important if you are working with a burner.

J. First Aid: Cuts, Minor Burns, and Acid or Base Burns

If any chemical enters your eyes, immediately irrigate the eyes with copious quantities of water. Tempered (slightly warm) water, if available, is preferable. Be sure that the eyelids are kept open. Continue flushing the eyes in this way for 15 minutes.

In case of a cut, wash the wound well with water unless you are specifically instructed to do otherwise. If necessary, apply pressure to the wound to stop the flow of blood.

Minor burns caused by flames or contact with hot objects may be soothed by immediately immersing the burned area in cold water or cracked ice until you no longer feel a burning sensation. Applying salves to burns is discouraged. Severe burns must be examined and treated by a physician. For chemical acid or base burns, rinse the burned area with copious quantities of water for at least 15 minutes.

If you accidentally ingest a chemical, call the local poison control center for instructions. Do not drink anything until you have been told to do so. It is important that the examining physician be informed of the exact nature of the substance ingested.

1.2 Right-to-Know Laws

The federal government and most state governments now require that employers provide their employees with complete information about hazards in the workplace. These regulations are often referred to as **Right-to-Know Laws.** At the federal level, the Occupational Safety and Health Administration (OSHA) is charged with enforcing these regulations.

In 1990, the federal government extended the Hazard Communication Act, which established the Right-to-Know Laws, to include a provision that requires the establishment of a Chemical Hygiene Plan at all academic laboratories. Every college and university chemistry department should have a Chemical Hygiene Plan. Having this plan means that all of the safety regulations and laboratory safety procedures should be written in a manual. The plan also provides for the training of all employees in laboratory safety. Your laboratory instructor and assistants should have this training.

One of the components of Right-to-Know Laws is that employees and students have access to information about the hazards of any chemicals with which they are working. Your instructor will alert you to dangers to which you need to pay particular attention. However, you may want to seek additional information. Two excellent sources of information are labels on the bottles that come from a chemical manufacturer and **Material Safety Data Sheets** (MSDSs). The MSDSs are also provided by the manufacturer and must be kept available for all chemicals used at educational institutions.

A. Material Safety Data Sheets

Reading an MSDS for a chemical can be a daunting experience, even for an experienced chemist. MSDSs contain a wealth of information, some of which must be decoded to understand. The MSDS for methanol is shown below. Only the information that might be of interest to you is described in the paragraphs that follow.

Section 1. The first part of Section 1 identifies the substance by name, formula, and various numbers and codes. Most organic compounds have more than one name. In this case, the systematic (or International Union of Pure and Applied Chemistry [IUPAC]) name is methanol, and the other names are common names or are from an older system of nomenclature. The Chemical Abstract Service Number (CAS No.) is often used to identify a substance, and it may be used to access extensive information about a substance found in many computer databases or in the library.

Section 3. The Baker SAF-T-DATA System is found on all MSDSs and bottle labels for chemicals supplied by J. T. Baker, Inc. For each category listed, the number indicates the degree of hazard. The lowest number is 0 (very low hazard), and the highest number is 4 (extreme hazard). The Health category refers to damage involved when the substance is inhaled, ingested, or absorbed. Flammability indicates the tendency of a substance to burn. Reactivity refers to how reactive a substance is with air, water, or other substances. The last category, Contact, refers to how hazardous a substance is when it comes in contact with external parts of the body. Note that this rating scale is applicable only to Baker MSDSs and labels; other rating scales with different meanings are also in common use.

Section 4. This section provides helpful information for emergency and first aid procedures.

Section 6. This part of the MSDS deals with procedures for handling spills and disposal. The information could be very helpful, particularly if a large amount of a chemical was spilled. More information about disposal is also given in Section 13.

Section 8. Much valuable information is found in Section 8. To help you understand this material, some of the more important terms used in this section are defined:

> *Threshold Limit Value (TLV).* The American Conference of Governmental Industrial Hygienists (ACGIH) developed the TLV: This is the maximum concentration of a substance in air that a person should be exposed to on a regular basis. It is usually expressed in ppm or mg/m^3. Note that this value assumes that a person is exposed to the substance 40 hours per week, on a long-term basis. This value may not be particularly applicable in the case of a student performing an experiment in a single laboratory period.

> *Permissible Exposure Limit (PEL).* This has the same meaning as TLV; however, PELs were developed by OSHA. Note that for methanol, the TLV and PEL are both 200 ppm.

MSDS Number: M2015   Effective Date: 12/8/96

Material Safety Data Sheet

From: Mallinckrodt Baker, Inc.
222 Red School Lane
Phillipsburg, NJ 08865

MALLINCKRODT   J.T.Baker

24 Hour Emergency Telephone: 908-859-2151
CHEMTREC: 1-800-424-9300

National Response in Canada
CANUTEC: 613-996-6666

Outside U.S. and Canada
Chemtrec: 202-483-7616

NOTE: CHEMTREC, CANUTEC and National
Response Center emergency numbers to be
used only in the event of chemical
emergencies involving a spill, leak, fire,
exposure or accident involving chemicals.

All non-emergency questions should be directed to Customer Service (1-800-582-2537) for assistance.

METHYL ALCOHOL

1. Product Identification

Synonyms:	Wood alcohol; methanol; carbinol
CAS No:	67-56-1
Molecular Weight:	32.04
Chemical Formula:	CH_3OH
Product Codes:	**J.T. Baker:**

5217, 5370, 5794, 5807, 5811, 5842, 5869, 9049, 9063, 9066, 9067, 9069, 9070, 9071, 9073, 9075, 9076, 9077, 9091, 9093, 9096, 9097, 9098, 9263, 9893

Mallinckrodt:

3004, 3006, 3016, 3017, 3018, 3024, 3041, 3701, 4295, 5160, 8814, H080, H488, H603, V079, V571

2. Composition/Information on Ingredients

Ingredient	CAS No.	Percent	Hazardous
Methyl Alcohol	67-56-1	100%	Yes

3. Hazards Identification

Emergency Overview

POISON! DANGER! VAPOR HARMFUL. MAY BE FATAL OR CAUSE BLINDNESS IF SWALLOWED. HARMFUL IF INHALED OR ABSORBED THROUGH SKIN. CANNOT BE MADE NONPOISONOUS. FLAMMABLE LIQUID AND VAPOR. CAUSES IRRITATION TO SKIN, EYES AND RESPIRATORY TRACT. AFFECTS THE LIVER.

J.T. Baker SAF-T-DATA(tm) Ratings
(Provided here for your convenience)

Health:	Flammability:	Reactivity:	Contact:
3 - Severe (Poison)	4 - Extreme (Flammable)	1 - Slight	1 - Slight
Lab Protection Equip:	GOGGLES & SHIELD; LAB COAT & APRON; VENT HOOD; PROPER GLOVES; CLASS B EXTINGUISHER		
Storage Color Code:	Red (Flammable)		

Potential Health Effects

Inhalation:

A slight irritant to the mucous membranes. Toxic effects exerted upon nervous system, particularly the optic nerve. Once absorbed into the body, it is very slowly eliminated. Symptoms of overexposure may include headache, drowsiness, nausea, vomiting, blurred vision, blindness, coma, and death. A person may get better but then worse again up to 30 hours later.

Ingestion:

Toxic. Symptoms parallel inhalation. Can intoxicate and cause blindness. Usual fatal dose: 100-125 milliliters.

Skin Contact:

Methyl alcohol is a defatting agent and may cause skin to become dry and cracked. Skin absorption can occur; symptoms may parallel inhalation exposure.

Eye Contact:

Irritant. Continued exposure may cause eye lesions.

Chronic Exposure:

Marked impairment of vision and enlargement of the liver has been reported. Repeated or prolonged exposure may cause skin irritation.

Aggravation of Pre-existing Conditions:

Persons with pre-existing skin disorders or eye problems or impaired liver or kidney function may be more susceptible to the effects of the substance.

4.   First Aid Measures

Inhalation:

Remove to fresh air. If not breathing, give artificial respiration. If breathing is difficult, give oxygen. Call a physician.

Ingestion:

Induce vomiting immediately as directed by medical personnel. Never give anything by mouth to an unconscious person.

Skin Contact:

Remove any contaminated clothing. Wash skin with soap or mild detergent and water for at least 15 minutes. Get medical attention if irritation develops or persists.

Eye Contact:

Immediately flush eyes with plenty of water for at least 15 minutes, lifting lower and upper eyelids occasionally. Get medical attention immediately.

5.   Fire Fighting Measures

Fire:

Flash point: 12°C (54°F) CC
Autoignition temperature: 464°C (867°F)
Flammable limits in air % by volume:
lel: 7.3; uel: 36
Flammable.

Explosion:

Above flash point, vapor-air mixtures are explosive within flammable limits noted above. Moderate explosion hazard and dangerous fire hazard when exposed to heat, sparks or flames. Sensitive to static discharge.

Fire Extinguishing Media:

Water spray, dry chemical, alcohol foam, or carbon dioxide.

Special Information:

In the event of a fire, wear full protective clothing and NIOSH-approved self-contained breathing apparatus with full facepiece operated in the pressure demand or other positive pressure mode. Use water spray to blanket fire, cool fire exposed containers, and to flush non-ignited spills or vapors away from fire. Vapors can flow along surfaces to distant ignition source and flash back.

6. Accidental Release Measures

Ventilate area of leak or spill. Remove all sources of ignition. Wear appropriate personal protective equipment as specified in Section 8. Isolate hazard area. Keep unnecessary and unprotected personnel from entering. Contain and recover liquid when possible. Use non-sparking tools and equipment. Collect liquid in an appropriate container or absorb with an inert material (e. g., vermiculite, dry sand, earth), and place in a chemical waste container. Do not use combustible materials, such as saw dust. Do not flush to sewer! J. T. Baker SOLUSORB® solvent adsorbent is recommended for spills of this product.

7. Handling and Storage

Protect against physical damage. Store in a cool, dry well-ventilated location, away from any area where the fire hazard may be acute. Outside or detached storage is preferred. Separate from incompatibles. Containers should be bonded and grounded for transfers to avoid static sparks. Storage and use areas should be No Smoking areas. Use non-sparking type tools and equipment, including explosion proof ventilation. Containers of this material may be hazardous when empty since they retain product residues (vapors, liquid); observe all warnings and precautions listed for the product.

8. Exposure Controls/Personal Protection

Airborne Exposure Limits:
For Methyl Alcohol:
- OSHA Permissible Exposure Limit (PEL):
    200 ppm (TWA)
- ACGIH Threshold Limit Value (TLV):
    200 ppm (TWA), 250 ppm (STEL) skin

Ventilation System:
A system of local and/or general exhaust is recommended to keep employee exposures below the Airborne Exposure Limits. Local exhaust ventilation is generally preferred because it can control the emissions of the contaminant at its source, preventing dispersion of it into the general work area. Please refer to the ACGIH document, "Industrial Ventilation, A Manual of Recommended Practices", most recent edition, for details.

Personal Respirator (NIOSH Approved)
If the exposure limit is exceeded, wear a supplied air, full-facepiece respirator, airlined hood, or full-facepiece self-contained breathing apparatus.

Skin Protection:
Rubber or neoprene gloves and additional protection including impervious boots, apron, or coveralls, as needed in areas of unusual exposure.

Eye Protection:
Use chemical safety goggles. Maintain eye wash fountain and quick-drench facilities in work area.

9. Physical and Chemical Properties

Appearance:	**Boiling Point:**
Clear, colorless liquid.	64.5°C (147°F)
Odor:	**Melting Point:**
Characteristic odor.	-98°C (-144°F)
Solubility:	**Vapor Density (Air=1):**
Miscible in water.	1.1
Specific Gravity:	**Vapor Pressure (mm Hg):**
0.8	97 @ 20°C (68°F)
pH:	**Evaporation Rate (BuAc=1):**
No information found.	5.9
% Volatiles by volume @ 21°C (70°F):	
100	

10. Stability and Reactivity

Stability:
Stable under ordinary conditions of use and storage.

Hazardous Decomposition Products:
May form carbon dioxide, carbon monoxide, and formaldehyde when heated to decomposition.

Hazardous Polymerization:
Will not occur.

Incompatabilities:
Strong oxidizing agents such as nitrates, perchlorates or sulfuric acid. Will attack some forms of plastics, rubber, and coatings. May react with metallic aluminum and generate hydrogen gas.

Conditions to Avoid:
Heat, flames, ignition sources and incompatibles.

11. Toxicological Information

Methyl Alcohol (Methanol) Oral rat LD50: 5628 mg/kg; inhalation rat LC50: 64000 ppm/4H; skin rabbit LD50: 15800 mg/kg; Irritation data-standard Draize test: skin, rabbit: 20mg/24 hr. Moderate; eye, rabbit: 100 mg/24 hr. Moderate; Investigated as a mutagen, reproductive effector.

Cancer Lists			
	—NTP Carcinogen—		
Ingredient	Known	Anticipated	IARC Category
Methyl Alcohol (67-56-1)	No	No	None

12. Ecological Information

Environmental Fate:
When released into the soil, this material is expected to readily biodegrade. When released into the soil, this material is expected to leach into groundwater. When released into the soil, this material is expected to quickly evaporate. When released into the water, this material is expected to have a half-life between 1 and 10 days. When released into water, this material is expected to readily biodegrade. When released into the air, this material is expected to exist in the aerosol phase with a short half-life. When released into the air, this material is expected to be readily degraded by reaction with photochemically produced hydroxyl radicals. When released into air, this material is expected to have a half-life between 10 and 30 days. When released into the air, this material is expected to be readily removed from the atmosphere by wet deposition.

Environmental Toxicity:
This material is expected to be slightly toxic to aquatic life.

13. Disposal Considerations

Whatever cannot be saved for recovery or recycling should be handled as hazardous waste and sent to a RCRA approved incinerator or disposed in a RCRA approved waste facility. Processing, use or contamination of this product may change the waste management options. State and local disposal regulations may differ from federal disposal regulations.

Dispose of container and unused contents in accordance with federal, state and local requirements.

14. Transport Information

Domestic (Land, D.O.T.)

Proper Shipping Name:	METHANOL		
Hazard Class:	3		
UN/NA:	UN1230	**Packing Group:**	II

Information reported for product/size:	350LB

International (Water, I.M.O.)

Proper Shipping Name:	METHANOL
Hazard Class:	3.2, 6.1
UN/NA:	UN1230
Information reported for product/size:	350LB

Packing Group: II (appears to the right of UN/NA line)

15. Regulatory Information

Chemical Inventory Status

						—Canada—		
Ingredient	TSCA	EC	Japan	Australia	Korea	DSL	NDSL	Phil.
Methyl Alcohol (67-56-1)	Yes	Yes	Yes	Yes	Yes	Yes	No	Yes

Federal, State & International Regulations

	--SARA 302--		------SARA 313------			-RCRA-	-TSCA-
Ingredient	RQ	TPQ	List	Chemical Catg.	CERCLA	261.33	8(d)
Methyl Alcohol (67-56-1)	No	No	Yes	No	5000	U154	No

Chemical Weapons Convention: No   **TSCA 12(b):** No   **CDTA:** No

SARA 311/312: Acute: Yes Chronic: Yes Fire: Yes Pressure: No Reactivity: No   (Pure / Liquid)

Australian Hazchem Code: 2PE   **Australian Poison Schedule:** S6

WHMIS: This MSDS has been prepared according to the hazard criteria of the Controlled Products Regulations (CPR) and the MSDS contains all of the information required by the CPR.

16. Other Information

NFPA Ratings:

Health: 1 Flammability: 3 Reactivity: 0

Label Hazard Warning:

POISON! DANGER! VAPOR HARMFUL. MAY BE FATAL OR CAUSE BLINDNESS IF SWALLOWED. HARMFUL IF INHALED OR ABSORBED THROUGH SKIN. CANNOT BE MADE NONPOISONOUS. FLAMMABLE LIQUID AND VAPOR. CAUSES IRRITATION TO SKIN, EYES AND RESPIRATORY TRACT. AFFECTS THE LIVER.

Label Precautions:

Keep away from heat, sparks and flame.
Keep container closed.
Use only with adequate ventilation.
Wash thoroughly after handling.
Avoid breathing vapor.
Avoid contact with eyes, skin and clothing.

Label First Aid:

If swallowed, induce vomiting immediately as directed by medical personnel. Never give anything by mouth to an unconscious person. In case of contact, immediately flush eyes or skin with plenty of water for at least 15 minutes while removing contaminated clothing and shoes. Wash clothing before reuse. If inhaled, remove to fresh air. If not breathing give artificial respiration. If breathing is difficult, give oxygen. In all cases get medical attention immediately.

Product Use:

Laboratory Reagent.

Revision Information:

New 16 section MSDS format, all sections have been revised.

Disclaimer:

Mallinckrodt Baker, Inc. provides the information contained herein in good faith but makes no representation as to its comprehensiveness or accuracy. This document is intended only as a guide to the appropriate precautionary handling of the material by a properly trained person using this product. Individuals receiving the information must exercise their independent judgment in determining its appropriateness for a particular purpose. MALLINCKRODT BAKER, INC. MAKES NO REPRESENTATIONS OR WARRANTIES, EITHER EXPRESS OR IMPLIED, INCLUDING WITHOUT LIMITATION ANY WARRANTIES OR MERCHANTABILITY, FITNESS FOR A PARTICULAR PURPOSE WITH RESPECT TO THE INFORMATION SET FORTH HEREIN OR THE PRODUCT TO WHICH THE INFORMATION REFERS. ACCORDINGLY, MALLINCKRODT BAKER, INC. WILL NOT BE RESPONSIBLE FOR DAMAGES RESULTING FROM USE OF OR RELIANCE UPON THIS INFORMATION.

Prepared By: Strategic Services Division
        Phone Number: (314) 539-1600 (U.S.A.)

Section 10. The information contained in Section 10 refers to the stability of the compound and the hazards associated with mixing of chemicals. It is important to consider this information before carrying out an experiment not previously done.

Section 11. More information about the toxicity is given in this section. Another important term must first be defined:

> *Lethal Dose, 50% Mortality (LD_{50}).* This is the dose of a substance that will kill 50% of the animals administered a single dose. Different means of administration are used, such as oral, intraperitoneal (injected into the lining of the abdominal cavity), subcutaneous (injected under the skin), and application to the surface of the skin. The LD_{50} is usually expressed in milligrams (mg) of substance per kilogram (kg) of animal weight. The lower the value of LD_{50}, the more toxic the substance. It is assumed that the toxicity in humans will be similar.

Unless you have considerably more knowledge about chemical toxicity, the information in Sections 8 and 11 is most useful for comparing the toxicity of one substance with another. For example, the TLV for methanol is 200 ppm, whereas the TLV for benzene is 10 ppm. Clearly, performing an experiment involving benzene would require much more stringent precautions than an experiment involving methanol. One of the LD_{50} values for methanol is 5628 mg/kg. The comparable LD_{50} value of aniline is 250 mg/kg. Clearly, aniline is much more toxic, and because it is easily absorbed through the skin, it presents a significant hazard. It should also be mentioned that both TLV and PEL ratings assume that the worker comes in contact with a substance on a repeated and long-term basis. Thus, even if a chemical has a relatively low TLV or PEL, it does not mean that using it for one experiment will present a danger to you. Furthermore, by performing experiments using small amounts of chemicals and with proper safety precautions, your exposure to organic chemicals in this course will be minimal.

Section 16. Section 16 contains the National Fire Protection Association (NFPA) rating. This is similar to the Baker SAF-T-DATA (discussed in Section 3), except that the number represents the hazards when a fire is present. The order here is Health, Flammability, and Reactivity. Often, this is presented in graphic form on a label (see figure). The small diamonds are often color coded: blue for Health, red for Flammability, and yellow for Reactivity. The bottom diamond (white) is sometimes used to display graphic symbols denoting unusual reactivity, hazards, or special precautions to be taken.

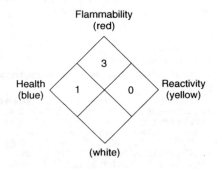

B. Bottle Labels

Reading the label on a bottle can be a very helpful way of learning about the hazards of a chemical. The amount of information varies greatly, depending on which company supplied the chemical.

Apply some common sense when you read MSDSs and bottle labels. Using these chemicals does not mean you will experience the consequences that can potentially result from exposure to each chemical. For example, an MSDS for sodium chloride states, "Exposure to this product may have serious adverse health effects." Despite the apparent severity of this cautionary statement, it would not be reasonable to expect people to stop using sodium chloride in a chemistry experiment or to stop sprinkling a small amount of it (as table salt) on eggs to enhance their flavor. In many cases, the consequences described in MSDSs from exposure to chemicals are somewhat overstated, particularly for students using these chemicals to perform a laboratory experiment.

1.3 Common Solvents

Most organic chemistry experiments involve an organic solvent at some step in the procedure. A list of common organic solvents follows, with a discussion of toxicity, possible carcinogenic properties, and precautions that you should use when handling these solvents. A tabulation of the compounds currently suspected of being carcinogens appears at the end of Technique 1.

Acetic Acid. Glacial acetic acid is corrosive enough to cause serious acid burns on the skin. Its vapors can irritate the eyes and nasal passages. Care should be exercised not to breathe the vapors and not to allow them to escape into the laboratory.

Acetone. Relative to other organic solvents, acetone is not very toxic. It is flammable, however. Do not use acetone near open flames.

Benzene. Benzene can damage bone marrow, it causes various blood disorders, and its effects may lead to leukemia. Benzene is considered a serious carcinogenic hazard. It is absorbed rapidly through the skin and also poisons the liver and kidneys. In addition, benzene is flammable. Because of its toxicity and its carcinogenic properties, benzene should not be used in the laboratory; you should use some less dangerous solvent instead. Toluene is considered a safer alternative solvent in procedures that specify benzene.

Carbon Tetrachloride. Carbon tetrachloride can cause serious liver and kidney damage, as well as skin irritation and other problems. It is absorbed rapidly through the skin. In high concentrations, it can cause death as a result of respiratory failure. Moreover, carbon tetrachloride is suspected of being a carcinogenic material. Although this solvent has the advantage of being nonflammable (in the past, it was used on occasion as a fire extinguisher), it can cause health problems, so it should not be used routinely in the laboratory. If no reasonable substitute exists, however, it must be used in small quantities, as in preparing samples for infrared (IR) and nuclear magnetic resonance (NMR) spectroscopy. In such cases, you must use it in a hood.

Chloroform. Chloroform is similar to carbon tetrachloride in its toxicity. It has been used as an anesthetic. However, chloroform is currently on the list of suspected carcinogens. Because of this, do not use chloroform routinely as a solvent in the laboratory. If it is occasionally necessary to use chloroform as a solvent for special samples, then you must use it in a hood. Methylene chloride is usually found to be a safer substitute in procedures that specify chloroform as a solvent. Deuterochloroform, $CDCl_3$, is a common solvent for NMR spectroscopy. Caution dictates that you should treat it with the same respect as chloroform.

1,2-Dimethoxyethane (Ethylene Glycol Dimethyl Ether or Monoglyme). Because it is miscible with water, 1,2-dimethoxyethane is a useful alternative to solvents such as dioxane and tetrahydrofuran, which may be more hazardous. 1,2-Dimethoxyethane is flammable and should not be handled near an open flame. Upon long exposure of 1,2-dimethoxyethane to light and oxygen, explosive peroxides may form. 1,2-Dimethoxyethane is also a possible reproductive toxin.

Dioxane. Dioxane has been used widely because it is a convenient, water-miscible solvent. It is now suspected, however, of being carcinogenic. It is also toxic, affecting the central nervous system, liver, kidneys, skin, lungs, and mucous membranes. Dioxane is also flammable and tends to form explosive peroxides when it is exposed to light and air. Because of its carcinogenic properties, it is no longer used in the laboratory unless absolutely necessary. Either 1,2-dimethoxyethane or tetrahydrofuran is a suitable, water-miscible alternative solvent.

Ethanol. Ethanol has well-known properties as an intoxicant. In the laboratory, the principal danger arises from fires, because ethanol is a flammable solvent. When using ethanol, take care to work where there are no open flames.

Ether (diethyl ether). The principal hazard associated with diethyl ether is fire or explosion. Ether is probably the most flammable solvent found in the laboratory. Because ether vapors are much denser than air, they may travel along a laboratory bench for a considerable distance from their source before being ignited. Before using ether, it is very important to be sure that no one is working with matches or any open flame. Ether is not a particularly toxic solvent, although in high enough concentrations it can cause drowsiness and perhaps nausea. It has been used as a general anesthetic. Ether can form highly explosive peroxides when exposed to air. Consequently, you should never distill it to dryness.

Hexane. Hexane may be irritating to the respiratory tract. It can also act as an intoxicant and a depressant of the central nervous system. It can cause skin irritation because it is an excellent solvent for skin oils. The most serious hazard, however, comes from its flammability. The precautions recommended for using diethyl ether in the presence of open flames apply equally to hexane.

Ligroin. See Hexane.

Methanol. Much of the material outlining the hazards of ethanol applies to methanol. Methanol is more toxic than ethanol; ingestion can cause blindness and even death. Because methanol is more volatile, the danger of fires is more acute.

Methylene Chloride (Dichloromethane). Methylene chloride is not flammable. Unlike other members of the class of chlorocarbons, it is not currently considered a serious carcinogenic hazard. Recently, however, it has been the subject of much serious investigation, and there have been proposals to regulate it in industrial situations in which workers have high levels of exposure on a day-to-day basis. Methylene chloride is less toxic than chloroform and carbon tetrachloride. It can cause liver damage when ingested, however, and its vapors may cause drowsiness or nausea.

Pentane. See Hexane.

Petroleum Ether. See Hexane.

Pyridine. Some fire hazard is associated with pyridine. However, the most serious hazard arises from its toxicity. Pyridine may depress the central nervous system; irritate the skin and respiratory tract; damage the liver, kidneys, and gastrointestinal system; and even cause temporary sterility. You should treat pyridine as a highly toxic solvent and handle it only in the fume hood.

Tetrahydrofuran. Tetrahydrofuran may cause irritation of the skin, eyes, and respiratory tract. It should never be distilled to dryness because it tends to form potentially explosive peroxides on exposure to air. Tetrahydrofuran does present a fire hazard.

Toluene. Unlike benzene, toluene is not considered a carcinogen. However, it is at least as toxic as benzene. It can act as an anesthetic and damage the central nervous system. If benzene is present as an impurity in toluene, expect the usual hazards associated with benzene. Toluene is also a flammable solvent, and the usual precautions about working near open flames should be applied.

You should not use certain solvents in the laboratory because of their carcinogenic properties. Benzene, carbon tetrachloride, chloroform, and dioxane are among these solvents. For certain applications, however, notably as solvents for infrared or NMR spectroscopy, there may be no suitable alternative. When it is necessary to use one of these solvents, use safety precautions and refer to the discussions in Techniques 25–28.

Because relatively large amounts of solvents may be used in a large organic laboratory class, your laboratory supervisor must take care to store these substances safely. Only the amount of solvent needed for a particular experiment should be kept in the laboratory. The preferred location for bottles of solvents being used during a class period is in a hood. When the solvents are not being used, they should be stored in a fireproof storage cabinet for solvents. If possible, this cabinet should be ventilated into the fume hood system.

1.4 Carcinogenic Substances

A **carcinogen** is a substance that causes cancer in living tissue. The usual procedures for determining whether a substance is carcinogenic is to expose laboratory animals to high dosages over a long period. It is not clear whether short-term exposure to these chemicals carries a comparable risk, but it is prudent to use these substances with special precautions.

Many regulatory agencies have compiled lists of carcinogenic substances or substances suspected of being carcinogenic. Because these lists are inconsistent, compiling a definitive list of carcinogenic substances is difficult. The following common substances are included in many of these lists.

Acetamide	4-Methyl-2-oxetanone (β-butyrolactone)
Acrylonitrile	1-Naphthylamine
Asbestos	2-Naphthylamine
Benzene	*N*-Nitroso compounds
Benzidine	2-Oxetanone (β-propiolactone)
Carbon tetrachloride	Phenacetin
Chloroform	Phenylhydrazine and its salts
Chromic oxide	Polychlorinated biphenyl (PCB)
Coumarin	Progesterone
Diazomethane	Styrene oxide
1,2-Dibromoethane	Tannins
Dimethyl sulfate	Testosterone
p-Dioxane	Thioacetamide
Ethylene oxide	Thiourea
Formaldehyde	*o*-Toluidine
Hydrazine and its salts	Trichloroethylene
Lead (II) acetate	Vinyl chloride

REFERENCES

Aldrich Catalog and Handbook of Fine Chemicals. Aldrich Chemical Co.: Milwaukee, WI, current edition.

Armour, M. A., *Pollution Prevention and Waste Minimization in Laboratories.* Reinhardt, P. A., Leonard, K. L., Ashbrook P. C., Eds.; Lewis Publishers: Boca Raton, Florida, 1996.

Fire Protection Guide on Hazardous Materials, 10th ed. National Fire Protection Quincy, MA: Association 1991.

Flinn Chemical Catalog Reference Manual. Flinn Scientific: Batavia, IL, current edition.

Gosselin, R. E., Smith, R. P., Hodge, H. C. *Clinical Toxicology of Commercial Products,* 5th ed. Williams & Wilkins: Baltimore, MD 1984.

Lenga, R. E., ed. *The Sigma-Aldrich Library of Chemical Safety Data.* Sigma-Aldrich: Milwaukee, WI 1985.

Lewis, R. J. *Carcinogenically Active Chemicals: A Reference Guide.* Van Nostrand Reinhold: New York 1990.

Lewis, R. J., *Sax's Dangerous Properties of Industrial Materials,* 11th edition, Van Nostrand Reinhold: New York 2007.

The Merck Index, 14th ed. Merck and Co.: Rahway, NJ 2006.

Prudent Practices in the Laboratory: Handling and Disposal of Chemicals. Washington, DC: Committee on Prudent Practices for Handling, Storage, and Disposal of Chemicals in Laboratories; Board on Chemical Sciences and Technology; Commission on Physical Sciences, Mathematics, and Applications; National Research Council, National Academy Press, 1995.

Renfrew, M. M., ed. *Safety in the Chemical Laboratory.* Division of Chemical Education, American Chemical Society; Easton, PA 1967–1991.

Safety in Academic Chemistry Laboratories, 4th ed. Committee on Chemical Safety, American Chemical Society: Washington, DC 1985.

Sax, N. I., Lewis, R. J., eds. *Rapid Guide to Hazardous Chemicals in the Work Place,* 4th ed. Van Nostrand Reinhold: New York 2000.

Useful Safety-Related Internet Addresses

Interactive Learning Paradigms, Inc.
http://www.ilpi.com/msds/
This is an excellent general site for MSDS sheets. The site lists chemical manufacturers and suppliers. Selecting a company will take you directly to the appropriate place to obtain an MSDS sheet. Many of the sites listed require you to register in order to obtain an MSDS sheet for a particular chemical. Ask your departmental or college safety supervisor to obtain the information for you.

Acros chemicals and Fisher Scientific
https://www1.fishersci.com/

Alfa Aesar
http://www.alfa.com/alf/index.htm

Cornell University, Department of Environmental Health and Safety
http://msds.pdc.cornell.edu/msdssrch.asp
This is an excellent searchable database of more than 325,000 MSDS files. No registration is required.

Eastman Kodak
http://msds.kodak.com/ehswww/external/index.jsp

EMD Chemicals (formerly EM Science) and Merck
http://www.emdchemicals.com/corporate/emd_corporate.asp

J. T. Baker and Mallinckrodt Laboratory Chemicals
http://www.jtbaker.com/asp/Catalog.asp

National Institute for Occupational Safety and Health (NIOSH) has an excellent "Website" that includes databases and information resources, including links:
http://www.cdc.gov/niosh/topics/chemical-safety/default.html

Sigma, Aldrich and Fluka
http://www.sigmaaldrich.com/Area_of_Interest/The_Americas/United_States.html

VWR Scientific Products
http://www.vwrsp.com/search/index.cgi?tmpl=msds

---

2   **TECHNIQUE 2**

The Laboratory Notebook, Calculations, and Laboratory Records

In the Introduction to this book, we mentioned the importance of advance preparation for laboratory work. Presented here are some suggestions about what specific information you should try to obtain in your advance studying. Because much of this information must be obtained while preparing your laboratory notebook, the two subjects, advance study and notebook preparation, are developed simultaneously.

An important part of any laboratory experience is learning to maintain very complete records of every experiment undertaken and every item of data obtained. Far too often, careless recording of data and observations has resulted in mistakes, frustration, and lost time due to needless repetition of experiments. If reports are required, you will find that proper collection and recording of data can make your report writing much easier.

Because organic reactions are seldom quantitative, special problems result. Frequently, reagents must be used in large excess to increase the amount of product. Some reagents are expensive, and, therefore, care must be used in measuring the amounts of these substances. Very often, many more reactions take place than you desire. These extra reactions, or **side reactions**, may form products other than the desired product. These are called **side products**. For all of these reasons, you must plan your experimental procedure carefully before undertaking the actual experiment.

2.1 The Notebook

For recording data and observations during experiments, use a *bound notebook*. The notebook should have consecutively numbered pages. If it does not, number the pages immediately. A spiral-bound notebook or any other notebook from which the pages can be removed easily is not acceptable, because the possibility of losing the pages is great.

All data and observations must be recorded in the notebook. Paper towels, napkins, toilet tissue, or scratch paper tend to become lost or destroyed. It is bad laboratory practice to record information on such random and perishable pieces of paper. All entries must be recorded in *permanent ink*. It can be frustrating to have important information disappear from the notebook because it was recorded in washable ink or pencil and could not survive a flood caused by the student at the next position on the bench. Because you will be using your notebook in the laboratory, the book will probably become soiled or stained by chemicals, filled with scratched-out entries, or even slightly burned. That is expected and is a normal part of laboratory work.

Your instructor may check your notebook at any time, so you should always have it up to date. If your instructor requires reports, you can prepare them quickly from the material recorded in the laboratory notebook.

2.2 Notebook Format

A. Advance Preparation

Individual instructors vary greatly in the type of notebook format they prefer; such variation stems from differences in philosophies and experience. You must obtain specific directions from your own instructor for preparing a notebook. Certain features, however, are common to most notebook formats. The following discussion indicates what might be included in a typical notebook.

It will be very helpful and you can save much time in the laboratory if for each experiment you know the main reactions, the potential side reactions, the mechanism, and the stoichiometry, and you understand fully the procedure and the theory underlying it before you come to the laboratory. Understanding the procedure by which the desired product is to be separated from undesired materials is also very important. If you examine each of these topics before coming to class, you will be prepared to do the experiment efficiently. You will have your equipment and reagents already prepared when they are to be used. Your reference material will be at hand when you need it. Finally, with your time efficiently organized, you will be able to take advantage of long reaction or reflux periods to perform other tasks, such as doing shorter experiments or finishing previous ones.

For experiments in which a compound is synthesized from other reagents, that is, **preparative experiments**, it is essential to know the main reaction. To perform stoichiometric calculations, you should balance the equation for the main reaction. Therefore, before you begin the experiment, your notebook should contain the balanced equation for the pertinent reaction. Using the preparation of isopentyl acetate, or banana oil, as an example, you should write the following:

$$CH_3-\overset{\overset{\displaystyle O}{\|}}{C}-OH \;+\; CH_3-\overset{\overset{\displaystyle CH_3}{|}}{CH}-CH_2-CH_2-OH \;\xrightarrow{\;H^+\;}$$

Acetic acid   Isopentyl alcohol

$$CH_3-\overset{\overset{\displaystyle O}{\|}}{C}-O-CH_2-CH_2-\overset{\overset{\displaystyle CH_3}{|}}{CH}-CH_3 \;+\; H_2O$$

Isopentyl acetate

Also, before beginning the experiment enter in the notebook the possible side reactions that divert reagents into contaminants (side products). You will have to separate these side products from the major product during purification.

You should list physical constants such as melting points, boiling points, densities, and molecular weights in the notebook when this information is needed to perform an experiment or to do calculations. These data are located in sources such as the *CRC Handbook of Chemistry and Physics, The Merck Index, Lange's Handbook of Chemistry,* or the *Aldrich Handbook of Fine Chemicals.* Write physical constants required for an experiment in your notebook before you come to class.

Advance preparation may also include examining some subjects, information not necessarily recorded in the notebook, that should prove useful in understanding the experiment. Included among these subjects are an understanding of the mechanism of the reaction, an examination of other methods by which the same compound might be prepared, and a detailed study of the experimental procedure. Many students find that an outline of the procedure, prepared *before* they come to class, helps them use their time more efficiently once they begin the experiment. Such an outline could very well be prepared on some loose sheet of paper rather than in the notebook itself.

Once the reaction has been completed, the desired product does not magically appear as purified material; it must be isolated from a frequently complex mixture of side products, unreacted starting materials, solvents, and catalysts. You should try to outline a **separation scheme** in your notebook for isolating the product from its contaminants. At each stage, you should try to understand the reason for the particular instruction given in the experimental procedure. This not only will familiarize you with the basic separation and purification techniques used in organic chemistry but also will help you understand when to use these techniques. Such an outline might take the form of a flowchart. For example, see the separation scheme for isopentyl acetate (see Figure 2.1). Careful attention to understanding the separation, besides familiarizing you with the procedure by which the desired product is separated from impurities in your particular experiments, may prepare you for original research in which no experimental procedure exists.

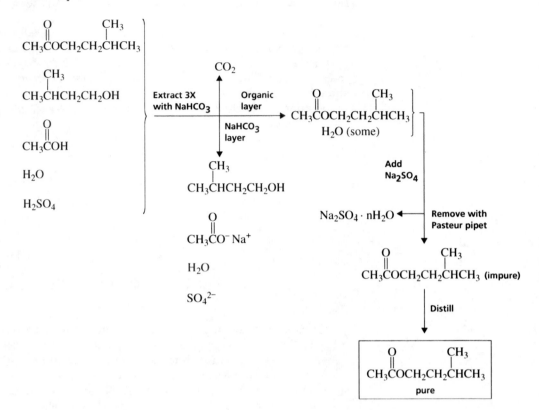

Figure 2.1   Separation scheme for isopentyl acetate.

In designing a separation scheme, note that the scheme outlines those steps undertaken once the reaction period has been concluded. For this reason, the represented scheme does not include steps such as the addition of the reactants (isopentyl alcohol and acetic acid) and the catalyst (sulfuric acid) or the heating of the reaction mixture.

For experiments in which a compound is isolated from a particular source and is not prepared from other reagents, some information described in this section will not be applicable. Such experiments are called **isolation experiments**. A typical isolation experiment involves isolating a pure compound from a natural source. Examples include isolating caffeine from tea or isolating cinnamaldehyde from cinnamon. Although isolation experiments require somewhat different advance preparation, this advance study may include looking up physical constants for the compound isolated and outlining the isolation procedure. A detailed examination of the separation scheme is very important here because it is the heart of such an experiment.

B. Laboratory Records

When you begin the actual experiment, keep your notebook nearby so you will be able to record those operations you perform. When working in the laboratory, your notebook serves as a place in which to record a rough transcript of your experimental method. Data from actual weighings, volume measurements, and determinations of physical constants are also noted. This section of your notebook should *not* be prepared in advance. The purpose is not to write a recipe but rather to record what you *did* and what you *observed*. These observations will help you write reports without resorting to memory. They will also help you or other workers repeat the experiment in as nearly as possible the same way. The sample notebook pages found in Figures 2.2 and 2.3 illustrate the type of data and observations that should be written in your notebook.

When your product has been prepared and purified, or isolated if it is an isolation experiment, record pertinent data such as the melting point or boiling point of the substance, its density, its index of refraction, and the conditions under which spectra were determined.

C. Calculations

A chemical equation for the overall conversion of the starting materials to products is written on the assumption of simple ideal stoichiometry. Actually, this assumption is seldom realized. Side reactions or competing reactions will also occur, giving other products. For some synthetic reactions, an equilibrium state will be reached in which an appreciable amount of starting material is still present and can be recovered. Some of the reactant may also remain if it is present in excess or if the reaction was incomplete. A reaction involving an expensive reagent illustrates another reason for needing to know how far a particular type of reaction converts reactants to products. In such a case, it is preferable to use the most efficient method for this conversion. Thus, information about the efficiency of conversion for various reactions is of interest to the person contemplating the use of these reactions.

The quantitative expression for the efficiency of a reaction is found by calculating the **yield** for the reaction. The **theoretical yield** is the number of grams of the product expected from the reaction on the basis of ideal stoichiometry, with side reactions, reversibility, and losses ignored. To calculate the theoretical yield, it is first necessary to determine the **limiting reagent**. The limiting reagent is the reagent that is not present in excess and on which the overall yield of product depends. The method for determining the limiting reagent in the isopentyl acetate experiment is illustrated in the sample notebook pages shown in Figures 2.2 and 2.3. You should consult your general chemistry textbook for more complicated examples. The theoretical yield is then calculated from the expression:

Theoretical yield = (moles of limiting reagent)(ratio)(molecular weight of product)

The ratio here is the stoichiometric ratio of product to limiting reagent. In preparing isopentyl acetate, that ratio is 1:1. One mole of isopentyl alcohol, under ideal circumstances, should yield 1 mole of isopentyl acetate.

The **actual yield** is simply the number of grams of desired product obtained. The **percentage yield** describes the efficiency of the reaction and is determined by

$$\text{Percentage yield} = \frac{\text{Actual yield}}{\text{Theoretical yield}} \times 100$$

THE PREPARATION OF ISOPENTYLACETATE (BANANA OIL)

Main Reaction

$$CH_3-\overset{\overset{\displaystyle O}{\|}}{C}-OH + CH_3-\overset{\overset{\displaystyle CH_3}{|}}{CH}-CH_2-CH_2-OH \xrightarrow{\ H^+\ } CH_3-\overset{\overset{\displaystyle O}{\|}}{C}-O-CH_2-CH_2-\overset{\overset{\displaystyle CH_3}{|}}{CH}-CH_3 + H_2O$$

Acetic acid   Isopentyl alcohol   Isopentyl acetate

Table of Physical Constants

	MW	BP	Density
Isopentyl alcohol	88.2	132°C	0.813 g/ml
Acetic acid	60.1	118	1.06
Isopentyl acetate	130.2	142	0.876

Separation Scheme

$$CH_3\overset{\overset{\displaystyle O}{\|}}{C}OCH_2CH_2\overset{\overset{\displaystyle CH_3}{|}}{CH}-CH_3$$

$$\overset{\overset{\displaystyle CH_3}{|}}{CH_3CHCH_2CH_2OH}$$

$$CH_3\overset{\overset{\displaystyle O}{\|}}{C}OH$$

$$H_2O$$

$$H_2SO_4$$

Extract 3x NaHCO₃ → CO₂ ↗

$$CH_3\overset{\overset{\displaystyle O}{\|}}{C}OCH_2CH_2\overset{\overset{\displaystyle CH_3}{|}}{CH}CH_3$$

$$H_2O \ (trace)$$

$$NaHCO_3 \ (trace)$$

Extract H₂O + NaCl →

$$CH_3\overset{\overset{\displaystyle O}{\|}}{C}OCH_2CH_2\overset{\overset{\displaystyle CH_3}{|}}{CH}CH_3$$

$$H_2O \ (trace)$$

NaHCO₃ layer ↓

$$\overset{\overset{\displaystyle CH_3}{|}}{CH_3CHCH_2CH_2OH}$$

$$CH_3\overset{\overset{\displaystyle O}{\|}}{C}O^- Na^+$$

$$H_2O$$

$$NaHCO_3$$

$$SO_4{}^{2-}$$

NaHCO₃ / H₂O ↓

Na₂SO₄ ↓   H₂O ←

$$CH_3\overset{\overset{\displaystyle O}{\|}}{C}OCH_2CH_2\overset{\overset{\displaystyle CH_3}{|}}{CH}CH_3$$

(IMPURE)

DISTILL ↓

$$CH_3\overset{\overset{\displaystyle O}{\|}}{C}OCH_2CH_2\overset{\overset{\displaystyle CH_3}{|}}{CH}CH_3$$

PURE

Figure 2.2   A sample notebook, page 1.

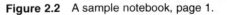

Data and Observations

7.5 mL of isopentyl alcohol was added to a pre-weighed 50-mL round-bottomed flask:

Flask + alcohol	139.75 g
Flask	133.63 g
	6.12 g isopentyl alcohol

Glacial acetic acid (10 mL) and 2 mL of concentrated sulfuric acid were also added to the flask, with swirling, along with several boiling stones. A water-cooled condenser was attached to the flask. The reaction was allowed to boil, using a heating mantle, for about one hour. The color of the reaction mixture was brownish-yellow.

After the reaction mixture had cooled to room temperature, the boiling stones were removed, and the reaction mixture was poured into a separatory funnel. About 30 mL of cold water was added to the separatory funnel. The reaction flask was rinsed with 5 mL of cold water, and the water was also added to the separatory funnel. The separatory funnel was shaken, and the lower aqueous layer was removed and discarded. The organic layer was extracted twice with two 10–15-mL portions of 5% aqueous sodium bicarbonate. During the first extraction, much CO_2 was given off, but the amount of gas evolved was markedly diminished during the second extraction. The organic layer was a light yellow in color. After the second extraction, the aqueous layer turned red litmus blue. The bicarbonate layers were discarded, and the organic layer was extracted with a 10–15-mL portion of water. A 2–3 mL portion of saturated sodium chloride solution was added during this extraction. When the aqueous layer had been removed, the upper, organic phase was transferred to a 15-mL Erlenmeyer flask. 2 g of anhydrous magnesium sulfate was added. The flask was stoppered, swirled gently, and allowed to stand for 15 mins.

The product was transferred to a 25-mL round-bottomed flask, and it was distilled by simple distillation. The distillation continued until no liquid could be observed dripping into the collection flask. After the distillation, the ester was transferred to a pre-weighed sample vial.

Sample vial + product	9.92 g
Sample vial	6.11 g
	3.81 g isopentyl acetate

The product was colorless and clear. The observed boiling point obtained during the distillation, was 140°C. An IR spectrum was obtained of the product.

Calculations

Determine limiting reagent:

$$\text{isopentyl alcohol } 6.12 \text{ g}\left(\frac{1 \text{ mol isopentyl alcohol}}{88.2 \text{ g}}\right) = 6.94 \times 10^{-2} \text{ mol}$$

$$\text{acetic acid: } (10 \text{ mL})\left(\frac{1.06 \text{ g}}{\text{mL}}\right)\left(\frac{1 \text{ mol acetic acid}}{60.1 \text{ g}}\right) = 1.76 \times 10^{-1} \text{ mol}$$

Since they react in a 1:1 ratio, isopentyl alcohol is the limiting reagent. Theoretical yield:

$$(6.94 \times 10^{-2} \text{ mol isopentyl alcohol})\left(\frac{1 \text{ mol isopentyl acetate}}{1 \text{ mol isopentyl alcohol}}\right)\left(\frac{130.2 \text{ g isopentyl acetate}}{1 \text{ mol isopentyl acetate}}\right)$$

$$= 9.03 \text{ g isopentyl acetate}$$

$$\text{Percentage yield} = \frac{3.81 \text{ g}}{9.03 \text{ g}} \times 100 = 42.2\%$$

Figure 2.3   A sample notebook, page 2.

Calculation of the theoretical yield and percentage yield can be illustrated using hypothetical data for the isopentyl acetate preparation:

$$\text{Theoretical yield} = (6.94 \times 10^{-2} \, \text{mol isopentyl alcohol})\left(\frac{1 \, \text{mol isopentyl acetate}}{1 \, \text{mol isopentyl alcohol}}\right)$$

$$\times \left(\frac{130.2 \, \text{g isopentyl acetate}}{1 \, \text{mol isopentyl acetate}}\right) = 9.03 \, \text{g isopentyl acetate}$$

$$\text{Actual yield} = 3.81 \, \text{g isopentyl acetate}$$

$$\text{Percentage yield} = \frac{3.81 \, \text{g}}{9.03 \, \text{g}} \times 100 = 42.2\%$$

For experiments that have the principal objective of isolating a substance such as a natural product rather than preparing and purifying some reaction product, the **weight percentage recovery** and not the percentage yield is calculated. This value is determined by

$$\text{Weight percentage recovery} = \frac{\text{Weight of substance isolated}}{\text{Weight of original material}} \times 100$$

Thus, for instance, if 0.014 g of caffeine was obtained from 2.3 g of tea, the weight percentage recovery of caffeine would be

$$\text{Weight percentage recovery} = \frac{0.014 \, \text{g caffeine}}{2.3 \, \text{g tea}} \times 100 = 0.61\%$$

2.3 Laboratory Reports

Various formats for reporting the results of the laboratory experiments may be used. You may write the report directly in your notebook in a format similar to the sample notebook pages included in this section. Alternatively, your instructor may require a more formal report that is not written in your notebook. When you do original research, these reports should include a detailed description of all the experimental steps undertaken. Frequently, the style used in scientific periodicals such as *Journal of the American Chemical Society* is applied to writing laboratory reports. Your instructor is likely to have his or her own requirements for laboratory reports and should describe the requirements to you.

2.4 Submission of Samples

In all preparative experiments and in some isolation experiments, you will be required to submit to your instructor the sample of the substance you prepared or isolated. How this sample is labeled is very important. Again, learning a correct method of labeling bottles and vials can save time in the laboratory, because fewer mistakes will be made. More importantly, learning to label properly can decrease the danger inherent in having samples of material that cannot be identified correctly at a later date.

Solid materials should be stored and submitted in containers that permit the substance to be removed easily. For this reason, narrow-mouthed bottles or vials are not used for solid substances. Liquids should be stored in containers that will not let them escape through leakage. Be careful not to store volatile liquids in containers that have plastic caps, unless the cap is lined with an inert material such as Teflon. Otherwise, the vapors from the liquid are likely to contact the plastic and dissolve some of it, thus contaminating the substance being stored.

On the label, print the name of the substance, its melting or boiling point, the actual and percentage yields, and your name. An illustration of a properly prepared label follows:

> **Isopentyl Acetate**
> **BP 140°C**
> **Yield 3.81 g (42.2%)**
> **Joe Schmedlock**

---

3   **T E C H N I Q U E   3**

Laboratory Glassware: Care and Cleaning

Because your glassware is expensive and you are responsible for it, you will want to give it proper care and respect. If you read this section carefully and follow the procedures presented here, you may be able to avoid some unnecessary expense. You may also save time, because cleaning problems and replacing broken glassware are time consuming.

If you are unfamiliar with the equipment found in an organic chemistry laboratory or are uncertain about how such equipment should be treated, this section provides some useful information, such as how to clean and care for glassware when using corrosive or caustic reagents. At the end of this section are illustrations that show and name most of the equipment you are likely to find in your drawer or locker.

3.1 Cleaning Glassware

Glassware can be cleaned easily if you clean it immediately after use. It is good practice to do your "dishwashing" right away. With time, organic tarry materials left in a container begin to attack the surface of the glass. The longer you wait to clean glassware, the more extensively this interaction will have progressed. If you wait, cleaning is more difficult, because water will no longer wet the surface of the glass as effectively. If you cannot wash your glassware immediately after use, soak the dirty pieces of glassware in soapy water. A half-gallon plastic container is convenient for soaking and washing glassware. Using a plastic container also helps prevent the loss of small pieces of equipment.

Various soaps and detergents are available for washing glassware. They should be tried first when washing dirty glassware. Organic solvents can also be used, because the residue remaining in dirty glassware is likely to be soluble. After the solvent has been used, the glass item probably will have to be washed with soap and water to remove the residual solvent. When you use solvents to clean glassware, use caution, because the solvents are hazardous (see Technique 1). Use fairly small amounts of a solvent for cleaning purposes. Usually less than 5 mL (or 1–2 mL for microscale glassware) will be sufficient. Acetone is commonly used, but it is expensive. Your **wash acetone** can be used effectively several times before it is "spent." Once your acetone is spent, dispose of it as your instructor directs. If acetone does not work, other organic solvents such as methylene chloride or toluene can be used.

> **CAUTION**
>
> Acetone is very flammable. Do not use it around flames.

For troublesome stains and residues that adhere to the glass despite your best efforts, use a mixture of sulfuric acid and nitric acid. Cautiously add about 20 drops of concentrated sulfuric acid and 5 drops of concentrated nitric acid to the flask or vial.

> **CAUTION**
>
> You must wear safety glasses when you are using a cleaning solution made from sulfuric acid and nitric acid. Do not allow the solution to come into contact with your skin or clothing. It will cause severe burns on your skin and create holes in your clothing. The acids may also react with the residue in the container.

Swirl the acid mixture in the container for a few minutes. If necessary, place the glassware in a warm water bath and heat it cautiously to accelerate the cleaning process. Continue heating the glassware until any sign of a reaction ceases. When the cleaning procedure is completed, decant the mixture into an appropriate waste container.

> **CAUTION**
>
> Do not pour the acid solution into a waste container that is intended for organic wastes.

Rinse the piece of glassware thoroughly with water and then wash it with soap and water. For most common organic chemistry applications, any stains that survive this treatment are not likely to cause difficulty in subsequent laboratory procedures.

If the glassware is contaminated with stopcock grease, rinse the glassware with a small amount (1–2 mL) of methylene chloride. Discard the rinse solution into an appropriate waste container. Once the grease is removed, wash the glassware with soap or detergent and water.

3.2 Drying Glassware

The easiest way to dry glassware is to let it stand overnight. Store vials, flasks, and beakers upside down on a piece of paper towel to permit the water to drain from them. Drying ovens can be used to dry glassware if they are available and if they are not being used for other purposes. Rapid drying can be achieved by rinsing the glassware with acetone and air drying it or placing it in an oven. First, thoroughly drain the glassware of water. Then rinse it with one or two *small* portions (1–2 mL) of acetone. Do not use any more acetone than is suggested here. Return the used acetone to an acetone waste container for recycling. After you rinse the glassware with acetone, dry it by placing it in a drying oven for a few minutes or allow it to air dry at room temperature. The acetone can also be removed by aspirator suction. In some laboratories, it may be possible to dry the glassware by blowing a *gentle* stream of dry air into the container. (Your laboratory instructor will indicate if you should do this.) Before drying the glassware with air, make sure that the air line is not filled with oil. Otherwise, the oil will be blown into the container, and you will have to clean it again. It is not necessary to blast the acetone out of the glassware with a wide-open stream of air; a gentle stream of air is just as effective and will not startle other people in the room.

Do not dry your glassware with a paper towel unless the towel is lint-free. Most paper will leave lint on the glass that can interfere with subsequent procedures. Sometimes it is not necessary to dry a piece of equipment thoroughly. For example, if you are going to place water or an aqueous solution in a container, it does not need to be completely dry.

3.3 Ground-Glass Joints

It is likely that the glassware in your organic kit has **standard-taper ground-glass joints**. For example, the Claisen head in Figure 3.1 consists of an inner (male) ground-glass joint at the bottom and two outer (female) joints at the top. Each end is ground to a precise size, which is designated by the symbol T followed by two numbers. A common joint size in many macroscale organic glassware kits is T 19/22. The first number indicates the diameter (in millimeters) of the joint at its widest point, and the second number refers to its length (see Figure 3.1). One advantage of standard-taper joints is that the pieces fit together snugly and form a good seal. In addition, standard-taper joints allow all glassware components with the same joint size to be connected, thus permitting the assembly of a wide variety of apparatuses. One disadvantage of glassware with ground-glass joints, however, is that it is expensive.

3.4 Connecting Ground-Glass Joints

It is a simple matter to connect pieces of macroscale glassware using standard-taper ground-glass joints. Figure 3.2B illustrates the connection of a condenser to a round-bottom flask. At times, however, it may be difficult to secure the connection so that it does not come apart unexpectedly. Figure 3.2A shows a plastic clip that serves to secure the connection. Methods to secure ground-glass connections with macroscale apparatus, including the use of plastic clips, are covered in Technique 7.

It is important to make sure no solid or liquid is on the joint surfaces. Either of these will decrease the efficiency of the seal, and the joints may leak. With microscale glassware, the presence of solid particles could cause the ground-glass joints to break when the plastic cap is tightened. Also, if the apparatus is to be heated, material caught between the joint surfaces will increase the tendency for the joints to stick. If the joint surfaces are coated with liquid or adhering solid, you should wipe the surfaces with a cloth or a lint-free paper towel before assembling.

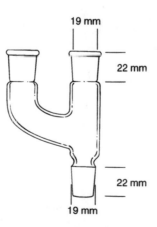

Figure 3.1   Illustration of inner and outer joints, showing dimensions. A Claisen head with T 19/22 joints.

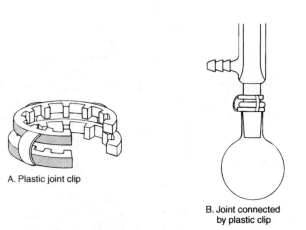

A. Plastic joint clip

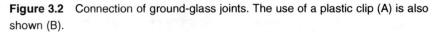

B. Joint connected
by plastic clip

Figure 3.2   Connection of ground-glass joints. The use of a plastic clip (A) is also shown (B).

3.5 Capping Flasks, Conical Vials, and Openings

The sidearms in two-necked or three-necked round-bottom flasks can be capped using the ℑ 19/22 ground-glass stoppers that are part of a normal macroscale organic kit. Figure 3.3 shows such a stopper being used to cap the sidearm of a three-necked flask.

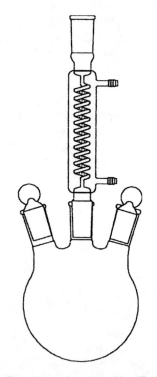

Figure 3.3   Capping a sidearm with a ℑ 19/22 stopper.

3.6 Separating Ground-Glass Joints

When ground-glass joints become "frozen" or stuck together, you are faced with the often vexing problem of separating them. The techniques for separating ground-glass joints, or for removing stoppers that are stuck in the openings of flasks and vials, are the same for both macroscale and microscale glassware.

The most important thing you can do to prevent ground-glass joints from becoming frozen is to disassemble the glassware as soon as possible after a procedure is completed. Even when this precaution is followed, ground-glass joints may become stuck tightly together. The same is true of glass stoppers in bottles or conical vials. Because certain items of microscale glassware may be small and very fragile, it is relatively easy to break a piece of glassware when trying to pull two pieces apart. If the pieces do not separate easily, you must be careful when you try to pull them apart. The best way is to hold the two pieces, with both hands touching, as close as possible to the joint. With a firm grasp, try to loosen the joint with a slight twisting motion (do not twist very hard). If this does not work, try to pull your hands apart without pushing sideways on the glassware.

If it is not possible to pull the pieces apart, the following methods may help. A frozen joint can sometimes be loosened if you tap it *gently* with the wooden handle of a spatula. Then try to pull it apart as already described. If this procedure fails, you may try heating the joint in hot water or a steam bath. If heating fails, the instructor may be able to advise you. As a last resort, you may try heating the joint in a flame. You should not try this unless the apparatus is hopelessly stuck, because heating by flame often causes the joint to expand rapidly and crack or break. If you use a flame, make sure the joint is clean and dry. Heat the outer part of the joint slowly, in the yellow portion of a low flame, until it expands and separates from the inner section. Heat the joint very slowly and carefully, or it may break.

3.7 Etching Glassware

Glassware that has been used for reactions involving strong bases such as sodium hydroxide or sodium alkoxides must be cleaned thoroughly *immediately* after use. If these caustic materials are allowed to remain in contact with the glass, they will etch the glass permanently. The etching makes later cleaning more difficult, because dirt particles may become trapped within the microscopic surface irregularities of the etched glass. Furthermore, the glass is weakened, so the lifetime of the glassware is shortened. If caustic materials are allowed to come into contact with ground-glass joints without being removed promptly, the joints will become fused or "frozen." It is extremely difficult to separate fused joints without breaking them.

3.8 Attaching Rubber Tubing to Equipment

When you attach rubber tubing to the glass apparatus or when you insert glass tubing into rubber stoppers, first lubricate the rubber tubing or the rubber stopper with either water or glycerin. Without such lubrication, it can be difficult to attach rubber tubing to the sidearms of items of glassware such as condensers and filter flasks. Furthermore, glass tubing may break when it is inserted into rubber stoppers. Water is a good lubricant for most purposes. Do not use water as a lubricant when it might contaminate the reaction. Glycerin is a better lubricant than water and should be used when there is considerable friction between the glass and rubber. If glycerin is the lubricant, be careful not to use too much.

3.9 Description of Equipment

Figures 3.4 and 3.5 include examples of glassware and equipment that are commonly used in the organic laboratory. Your glassware and equipment may vary slightly from the pieces shown.

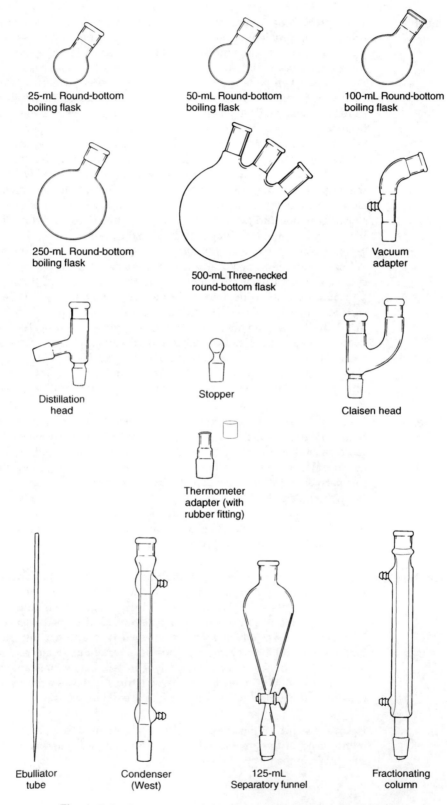

25-mL Round-bottom
boiling flask

50-mL Round-bottom
boiling flask

100-mL Round-bottom
boiling flask

250-mL Round-bottom
boiling flask

500-mL Three-necked
round-bottom flask

Vacuum
adapter

Distillation
head

Stopper

Claisen head

Thermometer
adapter (with
rubber fitting)

Ebulliator
tube

Condenser
(West)

125-mL
Separatory funnel

Fractionating
column

Figure 3.4 Components of the macroscale organic laboratory kit.

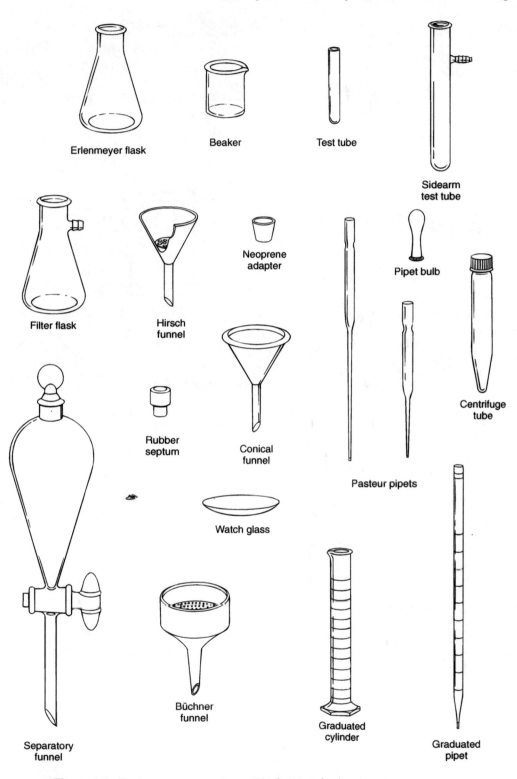

Erlenmeyer flask

Beaker

Test tube

Sidearm
test tube

Filter flask

Hirsch
funnel

Neoprene
adapter

Pipet bulb

Rubber
septum

Conical
funnel

Centrifuge
tube

Pasteur pipets

Watch glass

Separatory
funnel

Büchner
funnel

Graduated
cylinder

Graduated
pipet

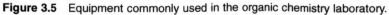

Figure 3.5   Equipment commonly used in the organic chemistry laboratory.

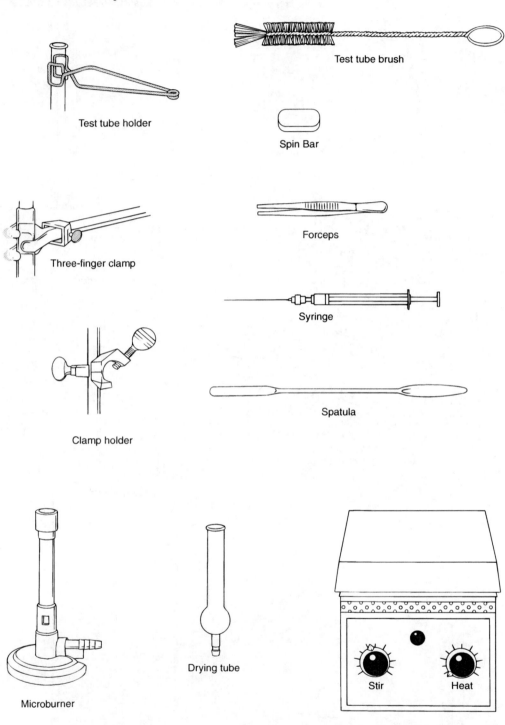

Test tube holder

Test tube brush

Spin Bar

Three-finger clamp

Forceps

Syringe

Spatula

Clamp holder

Microburner

Drying tube

Stir   Heat

Hot plate / Stirrer

6   TECHNIQUE 6

Heating and Cooling Methods

Most organic reaction mixtures need to be heated in order to complete the reaction. In general chemistry, you used a Bunsen burner for heating because nonflammable aqueous solutions were used. In an organic chemistry laboratory, however, the student must heat nonaqueous solutions that may contain *highly flammable* solvents. You *should not heat organic mixtures with a Bunsen burner* unless you are directed to do so by your laboratory instructor. Open flames present a potential fire hazard. Whenever possible you should use one of the alternative heating methods, as described in the following sections.

6.1 Heating Mantles

A useful source of heat for most macroscale experiments is the heating mantle, illustrated in Figure 6.1. The heating mantle shown here consists of a ceramic heating shell with electric heating coils embedded within the shell. The temperature of a heating mantle is regulated with the heat controller. Although it is difficult to monitor the actual temperature of the heating mantle, the controller is calibrated so that it is fairly easy to duplicate approximate heating levels after one has gained some experience with this apparatus. Reactions or distillations requiring relatively high temperatures can be easily performed with a heating mantle. For temperatures in the range of 50–80°C, you should use a water bath (see Section 6.3) or a steam bath (see Section 6.8).

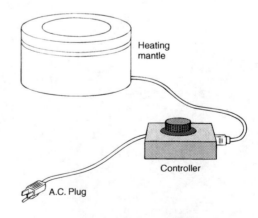

Figure 6.1   A heating mantle.

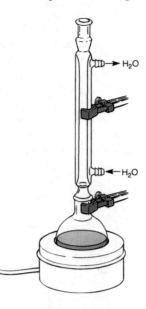

Figure 6.2   Heating with a heating mantle.

In the center of the heating mantle shown in Figure 6.1 is a well that can accommodate round-bottom flasks of several different sizes. Some heating mantles, however, are designed to fit only specific sizes of round-bottom flasks. Some heating mantles are also made to be used with a magnetic stirrer so that the reaction mixture can be heated and stirred at the same time. Figure 6.2 shows a reaction mixture being heated with a heating mantle.

Heating mantles are very easy to use and safe to operate. The metal housing is grounded to prevent electrical shock if liquid is spilled into the well; however, flammable liquids may ignite if spilled into the well of a hot heating mantle.

CAUTION   ⚠️

You should be very careful to avoid spilling liquids into the well of the heating mantle. The surface of the ceramic shell may be very hot and could cause the liquid to ignite.

Raising and lowering the apparatus is a much more rapid method of changing the temperature within the flask than changing the temperature with the controller. For this reason, the entire apparatus should be clamped above the heating mantle so that it can be raised if overheating occurs. Some laboratories may provide a lab jack or blocks of wood that can be placed under the heating mantle. In this case, the heating mantle itself is lowered and the apparatus remains clamped in the same position.

There are two situations in which it is relatively easy to overheat the reaction mixture. The first situation occurs when a larger heating mantle is used to heat a relatively small flask. You should be very careful when doing this. Many laboratories provide heating mantles of different sizes to prevent this from happening. The second situation occurs when the reaction mixture is first brought to a boil. To bring the mixture to a boil as rapidly as possible, the heat controller is often turned up higher than it will need to be set in order to keep the mixture boiling. When the mixture begins boiling very rapidly, turn the controller to a lower setting and raise the apparatus until the mixture boils less rapidly. As the temperature of the heating mantle cools down, lower the apparatus until the flask is resting on the bottom of the well.

6.2 Hot Plates

Hot plates are a very convenient source of heat; however, it is difficult to monitor the actual temperature, and changes in temperature occur somewhat slowly. Care must be taken with flammable solvents to ensure against fires caused by "flashing" when solvent vapors come into contact with the hot-plate surface. Never evaporate large quantities of a solvent by this method; the fire hazard is too great.

Some hot plates *heat constantly* at a given setting. They have no thermostat, and you will have to control the temperature manually, either by removing the container being heated or by adjusting the temperature up or down until a balance point is found. Some hot plates have a thermostat to control the temperature. A good thermostat will maintain a very even temperature. With many hot plates, however, the temperature may vary greatly ($>10–20°C$), depending upon whether the heater is in its "on" cycle or its "off" cycle. These hot plates will have a cycling (or oscillating) temperature, as shown in Figure 6.3. They, too, will have to be adjusted continually to maintain even heat.

Some hot plates also have built-in magnetic stirring motors that enable the reaction mixture to be stirred and heated at the same time. Their use is described in Section 6.5.

6.3 Water Bath with Hot Plate/Stirrer

A hot-water bath is a very effective heat source when a temperature below 80°C is required. A beaker (250-mL or 400-mL) is partially filled with water and heated on a hot plate. A thermometer is clamped into position in the water bath. You may need to cover the water bath with aluminum foil to prevent evaporation, especially at higher temperatures. The water bath is illustrated in Technique 6, Figure 6.4. A mixture can be stirred with a magnetic stir bar (see Technique 7, Section 7.3). A hot-water bath has some advantage over a heating mantle in that the temperature in the bath is uniform. In addition, it is sometimes easier to establish a lower temperature with a water bath than with other heating devices. Finally, the temperature of the reaction mixture will be closer to the temperature of the water, which allows for more precise control of the reaction conditions.

6.4 Oil Bath with Hot Plate/Stirrer

In some laboratories, oil baths may be available. An oil bath can be used when carrying out a distillation or heating a reaction mixture that needs a temperature above 100°C. An oil bath can be heated most conveniently with a hot plate, and a *heavy-walled* beaker provides a suitable container for the oil.[1] A thermometer is clamped into position in the oil bath. In some laboratories, the oil may be heated electrically by an immersion coil. Because oil baths have a high heat capacity and heat slowly, it is advisable to heat the oil bath partially before the actual time at which it is to be used.

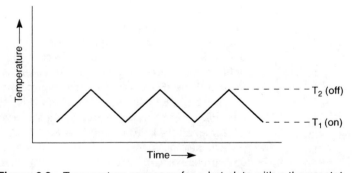

Figure 6.3   Temperature response for a hot plate with a thermostat.

---

[1]It is very dangerous to use a thin-walled beaker for an oil bath. Breakage due to heating can occur, spilling hot oil everywhere!

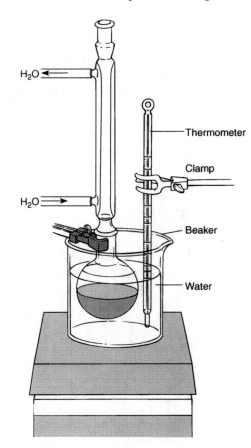

Figure 6.4   A water bath with a hot plate/stirrer.

An oil bath with ordinary mineral oil cannot be used above 200–220 °C. Above this temperature, the oil bath may "flash," or suddenly burst into flame. A hot oil fire is not extinguished easily. If the oil starts smoking, it may be near its flash temperature; discontinue heating. Old oil, which is dark, is more likely to flash than new oil. Also, hot oil causes bad burns. Water should be kept away from a hot oil bath, because water in the oil will cause it to splatter. Never use an oil bath when it is obvious that there is water in the oil. If water is present, replace the oil before using the heating bath. An oil bath has only a finite lifetime. New oil is clear and colorless but, after extended use, becomes dark brown and gummy from oxidation.

Besides ordinary mineral oil, a variety of other types of oils can be used in an oil bath. Silicone oil does not begin to decompose at as low a temperature as does mineral oil. When silicone oil is heated high enough to decompose, however, its vapors are far more hazardous than mineral oil vapors. The polyethylene glycols may be used in oil baths. They are water-soluble, which makes cleaning up after using an oil bath much easier than with mineral oil. One may select any one of a variety of polymer sizes of polyethylene glycol, depending on the temperature range required. The polymers of large molecular weight are often solid at room temperature. Wax may also be used for higher temperatures, but this material also becomes solid at room temperature. Some workers prefer to use a material that solidifies when not in use because it minimizes both storage and spillage problems.

6.5 Aluminum Block with a Hot Plate/Stirrer

Although aluminum blocks are most commonly used in microscale organic chemistry laboratories, they can also be used with the smaller round-bottom flasks used in macroscale experiments.[2] The aluminum block shown in Figure 6.5A can be used to hold 25-, 50-, or 100-mL round-bottom flasks, as well as a thermometer. Heating will occur more rapidly if the flask fits all the way into the hole; however, heating is also effective if the flask only partially fits into the hole. The aluminum block with smaller holes, as shown in Figure 6.5B, is designed for microscale glassware. It will hold a conical vial, a Craig tube or small test tubes, and a thermometer.

There are several advantages to heating with an aluminum block. The metal heats very quickly, high temperatures can be obtained, and you can cool the aluminum rapidly by removing it with crucible tongs and immersing it in cold water. Aluminum blocks are also inexpensive or can be fabricated readily in a machine shop.

Figure 6.6 shows a reaction mixture being heated with an aluminum block on a hot plate/stirrer unit. The thermometer in the figure is used to determine the temperature of the aluminum block. *Do not use a mercury thermometer:* use a thermometer containing a liquid other than mercury or use a metal dial thermometer that can be inserted into a smaller-diameter hole drilled into the side of the block.[3] Make sure that the thermometer fits loosely in the hole, or it may break. Secure the thermometer with a clamp.

To avoid the possibility of breaking a glass thermometer, your hot plate may have a hole drilled into the metal plate so that a metal dial thermometer can be inserted into the unit (see Figure 6.7A). These metal thermometers, such as the one shown in Figure 6.7B, can be obtained in a number of temperature ranges. For example, a 0–250°C thermometer with 2-degree divisions can be obtained at a reasonable price. Also shown in Figure 6.7 (inset) is an aluminum block with a small hole drilled into it so that a metal thermometer can be inserted. An alternative to the metal thermometer is a digital electronic temperature measuring device that can be inserted into the aluminum block or hot plate. It is strongly recommended that mercury thermometers be avoided when measuring the surface temperature of the hot plate or aluminum block. If a mercury thermometer is broken on a hot surface, you will introduce toxic mercury vapors into the laboratory. Nonmercury thermometers filled with high-boiling colored liquids are available as alternatives.

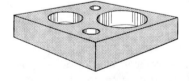

A. Large holes for 25-, 50-, or
   100-mL round-bottom flasks

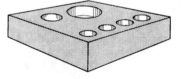

B. Small holes for Craig tube, 3-mL and
   5-mL conical vials, and small test tubes

Figure 6.5 Aluminum heating blocks.

---

[2] The use of solid aluminum heating devices was developed by Siegfried Lodwig at Centralia College, Centralia, WA: Lodwig, S. N., *Journal of Chemical Education, 66* (1989): 77.
[3] C. M. Garner, "A Mercury-Free Alternative for Temperature Measurement in Aluminum Blocks," *Journal of Chemical Education, 68* (1991): A244.

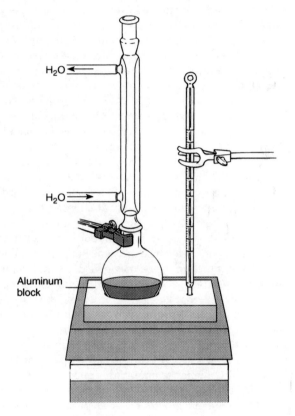

Figure 6.6 Heating with an aluminum block.

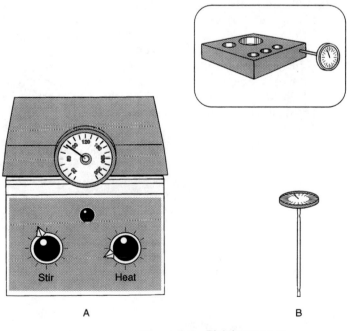

Figure 6.7 Dial thermometers.

As already mentioned, aluminum blocks are often used in the microscale organic chemistry laboratory. The use of an aluminum block to heat a microscale reflux apparatus is shown in Figure 6.8. The reaction vessel in the figure is a conical vial, which is used in many microscale experiments. Also shown in Figure 6.8 is a split aluminum collar that may be used when very high temperatures are required. The collar is split to facilitate easy placement around a 5-mL conical vial. The collar helps to distribute heat further up the wall of the vial.

You should first calibrate the aluminum block so that you have an approximate idea where to set the control on the hot plate to achieve a desired temperature. Place the aluminum block on the hot plate and insert a thermometer into the small hole in the block. Select five equally spaced temperature settings, including the lowest and highest settings, on the heating control of the hot plate. Set the dial to the first of these settings and monitor the temperature recorded on the thermometer. When the thermometer reading arrives at a constant value,[4] record this final temperature, along with the dial setting. Repeat this procedure with the remaining four settings. Using these data, prepare a calibration curve for future reference.

It is a good idea to use the same hot plate each time, as it is very likely that two hot plates of the same type may give different temperatures with identical settings. Record in your notebook the identification number printed on the unit that you are using to ensure that you always use the same hot plate.

For many experiments, you can determine what the approximate setting on the hot plate should be from the boiling point of the liquid being heated. Because the temperature inside the flask is lower than the aluminum block temperature, you should add at least 20°C to the boiling point of the liquid and set the aluminum block at this higher temperature. In fact, you may need to raise the temperature even higher than this value in order to bring the liquid to a boil.

Many organic mixtures need to be stirred as well as heated to achieve satisfactory results. To stir a mixture, place a magnetic stir bar (see Technique 7, Figure 7.8A) in a round-bottom flask containing the reaction mixture as shown in Figure 6.9A. If the mixture is to be heated as well as stirred, attach a water condenser as shown in Figure 6.6. With the combination hot plate/stirrer unit, it is possible to stir and heat a mixture simultaneously. With conical vials, a magnetic spin vane must be used to stir mixtures (see Technique 7, Figure 7.8B). This is shown in Figure 6.9B. More uniform stirring will be obtained if the flask or vial is placed in the aluminum block so that it is centered on the hot plate. Mixing may also be achieved by boiling the mixture. A boiling stone (see Technique 7, Section 7.4) must be added when a mixture is boiled without magnetic stirring.

6.6 Sand Bath with Hot Plate/Stirrer

The sand bath is used in some microscale laboratories to heat organic mixtures. It can also be used as a heat source in some macroscale experiments. Sand provides a clean way of distributing heat to a reaction mixture. To prepare a sand bath for microscale use, place about a 1-cm depth of sand in a crystallizing dish and then set the dish on a hot plate/stirrer unit. The apparatus is shown in Figure 6.10. Clamp the thermometer into position in the sand bath. You should calibrate the sand bath in a manner similar to that used with the aluminum block (see previous section). Because sand heats more slowly than an aluminum block, you will need to begin heating the sand bath well before using it.

---

[4] See, however, Section 6.2.

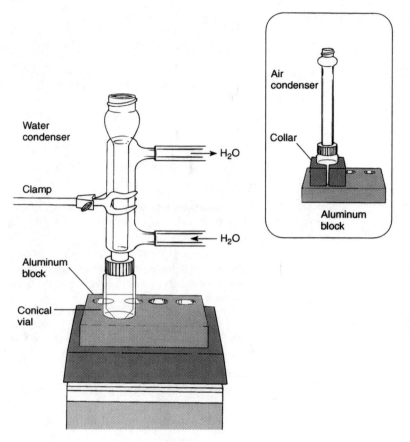

Figure 6.8 Heating with an aluminum block (microscale).

Do not heat the sand bath much above 200°C, or you may break the dish. If you need to heat at very high temperatures, you should use a heating mantle or an aluminum block rather than a sand bath. With sand baths, it may be necessary to cover the dish with aluminum foil to achieve a temperature near 200°C. Because of the relatively poor heat conductivity of sand, a temperature gradient is established within the sand bath. It is warmer near the bottom of the sand bath and cooler near the top for a given setting on the hot plate. To make use of this gradient, you may find it convenient to bury the flask or vial in the sand to heat a mixture more rapidly. Once the mixture is boiling, you can then slow the rate of heating by raising the flask or vial. These adjustments may be made easily and do not require a change in the setting on the hot plate.

6.7 Flames

The simplest technique for heating mixtures is to use a Bunsen burner. Because of the high danger of fires, however, the use of a Bunsen burner should be strictly limited to those cases for which the danger of fire is low or for which no reasonable alternative source of heat is available. A flame should generally be used only to heat aqueous solutions or solutions with very high boiling points. You should always check with your instructor about using a burner. If you use a burner at your bench, great care should be taken to ensure that others in the vicinity are not using flammable solvents.

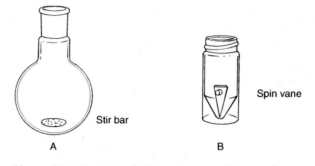

Figure 6.9   Methods of stirring in a round-bottom flask or conical vial.

In heating a flask with a Bunsen burner, you will find that using a wire gauze can produce more even heating over a broader area. The wire gauze, when placed under the object being heated, spreads the flame to keep the flask from being heated in one small area only.

Bunsen burners may be used to prepare capillary micropipets for thin-layer chromatography or to prepare other pieces of glassware requiring an open flame. For these purposes, burners should be used in designated areas in the laboratory and not at your laboratory bench.

6.8 Steam Baths

The steam cone or steam bath is a good source of heat when temperatures around 100°C are needed. Steam baths are used to heat reaction mixtures and solvents needed for crystallization. A steam cone and a portable steam bath are shown in

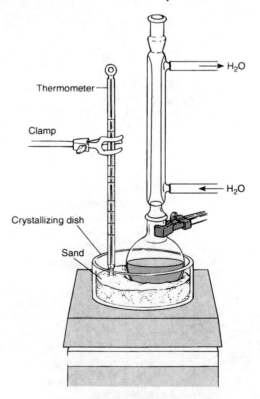

Figure 6.10   Heating with a sand bath.

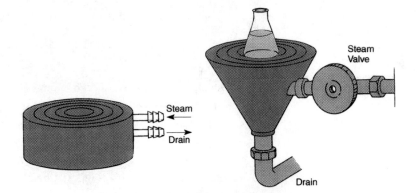

Figure 6.11 A steam bath and a steam cone.

Figure 6.11. These methods of heating have the disadvantage that water vapor may be introduced, through condensation of steam, into the mixture being heated. A slow flow of steam may minimize this difficulty.

Because water condenses in the steam line when it is not in use, it is necessary to purge the line of water before the steam will begin to flow. This purging should be accomplished before the flask is placed on the steam bath. The steam flow should be started with a high rate to purge the line; then the flow should be reduced to the desired rate. When using a portable steam bath, be certain that condensate (water) is drained into a sink. Once the steam bath or cone is heated, a slow steam flow will maintain the temperature of the mixture being heated. There is no advantage to having a Vesuvius on your desk! An excessive steam flow may cause problems with condensation in the flask. This condensation problem can often be avoided by selecting the correct place at which to locate the flask on top of the steam bath.

The top of the steam bath consists of several flat concentric rings. The amount of heat delivered to the flask being heated can be controlled by selecting the correct sizes of these rings. Heating is most efficient when the largest opening that will still support the flask is used. Heating large flasks on a steam bath while using the smallest opening leads to slow heating and wastes laboratory time.

6.9 Cold Baths

At times, you may need to cool an Erlenmeyer flask or round-bottom flask below room temperature. A cold bath is used for this purpose. The most common cold bath is an **ice bath**, which is a highly convenient source of 0°C temperature. An ice bath requires water along with ice to work well. If an ice bath is made up of only ice, it is not a very efficient cooler because the large pieces of ice do not make good contact with the flask. Enough water should be present with ice so that the flask is surrounded by water but not so much that the temperature is no longer maintained at 0°C. In addition, if too much water is present, the buoyancy of a flask resting in the ice bath may cause it to tip over. There should be enough ice in the bath to allow the flask to rest firmly.

For temperatures somewhat below 0°C, you may add some solid sodium chloride to the ice-water bath. The ionic salt lowers the freezing point of the ice so that temperatures in the range of 0 to −10°C can be reached. The lowest temperatures are reached with ice-water mixtures that contain relatively little water.

A temperature of −78.5°C can be obtained with solid carbon dioxide or dry ice. However, large chunks of dry ice do not provide uniform contact with a flask being cooled. A liquid such as isopropyl alcohol is mixed with small pieces of dry ice to provide an efficient cooling mixture. Acetone and ethanol can be used in place of isopropyl alcohol. Be careful when handling dry ice because it can inflict severe frost-bite. Extremely low temperatures can be obtained with liquid nitrogen ($-195.8°C$).

PROBLEMS

1. What would be the preferred heating device(s) in each of the following situations?
   a. Reflux a solvent with a 56°C boiling point
   b. Reflux a solvent with a 110°C boiling point
   c. Distillation of a substance that boils at 220°C

2. Obtain the boiling points for the following compounds by using a handbook (see Technique 4). In each case, suggest a heating device(s) that should be used for refluxing the substance.
   a. Butyl benzoate
   b. 1-Pentanol
   c. 1-Chloropropane

3. What type of bath would you use to get a temperature of $-10°C$?

4. Obtain the melting point and boiling point for benzene and ammonia from a handbook (see Technique 4) and answer the following questions.
   a. A reaction was conducted in benzene as the solvent. Because the reaction was very exothermic, the mixture was cooled in a salt-ice bath. This was a bad choice. Why?
   b. What bath should be used for a reaction that is conducted in liquid ammonia as the solvent?

5. Criticize the following techniques:
   a. Refluxing a mixture that contains diethyl ether using a Bunsen burner
   b. Refluxing a mixture that contains a large amount of toluene using a hot-water bath
   c. Refluxing a mixture using the apparatus shown in Figure 6.6, but with an unclamped thermometer
   d. Using a mercury thermometer that is inserted into an aluminum block on a hot plate
   e. Running a reaction with *tert*-butyl alcohol (2-methyl-2-propanol) that is cooled to 0°C in an ice bath

| 9 | TECHNIQUE 9 |

Physical Constants of Solids: The Melting Point

9.1 Physical Properties

The physical properties of a compound are those properties that are intrinsic to a given compound when it is pure. A compound may often be identified simply by determining a number of its physical properties. The most commonly recognized physical properties of a compound include its color, melting point, boiling point, density, refractive index, molecular weight, and optical rotation. Modern chemists would include the various types of spectra (infrared, nuclear magnetic resonance, mass, and ultraviolet-visible) among the physical properties of a compound. A compound's spectra do not vary from one pure sample to another. Here, we look at methods of determining the melting point. Boiling point and density of compounds are covered in Technique 13. Refractive index, optical rotation, and spectra are also considered separately.

Many reference books list the physical properties of substances. You should consult Technique 4 for a complete discussion on how to find data for specific compounds. The works most useful for finding lists of values for the nonspectroscopic physical properties include:

The Merck Index

The CRC Handbook of Chemistry and Physics

Lange's Handbook of Chemistry

Aldrich Handbook of Fine Chemicals

Complete citations for these references can be found in Technique 29. Although the *CRC Handbook* has very good tables, it adheres strictly to IUPAC nomenclature. For this reason, it may be easier to use one of the other references, particularly *The Merck Index* or the *Aldrich Handbook of Fine Chemicals*, in your first attempt to locate information (see Technique 4).

9.2 The Melting Point

The melting point of a compound is used by the organic chemist not only to identify the compound, but also to establish its purity. A small amount of material is heated *slowly* in a special apparatus equipped with a thermometer or thermocouple, a heating bath or heating coil, and a magnifying eyepiece for observing the sample. Two temperatures are noted. The first is the point at which the first drop of liquid forms among the crystals; the second is the point at which the whole mass of crystals turns to a *clear* liquid. The melting point is recorded by giving this range of melting. You might say, for example, that the melting point of a substance is 51–54°C. That is, the substance melted over a 3-degree range.

The melting point indicates purity in two ways. First, the purer the material, the higher its melting point. Second, the purer the material, the narrower its melting-point range. Adding successive amounts of an impurity to a pure substance generally causes its melting point to decrease in proportion to the amount of impurity. Looking at it another way, adding impurities lowers the freezing point. The freezing point, a colligative property, is simply the melting point (solid → liquid) approached from the opposite direction (liquid → solid).

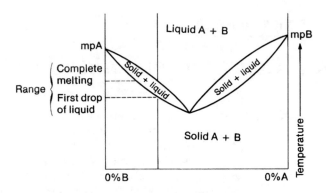

Figure 9.1   A melting-point–composition curve.

Figure 9.1 is a graph of the usual melting-point behavior of mixtures of two substances, A and B. The two extremes of the melting range (the low and high temperature) are shown for various mixtures of the two. The upper curves indicate the temperatures at which all the sample has melted. The lower curves indicate the temperature at which melting is observed to begin. With pure compounds, melting is sharp and without any range. This is shown at the left- and right-hand edges of the graph. If you begin with pure A, the melting point decreases as impurity B is added. At some point, a minimum temperature, or **eutectic**, is reached, and the melting point begins to increase to that of substance B. The vertical distance between the lower and upper curves represents the melting range. Notice that for mixtures that contain relatively small amounts of impurity (< 15%) and are not close to the eutectic, the melting range increases as the sample becomes less pure. The range indicated by the lines in Figure 9.1 represents the typical behavior.

We can generalize the behavior shown in Figure 9.1. Pure substances melt with a narrow range of melting. With impure substances, the melting range becomes wider, and the entire melting range is lowered. Be careful to note, however, that at the minimum point of the melting-point–composition curves, the mixture often forms a eutectic, which also melts sharply. Not all binary mixtures form eutectics, and some caution must be exercised in assuming that every binary mixture follows the previously described behavior. Some mixtures may form more than one eutectic; others might not form even one. In spite of these variations, both the melting point and its range are useful indications of purity, and they are easily determined by simple experimental methods.

9.3 Melting-Point Theory

Figure 9.2 is a phase diagram describing the usual behavior of a two-component mixture (A + B) on melting. The behavior on melting depends on the relative amounts of A and B in the mixture. If A is a pure substance (no B), then A melts sharply at its melting point t_A. This is represented by point A on the left side of the diagram. When B is a pure substance, it melts at t_B; its melting point is represented by point B on the right side of the diagram. At either point A or point B, the pure solid passes cleanly, with a narrow range, from solid to liquid.

In mixtures of A and B, the behavior is different. Using Figure 9.2, consider a mixture of 80% A and 20% B on a mole-per-mole basis (that is, mole percentage). The melting point of this mixture is given by t_M at point M on the diagram. That is, adding B to A has lowered the melting point of A from t_A to t_M. It has also expanded

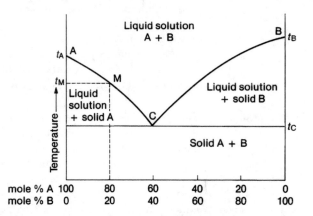

Figure 9.2   A phase diagram for melting in a two-component system.

the melting range. The temperature t_M corresponds to the **upper limit** of the melting range.

Lowering the melting point of A by adding impurity B comes about in the following way. Substance A has the lower melting point in the phase diagram shown, and if heated, it begins to melt first. As A begins to melt, solid B begins to dissolve in the liquid A that is formed. When solid B dissolves in liquid A, the melting point is depressed. To understand this, consider the melting point from the opposite direction. When a liquid at a high temperature cools, it reaches a point at which it solidifies, or "freezes." The temperature at which a liquid freezes is identical to its melting point. Recall that the freezing point of a liquid can be lowered by adding an impurity. Because the freezing point and the melting point are identical, lowering the freezing point corresponds to lowering the melting point. Therefore, as more impurity is added to a solid, its melting point becomes lower. There is, however, a limit to how far the melting point can be depressed. You cannot dissolve an infinite amount of the impurity substance in the liquid. At some point, the liquid will become saturated with the impurity substance. The solubility of B in A has an upper limit. In Figure 9.2, the solubility limit of B in liquid A is reached at point C, the **eutectic point**. The melting point of the mixture cannot be lowered below t_C, the melting temperature of the eutectic.

Now consider what happens when the melting point of a mixture of 80% A and 20% B is approached. As the temperature is increased, A begins to "melt." This is not really a visible phenomenon in the beginning stages; it happens before liquid is visible. It is a softening of the compound to a point at which it can begin to mix with the impurity. As A begins to soften, it dissolves B. As it dissolves B, the melting point is lowered. The lowering continues until all B is dissolved or until the eutectic composition (saturation) is reached. When the maximum possible amount of B has been dissolved, actual melting begins, and one can observe the first appearance of liquid. The initial temperature of melting will be below t_A. The amount below t_A at which melting begins is determined by the amount of B dissolved in A, but will never be below t_C. Once all B has been dissolved, the melting point of the mixture begins to rise as more A begins to melt. As more A melts, the semisolid solution is diluted by more A, and its melting point rises. While all this is happening, you can observe *both* solid and liquid in the melting-point capillary. Once all A has begun to melt, the composition of the mixture M becomes uniform and will reach 80% A and 20% B. At this point, the mixture finally melts sharply, giving a clear solution.

The maximum melting-point range will be $t_C - t_M$, because t_A is depressed by the impurity B that is present. The lower end of the melting range will always be t_C; however, melting will not always be observed at this temperature. An observable melting at t_C comes about only when a large amount of B is present. Otherwise, the amount of liquid formed at t_C will be too small to observe. Therefore, the melting behavior that is actually observed will have a smaller range, as shown in Figure 9.1.

9.4 Mixture Melting Points

The melting point can be used as supporting evidence in identifying a compound in two different ways. Not only may the melting points of the two individual compounds be compared, but a special procedure called a **mixture melting point** may also be performed. The mixture melting point requires that an authentic sample of the same compound be available from another source. In this procedure, the two compounds (authentic and suspected) are finely pulverized and mixed together in equal quantities. Then the melting point of the mixture is determined. If there is a melting-point depression or if the range of melting is expanded by a large amount compared to that of the individual substances, you may conclude that one compound has acted as an impurity toward the other and that they are not the same compound. If there is no lowering of the melting point for the mixture (the melting point is identical with those of pure A and pure B), then A and B are almost certainly the same compound.

9.5 Packing the Melting-Point Tube

Melting points are usually determined by heating the sample in a piece of thin-walled capillary tubing (1 mm × 100 mm) that has been sealed at one end. To pack the tube, press the open end gently into a *pulverized* sample of the crystalline material. Crystals will stick in the open end of the tube. The amount of solid pressed into the tube should correspond to a column no more than 1–2 mm high. To transfer the crystals to the closed end of the tube, drop the capillary tube, closed end first, down a $\frac{2}{3}$-m length of glass tubing, which is held upright on the desktop. When the capillary tube hits the desktop, the crystals will pack down into the bottom of the tube. This procedure is repeated if necessary. Tapping the capillary on the desktop with fingers is not recommended because it is easy to drive the small tubing into a finger if the tubing should break.

Some commercial melting-point instruments have a built-in vibrating device that is designed to pack capillary tubes. With these instruments, the sample is pressed into the open end of the capillary tube, and the tube is placed in the vibrator slot. The action of the vibrator will transfer the sample to the bottom of the tube and pack it tightly.

9.6 Determining the Melting Point—The Thiele Tube

There are two principal types of melting-point apparatus available: the Thiele tube and commercially available, electrically heated instruments. The Thiele tube, shown in Figure 9.3, is the simpler device and was once widely used. It is a glass tube designed to contain a heating oil (mineral oil or silicone oil) and a thermometer to which a capillary tube containing the sample is attached. The shape of the Thiele tube allows convection currents to form in the oil when it is heated. These currents maintain a uniform temperature distribution through the oil in the tube. The sidearm of the tube is designed to generate these convection currents and thus transfer the heat from the flame evenly and rapidly throughout the oil. The sample, which is in a capillary tube attached to the thermometer, is held by a rubber band or a thin slice of rubber tubing. It is important that this rubber band be above the level of the

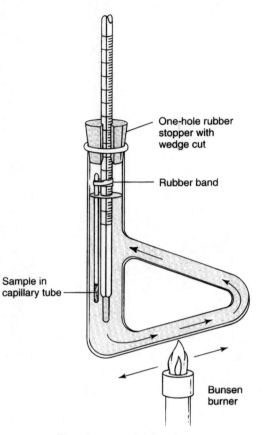

Figure 9.3   A Thiele tube.

oil (allowing for expansion of the oil on heating) so that the oil does not soften the rubber and allow the capillary tubing to fall into the oil. If a cork or a rubber stopper is used to hold the thermometer, a triangular wedge should be sliced in it to allow pressure equalization.

The Thiele tube is usually heated by a microburner. During the heating, the rate of temperature increase should be regulated. Hold the burner by its cool base and, using a low flame, move the burner slowly back and forth along the bottom of the arm of the Thiele tube. If the heating is too fast, remove the burner for a few seconds and then resume heating. The rate of heating should be *slow* near the melting point (about 1°C per minute) to ensure that the temperature increase is not faster than the rate at which heat can be transferred to the sample being observed. At the melting point, it is necessary that the mercury in the thermometer and the sample in the capillary tube be at temperature equilibrium.

9.7 Determining the Melting Point—Electrical Instruments

Three types of electrically heated melting-point instruments are illustrated in Figure 9.4. In each case, the melting-point tube is filled as described in Section 9.5 and placed in a holder located just behind the magnifying eyepiece. The apparatus is operated by moving the switch to the ON position, adjusting the potentiometric

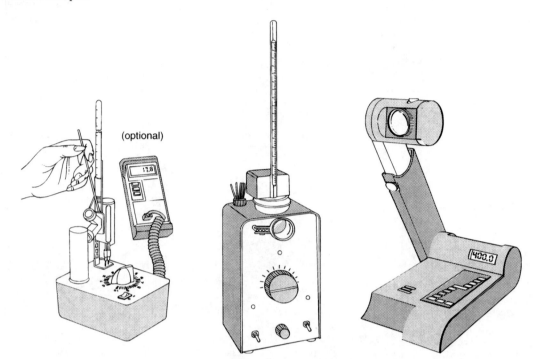

Figure 9.4   Melting-point apparatus.

control dial for the desired rate of heating, and observing the sample through the magnifying eyepiece. The temperature is read from a thermometer or, in the most modern instruments, from a digital display attached to a thermocouple. Your instructor will demonstrate and explain the type used in your laboratory.

Most electrically heated instruments do not heat or increase the temperature of the sample linearly. Although the rate of increase may be linear in the early stages of heating, it usually decreases and leads to a constant temperature at some upper limit. The upper-limit temperature is determined by the setting of the heating control. Thus, a family of heating curves is usually obtained for various control settings, as shown in Figure 9.5. The four hypothetical curves shown (1–4) might correspond to different control settings. For a compound melting at temperature t_1, the setting corresponding to curve 3 would be ideal. In the beginning of the curve, the temperature is increasing too rapidly to allow determination of an accurate melting point, but after the change in slope, the temperature increase will have slowed to a more usable rate.

If the melting point of the sample is unknown, you can often save time by preparing two samples for melting-point determination. With one sample, you can rapidly determine a crude melting-point value. Then repeat the experiment more carefully using the second sample. For the second determination, you already have an approximate idea of what the melting-point temperature should be, and a proper rate of heating can be chosen.

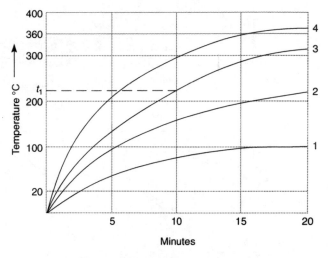

Figure 9.5   Heating-rate curves.

When measuring temperatures above 150°C, thermometer errors can become significant. For an accurate melting point with a high-melting solid, you may wish to apply a **stem correction** to the thermometer as described in Technique 13, Section 13.4. An even better solution is to calibrate the thermometer as described in Section 9.9.

9.8 Decomposition, Discoloration, Softening, Shrinkage, and Sublimation

Many solid substances undergo some degree of unusual behavior before melting. At times it may be difficult to distinguish these types of behavior from actual melting. You should learn, through experience, how to recognize melting and how to distinguish it from decomposition, discoloration, and, particularly, softening and shrinkage.

Some compounds decompose on melting. This decomposition is usually evidenced by discoloration of the sample. Frequently, this decomposition point is a reliable physical property to be used in lieu of an actual melting point. Such decomposition points are indicated in tables of melting points by placing the symbol *d* immediately after the listed temperature. An example of a decomposition point is thiamine hydrochloride, whose melting point would be listed as 248°d, indicating that this substance melts with decomposition at 248°C. When decomposition is a result of reaction with the oxygen in air, it may be avoided by determining the melting point in a sealed, evacuated melting-point tube.

Figure 9.6 shows two simple methods of evacuating a packed tube. Method A uses an ordinary melting-point tube, and method B constructs the melting-point tube from a disposable Pasteur pipet. Before using method B, be sure to determine that the tip of the pipet will fit into the sample holder in your melting-point instrument.

Method A

In method A, a hole is punched through a rubber septum using a large pin or a small nail, and the capillary tube is inserted from the inside, sealed end first. The septum is placed over a piece of glass tubing connected to a vacuum line. After the tube is evacuated, the upper end of the tube may be sealed by heating and pulling it closed.

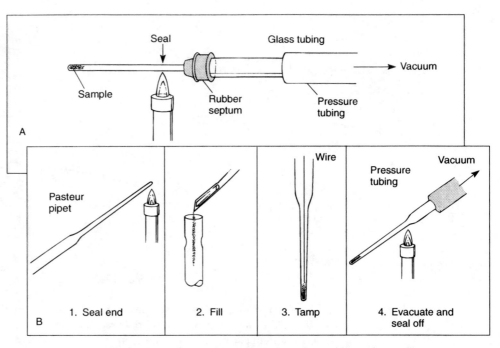

Figure 9.6 Evacuation and sealing of a melting-point capillary.

Method B

In method B, the thin section of a 9-inch Pasteur pipet is used to construct the melting-point tube. Carefully seal the tip of the pipet using a flame. Be sure to hold the tip *upward* as you seal it. This will prevent water vapor from condensing inside the pipet. When the sealed pipet has cooled, the sample may be added through the open end using a microspatula. A small wire may be used to compress the sample into the closed tip. (If your melting-point apparatus has a vibrator, it may be used in place of the wire to simplify the packing.) When the sample is in place, the pipet is connected to the vacuum line with tubing and evacuated. The evacuated sample tube is sealed by heating it with a flame and pulling it closed.

Some substances begin to decompose *below* their melting points. Thermally unstable substances may undergo elimination reactions or anhydride formation reactions during heating. The decomposition products formed represent impurities in the original sample, so the melting point of the substance may be lowered due to their presence.

It is normal for many compounds to soften or shrink immediately before melting. Such behavior represents not decomposition, but a change in the crystal structure or a mixing with impurities. Some substances "sweat," or release solvent of crystallization, before melting. These changes do not indicate the beginning of melting. Actual melting begins when the first drop of liquid becomes visible, and the melting range continues until the temperature is reached at which all the solid has been converted to the liquid state. With experience, you soon learn to distinguish between softening, or "sweating," and actual melting. If you wish, the temperature of the onset of softening or sweating may be reported as a part of your melting-point range: 211°C (softens), 223–225°C (melts).

Some solid substances have such a high vapor pressure that they sublime at or below their melting points. In many handbooks, the sublimation temperature is listed along with the melting point. The symbols *sub, subl,* and sometimes *s* are used

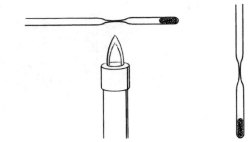

Figure 9.7   Sealing a tube for a substance that sublimes.

to designate a substance that sublimes. In such cases, the melting-point determination must be performed in a sealed capillary tube to avoid loss of the sample. The simplest way to accomplish sealing a packed tube is to heat the open end of the tube in a flame and pull it closed with tweezers or forceps. A better way, although more difficult to master, is to heat the center of the tube in a small flame, rotating it about its axis and keeping the tube straight until the center collapses. If this is not done quickly, the sample may melt or sublime while you are working. With the smaller chamber, the sample will not be able to migrate to the cool top of the tube that may be above the viewing area. Figure 9.7 illustrates the method.

9.9 Thermometer Calibration

When a melting-point or boiling-point determination has been completed, you expect to obtain a result that exactly duplicates the result recorded in a handbook or in the original literature. It is not unusual, however, to find a discrepancy of several degrees from the literature value. Such a discrepancy does not necessarily indicate that the experiment was incorrectly performed or that the material is impure; rather, it may indicate that the thermometer used for the determination was slightly in error. Most thermometers do not measure the temperature with perfect accuracy.

To determine accurate values, you must calibrate the thermometer that is used. This calibration is done by determining the melting points of a variety of standard substances with the thermometer. A plot is drawn of the observed temperature vs. the published value of each standard substance. A smooth line is drawn through the points to complete the chart. A correction chart prepared in this way is shown in Figure 9.8. This chart is used to correct any melting point determined with that particular thermometer. Each thermometer requires its own calibration curve. A list of suitable standard substances for calibrating thermometers is provided in Table 9.1. The standard substances, of course, must be pure in order for the corrections to be valid.

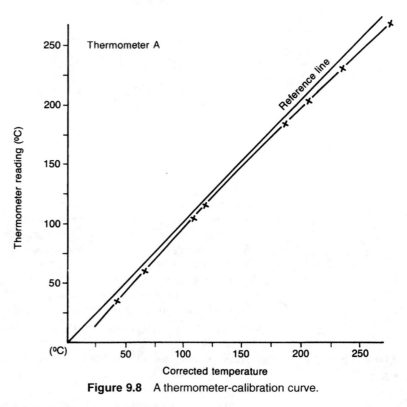

Figure 9.8   A thermometer-calibration curve.

TABLE 9.1   Melting-Point Standards

Compound	Melting Point (°C)
Ice (solid–liquid water)	0
Acetanilide	115
Benzamide	128
Urea	132
Succinic acid	189
3,5-Dinitrobenzoic acid	205

PROBLEMS

1. Two substances, A and B, have the same melting point. How can you determine if they are the same without using any form of spectroscopy? Explain in detail.

2. Using Figure 9.5, determine which heating curve would be most appropriate for a substance with a melting point of about 150°C.

3. What steps can you take to determine the melting point of a substance that sublimes before it melts?

4. A compound melting at 134°C was suspected to be either aspirin (mp 135°C) or urea (mp 133°C). Explain how you could determine whether one of these two suspected compounds was identical to the unknown compound without using any form of spectroscopy.

5. An unknown compound gave a melting point of 230°C. When the molten liquid solidified, the melting point was redetermined and found to be 131°C. Give a possible explanation for this discrepancy.

11   TECHNIQUE 11

Crystallization: Purification of Solids

In most organic chemistry experiments, the desired product is first isolated in an impure form. If this product is a solid, the most common method of purification is crystallization. The general technique involves dissolving the material to be crystallized in a *hot* solvent (or solvent mixture) and cooling the solution slowly. The dissolved material has a decreased solubility at lower temperatures and will separate from the solution as it is cooled. This phenomenon is called either **crystallization**, if the crystal growth is relatively slow and selective, or **precipitation**, if the process is rapid and nonselective. Crystallization is an equilibrium process and produces very pure material. A small seed crystal is formed initially, and it then grows layer by layer in a reversible manner. In a sense, the crystal "selects" the correct molecules from the solution. In precipitation, the crystal lattice is formed so rapidly that impurities are trapped within the lattice. Therefore, any attempt at purification with too rapid a process should be avoided. Because the impurities are usually present in much smaller amounts than the compound being crystallized, most of the impurities will remain in the solvent even when it is cooled. The purified substance can then be separated from the solvent and from the impurities by filtration.

The method of crystallization described here is called **macroscale crystallization**. This technique, which is carried out with an Erlenmeyer flask to dissolve the material and a Büchner funnel to filter the crystals, is normally used when the weight of solid to be crystallized is more than 0.1 g. Another method, which is performed with a Craig tube, is used with smaller amounts of solid. Referred to as **microscale crystallization**, this technique is discussed briefly in Section 11.4.

When the macroscale crystallization procedure described in Section 11.3 is used with a Hirsch funnel, the procedure is sometimes referred to as a **semi-microscale crystallization**. This procedure is commonly used in microscale work when the amount of solid is greater than 0.1 g or in macroscale work when the amount of solid is less than about 0.5 g.

PART A. THEORY

11.1 Solubility

The first problem in performing a crystallization is selecting a solvent in which the material to be crystallized shows the desired solubility behavior. In an ideal case, the material should be sparingly soluble at room temperature and yet quite soluble at the boiling point of the solvent selected. The solubility curve should be steep, as can be seen in line A of Figure 11.1. A curve with a low slope (line B) would not cause significant crystallization when the temperature of the solution was lowered. A solvent in which the material is very soluble at all temperatures (line C) also would not be a suitable crystallization solvent. The basic problem in performing a crystallization is to select a solvent (or mixed solvent) that provides a steep solubility-vs.-temperature curve for the material to be crystallized. A solvent that allows the

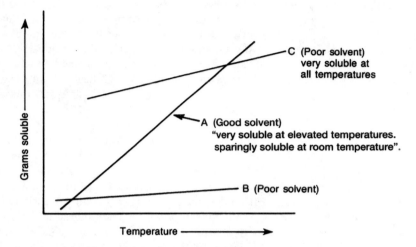

Figure 11.1   Graph of solubility vs. temperature.

behavior shown in line A is an ideal crystallization solvent. It should also be mentioned that solubility curves are not always linear, as they are depicted in Figure 11.1. This figure represents an idealized form of solubility behavior. The solubility curve for sulfanilamide in 95% ethyl alcohol, shown in Figure 11.2, is typical of many organic compounds and shows what solubility behavior might look like for a real substance.

The solubility of organic compounds is a function of the polarities of both the solvent and the **solute** (dissolved material). A general rule is "Like dissolves like." If the solute is very polar, a very polar solvent is needed to dissolve it; if the solute is nonpolar, a nonpolar solvent is needed. Applications of this rule are discussed extensively in Technique 10, Section 10.2, and in Technique 11, Section 11.5.

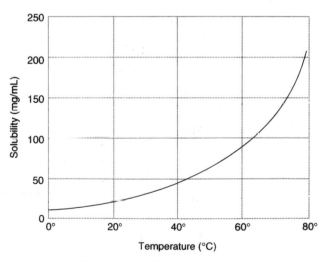

Figure 11.2   Solubility of sulfanilamide in 95% ethyl alcohol.

11.2 Theory Of Crystallization   A successful crystallization depends on a large difference between the solubility of a material in a hot solvent and its solubility in the same solvent when it is cold. When the impurities in a substance are equally soluble in both the hot and the cold solvent, an effective purification is not easily achieved through crystallization. A material can be purified by crystallization when both the desired substance and the impurity have similar solubilities, but only when the impurity represents a small fraction of the total solid. The desired substance will crystallize on cooling, but the impurities will not.

For example, consider a case in which the solubilities of substance A and its impurity B are both 1 g/100 mL of solvent at 20°C and 10 g/100 mL of solvent at 100°C. In the impure sample of A, the composition is 9 g of A and 2 g of B. In the calculations for this example, it is assumed that the solubilities of both A and B are unaffected by the presence of the other substance. To make the calculations easier ·to understand, 100 mL of solvent are used in each crystallization. Normally, the minimum amount of solvent required to dissolve the solid would be used.

At 20°C, this total amount of material will not dissolve in 100 mL of solvent. However, if the solvent is heated to 100°C, all 11 g dissolve. The solvent has the capacity to dissolve 10 g of A *and* 10 g of B at this temperature. If the solution is cooled to 20°C, only 1 g of each solute can remain dissolved, so 8 g of A and 1 g of B crystallize, leaving 2 g of material in the solution. This crystallization is shown in Figure 11.3. The solution that remains after a crystallization is called the **mother liquor**. If the process is now repeated by treating the crystals with 100 mL of fresh solvent, 7 g of A will crystallize again, leaving 1 g of A and 1 g of B in the mother liquor. As a result of these operations, 7 g of pure A are obtained, but with the loss of 4 g of material (2 g of A plus 2 g of B). Again, this second crystallization step is illustrated in Figure 11.3. The final result illustrates an important aspect of crystallization—it is wasteful. Nothing can be done to prevent this waste; some A must be lost along with the impurity B for the method to be successful. Of course, if the impurity B were *more* soluble than A in the solvent, the losses would be reduced. Losses could also be reduced if the impurity were present in *much smaller* amounts than the desired material.

Note that in the preceding case, the method operated successfully because A was present in substantially larger quantity than its impurity B. If there had been a

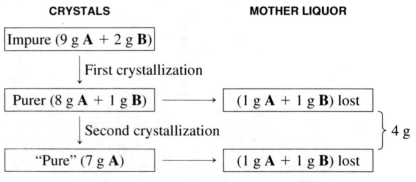

Figure 11.3 Purification of a mixture by crystallization.

50–50 mixture of A and B initially, no separation would have been achieved. In general, a crystallization is successful only if there is a *small* amount of impurity. As the amount of impurity increases, the loss of material must also increase. Two substances with nearly equal solubility behavior, present in equal amounts, cannot be separated. If the solubility behavior of two components present in equal amounts is different, however, a separation or purification is frequently possible.

In the preceding example, two crystallization procedures were performed. Normally, this is not necessary; however, when it is, the second crystallization is more appropriately called **recrystallization**. As illustrated in this example, a second crystallization results in purer crystals, but the yield is lower.

In some experiments, you will be instructed to cool the crystallizing mixture in an ice-water bath before collecting the crystals by filtration. Cooling the mixture increases the yield by decreasing the solubility of the substance; however, even at this reduced temperature, some of the product will be soluble in the solvent. It is not possible to recover all your product in a crystallization procedure even when the mixture is cooled in an ice-water bath. A good example of this is illustrated by the solubility curve for sulfanilamide shown in Figure 11.2. The solubility of sulfanilamide at 0°C is still significant, 14 mg/mL.

PART B. MACROSCALE CRYSTALLIZATION

11.3 Macroscale Crystallization

The crystallization technique described in this section is used when the weight of solid to be crystallized is more than 0.1 g. There are four main steps in a macroscale crystallization:

1. Dissolving the solid
2. Removing insoluble impurities (when necessary)
3. Crystallizing
4. Collecting and drying

These steps are illustrated in Figure 11.4. An Erlenmeyer flask of an appropriate size must be chosen. It should be pointed out that a microscale crystallization with a Craig tube involves the same four steps, although the apparatus and procedures are somewhat different (see Section 11.4).

A. Dissolving the Solid

To minimize losses of material to the mother liquor, it is desirable to *saturate* the boiling solvent with solute. This solution, when cooled, will return the maximum possible amount of solute as crystals. To achieve this high return, the solvent is brought to its boiling point, and the solute is dissolved in the *minimum amount* (!) *of boiling solvent*. For this procedure, it is advisable to maintain a container of boiling solvent (on a hot plate). From this container, a small portion (about 1–2 mL) of the solvent is added to the Erlenmeyer flask containing the solid to be crystallized, and this mixture is heated while swirling occasionally until it resumes boiling.

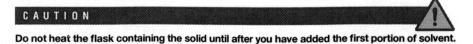

CAUTION

Do not heat the flask containing the solid until after you have added the first portion of solvent.

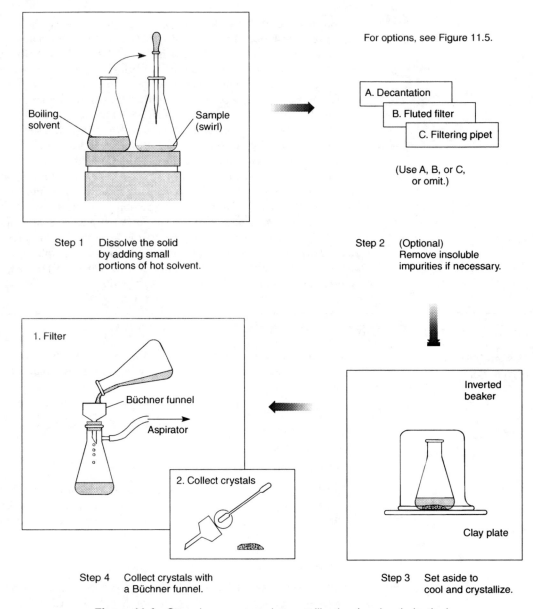

Step 1   Dissolve the solid
         by adding small
         portions of hot solvent.

For options, see Figure 11.5.

A. Decantation
  B. Fluted filter
    C. Filtering pipet

(Use A, B, or C,
   or omit.)

Step 2   (Optional)
         Remove insoluble
         impurities if necessary.

1. Filter

Büchner funnel

Aspirator

2. Collect crystals

Step 4   Collect crystals with
         a Büchner funnel.

Inverted
beaker

Clay plate

Step 3   Set aside to
         cool and crystallize.

Figure 11.4   Steps in a macroscale crystallization (no decolorization).

If the solid does not dissolve in the first portion of boiling solvent, then another small portion of boiling solvent is added to the flask. The mixture is swirled and heated again until it resumes boiling. If the solid dissolves, no more solvent is added. But if the solid has not dissolved, another portion of boiling solvent is added, as before, and the process is repeated until the solid dissolves. It is important to stress that the portions of solvent added each time are small, so only the *minimum* amount of solvent necessary for dissolving the solid is added. It is also important to emphasize that the procedure requires the addition of solvent to solid.

You must never add portions of solid to a fixed quantity of boiling solvent. By this latter method, it may be impossible to determine when saturation has been achieved. This entire procedure should be performed fairly rapidly, or you may lose solvent through evaporation nearly as quickly as you are adding it, and this procedure will then take a very long time. This is most likely to happen when using highly volatile solvents such as methyl alcohol or ethyl alcohol. The time from the first addition of solvent until the solid dissolves completely should not be longer than 15–20 minutes.

Comments on This Procedure for Dissolving the Solid

1. One of the most common mistakes is to add too much solvent. This can happen most easily if the solvent is not hot enough or if the mixture is not stirred sufficiently. If too much solvent is added, the percentage recovery will be reduced; it is even possible that no crystals will form when the solution is cooled. If too much solvent is added, you must evaporate the excess by heating the mixture. A nitrogen or air stream directed into the container will accelerate the evaporation process (see Technique 7, Section 7.10).

2. It is very important not to heat the solid until you have added some solvent. Otherwise, the solid may melt and possibly form an oil or decompose, and it may not crystallize easily (see Section 11.5).

3. It is also important to use an Erlenmeyer flask rather than a beaker for performing the crystallization. A beaker should not be used because the large opening allows the solvent to evaporate too rapidly and allows dust particles to get in too easily.

4. In some experiments, a specified amount of solvent for a given weight of solid will be recommended. In these cases, you should use the amount specified rather than the minimum amount of solvent necessary to dissolve the solid. The amount of solvent recommended has been selected to provide the optimum conditions for good crystal formation.

5. Occasionally, you may encounter an impure solid that contains small particles of insoluble impurities, pieces of dust, or paper fibers that will not dissolve in the hot crystallizing solvent. A common error is to add too much of the hot solvent in an attempt to dissolve these small particles, not realizing that they are insoluble. In such cases, you must be careful not to add too much solvent.

6. It is sometimes necessary to decolorize the solution by adding activated charcoal or by passing the solution through a column containing alumina or silica gel (see Section 11.7 and Technique 19, Section 19.15). A decolorization step should be performed only if the mixture is *highly* colored and it is clear that the color is due to impurities and not due to the actual color of the substance being crystallized. If decolorization is necessary, it should be accomplished before the following filtration step.

B. Removing Insoluble Impurities

It is necessary to use one of the following three methods only if insoluble material remains in the hot solution or if decolorizing charcoal has been used.

Indiscriminate use of the procedure can lead to needless loss of your product.

Decantation is the easiest method of removing solid impurities and should be considered first. If filtration is required, a filtering pipet is used when the volume of liquid to be filtered is less than 10 mL (see Technique 8, Section 8.1C), and you should use gravity filtration through a fluted filter when the volume is 10 mL or greater (see Technique 8, Section 8.1B). These three methods are illustrated in Figure 11.5, and each is discussed below.

Decantation. If the solid particles are relatively large in size or they easily settle to the bottom of the flask, it may be possible to separate the hot solution from the impurities by carefully pouring off the liquid, leaving the solid behind. This is accomplished most easily by holding a glass stirring rod along the top of the flask and tilting the flask so that the liquid pours out along one end of the glass rod into another container. A technique similar in principle to decantation, which may be easier to perform with smaller amounts of liquid, is to use a **preheated Pasteur pipet** to remove the hot solution. With this method, it may be helpful to place the tip of the pipet against the bottom of the flask when removing the last portion of solution. The small space between the tip of the pipet and the inside surface of the flask prevents solid material from being drawn into the pipet. An easy way to preheat the pipet is to draw up a small portion of hot *solvent* (not the *solution* being transferred) into the pipet and expel the liquid. Repeat this process several times.

Fluted Filter. This method is the most effective way to remove solid impurities when the volume of liquid is greater than 10 mL or when decolorizing charcoal has been used (see Technique 8, Section 8.1B and Section 11.7). You should first add a small amount of extra solvent to the hot mixture. This action helps prevent crystal formation in the filter paper or the stem of the funnel during the filtration. The funnel is then fitted with a fluted filter and installed at the top of the Erlenmeyer flask to be used for the actual filtration. It is advisable to place a small piece of wire between the funnel and the mouth of the flask to relieve any increase in pressure caused by hot filtrate.

The Erlenmeyer flask containing the funnel and fluted paper is placed on top of a hot plate (low setting). The liquid to be filtered is brought to its boiling point and poured through the filter in portions. (If the volume of the mixture is less than 10 mL, it may be more convenient to transfer the mixture to the filter with a preheated Pasteur pipet.) It is necessary to keep the solutions in both flasks at their boiling temperatures to prevent premature crystallization. The refluxing action of the filtrate keeps the funnel warm and reduces the chance that the filter will clog with crystals that may have formed during the filtration. With low-boiling solvents, be aware that some solvent may be lost through evaporation. Consequently, extra solvent must be added to make up for this loss. If crystals begin to form in the filter during filtration, a minimum amount of boiling solvent is added to redissolve the crystals and to allow the solution to pass through the funnel. If the volume of liquid being filtered is less than 10 mL, a small amount of hot solvent should be used to rinse the filter after all the filtrate has been collected. The rinse solvent is then combined with the original filtrate.

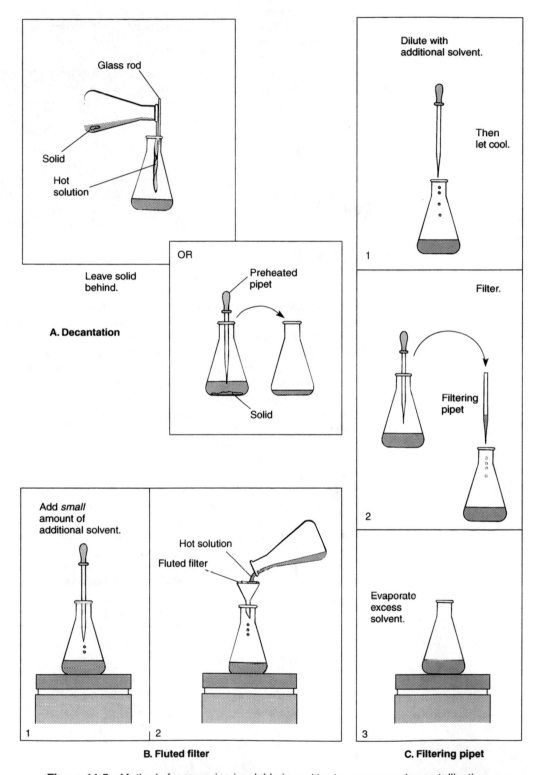

Figure 11.5   Methods for removing insoluble impurities in a macroscale crystallization.

After the filtration, it may be necessary to remove extra solvent by evaporation until the solution is once again saturated at the boiling point of the solvent (see Technique 7, Section 7.10).

Filtering Pipet. If the volume of solution after dissolving the solid in hot solvent is less than 10 mL, gravity filtration with a filtering pipet may be used to remove solid impurities. However, using a filtering pipet to filter a hot solution saturated with solute can be difficult without premature crystallization. The best way to prevent this from occurring is to add enough solvent to dissolve the desired product at room temperature (be sure not to add too much solvent) and perform the filtration at room temperature, as described in Technique 8, Section 8.1C. After filtration, the excess solvent is evaporated by boiling until the solution is saturated at the boiling point of the mixture (see Technique 7, Section 7.10). If powdered decolorizing charcoal was used, it will probably be necessary to perform two filtrations with a filtering pipet to remove all of the charcoal, or a fluted filter can be used.

C. Crystallizing

An Erlenmeyer flask, not a beaker, should be used for crystallization. The large open top of a beaker makes it an excellent dust catcher. The narrow opening of the Erlenmeyer flask reduces contamination by dust and allows the flask to be stoppered if it is to be set aside for a long period. Mixtures set aside for long periods must be stoppered after cooling to room temperature to prevent evaporation of solvent. If all of the solvent evaporates, no purification is achieved, and the crystals originally formed become coated with the dried contents of the mother liquor. Even if the time required for crystallization to occur is relatively short, it is advisable to cover the top of the Erlenmeyer flask with a small watch glass or inverted beaker to prevent evaporation of solvent while the solution is cooling to room temperature.

The chances of obtaining pure crystals are improved if the solution cools to room temperature slowly. When the volume of solution is 10 mL or less, the solution is likely to cool more rapidly than is desired. This can be prevented by placing the flask on a surface that is a poor heat conductor and covering the flask with a beaker to provide a layer of insulating air. Appropriate surfaces include a clay plate or several pieces of filter paper on top of the laboratory bench. It may also be helpful to use a clay plate that has been warmed slightly on a hot plate or in an oven.

After crystallization has occurred, it is sometimes desirable to cool the flask in an ice-water bath. Because the solute is less soluble at lower temperatures, this will increase the yield of crystals.

If a cooled solution does not crystallize, it will be necessary to induce crystallization. Several techniques are described in Section 11.8A.

D. Collecting and Drying

After the flask has been cooled, the crystals are collected by vacuum filtration through a Büchner (or Hirsch) funnel (see Technique 8, Section 8.3 and Figure 8.5). The crystals should be washed with a small amount of *cold* solvent to remove any mother liquor adhering to their surface. Hot or warm solvent will dissolve some of the crystals. The crystals should then be left for a short time (usually 5–10 minutes) in the funnel, where air, as it passes, will dry them free of most of the solvent. It is often wise to cover the Büchner funnel with an oversized filter paper or towel during this air drying. This precaution prevents accumulation of dust in the crystals. When the crystals are nearly dry, they should be gently scraped off the filter paper (so paper fibers are not removed with the crystals) onto a watch glass or clay plate for further drying (see Section 11.9).

The four steps in a macroscale crystallization are summarized in Table 11.1.

TABLE 11.1   Steps in a Macroscale Crystallization

A. Dissolving the Solid
1. Find a solvent with a steep solubility-vs.-temperature characteristic (done by trial and error using small amounts of material or by consulting a handbook).
2. Heat the desired solvent to its boiling point.
3. Dissolve the solid in a **minimum** of boiling solvent in a flask.
4. If necessary, add decolorizing charcoal or decolorize the solution on a silicagel or alumina column.

B. Removing Insoluble Impurities
1. Decant or remove the solution with a Pasteur pipet.
2. Alternatively, filter the hot solution through a fluted filter, a filtering pipet, or a filter-tip pipet to remove insoluble impurities or charcoal.

NOTE: If no decolorizing charcoal has been added or if there are no undissolved particles, Part B should be omitted.

C. Crystallizing
1. Allow the solution to cool.
2. If crystals appear, cool the mixture in an ice-water bath (if desired) and go to Part D. If crystals do not appear, go to the next step.
3. Inducing crystallization.
    a. Scratch the flask with a glass rod.
    b. Seed the solution with original solid, if available.
    c. Cool the solution in an ice-water bath.
    d. Evaporate excess solvent and allow the solution to cool again.

D. Collecting and Drying
1. Collect crystals by vacuum filtration using a Büchner funnel.
2. Rinse crystals with a small portion of **cold** solvent.
3. Continue suction until crystals are nearly dry.
4. Drying (three options).
    a. Air-dry the crystals.
    b. Place the crystals in a drying oven.
    c. Dry the crystals under a vacuum.

PART C. MICROSCALE CRYSTALLIZATION

11.4 Microscale Crystallization   In many microscale experiments, the amount of solid to be crystallized is small enough (generally less than 0.1 g) that a **Craig tube** (see Technique 8, Figure 8.10) is the preferred method for crystallization. The main advantage of the Craig tube is that it minimizes the number of transfers of solid material, thus resulting in a greater yield of crystals. Also, the separation of the crystals from the mother liquor with the Craig tube is very efficient, and little time is required for drying the crystals. The steps involved are, in principle, the same as those performed when a crystallization is accomplished with an Erlenmeyer flask and a Büchner funnel.

The solid is transferred to the Craig tube, and small portions of hot solvent are added to the tube while the mixture is stirred with a spatula and heated. If there are any insoluble impurities present, they can be removed with a filter-tip pipet. The inner plug is then inserted into the Craig tube and the hot solution is cooled slowly to room temperature. When the crystals have formed, the Craig tube is placed into a centrifuge tube, and the crystals are separated from the mother liquor by centrifugation (see Technique 8, Section 8.7). The crystals are then scraped off the end of the inner plug or from inside the Craig tube onto a watch glass or piece of paper. Minimal drying will be necessary (see Section 11.9).

PART D. ADDITIONAL EXPERIMENTAL CONSIDERATIONS: MACROSCALE AND MICROSCALE

11.5 Selecting a Solvent   A solvent that dissolves little of the material to be crystallized when it is cold but a great deal of the material when it is hot is a good solvent for crystallization. Quite often, correct crystallization solvents are indicated in the experimental procedures that you will be following. When a solvent is not specified in a procedure, you can determine a good crystallization solvent by consulting a handbook or making an educated guess based on polarities, both discussed in this section. A third approach, involving experimentation, is discussed in Section 11.6.

With compounds that are well known, the correct crystallization solvent has already been determined through the experiments of earlier researchers. In such cases, the chemical literature can be consulted to determine which solvent should be used. Sources such as *The Merck Index* or the *CRC Handbook of Chemistry and Physics* may provide this information.

For example, consider naphthalene, which is found in *The Merck Index*. It states under the entry for naphthalene: "Monoclinic prismatic plates from ether." This statement means that naphthalene can be crystallized from ether. It also gives the type of crystal structure. Unfortunately, the crystal structure may be given without reference to the solvent. Another way to determine the best solvent is by looking at solubility-vs.-temperature data. When this is given, a good solvent is one in which the solubility of the compound increases significantly as the temperature increases. Sometimes, the solubility data will be given for only cold solvent and boiling solvent. This should provide enough information to determine whether this would be a good solvent for crystallization.

In most cases, however, the handbooks will state only whether a compound is soluble or not in a given solvent, usually at room temperature. Determining a good solvent for crystallization from this information can be somewhat difficult. The solvent in which the compound is soluble may or may not be an appropriate solvent for crystallization. Sometimes, the compound may be too soluble in the solvent at all temperatures, and you would recover very little of your product if this solvent were used for crystallization. It is possible that an appropriate solvent would be the one in which the compound is nearly insoluble at room temperature because the solubility-vs.-temperature curve is very steep. Although the solubility information may give you some ideas about what solvents to try, you will most likely need to determine a good crystallizing solvent by experimentation as described in Section 11.6.

When using *The Merck Index* or *Handbook of Chemistry and Physics,* you should be aware that alcohol is frequently listed as a solvent. This generally refers to 95% or 100% ethyl alcohol. Because 100% (absolute) ethyl alcohol is more expensive than 95% ethyl alcohol, the cheaper grade is usually used in the chemistry laboratory. Another solvent frequently listed is benzene. Benzene is a known carcinogen, so it is rarely used in student laboratories. Toluene is a suitable substitute; the solubility behavior of a substance in benzene and toluene is so similar that you may assume any statement made about benzene also applies to toluene.

Another way to identify a solvent for crystallization is to consider the polarities of the compound and the solvents. Generally, you would look for a solvent that has a polarity somewhat similar to that of the compound to be crystallized. Consider the compound sulfanilamide, shown in the figure. There are several polar bonds in sulfanilamide, the NH and the SO bonds. In addition, the NH_2 groups and the oxygen

Sulfanilamide

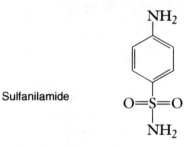

atoms in sulfanilamide can form hydrogen bonds. Although the benzene ring portion of sulfanilamide is nonpolar, sulfanilamide has an intermediate polarity because of the polar groups. A common organic solvent of intermediate polarity is 95% ethyl alcohol. Therefore, it is likely that sulfanilamide would be soluble in 95% ethyl alcohol because they have similar polarities. (Note that the other 5% in 95% ethyl alcohol is usually a substance such as water or isopropyl alcohol, which does not alter the overall polarity of the solvent.) Although this kind of analysis is a good first step in determining an appropriate solvent for crystallization, without more information it is not enough to predict the shape of the solubility curve for the temperature-vs.-solubility data (see Figure 11.1). Therefore, knowing that sulfanilamide is soluble in 95% ethyl alcohol does not necessarily mean that this is a good solvent for crystallizing sulfanilamide. You would still need to test the solvent to see if it is appropriate. The solubility curve for sulfanilamide (see Figure 11.2) indicates that 95% ethyl alcohol is a good solvent for crystallizing this substance.

When choosing a crystallization solvent, do not select one whose boiling point is higher than the melting point of the substance (solute) to be crystallized. If the boiling point of the solvent is too high, the substance may come out of solution as a liquid rather than a crystalline solid. In such a case, the solid may **oil out**. oiling out occurs when upon cooling the solution to induce crystallization, the solute begins to come out of solution at a temperature above its melting point. The solute will then come out of solution as a liquid. Furthermore, as cooling continues, the substance may still not

TABLE 11.2   Common Solvents for Crystallization

	Boils (°C)	Freezes (°C)	Soluble in H_2O	Flammability
Water	100	0	+	−
Methanol	65	*	+	+
95% Ethanol	78	*	+	+
Ligroin	60–90	*	−	+
Toluene	111	*	−	+
Chloroform[**]	61	*	−	−
Acetic acid	118	17	+	+
Dioxane[**]	101	11	+	+
Acetone	56	*	+	+
Diethyl ether	35	*	Slightly	++
Petroleum ether	30–60	*	−	++
Methylene chloride	41	*	−	−
Carbon tetrachloride[**]	77	*	−	−

[*]Lower than 0°C (ice temperature).
[**]Suspected carcinogen.

crystallize; rather, it will become a supercooled liquid. Oils may eventually solidify if the temperature is lowered, but often they will not actually crystallize. Instead, the solidified oil will be an amorphous solid or a hardened mass. In this case, purification of the substance will not have occurred as it does when the solid is crystalline. It can be very difficult to deal with oils when trying to obtain a pure substance. You must try to redissolve them and hope that the substance will crystallize with slow, careful cooling. During the cooling period, it may be helpful to scratch the glass container where the oil is present with a glass stirring rod that has not been fire polished. Seeding the oil as it cools with a small sample of the original solid is another technique that is sometimes helpful in working with difficult oils. Other methods of inducing crystallization are discussed in Section 11.8.

One additional criterion for selecting the correct crystallization solvent is the **volatility** of that solvent. Volatile solvents have low boiling points or evaporate easily. A solvent with a low boiling point may be removed from the crystals through evaporation without much difficulty. It will be difficult to remove a solvent with a high boiling point from the crystals without heating them under vacuum. On the other hand, solvents with very low boiling points are not ideal for crystallizations. The recovery will not be as great with low-boiling solvents because they cannot be heated past the boiling point. Diethyl ether (bp = 35°C) and methylene chloride (bp = 41°C) are not often used as crystallization solvents.

Table 11.2 lists common crystallization solvents. The solvents used most commonly are listed in the table first.

11.6 Testing Solvents for Crystallization

When the appropriate solvent is not known, select a solvent for crystallization by experimenting with various solvents and a very small amount of the material to be crystallized. Experiments are conducted on a small test tube scale before the entire quantity of material is committed to a particular solvent. Such trial-and-error methods are common when trying to purify a solid material that has not been previously studied.

Procedure

1. Place about 0.05 g of the sample in a test tube.

2. Add about 0.5 mL of solvent at room temperature and stir the mixture by rapidly twirling a microspatula between your fingers. If all (or almost all) of the solid dissolves at room temperature, then your solid is *probably* too soluble in this solvent and little compound would be recovered if this solvent were used. Select another solvent.

3. If none (or very little) of the solid dissolves at room temperature, heat the tube carefully and stir with a spatula. (A hotwater bath is perhaps better than an aluminum block because you can more easily control the temperature of the hot-water bath. The temperature of the hot-water bath should be slightly higher than the boiling point of the solvent.) Add more solvent dropwise, while continuing to heat and stir. Continue adding solvent until the solid dissolves, but do not add more than about 1.5 mL (total) of solvent. If all of the solid dissolves, go to step 4. If all of the solid has not dissolved by the time you have added 1.5 mL of solvent, this is probably not a good solvent. However, if most of the solid has dissolved at this point, you might try adding a little more solvent. Remember to heat and stir at all times during this step.

4. If the solid dissolves in about 1.5 mL or less of boiling solvent, then remove the test tube from the heat source, stopper the tube, and allow it to cool to room temperature. Then place it in an ice-water bath. If a lot of crystals come out, this is most likely a good solvent. If crystals do not come out, scratch the sides of the tube with a glass stirring rod to induce crystallization. If crystals still do not form, this is probably not a good solvent.

Comments about This Procedure

1. Selecting a good solvent is something of an art. There is no perfect procedure that can be used in all cases. You must think about what you are doing and use some common sense in deciding whether to use a particular solvent.

2. Do not heat the mixture above the melting point of your solid. This can occur most easily when the boiling point of the solvent is higher than the melting point of the solid. Normally, do not select a solvent that has a higher boiling point than the melting point of the substance. If you do, make certain that you do not heat the mixture beyond the melting point of your solid.

11.7 Decolorization

Small amounts of highly colored impurities may make the original crystallization solution appear colored; this color can often be removed by **decolorization**, either by using activated charcoal (often called Norit) or by passing the solution through a column packed with alumina or silica gel. A decolorizing step should be performed only if the color is due to impurities, not due to the color of the desired product, and if the color is significant. Small amounts of colored impurities will remain in solution during crystallization, making the decolorizing step unnecessary. The use of activated charcoal is described separately for macroscale and microscale crystallizations, and the column technique, which can be used with both crystallization techniques, is then described.

A. Macroscale—Powdered Charcoal

As soon as the solute is dissolved in the minimum amount of boiling solvent, the solution is allowed to cool slightly, and a small amount of Norit (powdered charcoal) is added to the mixture. The Norit adsorbs the impurities. When performing a crystallization in which the filtration is performed with a fluted filter, you should add powdered Norit because it has a larger surface area and can remove impurities more effectively. A reasonable amount of Norit is what could be held on the end of a microspatula, or about 0.01–0.02 g. If too much Norit is used, it will adsorb product as well as impurities. A small amount of Norit should be used, and its use should be repeated if necessary. (It is difficult to determine if the initial amount added is sufficient until after the solution is filtered, because the suspended particles of charcoal will obscure the color of the liquid.) Caution should be exercised so that the solution does not froth or erupt when the finely divided charcoal is added. The mixture is boiled with the Norit for several minutes and then filtered by gravity, using a fluted filter (see Section 11.3 and Technique 8, Section 8.1B), and the crystallization is carried forward as described in Section 11.3.

The Norit preferentially adsorbs the colored impurities and removes them from the solution. The technique seems to be most effective with hydroxylic solvents. In using Norit, be careful not to breathe the dust. Normally, small quantities are used so that little risk of lung irritation exists.

B. Microscale—Pelletized Norit

If the crystallization is being performed in a Craig tube, it is advisable to use pelletized Norit. Although this is not as effective in removing impurities as powdered Norit, it is easier to remove, and the amount of pelletized Norit required is more easily determined because you can see the solution as it is being decolorized. Again, the Norit is added to the hot solution (the solution should not be boiling) after the solid has dissolved. This should be performed in a test tube rather than in a Craig tube. About 0.02 g is added, and the mixture is boiled for a minute or so to see if more Norit is required. More Norit is added, if necessary, and the liquid is boiled again. It is important not to add too much pelletized Norit because the Norit will also adsorb some of the desired material, and it is possible that not all of the color can be removed no matter how much Norit is added. The decolorized solution is then removed with a preheated filter-tip pipet (see Technique 8, Section 8.6) to filter the mixture and transferred to a Craig tube for crystallization as described in Section 11.4.

C. Decolorization on a Column

The other method for decolorizing a solution is to pass the solution through a column containing alumina or silica gel. The adsorbent removes the colored impurities while allowing the desired material to pass through (see Technique 8, Figure 8.6, and Technique 19, Section 19.15). If this technique is used, it will be necessary to dilute the solution with additional solvent to prevent crystallization from occurring during the process. The excess solvent must be evaporated after the solution is passed through the column (see Technique 7, Section 7.10), and the crystallization procedure is continued as described in Sections 11.3 or 11.4.

11.8 Inducing Crystallization

If a cooled solution does not crystallize, several techniques may be used to induce crystallization. Although identical in principle, the actual procedures vary slightly when performing macroscale and microscale crystallizations.

A. Macroscale

In the first technique, you should try scratching the inside surface of the flask vigorously with a glass rod that *has not been* fire polished. The motion of the rod should be vertical (in and out of the solution) and should be vigorous enough to produce an audible scratching. Such scratching often induces crystallization, although the effect is not well understood. The high-frequency vibrations may have something to do with initiating crystallization; or perhaps—a more likely possibility—small amounts of solution dry by evaporation on the side of the flask, and the dried solute is pushed into the solution. These small amounts of material provide "seed crystals," or nuclei, on which crystallization may begin.

A second technique that can be used to induce crystallization is to cool the solution in an ice bath. This method decreases the solubility of the solute.

A third technique is useful when small amounts of the original material to be crystallized are saved. The saved material can be used to "seed" the cooled solution. A small crystal dropped into the cooled flask often will start the crystallization—this is called **seeding**.

If all of these measures fail to induce crystallization, it is likely that too much solvent was added. The excess solvent must then be evaporated (see Technique 7, Section 7.10) and the solution allowed to cool.

B. Microscale

The strategy is basically the same as described for macroscale crystallizations. Scratching vigorously with a glass rod *should be avoided*, however, because the Craig tube is fragile and expensive. Scratching *gently* is allowed.

Another measure is to dip a spatula or glass stirring rod into the solution and allow the solvent to evaporate so that a small amount of solid will form on the surface of the spatula or glass rod. When placed back into the solution, the solid will seed the solution. A small amount of the original material, if some was saved, may also be used to seed the solution.

A third technique is to cool the Craig tube in an ice-water bath. This method may also be combined with either of the previous suggestions.

If none of these measures is successful, it is possible that too much solvent is present, and it may be necessary to evaporate some of the solvent (see Technique 7, Section 7.10) and allow the solution to cool again.

11.9 Drying Crystals

The most common method of drying crystals involves allowing them to dry in air. Several different methods are illustrated in Figure 11.6 below. In all three methods, the crystals must be covered to prevent accumulation of dust particles. Note that in each method, the spout on the beaker provides an opening so that solvent vapor can escape from the system. The advantage of this method is that heat is not required, thus reducing the danger of decomposition or melting; however, exposure to atmospheric moisture may cause the hydration of strongly hygroscopic materials. A **hygroscopic** substance is a substance that absorbs moisture from the air.

Another method of drying crystals is to place the crystals on a watch glass, a clay plate, or a piece of absorbent paper in an oven. Although this method is simple, some possible difficulties deserve mention. Crystals that sublime readily should not be dried in an oven because they might vaporize and disappear. Care should be taken that the temperature of the oven does not exceed the melting point of the crystals. Remember that the melting point of crystals is lowered by the presence of solvent; allow for this melting-point depression when selecting a suitable oven temperature. Some materials decompose on exposure to heat, and they should not be dried in an oven. Finally, when many different samples are being dried in the same oven, crystals might be lost due to confusion or reaction with another person's sample. It is important to label the crystals when they are placed in the oven.

A third method, which requires neither heat nor exposure to atmospheric moisture, is drying *in vacuo*. Two procedures are illustrated in Figure 11.7.

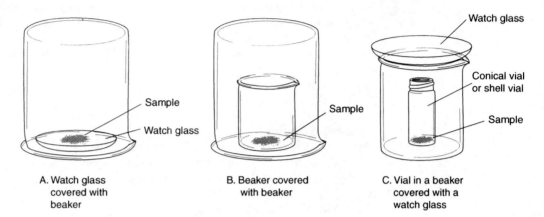

A. Watch glass
covered with
beaker

B. Beaker covered
with beaker

C. Vial in a beaker
covered with a
watch glass

Figure 11.6   Methods for drying crystals in air.

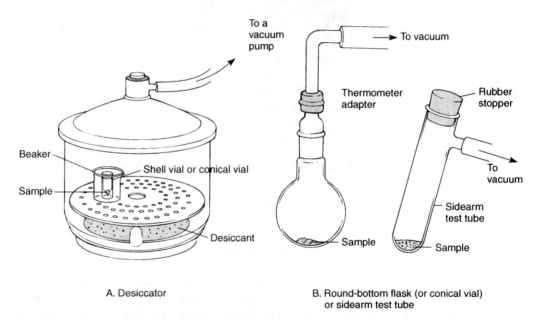

A. Desiccator

B. Round-bottom flask (or conical vial)
or sidearm test tube

Figure 11.7   Methods for drying crystals in vacuum.

Procedure A

In this method, a desiccator is used. The sample is placed under vacuum in the presence of a drying agent. Two potential problems must be noted. The first deals with samples that sublime readily. Under vacuum, the likelihood of sublimation is increased. The second problem deals with the vacuum desiccator itself. Because the surface area of glass that is under vacuum is large, there is some danger that the desiccator could implode. A vacuum desiccator should never be used unless it has been placed within a protective metal container (cage). If a cage is not available, the desiccator can be wrapped with electrical or duct tape. If you use an aspirator as a source of vacuum, you should use a water trap (see Technique 8, Figure 8.5).

Procedure B

This method can be accomplished with a round-bottom flask and a thermometer adapter equipped with a short piece of glass tubing, as illustrated in Figure 11.7B. In microscale work, the apparatus with the round-bottom flask can be modified by replacing the round-bottom flask with a conical vial. The glass tubing is connected by vacuum tubing to either an aspirator or a vacuum pump. A convenient alternative, using a sidearm test tube, is also shown in Figure 11.7B. With either apparatus, install a water trap when an aspirator is used.

11.10 Mixed Solvents

Often, the desired solubility characteristics for a particular compound are not found in a single solvent. In these cases, a mixed solvent may be used. You simply select a first solvent in which the solute is soluble and a second solvent, miscible with the first, in which the solute is relatively insoluble. The compound is dissolved in a minimum amount of the boiling solvent in which it is soluble. Following this, the second hot solvent is added to the boiling mixture, dropwise, until the mixture barely becomes cloudy. The cloudiness indicates precipitation. At this point, more of the first solvent should be added. Just enough is added to clear the cloudy mixture. At that point, the solution is saturated, and as it cools, crystals should separate. Common solvent mixtures are listed in Table 11.3.

It is important not to add an excess of the second solvent or to cool the solution too rapidly. Either of these actions may cause the solute to oil out, or separate as a viscous liquid. If this happens, reheat the solution and add more of the first solvent.

TABLE 11.3   Common Solvent Pairs for Crystallization

Methanol–water	Ether–acetone
Ethanol–water	Ether–petroleum ether
Acetic acid–water	Toluene–ligroin
Acetone–water	Methylene chloride–methanol
Ether–methanol	Dioxane[a]–water

[a] Suspected carcinogen.

PROBLEMS

1. Listed below are solubility-vs.-temperature data for an organic substance A dissolved in water.

Temperature (°C)	Solubility of A in 100 mL of Water (g)
0	1.5
20	3.0
40	6.5
60	11.0
80	17.0

a. Graph the solubility of A vs. temperature. Use the data given in the table. Connect the data points with a smooth curve.

b. Suppose 0.1 g of A and 1.0 mL of water were mixed and heated to 80°C. Would all of substance A dissolve?

c. The solution prepared in (b) is cooled. At what temperature will crystals of A appear?

d. Suppose the cooling described in (c) were continued to 0°C. How many grams of A would come out of solution? Explain how you obtained your answer.

2. What would likely happen if a hot saturated solution were filtered by vacuum filtration using a Büchner funnel? (*Hint:* The mixture will cool as it comes in contact with the Büchner funnel.)

3. A compound you have prepared is reported in the literature to have a pale yellow color. When the substance is dissolved in hot solvent to purify it by crystallization, the resulting solution is yellow. Should you use decolorizing charcoal before allowing the hot solution to cool? Explain your answer.

4. While performing a crystallization, you obtain a light tan solution after dissolving your crude product in hot solvent. A decolorizing step is determined to be unnecessary, and there are no solid impurities present. Should you perform a filtration to remove impurities before allowing the solution to cool? Why or why not?

5. **a.** Draw a graph of a cooling curve (temperature vs. time) for a solution of a solid substance that shows no supercooling effects. Assume that the solvent does not freeze.

b. Repeat the instructions in (a) for a solution for a solid substance that shows some supercooling behavior, but eventually yields crystals if the solution is cooled sufficiently.

6. A solid substance A is soluble in water to the extent of 10 mg/mL of water at 25°C and 100 mg/mL of water at 100°C. You have a sample that contains 100 mg of A and an impurity B.

a. Assuming that 2 mg of B are present along with 100 mg of A, describe how you can purify A if B is completely insoluble in water. Your description should include the volume of solvent required.

b. Assuming that 2 mg of the impurity B are present along with 100 mg of A, describe how you can purify A if B has the same solubility behavior as A. Will one crystallization produce pure A? (Assume that the solubilities of both A and B are unaffected by the presence of the other substance.)

c. Assume that 25 mg of the impurity B are present along with 100 mg of A. Describe how you can purify A if B has the same solubility behavior as A. Each time, use the minimum amount of water to just dissolve the solid. Will one crystallization produce absolutely pure A? How many crystallizations would be needed to produce pure A? How much A will have been recovered when the crystallizations have been completed?

7. Consider the crystallization of sulfanilamide from 95% ethyl alcohol. If impure sulfanilamide is dissolved in the minimum amount of 95% ethyl alcohol at 40°C rather than 78°C (the boiling point of ethyl alcohol), how would this affect the percent recovery of pure sulfanilamide? Explain your answer.

12   T E C H N I Q U E   1 2

Extractions, Separations, and Drying Agents

PART A. THEORY

12.1 Extraction

Sign in at www .cengage.com/login to access the Pre-Lab Video Exercise for this technique.

Transferring a solute from one solvent into another is called **extraction**, or, more precisely, liquid–liquid extraction. The solute is extracted from one solvent into the other because the solute is more soluble in the second solvent than in the first. The two solvents must not be **miscible** (mix freely), and they must form two separate **phases** or layers, in order for this procedure to work. Extraction is used in many ways in organic chemistry. Many **natural products** (organic chemicals that exist in nature) are present in animal and plant tissues having high water content. Extracting these tissues with a water-immiscible solvent is useful for isolating the natural products. Often, diethyl ether (commonly referred to as "ether") is used for this purpose. Sometimes, alternative water-immiscible solvents such as hexane, petroleum ether, ligroin, and methylene chloride are used. For instance, caffeine, a natural product, can be extracted from an aqueous tea solution by shaking the solution successively with several portions of methylene chloride.

A generalized extraction process, using a specialized piece of glassware called a **separatory funnel**, is illustrated in Figure 12.1. The first solvent contains a

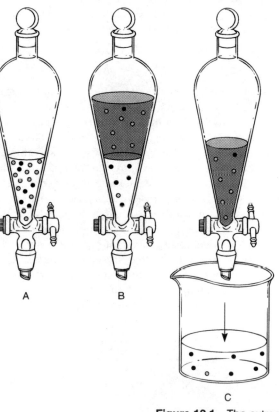

A. Solvent 1 contains a mixture of molecules (black and white).

B. After shaking with solvent 2 (shaded), most of the white molecules have been extracted into the new solvent. The white molecules are more soluble in the second solvent, whereas the black molecules are more soluble in the original solvent.

C. With removal of the lower phase, the black and white molecules have been partially separated.

Figure 12.1   The extraction process.

mixture of black-and-white molecules (see Figure 12.1A). A second solvent that is not miscible with the first is added. After the separatory funnel is capped and shaken, the layers separate. In this example, the second solvent (shaded) is less dense than the first, so it becomes the top layer (see Figure 12.1B). Because of differences in physical properties, the white molecules are more soluble in the second solvent, whereas the black molecules are more soluble in the first solvent. Most of the white molecules are in the upper layer, but there are some black molecules there, too. Likewise, most of the black molecules are in the lower layer. However, there are still a few white molecules in this lower phase. The lower phase may be separated from the upper phase by opening the stopcock at the bottom of the separatory funnel and allowing the lower layer to drain into a beaker (see Figure 12.1C). In this example, notice that it was not possible to effect a complete separation of the two types of molecules with a single extraction. This is a common occurrence in organic chemistry.

Many substances are soluble in both water and organic solvents. Water can be used to extract, or "wash," water-soluble impurities from an organic reaction mixture. To carry out a "washing" operation, you add water and an immiscible organic solvent to the reaction mixture contained in a separatory funnel. After stoppering the funnel and shaking it, you allow the organic layer and the aqueous (water) layer to separate. A water wash removes highly polar and water-soluble materials, such as sulfuric acid, hydrochloric acid, and sodium hydroxide, from the organic layer. The washing operation helps to purify the desired organic compound present in the original reaction mixture.

12.2 Distribution Coefficient

When a solution (solute A in solvent 1) is shaken with a second solvent (solvent 2) with which it is not miscible, the solute distributes itself between the two liquid phases. When the two phases have separated again into two distinct solvent layers, an equilibrium will have been achieved such that the ratio of the concentrations of the solute in each layer defines a constant. The constant, called the **distribution coefficient** (or partition coefficient) K, is defined by

$$K = \frac{C_2}{C_1}$$

where C_1 and C_2 are the concentrations at equilibrium, in grams per liter or milligrams per milliliter of solute A in solvent 1 and in solvent 2, respectively. This relationship is a ratio of two concentrations and is independent of the actual amounts of the two solvents mixed. The distribution coefficient has a constant value for each solute considered and depends on the nature of the solvents used in each case.

Not all of the solute will be transferred to solvent 2 in a single extraction unless K is very large. Usually, it takes several extractions to remove all of the solute from solvent 1. In extracting a solute from a solution, it is always better to use several small portions of the second solvent than to make a single extraction with a large portion. Suppose, as an illustration, a particular extraction proceeds with a distribution coefficient of 10. The system consists of 5.0 g of organic compound dissolved in 100 mL of water (solvent 1). In this illustration, the effectiveness of three 50-mL extractions with ether (solvent 2) is compared with one 150-mL extraction with ether. In the first 50-mL extraction, the amount extracted into the ether layer is given by the following calculation. The amount of compound remaining in the aqueous phase is given by x.

$$K = 10 = \frac{C_2}{C_1} = \frac{\left(\dfrac{5.0 - x}{50}\dfrac{\text{g}}{\text{mL ether}}\right)}{\left(\dfrac{x}{100}\dfrac{\text{g}}{\text{mL H}_2\text{O}}\right)}; \qquad 10 = \frac{(5.0 - x)(100)}{50x}$$

$$500x = 500 - 100x$$
$$600x = 500$$
$$x = 0.83 \text{ g remaining in the aqueous phase}$$
$$5.0 - x = 4.17 \text{ g in the ether layer}$$

As a check on the calculation, it is possible to substitute the value 0.83 g for x in the original equation and demonstrate that the concentration in the ether layer divided by the concentration in the water layer equals the distribution coefficient.

$$\frac{\left(\dfrac{5.0 - x}{50} \dfrac{g}{mL \ ether}\right)}{\left(\dfrac{x}{100} \dfrac{g}{mL \ H_2O}\right)} = \frac{\dfrac{4.17}{50}}{\dfrac{0.83}{100}} = \frac{0.083 \ g/mL}{0.0083 \ g/mL} = 10 = K$$

The second extraction with another 50-mL portion of fresh ether is performed on the aqueous phase, which now contains 0.83 g of the solute. The amount of solute extracted is given by the calculation shown in Figure 12.2. Also shown in the figure is a calculation for a third extraction with another 50-mL portion of ether. This third extraction will transfer 0.12 g of solute into the ether layer, leaving 0.02 g of solute remaining in the water layer. A total of 4.98 g of solute will be extracted into the combined ether layers, and 0.02 g will remain in the aqueous phase.

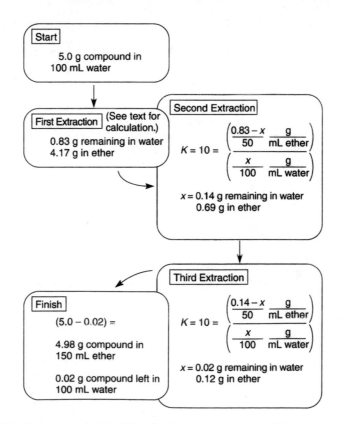

Figure 12.2 The result of extraction of 5.0 g of compound in 100 mL of water by three successive 50-mL portions of ether. Compare this result with that of Figure 12.3.

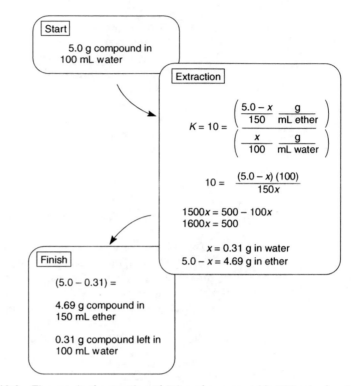

Figure 12.3 The result of extraction of 5.0 g of compound in 100 mL of water with one 150-mL portion of ether. Compare this result with that of Figure 12.2.

Figure 12.3 shows the result of a *single* extraction with 150 mL of ether. As shown there, 4.69 g of solute were extracted into the ether layer, leaving 0.31 g of compound in the aqueous phase. Three successive 50-mL ether extractions (see Figure 12.2) succeeded in removing 0.29 g more solute from the aqueous phase than using one 150-mL portion of ether (see Figure 12.3). This differential represents 5.8% of the total material.

NOTE: Several extractions with smaller amounts of solvent are more effective than one extraction with a larger amount of solvent.

12.3 Choosing an Extraction Method and a Solvent

Three types of apparatus are used for extractions: conical vials, centrifuge tubes, and separatory funnels (see Figure 12.4). Conical vials may be used with volumes of less than 4 mL; volumes of up to 10 mL may be handled in centrifuge tubes. A centrifuge tube equipped with a screw cap is particularly useful for extractions. Conical vials and centrifuge tubes are most often used in microscale experiments, although a centrifuge tube may also be used in some macroscale applications. The separatory funnel is used with larger volumes of liquid in macroscale experiments. The separatory funnel is discussed in Part B and the conical vial and centrifuge tube are discussed in Part C.

TABLE 12.1   Densities of Common Extraction Solvents

Solvent	Density (g/mL)
Ligroin	0.67–0.69
Diethyl ether	0.71
Toluene	0.87
Water	1.00
Methylene chloride	1.330

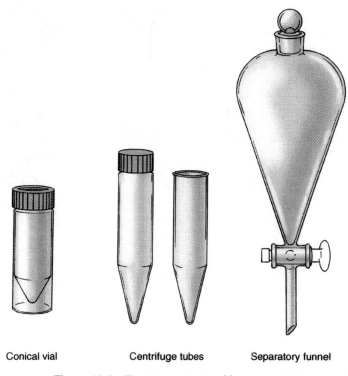

Conical vial   Centrifuge tubes   Separatory funnel

Figure 12.4   The apparatus used in extraction.

Most extractions consist of an aqueous phase and an organic phase. To extract a substance from an aqueous phase, you must use an organic solvent that is not miscible with water. Table 12.1 lists a number of the common organic solvents that are not miscible with water and are used for extractions.

Solvents that have a density less than that of water (1.00 g/mL) will separate as the top layer when shaken with water. Solvents that have a density greater than that of water will separate into the lower layer. For instance, diethyl ether ($d = 0.71$ g/mL) when shaken with water will form the upper layer, whereas methylene chloride ($d = 1.33$ g/mL) will form the lower layer. When an extraction is performed, slightly different methods are used to separate the lower layer (whether or not it is the aqueous layer or the organic layer) than to separate the upper layer.

PART B. MACROSCALE EXTRACTION

12.4 The Separatory Funnel

A separatory funnel is illustrated in Figure 12.5. It is the piece of equipment used for carrying out extractions with medium to large quantities of material. To fill the separatory funnel, support it in an iron ring attached to a ring stand. Since it is easy to break a separatory funnel by "clanking" it against the metal ring, pieces of rubber tubing are often attached to the ring to cushion the funnel, as shown in Figure 12.5. These are short pieces of tubing cut to a length of about 3 cm and slit open along their length. When slipped over the inside of the ring, they cushion the funnel in its resting place.

When beginning an extraction, first close the stopcock. (Don't forget!) Using a powder funnel (wide bore) placed in the top of the separatory funnel, fill the funnel with both the solution to be extracted and the extraction solvent. Swirl the funnel gently

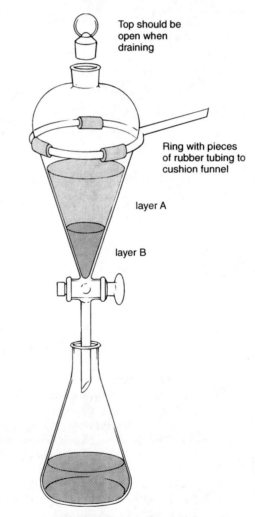

Figure 12.5   A separatory funnel.

by holding it by its upper neck and then stopper it. Pick up the separatory funnel with two hands and hold it as shown in Figure 12.6. Hold the stopper in place firmly because the two immiscible liquids will build pressure when they mix, and this pressure may force the stopper out of the separatory funnel. To release this pressure, vent the funnel by holding it upside down (hold the stopper securely) and slowly open the stopcock. Usually, the rush of vapors out of the opening can be heard. Continue shaking and venting until the "whoosh" is no longer audible. Now continue shaking the mixture gently for about 1 minute. This can be done by inverting the funnel in a rocking motion repeatedly or, if the formation of an emulsion is not a problem (see Section 12.10), by shaking the funnel more vigorously for less time.

NOTE: There is an art to shaking and venting a separatory funnel correctly, and this technique usually seems awkward to the beginner. The technique is best learned by observing a person, such as your instructor, who is thoroughly familiar with the separatory funnel's use.

When you have finished mixing the liquids, place the separatory funnel in the iron ring and remove the top stopper immediately. The two immiscible solvents separate into two layers after a short time, and they can be separated from one another by draining most of the lower layer through the stopcock.[1] Allow a few minutes to pass so that any of the lower phase adhering to the inner glass surfaces of the separatory funnel can drain down. Open the stopcock again and allow the remainder of the lower layer to drain until the interface between the upper and lower phases just begins to enter the bore of the stopcock. At this moment, close the stopcock and remove the remaining upper layer by pouring it from the top opening of the separatory funnel.

Figure 12.6   The correct way of shaking and venting a separatory funnel.

---

[1]A common error is to try to drain the separatory funnel without removing the top stopper. Under this circumstance, the funnel will not drain because a partial vacuum is in the space above the liquid.

NOTE: To minimize contamination of the two layers, the lower layer should always be drained from the bottom of the separatory funnel and the upper layer poured out from the top of the funnel.

When methylene chloride is used as the extracting solvent with an aqueous phase, it will settle to the bottom and be removed through the stopcock. The aqueous layer remains in the funnel. A second extraction of the remaining aqueous layer with fresh methylene chloride may be needed.

With a diethyl ether (ether) extraction of an aqueous phase, the organic layer will form on top. Remove the lower aqueous layer through the stopcock and pour the upper ether layer from the top of the separatory funnel. Pour the aqueous phase back into the separatory funnel and extract it a second time with fresh ether. The combined organic phases must be dried using a suitable drying agent (see Section 12.9) before the solvent is removed.

The usual macroscale procedure requires the use of a 125-mL or 250-mL separatory funnel. For microscale procedures, a 60-mL or 125-mL separatory funnel is recommended. Because of surface tension, water has a difficult time draining from the bore of smaller funnels.

PART C. MICROSCALE EXTRACTION

12.5 The Conical Vial—Separating the Lower Layer

Before using a conical vial for an extraction, make sure that the capped conical vial does not leak when shaken. To do this, place some water in the conical vial, place the Teflon liner in the cap, and screw the cap securely onto the conical vial. Shake the vial vigorously and check for leaks. Conical vials that are used for extractions must not be chipped on the edge of the vial or they will not seal adequately. If there is a leak, try tightening the cap or replacing the Teflon liner with another one. Sometimes it helps to use the silicone rubber side of the liner to seal the conical vial. Some laboratories are supplied with Teflon stoppers that fit into the 5-mL conical vials. You may find that this stopper eliminates leakage.

When shaking the conical vial, do it gently at first in a rocking motion. When it is clear that an emulsion will not form (see Section 12.10), you can shake it more vigorously.

In some cases, adequate mixing can be achieved by spinning your microspatula for at least 10 minutes in the conical vial. Another technique of mixing involves drawing the mixture up into a Pasteur pipet and squirting it rapidly back into the vial. Repeat this process for at least 5 minutes to obtain an adequate extraction.

The 5-mL conical vial is the most useful piece of equipment for carrying out extractions on a microscale level. In this section, we consider the method for removing the lower layer. A concrete example would be the extraction of a desired product from an aqueous layer using methylene chloride (d = 1.33 g/mL) as the extraction solvent. Methods for removal of the upper layer are discussed in the next section.

NOTE: Always place a conical vial in a small beaker to prevent the vial from falling over.

Removing the Lower Layer. Suppose that we extract an aqueous solution with methylene chloride. This solvent is denser than water and will settle to the bottom of the conical vial. Use the following procedure, which is illustrated in Figure 12.7, to remove the lower layer.

1. Place the aqueous phase containing the dissolved product into a 5-mL conical vial (see Figure 12.7A).

2. Add about 1 mL of methylene chloride, cap the vial, and shake the mixture gently at first in a rocking motion and then more vigorously when it is clear that an emulsion will not form. Vent or unscrew the cap slightly to release the pressure in the vial. Allow the phases to separate completely so that you can detect two distinct layers in the vial. The organic phase will be the lower layer in the vial (see Figure 12.7B). If necessary, tap the vial with your finger or stir the mixture gently if some of the organic phase is suspended in the aqueous layer.

3. Prepare a Pasteur filter-tip pipet (see Technique 8, Section 8.6) using a $5\frac{3}{4}$-inch pipet. Attach a 2-mL rubber bulb to the pipet, depress the bulb, and insert the pipet into the vial so that the tip touches the bottom (see Figure 12.7C). The filter-tip pipet gives you better control in removing the lower layer. In some cases, however, you may be able to use a Pasteur pipet (no filter tip), but considerably more care must be taken to avoid losing liquid from the pipet during the transfer operation. With experience, you should be able to judge how much to squeeze the bulb to draw in the desired volume of liquid.

4. Slowly draw the lower layer (methylene chloride) into the pipet in such a way that you exclude the aqueous layer and any emulsion (see Section 12.10) that might be at the interface between the layers (see Figure 12.7D). Be sure to keep the tip of the pipet squarely in the V at the bottom of the vial.

5. Transfer the withdrawn organic phase into a *dry* test tube or another *dry* conical vial if one is available. It is best to have the test tube or vial located next to the extraction vial. Hold the vials in the same hand between your index finger and thumb, as shown in Figure 12.8. This avoids messy and disastrous transfers. The aqueous layer (upper layer) is left in the original conical vial (see Figure 12.7E).

In performing an actual extraction in the laboratory, you would extract the aqueous phase with a second 1-mL portion of fresh methylene chloride to achieve a more complete extraction. Steps 2–5 would be repeated, and the organic layers from both extractions would be combined. In some cases, you may need to extract a third time with yet another 1-mL portion of methylene chloride. Again, the methylene chloride would be combined with the other extracts. The overall process would use three 1-mL portions of methylene chloride to transfer the product from the water layer into methylene chloride. Sometimes you will see the statement "extract the aqueous phase with three 1-mL portions of methylene chloride" in an experimental procedure. This statement describes in a shorter fashion the process described previously. Finally, the methylene chloride extracts will contain some water and must be dried with a drying agent as indicated in Section 12.9.

NOTE: If an organic solvent has been extracted with water, it should be dried with a drying agent (see Section 12.9) before proceeding.

A. The aqueous solution contains the desired product.

B. Methylene chloride is used to extract the aqueous phase.

C. The Pasteur filter-tip pipet is placed in the vial.

D. The lower organic layer is removed from the aqueous phase.

E. The organic layer is transferred to a dry test tube or conical vial. The aqueous layer remains in the original extraction vial.

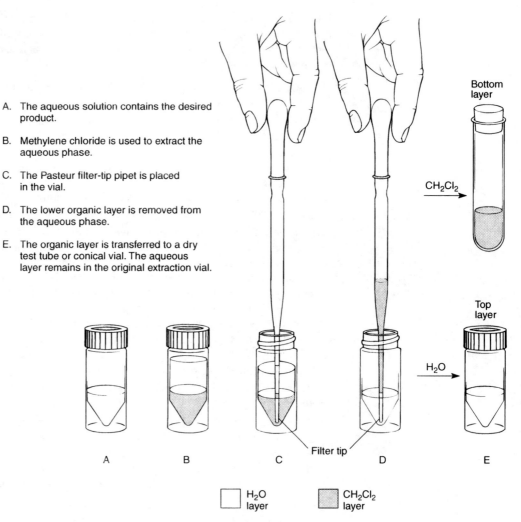

Figure 12.7 Extraction of an aqueous solution using a solvent denser than water: methylene chloride.

In this example, we extracted water with the heavy solvent methylene chloride and removed it as the lower layer. If you were extracting a light solvent (for instance, diethyl ether) with water and you wished to keep the water layer, the water would be the lower layer and would be removed using the same procedure. You would not dry the water layer, however.

12.6 The Conical Vial— Separating the Upper Layer

In this section, we consider the method used when you wish to remove the upper layer. A concrete example would be the extraction of a desired product from an aqueous layer using diethyl ether ($d = 0.71$ g/mL) as the extraction solvent. Methods for removing the lower layer were discussed previously.

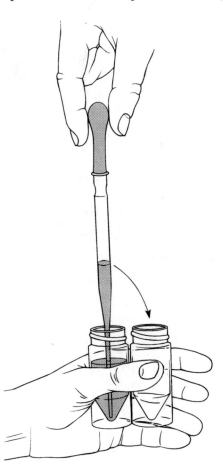

Figure 12.8   Method for holding vials while transferring liquids.

NOTE: Always place a conical vial in a small beaker to prevent the vial from falling over.

Removing the Upper Layer. Suppose we extract an aqueous solution with diethyl ether (ether). This solvent is less dense than water and will rise to the top of the conical vial. Use the following procedure, which is illustrated in Figure 12.9, to remove the upper layer.

1. Place the aqueous phase containing the dissolved product in a 5-mL conical vial (Figure 12.9A).

2. Add about 1 mL of ether, cap the vial, and shake the mixture vigorously. Vent or unscrew the cap slightly to release the pressure in the vial. Allow the phases to separate completely so that you can detect two distinct layers in the vial. The ether phase will be the upper layer in the vial (see Figure 12.9B).

3. Prepare a Pasteur filter-tip pipet (see Technique 8, Section 8.6) using a $5\frac{3}{4}$-inch pipet. Attach a 2-mL rubber bulb to the pipet, depress the bulb, and insert the pipet into the vial so that the tip touches the bottom. The filter-tip pipet gives you better control in removing the lower layer. In some cases, however, you may be able to use a Pasteur pipet (no filter tip), but considerably

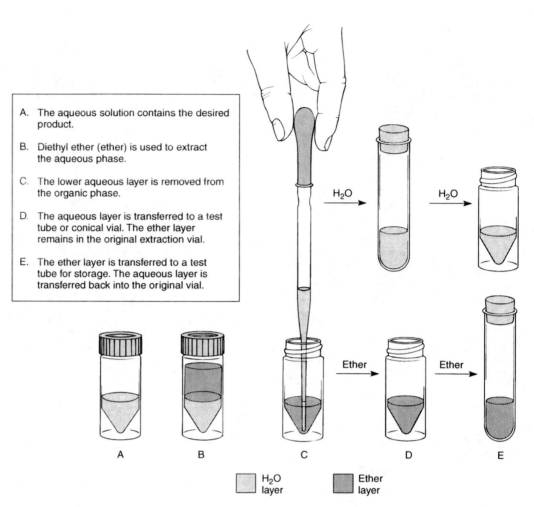

A. The aqueous solution contains the desired product.

B. Diethyl ether (ether) is used to extract the aqueous phase.

C. The lower aqueous layer is removed from the organic phase.

D. The aqueous layer is transferred to a test tube or conical vial. The ether layer remains in the original extraction vial.

E. The ether layer is transferred to a test tube for storage. The aqueous layer is transferred back into the original vial.

H_2O H_2O

Ether   Ether

A   B   C   D   E

H_2O layer   Ether layer

Figure 12.9   Extraction of an aqueous solution using a solvent less dense than water: diethyl ether.

more care must be taken to avoid losing liquid from the pipet during the transfer operation. With experience, you should be able to judge how much to squeeze the bulb to draw in the desired volume of liquid. Slowly draw the lower *aqueous* layer into the pipet. Be sure to keep the tip of the pipet squarely in the V at the bottom of the vial (see Figure 12.9C).

4. Transfer the withdrawn aqueous phase into a test tube or another conical vial for temporary storage. It is best to have the test tube or vial located next to the extraction vial. This avoids messy and disastrous transfers. Hold the vials in the same hand between your index finger and thumb, as shown in Figure 12.8. The ether layer is left behind in the conical vial (see Figure 12.9D).

5. The ether phase remaining in the original conical vial should be transferred with a Pasteur pipet into a test tube for storage and the aqueous phase returned to the original conical vial (see Figure 12.9E).

In performing an actual extraction, you would extract the aqueous phase with another 1-mL portion of fresh ether to achieve a more complete extraction. Steps 2–5 would be repeated, and the organic layers from both extractions would be combined in the test tube. In some cases, you may need to extract the aqueous layer a third time with yet another 1-mL portion of ether. Again, the ether would be combined with the other two layers. This overall process uses three 1-mL portions of ether to transfer the product from the water layer into ether. The ether extracts contain some water and must be dried with a drying agent as indicated in Section 12.9.

12.7 The Screw-Cap Centrifuge Tube

If you require an extraction that uses a larger volume than a conical vial can accommodate (about 4 mL), a centrifuge tube can often be used. A centrifuge tube can also be used instead of a separatory funnel for some macroscale applications in which the total volume of liquid is less than about 12 mL. A commonly available size of centrifuge tube has a volume of about 15 mL and is supplied with a screw cap. In performing an extraction with a screw-cap centrifuge tube, use the same procedures outlined for the conical vial (see Sections 12.5 and 12.6). As is the case for a conical vial, the tapered bottom of the centrifuge tube makes it easy to withdraw the lower layer with a Pasteur pipet.

NOTE: A centrifuge tube has a great advantage over other methods of extraction. If an emulsion (Section 12.10) forms, you can use a centrifuge to aid in the separation of the layers.

You should check the capped centrifuge tube for leaks by filling it with water and shaking it vigorously. If it leaks, try replacing the cap with a different one. A **vortex mixer**, if available, provides an alternative to shaking the tube. In fact, a vortex mixer works well with a variety of containers, including small flasks, test tubes, conical vials, and centrifuge tubes. You start the mixing action on a vortex mixer by holding the test tube or other container on one of the neoprene pads. The unit mixes the sample by high-frequency vibration.

PART D. ADDITIONAL EXPERIMENTAL CONSIDERATIONS: MACROSCALE AND MICROSCALE

12.8 How Do You Determine Which One Is the Organic Layer?

A common problem encountered during an extraction is trying to determine which of the two layers is the organic layer and which is the aqueous (water) layer. The most common situation occurs when the aqueous layer is on the bottom in the presence of an upper organic layer consisting of ether, ligroin, petroleum ether, or hexane (see densities in Table 12.1). However, the aqueous layer will be on the top when you use methylene chloride as a solvent (again, see Table 12.1). Although a laboratory procedure may frequently identify the expected relative positions of the organic and aqueous layers, sometimes their actual positions are reversed. Surprises usually occur in situations in which the aqueous layer contains a high concentration of sulfuric acid or a dissolved ionic compound, such as sodium chloride. Dissolved substances greatly increase the density of the aqueous layer, which may lead to the aqueous layer being found on the bottom even when coexisting with a relatively dense organic layer such as methylene chloride.

NOTE: Always keep both layers until you have actually isolated the desired compound or until you are certain where your desired substance is located.

To determine if a particular layer is the aqueous one, add a few drops of water to the layer. Observe closely as you add the water to see where it goes. If the layer is water, then the drops of added water will dissolve in the aqueous layer and increase its volume. If the added water forms droplets or a new layer, however, you can assume that the suspected aqueous layer is actually organic. You can use a similar procedure to identify a suspected organic layer. This time, try adding more of the solvent, such as methylene chloride. The organic layer should increase in size, without separation of a new layer, if the tested layer is actually organic.

When performing an extraction procedure on the microscale level, you can use the following approach to identify the layers. When both layers are present, it is always a good idea to think carefully about the volumes of materials that you have added to the conical vial. You can use the graduations on the vial to help determine the volumes of the layers in the vial. If, for example, you have 1 mL of methylene chloride in a vial and you add 2 mL of water, you should expect the water to be on top because it is less dense than methylene chloride. As you add the water, *watch to see where it goes.* By noting the relative volumes of the two layers, you should be able to tell which is the aqueous layer and which is the organic layer. This approach can also be used when performing an extraction procedure using a centrifuge tube. Of course, you can always test to see which layer is the aqueous layer by adding one or two drops of water, as described previously.

12.9 Drying Agents

After an organic solvent has been shaken with an aqueous solution, it will be "wet"; that is, it will have dissolved some water even though its solubility with water is not great. The amount of water dissolved varies from solvent to solvent; diethyl ether represents a solvent in which a fairly large amount of water dissolves. To remove water from the organic layer, use a **drying agent**. A drying agent is an *anhydrous* inorganic salt that acquires waters of hydration when exposed to moist air or a wet solution:

Insoluble   **Insoluble**
$$Na_2SO_4(s) \ + \ Wet \ Solution \ (nH_2O) \ \longrightarrow \ Na_2SO_4 \cdot nH_2O \ (s) \ + \ Dry \ Solution$$
Anhydrous   Hydrated
drying agent   drying agent

The insoluble drying agent is placed directly into the solution, where it acquires water molecules and becomes hydrated. If enough drying agent is used, all of the water can be removed from a wet solution, making it "dry," or free of water.

The following anhydrous salts are commonly used: sodium sulfate, magnesium sulfate, calcium chloride, calcium sulfate (Drierite), and potassium carbonate. These salts vary in their properties and applications. For instance, not all will absorb the same amount of water for a given weight, nor will they dry the solution to the same extent. **Capacity** refers to the amount of water a drying agent absorbs per unit weight. Sodium and magnesium sulfates absorb a large amount of water (high capacity), but magnesium sulfate dries a solution more completely. **Completeness** refers to a compound's effectiveness in removing all the water from a solution by the time equilibrium has been reached. Magnesium ion, a strong Lewis acid, sometimes causes rearrangements of compounds such as epoxides. Calcium chloride is a good drying agent, but cannot be used with many compounds containing oxygen or nitrogen because it forms complexes. Calcium chloride absorbs methanol and ethanol in addition to water, so it is useful for removing these materials when they are present as impurities. Potassium carbonate is a base and is used for drying solutions of basic substances, such as amines. Calcium sulfate dries a solution completely, but has a low capacity.

Anhydrous sodium sulfate is the most widely used drying agent. The granular variety is recommended because it is easier to remove the dried solution from it than from the powdered variety. Sodium sulfate is mild and effective. It will remove water from most common solvents, with the possible exception of diethyl ether, in which case a prior drying with saturated salt solution may be advised. Sodium sulfate must be used at room temperature to be effective; it cannot be used with boiling solutions. Table 12.2 compares the various common drying agents.

Drying Procedure with Snhydrous Sodium Sulfate. In experiments that require a drying step, the instructions are usually given in the following way: dry the organic layer (or phase) over granular anhydrous sodium sulfate (or some other drying agent). More specific instructions, such as the amount of drying agent to add, usually will not be given, and you will need to determine this each time that you perform a drying step. The drying procedure consists of four steps:

1. Remove the organic layer from any visible water.
2. Add the appropriate amount of granular anhydrous sodium sulfate (or other drying agent).
3. Allow a drying period during which dissolved water is removed from the organic layer by the drying agent.
4. Separate the dried organic layer from the drying agent.

More specific instructions are given below for both macroscale and microscale procedures. The only differences between these two procedures is that they are

TABLE 12.2   Common Drying Agents

	Acidity	**Hydrated**	**Capacity[a]**	**Completeness[b]**	**Rate[c]**	**Use**
Magnesium sulfate	Neutral	$MgSO_4 \cdot 7H_2O$	High	Medium	Rapid	General
Sodium sulfate	Neutral	$Na_2SO_4 \cdot 7H_2O$ $Na_2SO_4 \cdot 10H_2O$	High	Low	Medium	General
Calcium chloride	Neutral	$CaCl_2 \cdot 2H_2O$ $CaCl_2 \cdot 6H_2O$	Low	High	Rapid	Hydrocarbons Halides
Calcium sulfate (Drierite)	Neutral	$CaSO_4 \cdot \frac{1}{2}H_2O$ $CaSO_4 \cdot 2H_2O$	Low	High	Rapid	General
Potassium carbonate	Basic	$K_2CO_3 \cdot 1\frac{1}{2}H_2O$ $K_2CO_3 \cdot 2H_2O$	Medium	Medium	Medium	Amines, esters, bases, ketones
Potassium hydroxide	Basic	—	—	—	Rapid	Amines only
Molecular sieves (3 or 4 Å)	Neutral	—	High	Extremely high	—	General

[a]Amount of water removed per given weight of drying agent.
[b]Refers to amount of H_2O still in solution at equilibrium with drying agent.
[c]Refers to rate of action (drying).

intended for different volumes of liquid and they require different glassware. The microscale procedure is generally for volumes up to about 5 mL, and the macroscale procedure is usually appropriate for volumes of 5 mL or greater.

A. Macroscale Drying Procedure

Step 1. Removal of Visible Water. Before attempting to dry an organic layer, check closely to see that there are no visible signs of water. If there is a separate layer of water (top or bottom), droplets or a globule of water floating in the organic layer, or water droplets clinging to the sides of the container, then transfer the organic layer to a clean, dry Erlenmeyer flask before adding any drying agent. If there is a large amount of water, it may be best to separate the layers using a separatory funnel. Otherwise, you may use a dry Pasteur pipet to make the transfer. The size of the Erlenmeyer flask is not critical, but it's best that the flask not be filled more than half full with the solution and it is best to have a layer of liquid in the flask at least 1 cm deep. If there is any doubt whether water is present, it is advisable to make a transfer to a dry flask. Performing this step when necessary will save time later in the drying procedure and result in a greater recovery of the desired substance.

Step 2. Addition of Drying Agent. Each time a drying procedure is performed, it is necessary to determine how much granular anhydrous sodium sulfate (or other drying agent) should be added. This will depend on the total volume of the organic phase and how much water is dissolved in the solvent. Nonpolar organic solvents such as methylene chloride or hydrocarbons (hexane, pentane, etc.) can dissolve relatively small amounts of water and generally require less drying agent, whereas more polar organic solvents such as ether and ethyl acetate can dissolve more water, and more drying agent will be required. A common guideline is to add enough granular anhydrous sodium sulfate (or other drying agent) to give a 1- to 3-mm layer on the bottom of the flask, depending on the volume of the solution. However, it is best to add the drying agent in small portions in the following way. In this procedure, use the larger microspatula shown in Figure 12.10 to add the drying agent. Generally, an appropriate portion to add each time is about 0.5–1.0 g. (You should weigh this out the first time so that you will know how much to add.) Begin by adding one portion of granular anhydrous sodium sulfate (or other drying agent) into the solution. If all of the drying agent "clumps," add another portion of sodium sulfate. To determine if the drying agent has clumped, it is helpful to stir the mixture with a clean, dry spatula or to rapidly swirl the flask. If any portion of the drying agent flows freely (is not clumped) on the bottom of the container when stirred or swirled, then you can assume that enough of the drying agent has been added. Otherwise, you must continue adding one portion of drying agent at a time until it is clear that some of the drying agent has stopped clumping. Stir or swirl the mixture after adding each portion of the drying agent. It is likely that you will need to add at least several portions of drying agent. However, the actual amount must be determined by experimentation, as just described. It is best to use a slight excess of drying agent; but if too great an excess is used, the recovery may be poor because some of the solution always adheres to the solid drying agent after the liquid is separated from it (Step 4). Take care not to add so much drying agent that all of the liquid is absorbed (disappears). If you do this, you will have to add additional solvent to recover your product from the drying agent!

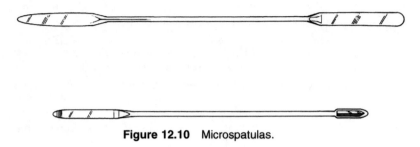

Figure 12.10   Microspatulas.

Step 3. Drying Period. Stopper or cap the container, and let the solution dry for at least 15 minutes.

NOTE: It is important that you stopper or cap the container to prevent evaporation and exposure to atmospheric moisture.

Swirl the mixture occasionally during the drying period. The mixture is dry if it appears clear (not cloudy) and shows the common signs of a dry solution given in Table 12.3. Note that a "clear" solution may be colorless or colored. If the solution remains cloudy after treatment with the first batch of drying agent, add more drying agent and repeat the drying procedure. However, if a water layer forms or if drops of water are visible, transfer the organic layer to a dry container before adding fresh drying agent, as described in Step 2. It will also be necessary to repeat the 15-minute drying step described in Step 3.

Step 4. Removal of Liquid from Drying Agent. When the solution is dry, the drying agent should be removed by using decantation (pouring carefully to leave the drying agent behind). Transfer the liquid to a dry Erlenmeyer flask. If the volume of liquid is relatively small (less than 10 mL), it may be easier to complete this step by using a dry Pasteur pipet or a dry filter-tip pipet (see Technique 8, Section 8.6) to remove the dried organic layer. With granular sodium sulfate, decantation is easy to perform because of the size of the drying-agent particles. If a powdered drying agent, such as magnesium sulfate, is used, it may be necessary to use gravity filtration (see Technique 8, Section 8.1B) to remove the drying agent. Finally, to isolate the desired material, remove the solvent by distillation (see Technique 14, Section 14.3) or evaporation (see Technique 7, Section 7.10).

B. Microscale Drying Procedure

To dry a small amount of organic liquid (less than about 5 mL), follow the same four steps just described for the "Macroscale Drying Procedure." The main differences

TABLE 12.3   Common Signs That Indicate a Solution Is Dry

---

1. There are no visible water droplets on the side of flask or suspended in solution.
2. There is not a separate layer of liquid or a "puddle."
3. The solution is clear, not cloudy. Cloudiness indicates water is present.
4. The drying agent (or a portion of it) flows freely on the bottom of the container when stirred or swirled and does not "clump" together as a solid mass.

---

are that a test tube or conical vial is used rather than an Erlenmeyer flask, and less drying agent will be required.

Step 1. Removal of visible water. Refer to Step 1 above for additional information. If there is a separate layer of water (top or bottom), droplets or a globule of water floating in the organic layer, or water droplets clinging to the sides of the container, then transfer the organic layer with a dry Pasteur pipet to a dry container, usually a conical vial or test tube, before adding any drying agent. If there is any doubt about whether water is present, it is advisable to make a transfer to a dry container.

Step 2. Addition of Drying Agent. Refer to Step 2 in the "Macroscale Drying Procedure" for the basic instructions. The only difference is that in this microscale procedure, less drying agent will be required. Begin by adding one spatulaful of granular anhydrous sodium sulfate (or other drying agent) from the V-grooved end of a microspatula (smaller microspatula in Figure 12.10) into the solution. If all of the drying agent "clumps," add another spatulaful of sodium sulfate. To determine if the drying agent has clumped, it is helpful to stir the mixture with a clean, dry spatula or to rapidly swirl the container. If any portion of the drying agent flows freely (does not clump) on the bottom of the container when stirred or swirled, then you can assume that enough of the drying agent has been added. Otherwise, you must continue adding one spatulaful of drying agent at a time until it is clear that the drying agent has stopped clumping. Stir or swirl the mixture after adding each spatulaful of the drying agent. For small amounts of liquid (less than 5 mL), about 1–6 microspatulafuls of drying agent will usually be required. However, the actual amount must be determined by experimentation, as just described. It is best to use a slight excess of drying agent; but if too great an excess is used, the recovery may be poor because some of the solution always adheres to the solid drying after the liquid is separated from the drying agent (Step 4). Take care not to add so much drying agent that all of the liquid is absorbed (disappears). If you do this, you will have to add additional solvent to recover your product from the drying agent!

Step 3. Drying Period. The instructions are the same as for Step 3 in the "Macroscale Drying Procedure."

Step 4. Removal of Liquid from Drying Agent. When the organic phase is dry, use a dry Pasteur pipet or a dry filter-tip pipet (see Technique 8, Section 8.6) to remove the dried organic layer from the drying agent and transfer the solution to a dry conical vial or test tube. Be careful not to transfer any of the drying agent when performing this step. Rinse the drying agent with a small amount of fresh solvent, and transfer this additional solvent to the vial containing the dried organic layer. To isolate the desired material, remove the solvent by evaporation using heat and a stream of air or nitrogen (see Technique 7, Section 7.10).

An alternative method of drying a small volume of organic phase is to pass it through a filtering pipet (see Technique 8, Section 8.1C) that has been packed with a small amount (about 2 cm) of drying agent. Again, the solvent is removed by evaporation.

Saturated Salt Solution. At room temperature, diethyl ether (ether) dissolves 1.5% by weight of water, and water dissolves 7.5% of ether. Ether, however, dissolves a much smaller amount of water from a saturated aqueous sodium chloride solution. Hence, the bulk of water in ether, or ether in water, can be removed by shaking it with a saturated aqueous sodium chloride solution. A solution of high ionic strength is usually not compatible with an organic solvent and forces separation of it from the aqueous layer. The water migrates into the concentrated salt solution. The ether phase (organic layer) will be on top, and the saturated sodium chloride solution will be on the bottom ($d = 1.2$ g/mL). After removing the organic phase from the aqueous sodium chloride, dry the organic layer completely with sodium sulfate or with one of the other drying agents listed in Table 12.2.

12.10 Emulsions

An **emulsion** is a colloidal suspension of one liquid in another. Minute droplets of an organic solvent are often held in suspension in an aqueous solution when the two are mixed or shaken vigorously; these droplets form an emulsion. This is especially true if any gummy or viscous material was present in the solution. Emulsions are often encountered in performing extractions. Emulsions may require a long time to separate into two layers and are a nuisance to the organic chemist.

Fortunately, several techniques may be used to break a difficult emulsion once it has formed.

1. Often an emulsion will break up if it is allowed to stand for some time. Patience is important here. Gently stirring with a stirring rod or spatula may also be useful.

2. If one of the solvents is water, adding a saturated aqueous sodium chloride solution will help destroy the emulsion. The water in the organic layer migrates into the concentrated salt solution.

3. If the total volume is less than 13 mL, the mixture may be transferred to a centrifuge tube. The emulsion will often break during centrifugation. Remember to place another tube filled with water on the opposite side of the centrifuge to balance it. Both tubes should weigh the same.

4. Adding a very small amount of a water-soluble detergent may also help. This method has been used in the past for combating oil spills. The detergent helps to solubilize the tightly-bound oil droplets.

5. Gravity filtration (see Technique 8, Section 8.1) may help to destroy an emulsion by removing gummy polymeric substances. With large volumes, you might try filtering the mixture through a fluted filter (see Technique 8, Section 8.1B) or a piece of cotton. With small-scale reactions, a filtering pipet may work (see Technique 8, Section 8.1C). In many cases, once the gum is removed, the emulsion breaks up rapidly.

6. If you are using a separatory funnel, you might try to use a gentle swirling action in the funnel to help break an emulsion. Gently stirring with a stirring rod may also be useful.

When you know through prior experience that a mixture may form a difficult emulsion, you should avoid shaking the mixture vigorously. When using conical vials for extractions, it may be better to use a magnetic spin vane for mixing and not shake the mixture at all. When using separatory funnels, extractions should be performed with gentle swirling instead of shaking, or with several gentle inversions of the separatory funnel. Do not shake the separatory funnel vigorously in these cases. It is important to use a longer extraction period if the more gentle techniques described in this paragraph are being employed. Otherwise, you will not transfer all of the material from the first phase to the second one.

12.11 Purification and Separation Methods

In nearly all synthetic experiments undertaken in the organic laboratory, a series of operations involving extractions is used after the actual reaction has been concluded. These extractions form an important part of the purification. Using them, you separate the desired product from unreacted starting materials or from undesired side products in the reaction mixture. These extractions may be grouped into three categories, depending on the nature of the impurities they are designed to remove.

The first category involves extracting or "washing" an organic mixture with water. Water washes are designed to remove highly polar materials, such as inorganic salts, strong acids or bases, and low-molecular-weight, polar substances including alcohols, carboxylic acids, and amines. Many organic compounds containing fewer than five carbons are water soluble. Water extractions are also used immediately following extractions of a mixture with either acid or base to ensure that all traces of acid or base have been removed.

The second category concerns extraction of an organic mixture with a dilute acid, usually 1–2 M hydrochloric acid. Acid extractions are intended to remove basic impurities, especially such basic impurities as organic amines. The bases are converted to their corresponding cationic salts by the acid used in the extraction. If an amine is one of the reactants or if pyridine or another amine is a solvent, such an extraction might be used to remove any excess amine present at the end of a reaction.

$$RNH_2 + HCl \longrightarrow RNH_3^+Cl^-$$
(water-soluble ammonium salt)

Cationic ammonium salts are usually soluble in the aqueous solution, and they are thus extracted from the organic material. A water extraction may be used immediately following the acid extraction to ensure that all traces of the acid have been removed from the organic material.

The third category is extraction of an organic mixture with a dilute base, usually 1 M sodium bicarbonate, although extractions with dilute sodium hydroxide can also be used. Such basic extractions are intended to convert acidic impurities, such as organic acids, to their corresponding anionic salts. For example, in the preparation of an ester, a sodium bicarbonate extraction might be used to remove any excess carboxylic acid that is present.

$$RCOOH + NaHCO_3 \longrightarrow RCOO^-Na^+ + H_2O + CO_2$$
(pK$_a$ ~ 5)   (water-soluble carboxylate salt)

Anionic carboxylate salts, being highly polar, are soluble in the aqueous phase. As a result, these acid impurities are extracted from the organic material into the basic solution. A water extraction may be used after the basic extraction to ensure that all of the base has been removed from the organic material.

Occasionally, phenols may be present in a reaction mixture as impurities, and removing them by extraction may be desired. Because phenols, although they are acidic, are about 10^5 times less acidic than carboxylic acids, basic extractions may be used to separate phenols from carboxylic acids by a careful selection of the base. If sodium bicarbonate is used as a base, carboxylic acids are extracted into the aqueous base, but phenols are not. Phenols are not sufficiently acidic to be deprotonated by the weak base bicarbonate. Extraction with sodium hydroxide, on the other hand, extracts both carboxylic acids and phenols into the aqueous basic solution, because hydroxide ion is a sufficiently strong base to deprotonate phenols.

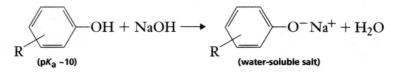

Mixtures of acidic, basic, and neutral compounds are easily separated by extraction techniques. One such example is shown in Figure 12.10.

Organic acids or bases that have been extracted can be regenerated by neutralizing the extraction reagent. This would be done if the organic acid or base were a product of a reaction rather than an impurity. For example, if a carboxylic acid has been extracted with the aqueous base, the compound can be regenerated by acidifying the extract with 6 M HCl until the solution becomes *just* acidic, as indicated by litmus or pH paper. When the solution becomes acidic, the carboxylic acid will separate from the aqueous solution. If the acid is a solid at room temperature, it will precipitate and can be purified by filtration and crystallization. If the acid is a liquid, it will form a separate layer. In this case, it would usually be necessary to extract the mixture with ether or methylene chloride. After removing the organic layer and drying it, the solvent can be evaporated to yield the carboxylic acid.

In the example shown in Figure 12.10, you also need to perform a drying step at (3) before isolating the neutral compound. When the solvent is ether, you should first extract the ether solution with saturated aqueous sodium chloride to remove much of the water. The ether layer is then dried over a drying agent such as anhydrous sodium sulfate. If the solvent were methylene chloride, it would not be necessary to do the step with saturated sodium chloride.

When performing acid–base extractions, it is common practice to extract a mixture several times with the appropriate reagent. For example, if you were extracting a carboxylic acid from a mixture, you might extract the mixture three times with 2-mL portions of 1 M NaOH. In most published experiments, the procedure will specify the volume and concentration of extracting reagent and the number of times to do the extractions. If this information is not given, you must devise your own procedure. Using a carboxylic acid as an example, if you know the identity of the acid and the approximate amount present, you can actually calculate how much sodium hydroxide is needed. Because the carboxylic acid (assuming it is monoprotic) will react with sodium hydroxide in a 1:1 ratio, you would need the same number of moles of sodium hydroxide as there are moles of acid. To ensure that all the carboxylic acid is extracted, you should use about a *twofold* excess of the base. From this, you could calculate the number of milliliters of base needed. This should be divided into two or three equal portions, one portion for each extraction. In a similar fashion, you could calculate the amount of 5% sodium bicarbonate required to extract an acid or the amount of 1 M HCl required to extract a base. If the amount of organic acid or base is not known, then the situation is more difficult. A guideline that sometimes works is to do two or three extractions so that the total volume of the extracting reagent is approximately equal to the volume of the organic layer. To test this procedure, neutralize the aqueous layer from the last extraction. If a precipitate or cloudiness results, perform another extraction and test again. When no precipitate forms, you know that all the organic acid or base has been removed.

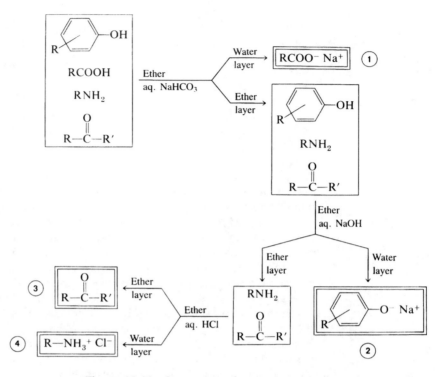

Figure 12.11   Separating a four-component mixture by extraction.

For some applications of acid base extraction, an additional step, called **back-washing** or **back extraction**, is added to the scheme shown in Figure 12.11. Consider the first step, in which the carboxylic acid is extracted by sodium bicarbonate. This aqueous layer may contain some unwanted neutral organic material from the original mixture. To remove this contamination, backwash the aqueous layer with an organic solvent such as ether or methylene chloride. After shaking the mixture and allowing the layers to separate, remove and discard the organic layer. This technique may also be used when an amine is extracted with hydrochloric acid. The resulting aqueous layer is backwashed with an organic solvent to remove unwanted neutral material.

PART E. OTHER EXTRACTION METHODS

12.12 Continuous Solid–Liquid Extraction

The technique of liquid–liquid extraction was described in Sections 12.1–12.8. In this section, solid–liquid extraction is described. Solid–liquid extraction is often used to extract a solid natural product from a natural source, such as a plant. A solvent is chosen that selectively dissolves the desired compound, but leaves behind the undesired insoluble solid. A continuous solid–liquid extraction apparatus, called a Soxhlet extractor, is commonly used in a research laboratory.

As shown in Figure 12.12, the solid to be extracted is placed in a thimble made from filter paper, and the thimble is inserted into the central chamber. A low-boiling solvent, such as diethyl ether, is placed in the round-bottom distilling flask and is

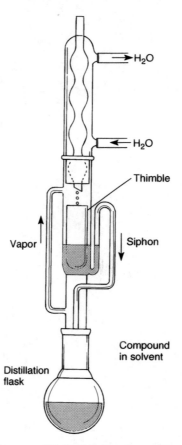

Figure 12.12   Continuous solid–liquid extraction using a Soxhlet extractor.

heated to reflux. The vapor rises through the left sidearm into the condenser where it liquefies. The condensate (liquid) drips into the thimble containing the solid. The hot solvent begins to fill the thimble and extracts the desired compound from the solid. Once the thimble is filled with solvent, the sidearm on the right acts as a siphon, and the solvent, which now contains the dissolved compound, drains back into the distillation flask. The vaporization–condensation–extraction–siphoning process is repeated hundreds of times, and the desired product is concentrated in the distillation flask. The product is concentrated in the flask because the product has a boiling point higher than that of the solvent or because it is a solid.

12.13 Continuous Liquid–Liquid Extraction

When a product is very soluble in water, it is often difficult to extract using the techniques described in Sections 12.4–12.7 because of an unfavorable distribution coefficient. In this case, you need to extract the aqueous solution numerous times with fresh batches of an immiscible organic solvent to remove the desired product from water. A less labor-intensive technique involves the use of a continuous liquid–liquid extraction apparatus. One type of extractor, used with solvents that are less dense than water, is shown in Figure 12.13. Diethyl ether is usually the solvent of choice.

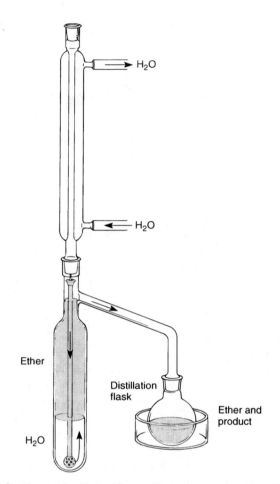

Figure 12.13   Continuous liquid–liquid extraction using a solvent less dense than water.

The aqueous phase is placed in the extractor, which is then filled with diethyl ether up to the sidearm. The round-bottom distillation flask is partially filled with ether. The ether is heated to reflux in the round-bottom flask, and the vapor is liquefied in the water-cooled condenser. The ether drips into the central tube, passes through the porous sintered glass tip, and flows through the aqueous layer. The solvent extracts the desired compound from the aqueous phase, and the ether is recycled back into the round-bottom flask. The product is concentrated in the flask. The extraction is rather inefficient and must be placed in operation for at least 24 hours to remove the compound from the aqueous phase.

12.14 Solid Phase Extraction   Solid phase extraction (SPE) is a relatively new technique, which is similar in appearance and function to column chromatography and high performance liquid chromatography (Techniques 19 and 21). In some applications, SPE is also similar to liquid-liquid extraction, discussed in this technique chapter. In addition to performing separation processes, SPE can also be used to carry out reactions in which new compounds are prepared.

A typical SPE column is constructed from the body of a plastic syringe, which is packed with a **sorbent**. The term *sorbent* is used by many manufactures as a general term for materials that can both adsorb (attract to the surface of the sorbent by a physical attraction) or absorb (penetrate into the material like a sponge). A frit is inserted at the bottom of the column to support the sorbent. After the sorbent is added, another frit is inserted on top of the sorbent to hold it in place. The remainder of the tube serves as a reservoir for the solvent. Generally, the column comes packed with the sorbent from the manufacturer, but unpacked columns can also be purchased and packed by the user for specific applications. The Luer-lock tip at the bottom is connected to a vacuum source that pulls the solvents through the column.

SPE columns can be packed with many kinds of sorbents, depending on how the column will be used. Some common types are identified in the same way that column chromatography adsorbents are classified (see Technique 21, Section 21.1): normal-phase, reversed-phase, and ion exchange. Examples of normal-phase sorbents, which are polar, include silica and alumina. These columns are used to isolate polar compounds from a nonpolar solvent. Reversed-phase sorbents are made by alkylating silica. As a result, nonpolar alkyl groups are bonded to the silica surface, making the sorbet nonpolar. A common column of this type, known as a C_{18} column, is prepared by attaching an octadecyl ($-C_8H_{18}$) group to the silica surface (see Figure 12.14). C_{18} columns most likely function by an adsorption process. Reversed-phase sorbents are used to isolate relatively nonpolar compounds from polar solvents. Ion-exchange sorbents consist of charged or highly polar materials and are used to isolate charged compounds, either as anions or cations.

A major advantage of SPE columns is that they are fast and convenient to use compared to traditional column chromatography or liquid-liquid extraction. However, there are many other advantages that are of benefit to the environment, and their use is a good example of green chemistry (see the essay "Green Chemistry" that precedes Experiment 27). These advantages include the use of more environmentally friendly solvents, higher recovery, elimination of emulsions, enormous decrease in the use of solvents, and reduced toxic waste generation.

A good example of the use of SPE columns for performing a task that is normally done by liquid-liquid extraction is the isolation of caffeine from tea or coffee. In this application, a C_{18} column is used. As the tea or coffee flows through the column, caffeine is attracted to the sorbent, and the polar impurities come off with water. Ethyl acetate is then used to remove the caffeine from the column. The experimental setup is shown in Figure 12.15. The SPE column[2] is attached to the filter flask by using two neoprene adapters (sizes #1 and #2). The filter flask is connected to either a vacuum line or a water aspirator to provide the vacuum. After each step, the solvents with impurities or desired product are drawn through the column into the filter flask using the vacuum.

The following steps are used with an SPE tube to remove caffeine from tea or coffee (see Figure 12.16):

A. Condition the C_{18} reversed-phase silica column by passing methanol and water through the tube.

B. Apply the sample of caffeinated drink to the column.

C. Wash the polar impurities from the column with water.

D. Elute the caffeine from the tube with ethyl acetate.

---

[2]This is a Strata SPE column available from Phenomenex, 411 Madrid Ave, Torrance, CA 90501-1430; phone: (310)212-0555. Part number: 8B-S001-JCH-S, Strata C-18-E, 1000 mg sorbent/6-mL tube.

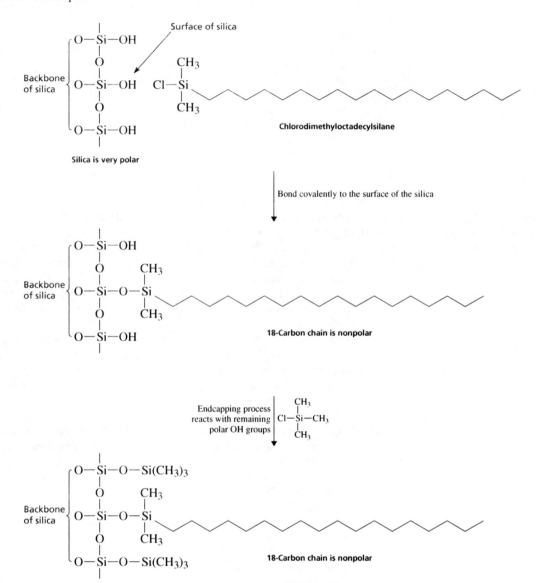

Figure 12.14 Preparation of C-18 silica for reversed-phase extractions using SPE tubes. The process changes polar silica (hydrophilic material) to nonpolar silica (hydrophobic material).

Even though Figure 12.16 is applied to the isolation of caffeine, the general scheme may be used in any application in which it is desired to separate polar substances, such as water, from a relatively nonpolar substance. Numerous applications are found in the medical field, in which analyzing body fluids is important.

There are many other diverse applications that SPE columns can be used for. By modifying the silica with specific chemical reagents, new compounds can be prepared in SPE columns. For example, oxidation reactions can be performed by mixing the silica with the appropriate oxidizing agents. Aldol condensation reactions can also be conducted in SPE columns. In another type of application, SPE has been adopted as an alternative to liquid–liquid extraction.

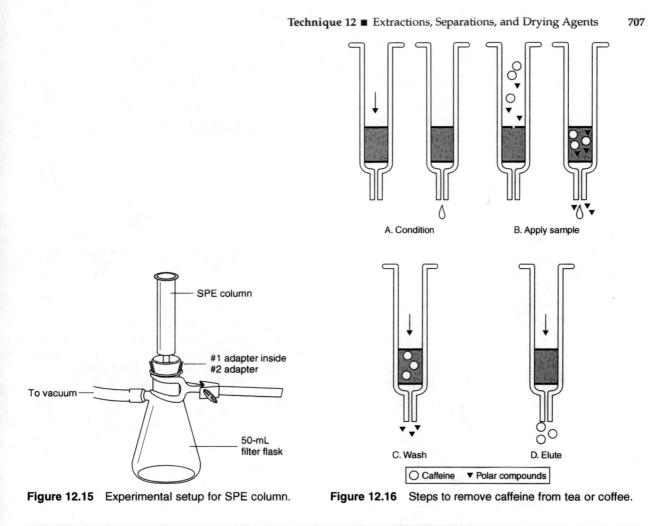

Figure 12.15 Experimental setup for SPE column.

Figure 12.16 Steps to remove caffeine from tea or coffee.

PROBLEMS

1. Suppose solute A has a distribution coefficient of 1.0 between water and diethyl ether. Demonstrate that if 100 mL of a solution of 5.0 g of A in water were extracted with two 25-mL portions of ether, a smaller amount of A would remain in the water than if the solution were extracted with one 50-mL portion of ether.

2. Write an equation to show how you could recover the parent compounds from their respective salts (1, 2, and 4) shown in Figure 12.11.

3. Aqueous hydrochloric acid was used *after* the sodium bicarbonate and sodium hydroxide extractions in the separation scheme shown in Figure 12.11. Is it possible to use this reagent earlier in the separation scheme to achieve the same overall result? If so, explain where you would perform this extraction.

4. Using aqueous hydrochloric acid, sodium bicarbonate, or sodium hydroxide solutions, devise a separation scheme using the style shown in Figure 12.11 to separate the following two-component mixtures. All the substances are soluble in ether. Also indicate how you would recover each of the compounds from its respective salts.

   a. Give two different methods for separating this mixture.

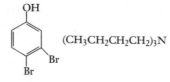

b. Give two different methods for separating this mixture.

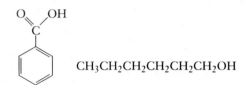

$CH_3CH_2CH_2CH_2CH_2CH_2OH$

c. Give one method for separating this mixture.

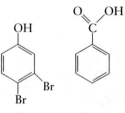

5. Solvents other than those in Table 12.1 may be used for extractions. Determine the relative positions of the organic layer and the aqueous layer in a conical vial or separatory funnel after shaking each of the following solvents with an aqueous phase. Find the densities for each of these solvents in a handbook (see Technique 4).

   a. 1,1,1-Trichloroethane

   b. Hexane

6. A student prepares ethyl benzoate by the reaction of benzoic acid with ethanol using a sulfuric acid catalyst. The following compounds are found in the crude reaction mixture: ethyl benzoate (major component), benzoic acid, ethanol, and sulfuric acid. Using a handbook, obtain the solubility properties in water for each of these compounds (see Technique 4). Indicate how you would remove benzoic acid, ethanol, and sulfuric acid from ethyl benzoate. At some point in the purification, you should also use an aqueous sodium bicarbonate solution.

7. Calculate the weight of water that could be removed from a wet organic phase using 50.0 mg of magnesium sulfate. Assume that it gives the hydrate listed in Table 12.2.

8. Explain exactly how you would perform the following laboratory instructions:

   a. "Wash the organic layer with 5.0 mL of 1 M aqueous sodium bicarbonate."

   b. "Extract the aqueous layer three times with 2-mL portions of methylene chloride."

9. Just prior to drying an organic layer with a drying agent, you notice water droplets in the organic layer. What should you do next?

10. What should you do if there is some question about which layer is the organic one during an extraction procedure?

11. Saturated aqueous sodium chloride ($d = 1.2$ g/mL) is added to the following mixtures in order to dry the organic layer. Which layer is likely to be on the bottom in each case?

    a. Sodium chloride layer or a layer containing a high-density organic compound dissolved in methylene chloride ($d = 1.4$ g/mL)

    b. Sodium chloride layer or a layer containing a low-density organic compound dissolved in methylene chloride ($d = 1.1$ g/mL)

13   **TECHNIQUE 13**

Physical Constants of Liquids: The Boiling Point and Density

PART A. BOILING POINTS AND THERMOMETER CORRECTION

13.1 The Boiling Point

As a liquid is heated, its vapor pressure increases to the point at which it just equals the applied pressure (usually atmospheric pressure). At this point, the liquid is observed to boil. The normal boiling point is measured at 760 mmHg (760 torr) or 1 atm. At a lower applied pressure, the vapor pressure needed for boiling is also lowered, and the liquid boils at a lower temperature. The relation between applied pressure and temperature of boiling for a liquid is determined by its vapor pressure–temperature behavior. Figure 13.1 is an idealization of the typical vapor pressure–temperature behavior of a liquid.

Because the boiling point is sensitive to pressure, it is important to record the barometric pressure when determining a boiling point if the determination is being conducted at an elevation significantly above or below sea level. Normal atmospheric variations may affect the boiling point, but they are usually of minor importance. However, if a boiling point is being monitored during the course of a vacuum distillation (Technique 16) that is being performed with an aspirator or a vacuum pump, the variation from the atmospheric value will be especially marked. In these cases, it is quite important to know the pressure as accurately as possible.

As a rule of thumb, the boiling point of many liquids drops about 0.5°C for a 10-mm decrease in pressure when in the vicinity of 760 mmHg. At lower pressures, a 10°C drop in boiling point is observed for each halving of the pressure. For example, if the observed boiling point of a liquid is 150°C at 10 mm pressure, then the boiling point would be about 140°C at 5 mmHg.

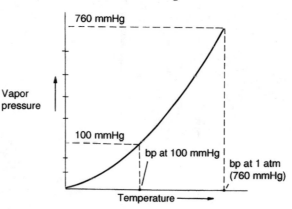

Figure 13.1 The vapor pressure–temperature curve for a typical liquid.

A more accurate estimate of the change in boiling point with a change of pressure can be made by using a nomograph. In Figure 13.2, a nomograph is given, and a method is described for using it to obtain boiling points at various pressures when the boiling point is known at some other pressure.

13.2 Determining the Boiling Point—Macroscale Methods

Two experimental methods of determining boiling points are easily available. When you have large quantities of material, you can simply record the boiling point (or boiling range) as viewed on a thermometer while you perform a simple distillation (see Technique 14).

Alternatively, you may find it convenient to use a direct method, shown in Figure 13.3. With this method, the bulb of the thermometer can be immersed in vapor from the boiling liquid for a period long enough to allow it to equilibrate and give a good temperature reading. A 13-mm × 100-mm test tube works well in this procedure. Use 0.3–0.5 mL of liquid and a small, inert carborundum (black) boiling stone. This method works best with a partial immersion (76 mm) mercury thermometer (see Section 13.4). It is not necessary to perform a stem correction with this type of thermometer. This method also works well with a temperature probe and computer interface (see Section 13.5).

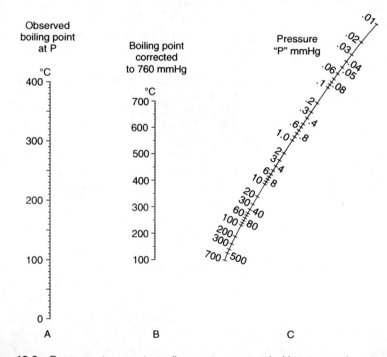

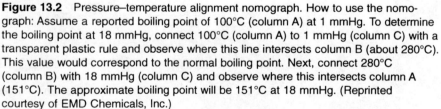

Figure 13.2 Pressure–temperature alignment nomograph. How to use the nomograph: Assume a reported boiling point of 100°C (column A) at 1 mmHg. To determine the boiling point at 18 mmHg, connect 100°C (column A) to 1 mmHg (column C) with a transparent plastic rule and observe where this line intersects column B (about 280°C). This value would correspond to the normal boiling point. Next, connect 280°C (column B) with 18 mmHg (column C) and observe where this intersects column A (151°C). The approximate boiling point will be 151°C at 18 mmHg. (Reprinted courtesy of EMD Chemicals, Inc.)

Place the bulb of the thermometer as close as possible to the boiling liquid without actually touching it. The best heating device is a hot plate with either an aluminum block or a sand bath.[1]

While you are heating the liquid, it is helpful to record the temperature at 1-minute intervals. This makes it easier to keep track of changes in the temperature and to know when you have reached the boiling point. The liquid must boil vigorously, such that you see a reflux ring above the bulb of the thermometer and drops of liquid condensing on the sides of the test tube. Note that with some liquids, the reflux ring will be very faint, and you must look closely to see it. The boiling point is reached when the temperature reading on the thermometer has remained constant at its highest observed value for 2–3 minutes. It is usually best to turn the heat control on the hot plate to a relatively high setting initially, especially if you are starting with a cold hot plate and aluminum block or sand bath. If the temperature begins to level off at a relatively low temperature (less than about 100°C) or if the reflux ring reaches the immersion ring on the thermometer, you should turn down the heat-control setting immediately.

Two problems can occur when you perform this boiling-point procedure. The first is much more common and occurs when the temperature appears to be leveling off at a temperature below the boiling point of the liquid. This is more likely to happen with a relatively high-boiling liquid (boiling points greater than about 150°C) or when the sample is not heated sufficiently. The best way to prevent this problem is to heat the sample more strongly. With high-boiling liquids, it may be helpful to wait for the temperature to remain constant for 3–4 minutes to make sure that you have reached the actual boiling point.

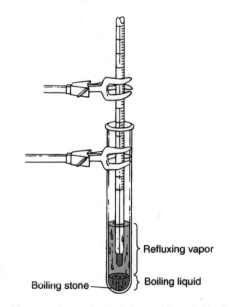

Figure 13.3   Macroscale method of determining the boiling point.

---

[1] Note to the instructor: The aluminum block should have a hole drilled in it that goes *all the way through* the block and is just slightly larger than the outside diameter of the test tube. A sand bath can be conveniently prepared by adding 40 mL of sand to a 150-mL beaker or by using a heating mantle partially filled with sand. For additional comments about these heating methods, see the Instructor's Manual, Experiment 7, "Infrared Spectroscopy and Boiling-Point Determination."

The second problem, which is rare, occurs when the liquid evaporates completely, and the temperature inside the dry test tube may rise higher than the actual boiling point of the liquid. This is more likely to happen with low-boiling liquids (boiling point less than 100°C), or if the temperature on the hot plate is set too high for too long. To check for this possibility, observe the amount of liquid remaining in the test tube as soon as you have finished the procedure. If there is no liquid remaining, it is possible that the highest temperature you observed is greater than the boiling point of the liquid. In this case, you should repeat the boiling-point determination, heating the sample less strongly or using more sample.

Depending on the skill of the person performing this technique, boiling points may be slightly inaccurate. When experimental boiling points are inaccurate, it is more common for them to be lower than the literature value, and inaccuracies are more likely to occur for higher-boiling liquids. With higher-boiling liquids, the difference may be as much as 5°C. Carefully following the previous instructions will make it more likely that your experimental value will be close to the literature value.

13.3 Determining the Boiling Point—Microscale Methods

With smaller amounts of material, you can carry out a microscale or semi-microscale determination of the boiling point by using the apparatus shown in Figure 13.4.

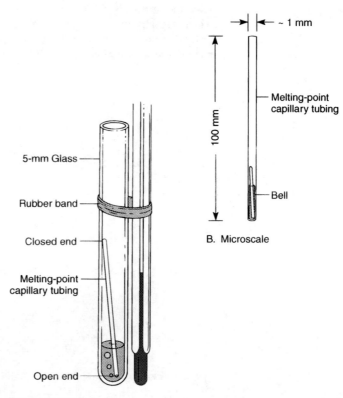

Figure 13.4 Boiling-point determinations.

Semi-microscale Method. To carry out the semi-microscale determination, attach a piece of 5-mm glass tubing (sealed at one end) to a thermometer with a rubber band or a thin slice of rubber tubing. The liquid whose boiling point is being determined is introduced with a Pasteur pipet into this piece of tubing, and a short piece of melting-point capillary (sealed at one end) is dropped in with the open end down. The whole unit is then placed in a Thiele tube. The rubber band should be placed above the level of the oil in the Thiele tube; otherwise the band may soften in the hot oil. When positioning the band, keep in mind that the oil will expand when heated. Next, the Thiele tube is heated in the same fashion as described in Technique 9, Section 9.6, for determining a melting point. Heating is continued until a rapid and continuous stream of bubbles emerges from the inverted capillary. At this point, you should stop heating. Soon, the stream of bubbles slows down and stops. When the bubbles stop, the liquid enters the capillary tube. The moment at which the liquid enters the capillary tube corresponds to the boiling point of the liquid, and the temperature is recorded.

Microscale Method. In microscale experiments, there often is too little product available to use the semi-microscale method just described. However, the method can be scaled down in the following manner. The liquid is placed in a 1-mm melting-point capillary tube to a depth of about 4–6 mm. Use a syringe or a Pasteur pipet that has had its tip drawn thinner to transfer the liquid into the capillary tube. It may be necessary to use a centrifuge to transfer the liquid to the bottom of the tube. Next, prepare an appropriately-sized inverted capillary, or **bell**.

The easiest way to prepare a bell is to use a commercial micropipet, such as a 10-μL Drummond "microcap." These are available in vials of 50 or 100 microcaps and are very inexpensive. To prepare the bell, cut the microcap in half with a file or scorer and then seal one end by inserting it a small distance into a flame, turning it on its axis until the opening closes.

If microcaps are not available, a piece of 1-mm open-end capillary tubing (same size as a melting-point capillary) can be rotated along its axis in a flame while being held horizontally. Use your index fingers and thumbs to rotate the tube; do not change the distance between your two hands while rotating. When the tubing is soft, remove it from the flame and pull it to a thinner diameter. When pulling, keep the tube straight by *moving both your hands and your elbows outward* by about 4 inches. Hold the pulled tube in place a few moments until it cools. Using the edge of a file or your fingernail, break out the thin center section. Seal one end of the thin section in the flame; then break it to a length that is about one and one-half times the height of your sample liquid (6–9 mm). Be sure the break is done squarely. Invert the bell (open end down), and place it in the capillary tube containing the sample liquid. Push the bell to the bottom with a fine copper wire if it adheres to the side of the capillary tube. A centrifuge may be used if you prefer. Figure 13.5 shows the construction method for the bell and the final assembly.

Place the microscale assembly in a standard melting-point apparatus (or a Thiele tube if an electrical apparatus is not available) to determine the boiling point. Heating is continued until a rapid and continuous stream of bubbles emerges from the inverted capillary. At this point, stop heating. Soon, the stream of bubbles slows down and stops. When the bubbles stop, the liquid enters the capillary tube. The moment at which the liquid enters the capillary tube corresponds to the boiling point of the liquid, and the temperature is recorded.

Explanation of the Method. During the initial heating, the air trapped in the inverted bell expands and leaves the tube, giving rise to a stream of bubbles. When the

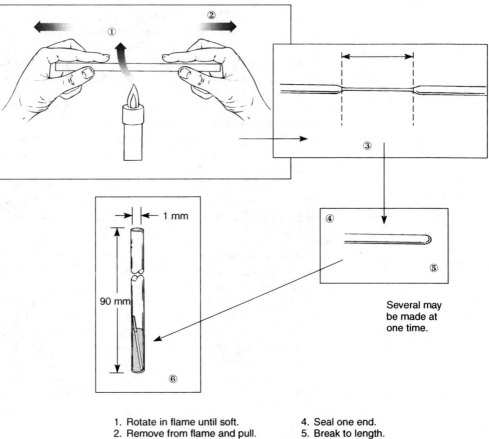

①
②
③
④
⑤
Several may
be made at
one time.

1 mm

90 mm

⑥

1. Rotate in flame until soft.
2. Remove from flame and pull.
3. Break pulled section out.

4. Seal one end.
5. Break to length.
6. Place bell in tube.

Figure 13.5   Construction of a microcapillary bell for microscale boiling-point determination.

liquid begins boiling, most of the air has been expelled; the bubbles of gas are due to the boiling action of the liquid. Once the heating is stopped, most of the vapor pressure left in the bell comes from the vapor of the heated liquid that seals its open end. There is always vapor in equilibrium with a heated liquid. If the temperature of the liquid is above its boiling point, the pressure of the trapped vapor will either exceed or equal the atmospheric pressure. As the liquid cools, its vapor pressure decreases. When the vapor pressure drops just below atmospheric pressure (just below the boiling point), the liquid is forced into the capillary tube.

Difficulties. Three problems are common to this method. The first arises when the liquid is heated so strongly that it evaporates or boils away. The second arises when the liquid is not heated above its boiling point before heating is discontinued. If the heating is stopped at any point below the actual boiling point of the sample, the liquid enters the bell *immediately,* giving an apparent boiling point that is too low. Be sure you observe a continuous stream of bubbles, too fast for individual bubbles to be distinguished, before lowering the temperature. Also be sure the bubbling action decreases slowly before the liquid enters the bell. If your melting-point apparatus has fine enough control and fast response, you can actually begin heating again and force the liquid out of the bell before it becomes completely filled with the liquid. This allows a second determination to be performed on the same sample. The third problem is that the bell may be so light that the bubbling action of the liquid causes the bell to move up the capillary tube. This problem can sometimes be solved by using a longer (heavier) bell or by sealing the bell so that a larger section of solid glass is formed at the sealed end of the bell.

When measuring temperatures above 150°C, thermometer errors can become significant. For an accurate boiling point with a high-boiling liquid, you may wish to apply a *stem correction* to the thermometer, as described in Section 13.4, or to calibrate the thermometer, as described in Technique 9, Section 9.9.

13.4 Thermometers and Stem Corrections

Three types of thermometers are available: bulb immersion, partial immersion (stem immersion), and total immersion. Bulb immersion thermometers are calibrated by the manufacturer to give correct temperature readings when only the bulb (not the rest of the thermometer) is placed in the medium to be measured. Partial immersion thermometers are calibrated to give correct temperature readings when they are immersed to a specified depth in the medium to be measured. Partial immersion thermometers are easily recognized because the manufacturer always scores a mark, or immersion ring, completely around the stem at the specified depth of immersion. The immersion ring is normally found below any of the temperature calibrations. Total immersion thermometers are calibrated when the entire thermometer is immersed in the medium to be measured. The three types of thermometers are often marked on the back (opposite side from the calibrations) by the words *bulb, immersion,* or *total,* but this may vary from one manufacturer to another.

Boiling-point determination and distillation are two techniques in which an accurate temperature reading may be obtained most easily with a partial immersion thermometer. A common immersion length for this type of thermometer is 76 mm. This length works well for these two techniques because the hot vapors are likely to surround the bottom of the thermometer up to a point fairly close to the immersion line. If a total immersion thermometer is used in these applications, a stem correction, which is described later, must be used to obtain an accurate temperature reading.

The liquid used in thermometers may be either mercury or a colored organic liquid such as an alcohol. Because mercury is highly poisonous and is difficult to clean up completely when a thermometer is broken, many laboratories now use nonmercury thermometers. When a highly accurate temperature reading is required, such as in a boiling-point determination or in some distillations, mercury thermometers may have an advantage over nonmercury thermometers for two reasons. Mercury has a lower coefficient of expansion than the liquids used in nonmercury thermometers. Therefore, a partial immersion mercury thermometer will give a more accurate reading when the thermometer is not immersed in the hot vapors exactly to the immersion line. In other words, the mercury thermometer is more forgiving. Furthermore, because mercury is a better conductor of heat, a mercury thermometer will respond more quickly to changes in the temperature of the hot vapors. If the temperature is read before the thermometer reading has stabilized, which is more likely to occur with a nonmercury thermometer, the temperature reading will be inaccurate.

Manufacturers design total immersion thermometers to read correctly only when they are immersed totally in the medium to be measured. The entire mercury thread must be covered. Because this situation is rare, a **stem correction** should be added to the observed temperature. This correction, which is positive, can be fairly large when high temperatures are being measured. Keep in mind, however, that if your thermometer has been calibrated for its desired use (such as described in Technique 9, Section 9.9, for a melting-point apparatus), a stem correction is not necessary for any temperature within the calibration limits. You are most likely to want a stem correction when you are performing a distillation. If you determine a melting point or boiling point using an uncalibrated, total immersion thermometer, you will also want to use a stem correction.

When you wish to make a stem correction for a total immersion thermometer, the following formula may be used. It is based on the fact that the portion of the mercury thread in the stem is cooler than the portion immersed in the vapor or the heated area around the thermometer. The mercury will not have expanded in the cool stem to the same extent as in the warmed section of the thermometer. The equation used is

$$(0.000154)(T - t_1)(T - t_2) = \text{correction to be added to } T \text{ observed}$$

1. The factor 0.000154 is a constant, the coefficient of expansion for the mercury in the thermometer.

2. The term $T - t_1$ corresponds to the length of the mercury thread not immersed in the heated area. Use the temperature scale on the thermometer itself for this measurement, rather than an actual length unit. T is the observed temperature, and t_1 is the *approximate* place where the heated part of the stem ends and the cooler part begins.

3. The term $T - t_2$ corresponds to the difference between the temperature of the mercury in the vapor T and the temperature of the mercury in the air outside the heated area (room temperature). The term T is the observed temperature, and t_2 is measured by hanging another thermometer so the bulb is close to the stem of the main thermometer.

Figure 13.6 shows how to apply this method for a distillation. By the formula just given, it can be shown that high temperatures are more likely to require a stem correction and that low temperatures need not be corrected. The following sample calculations illustrate this point.

Example 1	Example 2
$T = 200\ °C$	$T = 100\ °C$
$t_1 = 0\ °C$	$t_1 = 0\ °C$
$t_2 = 35\ °C$	$t_2 = 35\ °C$
$(0.000154)(200)(165) = 5.1\ °C$ stem correction	$(0.000154)(100)(165) = 1.0\ °C$ stem correction
$200\ °C + 5\ °C = 205\ °C$ corrected temperature	$100\ °C + 1\ °C = 101\ °C$ corrected temperature

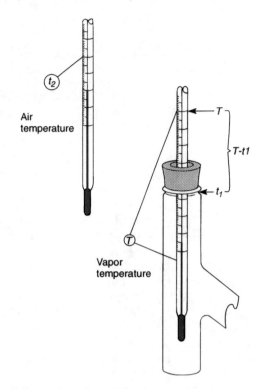

Figure 13.6   Measurement of a thermometer stem correction during distillation.

13.5 Computer Interface and Temperature Probe

Rather than using a thermometer to determine a boiling point or to monitor the temperature during a distillation, one can use a Vernier LabPro interface with a stainless-steel temperature probe and a laptop computer. This system provides a very accurate way of measuring the temperature. The data (temperature vs. time) is displayed on the monitor while it is being collected. When performing a boiling-point determination, the visual display of the temperature on the monitor makes it easy to know when the maximum temperature (the boiling point) has been reached. When a temperature probe is used with the macroscale method of determining a boiling point (see Section 13.2), the boiling point can usually be determined to within 2°C of the literature value. Being able to see a graph of temperature vs. time when performing a distillation gives students a better sense of when the different liquids are distilling.

The temperature probes (or thermocouples) work only in a given temperature range. It is therefore important to select a probe that has a maximum temperature that is somewhat higher than the boiling points of the liquids you will be working with. See the Instructor's Manual, Experiment 6, Simple and Fractional Distillation, for more specific information about selecting an appropriate temperature probe.

PART B. DENSITY

13.6 Density

Density is defined as mass per unit volume and is generally expressed in units of grams per milliliter (g/mL) for a liquid and grams per cubic centimeter (g/cm^3) for a solid.

$$\text{Density} = \frac{\text{mass}}{\text{volume}} \quad \text{or} \quad D = \frac{M}{V}$$

In organic chemistry, density is most commonly used in converting the weight of liquid to a corresponding volume, or vice versa. It is often easier to measure a volume of a liquid than to weigh it. As a physical property, density is also useful for identifying liquids in much the same way that boiling points are used.

Although precise methods that allow the measurements of the densities of liquids at the microscale level have been developed, they are often difficult to perform. An approximate method for measuring densities can be found in using a 100-μL (0.100-mL) automatic pipet (see Technique 5, Section 5.6). Clean, dry, and preweigh one or more conical vials (including their caps and liners) and record their weights. Handle these vials with a tissue to avoid getting your fingerprints on them. Adjust the automatic pipet to deliver 100 μL and fit it with a clean, new tip. Use the pipet to deliver 100 μL of the unknown liquid to each of your tared vials. Cap them so that the liquid does not evaporate. Reweigh the vials and use the weight of the 100 μL of liquid delivered to calculate a density for each case. It is recommended that from three to five determinations be performed, that the calculations be performed to three significant figures, and that all the calculations be averaged to obtain the final result. This determination of the density will be accurate to within two significant figures. Table 13.1 compares some literature values with those that could be obtained by this method.

TABLE 13.1 Densities determined by the automatic pipet method (g/mL)

Substance	BP	Literature	100 μL
Water	100	1.000	1.01
Hexane	69	0.660	0.66
Acetone	56	0.788	0.77
Dichloromethane	40	1.330	1.27
Diethyl ether	35	0.713	0.67

PROBLEMS

1. Using the pressure–temperature alignment chart in Figure 13.2, answer the following questions.

   a. What is the normal boiling point (at 760 mmHg) for a compound that boils at 150 °C at 10 mmHg pressure?

   b. At what temperature would the compound in (a) boil if the pressure were 40 mmHg?

   c. A compound was distilled at atmospheric pressure and had a boiling point of 285 °C. What would be the approximate boiling range for this compound at 15 mmHg?

2. Calculate the corrected boiling point for nitrobenzene by using the method given in Section 13.4. The boiling point was determined using an apparatus similar to that shown in Figure 13.3. Assume that a total immersion thermometer was used. The

observed boiling point was 205 °C. The reflux ring in the test tube just reached up to the 0 °C mark on the thermometer. A second thermometer suspended alongside the test tube, at a slightly higher level than the one inside, gave a reading of 35 °C.

3. Suppose that you had calibrated the thermometer in your melting-point apparatus against a series of melting-point standards. After reading the temperature and converting it using the calibration chart, should you also apply a stem correction? Explain.

4. The density of a liquid was determined by the automatic pipet method. A 100-μL automatic pipet was used. The liquid had a mass of 0.082 g. What was the density in grams per milliliter of the liquid?

5. During the microscale boiling-point determination of an unknown liquid, heating was discontinued at 154 °C and the liquid immediately began to enter the inverted bell. Heating was begun again at once, and the liquid was forced out of the bell. Heating was again discontinued at 165 °C, at which time a very rapid stream of bubbles emerged from the bell. On cooling, the rate of bubbling gradually diminished until the liquid reached a temperature of 161 °C and entered and filled the bell. Explain this sequence of events. What was the boiling point of the liquid?

14   TECHNIQUE 14

Simple Distillation

Sign in at www .cengage.com/login to access the Pre-Lab Video Exercise for this technique.

Distillation is the process of vaporizing a liquid, condensing the vapor, and collecting the condensate in another container. This technique is very useful for separating a liquid mixture when the components have different boiling points or when one of the components will not distill. It is one of the principal methods of purifying a liquid. Four basic distillation methods are available to the chemist: simple distillation, fractional distillation, vacuum distillation (distillation at reduced pressure), and steam distillation. Fractional distillation will be discussed in Technique 15; vacuum distillation in Technique 16; and steam distillation in Technique 18.

A typical modern distillation apparatus is shown in Figure 14.1. The liquid to be distilled is placed in the distilling flask and heated, usually by a heating mantle. The heated liquid vaporizes and is forced upward past the thermometer and into the condenser. The vapor is condensed to liquid in the cooling condenser, and the liquid flows downward through the vacuum adapter (no vacuum is used) and into the receiving flask.

14.1 The Evolution of Distillation Equipment

There are probably more types and styles of distillation apparatus than exist for any other technique in chemistry. Over the centuries, chemists have devised just about every conceivable design. The earliest known types of distillation apparatus were the **alembic** and the **retort** (see Figure 14.2). They were used by alchemists in the Middle Ages and the Renaissance, and probably even earlier by Arabic chemists. Most other distillation equipment has evolved as variations on these designs.

Figure 14.2 shows several stages in the evolution of distillation equipment as it relates to the organic laboratory. It is not intended to be a complete history; rather, it is representative. Up until recent years, equipment based on the retort design was

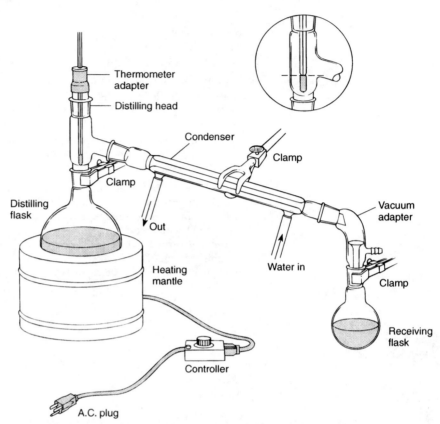

Figure 14.1 Distillation with the standard macroscale lab kit.

common in the laboratory. Although the retort itself was still in use early in the last century, it had evolved by that time into the distillation flask and water-cooled condenser combination. This early equipment was connected with drilled corks. By 1958, most introductory laboratories were beginning to use "organic lab kits" that included glassware connected by standard-taper glass joints. The original lab kits contained large Ⴠ 24/40 joints. Within a short time, they became smaller with Ⴠ 19/22 and even Ⴠ 14/20 joints. These later kits are still being used today in many "macroscale" laboratory courses such as yours.

In the 1960s, researchers developed even smaller versions of these kits for working at the "microscale" level (in Figure 14.2, see the box labeled "Research use only"), but this glassware is generally too expensive to use in an introductory laboratory. However, in the mid-1980s, several groups developed a different style of microscale distillation equipment based on the alembic design (see the box labeled "Modern microscale organic lab kit"). This new microscale equipment has Ⴠ 14/10 standard-taper joints, threaded outer joints with screw-cap connectors, and an internal O-ring for a compression seal. Microscale equipment similar to this is now used in many introductory courses. The advantages of this glassware are that there is less material used (lower cost), lower personal exposure to chemicals, and less waste generated. Because both types of equipment are in use today, after we describe macroscale equipment, we will also show the equivalent microscale distillation apparatus.

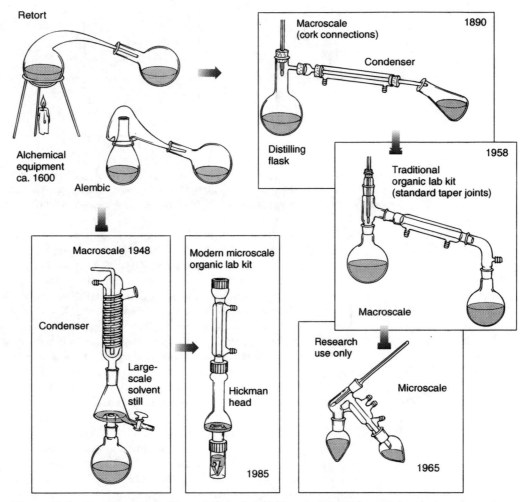

Figure 14.2 Some stages in the evolution of distillation equipment from alchemical equipment (dates represent approximate time of use).

14.2 Distillation Theory

In the traditional distillation of a pure substance, vapor rises from the distillation flask and comes into contact with a thermometer that records its temperature. The vapor then passes through a condenser, which reliquefies the vapor and passes it into the receiving flask. The temperature observed during the distillation of a **pure substance** remains constant throughout the distillation so long as both vapor *and* liquid are present in the system (see Figure 14.3A). When a **liquid mixture** is distilled, often the temperature does not remain constant but increases throughout the distillation. The reason for this is that the composition of the vapor that is distilling varies continuously during the distillation (see Figure 14.3B).

For a liquid mixture, the composition of the vapor in equilibrium with the heated solution is different from the composition of the solution itself. This is shown in Figure 14.4, which is a phase diagram of the typical vapor–liquid relation for a two-component system (A + B).

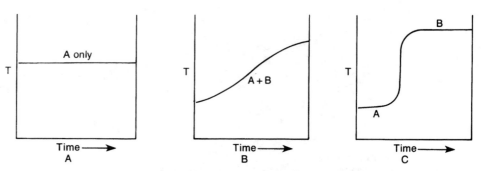

Figure 14.3   Three types of temperature behavior during a simple distillation. (A) A single pure component. (B) Two components of similar boiling points. (C) Two components with widely differing boiling points. Good separations are achieved in A and C.

In Figure 14.4, horizontal lines represent constant temperatures. The upper curve represents vapor composition, and the lower curve represents liquid composition. For any horizontal line (constant temperature), such as that shown at t, the intersections of the line with the curves give the compositions of the liquid and the vapor that are in equilibrium with each other at that temperature. In the diagram, at temperature t, the intersection of the curve at x indicates that liquid of composition w will be in equilibrium with vapor of composition z, which corresponds to the intersection at y. Composition is given as a mole percentage of A and B in the mixture. Pure A, which boils at temperature t_A, is represented at the left. Pure B, which boils at temperature t_B, is represented at the right. For either pure A or pure B, the vapor and liquid curves meet at the boiling point. Thus, either pure A or pure B will distill at a constant temperature (t_A or t_B). Both the vapor and the liquid must have the same composition in either of these cases. This is not the case for mixtures of A and B.

A mixture of A and B of composition w will have the following behavior when heated. The temperature of the liquid mixture will increase until the boiling point of the mixture is reached. This corresponds to following line wx from w to x, the boiling point of the mixture t. At temperature t the liquid begins to vaporize, which corresponds to line xy. The vapor has the composition corresponding to z. In other words, the first vapor obtained in distilling a mixture of A and B does not consist of pure A. It is richer in A than the original mixture but still contains a significant amount of the higher-boiling component B, *even from the very beginning of the distillation*. The result is that it is never possible to separate a mixture completely by a simple distillation. However, in two cases it is possible to get an acceptable separation into relatively pure components. In the first case, if the boiling points of A and B differ by a large amount (> 100°C) and if the distillation is carried out carefully, it will be possible to get a fair separation of A and B. In the second case, if A contains a fairly small amount of B (< 10%), a reasonable separation of A from B can be achieved. When the boiling-point differences are not large and when highly pure components are desired, it is necessary to perform a **fractional distillation**. Fractional distillation is described in Technique 15, where the behavior during a simple distillation is also considered in detail. Note only that as vapor distills from the mixture of composition w (see Figure 14.4) it is richer in A than is the solution. Thus, the composition of the material left behind in the distillation becomes richer in B (moves to the right from w toward pure B in the graph). A mixture of 90% B (dotted line on the right side in Figure 14.4) has a higher boiling point than at w. Hence, the temperature of the liquid in the distillation flask will increase during the distillation, and the composition of the distillate will change (as is shown in Figure 14.3B).

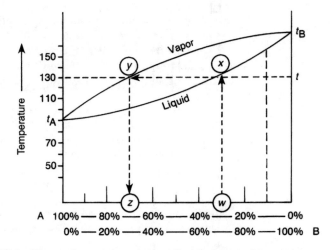

Figure 14.4   Phase diagram for a typical liquid mixture of two components.

When two components that have a large boiling-point difference are distilled, the temperature remains constant while the first component distills. If the temperature remains constant, a relatively pure substance is being distilled. After the first substance distills, the temperature of the vapors rises, and the second component distills, again at a constant temperature. This is shown in Figure 14.3C. A typical application of this type of distillation might be an instance of a reaction mixture containing the desired component A (bp 140°C) contaminated with a small amount of undesired component B (bp 250°C) and mixed with a solvent such as diethyl ether (bp 36°C). The ether is removed easily at low temperature. Pure A is removed at a higher temperature and collected in a separate receiver. Component B can then be distilled, but it is usually left as a residue and not distilled. The separation is not difficult and represents a case where simple distillation might be used to advantage.

14.3 Simple Distillation— Standard Apparatus

For a simple distillation, the apparatus shown in Figure 14.1 is used. Six pieces of specialized glassware are used:

1. Distilling flask
2. Distillation head
3. Thermometer adapter
4. Water condenser
5. Vacuum adapter
6. Receiving flask

The apparatus is usually heated electrically, using a heating mantle. The distilling flask, condenser, and vacuum adapter should be clamped. Two different methods of clamping this apparatus were shown in Technique 7 (Figure 7.2, p. 625 and Figure 7.4, p. 626). The receiving flask should be supported by removable wooden blocks or a wire gauze on an iron ring attached to a ring stand. The various components are each discussed in the following sections, along with some other important points.

Distilling Flask. The distilling flask should be a round-bottom flask. This type of flask is designed to withstand the required input of heat and to accommodate the boiling action. It gives a maximized heating surface. The size of the distilling flask should be chosen so that it is never filled more than two-thirds full. When the flask is filled beyond this point, the neck constricts and "chokes" the boiling action, resulting in bumping. The surface area of the boiling liquid should be kept as large as possible. However, too large a distilling flask should also be avoided. With too large a flask, the **holdup** is excessive; the holdup is the amount of material that cannot distill because some vapor must fill the empty flask. When you cool the apparatus at the end, this material drops back into the distilling flask.

Boiling Stones. A boiling stone (Technique 7, Section 7.4, p. 631) should be used during distillation to prevent bumping. As an alternative, the liquid being distilled may be rapidly stirred using a magnetic stirrer and stir bar (Technique 7, Section 7.3, p. 630). If you forget a boiling stone, cool the mixture before adding it. If you add a boiling stone to a hot superheated liquid, it may "erupt" into vigorous boiling, breaking your apparatus and spilling hot solvent everywhere.

Grease. In most cases, it is unnecessary to grease standard-taper joints for a simple distillation. The grease makes cleanup more difficult, and it may contaminate your product.

Distillation Head. The distillation head directs the distilling vapors into the condenser and allows the connection of a thermometer via the thermometer adapter. The thermometer should be positioned in the distillation head so that the thermometer is directly in the stream of vapor that is distilling. This can be accomplished if the entire bulb of the thermometer is positioned *below* the sidearm of the distilling head (see the circular inset in Figure 14.1). The entire bulb must be immersed in the vapor to achieve an accurate temperature reading. When distilling, you should be able to see a reflux ring (Technique 7, Section 7.2, p. 628) positioned well above both the thermometer bulb and the bottom of the sidearm.

Thermometer Adapter. The thermometer adapter connects to the top of the distillation head (see Figure 14.1). There are two parts to the thermometer adapter: a glass joint with an open rolled edge on the top, and a rubber adapter that fits over the rolled edge and holds the thermometer. The thermometer fits in a hole in the top of the rubber adapter and can be adjusted upward and downward by sliding it in the hole. Adjust the bulb to a point below the sidearm. The distillation temperature can be monitored most accurately by using a partial immersion mercury thermometer (see Technique 13, Section 13.4).

Water Condenser. The joint between the distillation head and the water condenser is the joint most prone to leak in this entire apparatus. Because the distilling liquid is both hot and vaporized when it reaches this joint, it will leak out of any small opening between the two joint surfaces. The odd angle of the joint, neither vertical or horizontal, also makes a good connection more difficult. Be sure this joint is well sealed. If possible, use one of the plastic joint clips described in Technique 7, Figure 7.3. Otherwise, adjust your clamps to be sure that the joint surfaces are pressed together and not pulled apart.

The condenser will remain full of cooling water only if the water flows *upward*, not downward. The water input hose should be connected to the lower opening in the jacket, and the exit hose should be attached to the upper opening. Place the other end of the exit hose in a sink. A moderate water flow will perform a good deal of cooling. A high rate of water flow may cause the tubing to pop off the joints and cause a flood. If you hold the exit hose horizontally and point the end into a sink, the flow rate is correct if the water stream continues horizontally for about two inches before bending downward.

If a distillation apparatus is to be left untended for a period of time, it is a good idea to wrap copper wire around the ends of the tubing and twist it tight. This will help to prevent the hoses from popping off of the connectors if there is an unexpected water-pressure change.

Vacuum Adapter. In a simple distillation, the vacuum adapter is not connected to a vacuum but is left open. It is merely an opening to the outside air so that pressure does not build up in the distillation system. If you plug this opening, you will have a **closed system** (no outlet). It is always dangerous to heat a closed system. Enough pressure can build up in the closed system to cause an explosion. The vacuum adapter, in this case, merely directs the distillate into the receiving, or collection, flask.

If the substance you are distilling is water sensitive, you can attach a calcium chloride drying tube to the vacuum connection to protect the freshly distilled liquid from atmospheric water vapor. Air that enters the apparatus will have to pass through the calcium chloride and be dried. Depending on the severity of the problem, drying agents other than calcium chloride may also be used.

The vacuum adapter has a disturbing tendency to obey the laws of Newtonian physics and fall off the slanted condenser onto the desk and break. If plastic joint clips are available, it is a good idea to use them on both ends of this piece. The top clip will secure the vacuum adapter to the condenser, and the bottom clip will secure the receiving flask, preventing it from falling.

Rate of Heating. The rate of heating for the distillation can be adjusted to the proper rate of **takeoff**, the rate at which distillate leaves the condenser, by watching drops of liquid emerge from the bottom of the vacuum adapter. A rate of from one to three drops per second is considered a proper rate of takeoff for most applications. At a greater rate, equilibrium is not established within the distillation apparatus, and the separation may be poor. A slower rate of takeoff is also unsatisfactory because the temperature recorded on the thermometer is not maintained by a constant vapor stream, thus leading to an inaccurate low boiling point.

Receiving Flask. The receiving flask, which is usually a round-bottom flask, collects the distilled liquid. If the liquid you are distilling is extremely volatile and there is danger of losing some of it to evaporation, it is sometimes advisable to cool the receiving flask in an ice-water bath.

Fractions. The material being distilled is called the **distillate**. Frequently, a distillate is collected in contiguous portions, called **fractions**. This is accomplished by replacing the collection flask with a clean one at regular intervals. If a small amount of liquid is collected at the beginning of a distillation and not saved or used further, it is called a **forerun**. Subsequent fractions will have higher boiling ranges, and each fraction should be labeled with its correct boiling range when the fraction is taken. For a simple distillation of a pure material, most of the material will be collected in a single, large **midrun** fraction, with only a small forerun. In some small-scale distillations, the volume of the forerun will be so small that you will not be able to collect it separately from the midrun fraction. The material left behind is called the **residue**. It is usually advised that you discontinue a distillation before the distilling flask becomes empty. Typically, the residue becomes increasingly dark in color during distillation, and it frequently contains thermal decomposition products.

In addition, a dry residue may explode on overheating, or the flask may melt or crack when it becomes dry. Don't distill until the distilling flask is completely dry!

14.4 Microscale and Semi-Microscale Equipment

When you wish to distill quantities that are smaller than 4–5 mL, different equipment is required. What you use depends on how small a quantity you wish to distill.

A. Semi-Microscale

One possibility is to use equipment identical in style to that used with conventional macroscale procedures, but to "downsize" it using ℑ14/10 joints. The major manufacturers do make distillation heads and vacuum takeoff adapters with ℑ 14/10 joints. This equipment will allow you to handle quantities of 5–15 mL. An example of such a "semi-microscale" apparatus is given in Figure 14.5. Although the manufacturers make ℑ14/10 condensers, the condenser has been left out in this example. This can be done if the material to be distilled is not extremely volatile or is high boiling. It is also possible to omit the condenser if you do not have a large amount of material and can cool the receiving flask in an ice-water bath as shown in the figure.

B. Microscale—Student Equipment

Figure 14.6 shows the typical distillation setup for those students who are taking a microscale laboratory course. Instead of a distillation head, condenser, and vacuum takeoff, this equipment uses a single piece of glassware called a **Hickman head**. The Hickman head provides a "short path" for the distilled liquid to travel

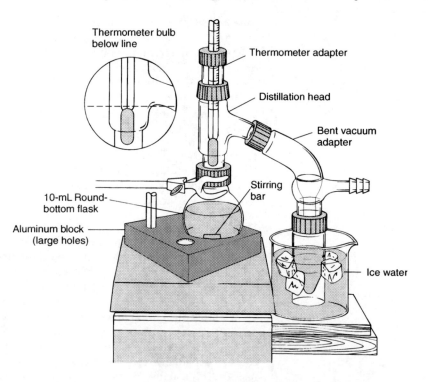

Figure 14.5 Semi-microscale distillation.

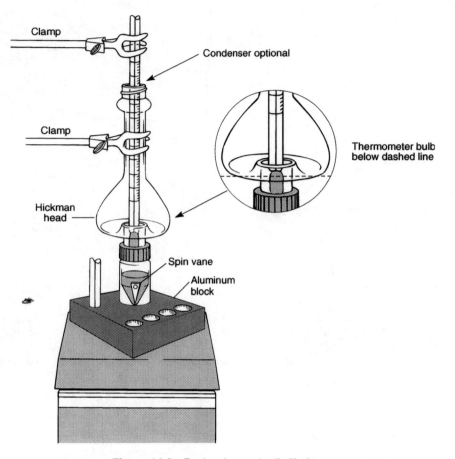

Figure 14.6   Basic microscale distillation.

before it is collected. The liquid is boiled, moves upward through the central stem of the Hickman head, condenses on the walls of the "chimney," and then runs down the sides into the circular well surrounding the stem. With very volatile liquids, a condenser can be placed on top of the Hickman head to improve its efficiency. The apparatus shown uses a 5-mL conical vial as the distilling flask, meaning that this apparatus can distill 1–3 mL of liquid. Unfortunately, the well in most Hickman heads holds only about 0.5–1.0 mL. Thus, the well must be emptied several times using a disposable Pasteur pipet, as shown in Figure 14.7. The figure shows two different styles of Hickman head. The one with the side port makes removal of the distillate easier.

C. Microscale—Research Equipment

Figure 14.8 shows a very well-designed research-style, short-path distillation head. Note how the equipment has been "unitized," eliminating several joints and decreasing the holdup.

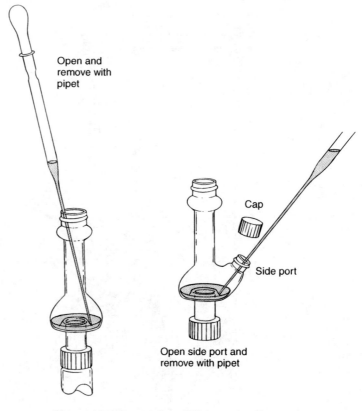

Figure 14.7 Two styles of Hickman head.

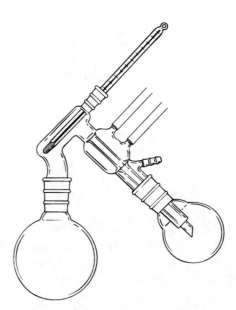

Figure 14.8   A research-style short-path distillation apparatus.

PROBLEMS

1. Using Figure 14.4, answer the following questions.

   a. What is the molar composition of the vapor in equilibrium with a boiling liquid that has a composition of 60% A and 40% B?

   b. A sample of vapor has the composition 50% A and 50% B. What is the composition of the boiling liquid that produced this vapor?

2. Use an apparatus similar to that shown in Figure 14.1 and assume that the round-bottom flask holds 100 mL and the distilling head has an internal volume of 12 mL in the vertical section. At the end of a distillation, vapor would fill this volume, but it could not be forced through the system. No liquid would remain in the distillation flask. Assuming this holdup volume of 112 mL, use the ideal gas law and assume a boiling point of 100 °C (760 mmHg) to calculate the number of milliliters of liquid (d = 0.9 g/mL, MW = 200) that would recondense into the distillation flask upon cooling.

3. Explain the significance of a horizontal line connecting a point on the lower curve with a point on the upper curve (such as line xy) in Figure 14.4.

4. Using Figure 14.4, determine the boiling point of a liquid having a molar composition of 50% A and 50% B.

5. Where should the thermometer bulb be located in the following setups:

   a. a microscale distillation apparatus using a Hickman head?

   b. a macroscale distillation apparatus using a distilling head, condenser, and vacuum takeoff adapter

6. Under what conditions can a good separation be achieved with a simple distillation?

---

15   TECHNIQUE 15

Fractional Distillation, Azeotropes

Sign in at www
.cengage.com/login to
access the Pre-Lab
Video Exercise for this
technique.

Simple distillation, described in Technique 14, works well for most routine separation and purification procedures for organic liquids. When the boiling-point differences of the components to be separated are not large, however, fractional distillation must be used to achieve a good separation.

A typical fractional distillation apparatus is shown in Figure 15.2 in Section 15.1, where the differences between simple and fractional distillation are discussed in detail. This apparatus differs from that for simple distillation by the insertion of a **fractionating column** between the distilling flask and the distillation head. The fractionating column is filled with a **packing**, a material that causes the liquid to condense and revaporize repeatedly as it passes through the column. With a good fractionating column, better separations are possible, and liquids with small boiling-point differences may be separated by using this technique.

PART A. FRACTIONAL DISTILLATION

15.1 Differences between Simple and Fractional Distillation

When an ideal solution of two liquids, such as benzene (bp 80°C) and toluene (bp 110°C), is distilled by simple distillation, the first vapor produced will be enriched in the lower-boiling component (benzene). However, when that initial vapor is condensed and analyzed, the distillate will not be pure benzene. The boiling point difference of benzene and toluene (30°C) is too small to achieve a complete separation by simple distillation. Following the principles outlined in Technique 14, Section 14.2 and using the vapor–liquid composition curve given in Figure 15.1, you can see what would happen if you started with an equimolar mixture of benzene and toluene.

Following the dashed lines shows that an equimolar mixture (50 mole percent benzene) would begin to boil at about 91°C and, far from being 100% benzene, the distillate would contain about 74 mole percent benzene and 26 mole percent toluene. As the distillation continued, the composition of the undistilled liquid would move in the direction of A′ (there would be increased toluene due to removal of more benzene than toluene), and the corresponding vapor would contain a progressively smaller amount of benzene. In effect, the temperature of the distillation would continue to increase throughout the distillation (as in Figure 14.3B), and it would be impossible to obtain any fraction that consisted of pure benzene.

Suppose, however, that we are able to collect a small quantity of the first distillate that was 74 mole percent benzene and redistill it. Using Figure 15.1, we can see that this liquid would begin to boil at about 84°C and would give an initial distillate containing 90 mole percent of benzene. If we were experimentally able to continue taking small fractions at the beginning of each distillation and redistill them, we would eventually reach a liquid with a composition of nearly 100 mole percent benzene. However, since we took only a small amount of material at the beginning of each distillation, we would have lost most of the material we started with. To recapture a reasonable amount of benzene, we would have to process each of the fractions

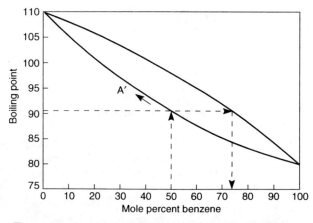

Figure 15.1 The vapor–liquid composition curve for mixtures of benzene and toluene.

left behind in the same way as our early fractions. As each of them was partially distilled, the material advanced would become progressively richer in benzene, and that left behind would become progressively richer in toluene. It would require thousands (maybe millions) of such microdistillations to separate benzene from toluene.

Obviously, the procedure just described would be very tedious; fortunately, it need not be performed in usual laboratory practice. **Fractional distillation** accomplishes the same result. You simply have to use a column inserted between the distillation flask and the distilling head, as shown in Figure 15.2. This **fractionating column** is filled, or **packed**, with a suitable material, such as a stainless-steel sponge. This packing allows a mixture of benzene and toluene to be subjected continuously to many vaporization–condensation cycles as the material moves up the column. With each cycle within the column, the composition of the vapor is progressively enriched in the lower-boiling component (benzene). Nearly pure benzene (bp 80°C) finally emerges from the top of the column, condenses, and passes into the receiving head or flask. This process continues until all of the benzene is removed. The distillation must be carried out slowly to ensure that numerous vaporization–condensation cycles occur. When nearly all of the benzene has been removed, the temperature begins to rise, and a small amount of a second fraction, which contains some benzene and toluene, may be collected. When the temperature reaches 110°C, the boiling point of pure toluene, the vapor is condensed and collected as the third fraction. A plot of boiling point versus volume of condensate (distillate) would resemble Figure 14.3C in Technique 14. This separation would be much better than that achieved by simple distillation (see Figure 14.3B).

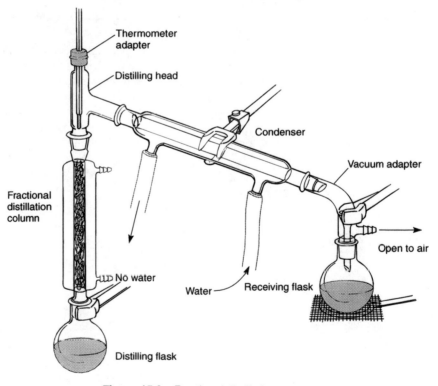

Figure 15.2   Fractional distillation apparatus.

15.2 Vapor–Liquid Composition Diagrams

A vapor–liquid composition phase diagram like the one in Figure 15.3 can be used to explain the operation of a fractionating column with an **ideal solution** of two liquids, A and B. An ideal solution is one in which the two liquids are chemically similar, are miscible (mutually soluble) in all proportions, and do not interact. Ideal solutions obey **Raoult's Law**. Raoult's Law is explained in detail in Section 15.3.

The phase diagram relates the compositions of the boiling liquid (lower curve) and its vapor (upper curve) as a function of temperature. Any horizontal line drawn across the diagram (a constant-temperature line) intersects the diagram in two places. These intersections relate the vapor composition to the composition of the boiling liquid that produces that vapor. By convention, composition is expressed either in **mole fraction** or in **mole percentage**. The mole fraction is defined as follows:

$$\text{Mole fraction A} = N_A = \frac{\text{Moles A}}{\text{Moles A} + \text{Moles B}}$$

$$\text{Mole fraction B} = N_B = \frac{\text{Moles B}}{\text{Moles A} + \text{Moles B}}$$

$$N_A + N_B = 1$$

$$\text{Mole percentage A} = N_A \times 100$$

$$\text{Mole percentage B} = N_B \times 100$$

The horizontal and vertical lines shown in Figure 15.3 represent the processes that occur during a fractional distillation. Each of the **horizontal lines** ($L_1 V_1, L_2 V_2,$ and so on) represents both the **vaporization** step of a given vaporization–condensation cycle and the composition of the vapor in equilibrium with liquid at a given temperature. For example, at 63°C a liquid with a composition of 50% A (L_3 on the diagram) would yield vapor of composition 80% A (V_3 on diagram) at equilibrium. The vapor is richer in the lower-boiling component A than the original liquid was.

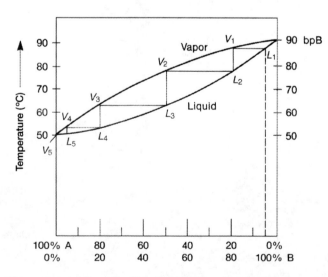

Figure 15.3   Phase diagram for a fractional distillation of an ideal two-component system.

Each of the **vertical lines** (V_1L_2, V_2L_3, and so on) represents the **condensation** step of a given vaporization–condensation cycle. The composition does not change as the temperature drops on condensation. The vapor at V_3, for example, condenses to give a liquid (L_4 on the diagram) of composition 80% A with a drop in temperature from 63°C to 53°C.

In the example shown in Figure 15.3, pure A boils at 50°C, and pure B boils at 90°C. These two boiling points are represented at the left- and right-hand edges of the diagram, respectively. Now consider a solution that contains only 5% of A but 95% of B. (Remember that these are *mole* percentages.) This solution is heated (following the dashed line) until it is observed to boil at L_1 (87°C). The resulting vapor has composition V_1 (20% A, 80% B). The vapor is richer in A than the original liquid was, but it is by no means pure A. In a simple distillation apparatus, this vapor would be condensed and passed into the receiver in a very impure state. However, with a fractionating column in place, the vapor is condensed in the **column** to give liquid L_2 (20% A, 80% B). Liquid L_2 is immediately revaporized (bp 78°C) to give a vapor of composition V_2 (50% A, 50% B), which is condensed to give liquid L_3. Liquid L_3 is revaporized (bp 63°C) to give vapor of composition V_3 (80% A, 20% B), which is condensed to give liquid L_4. Liquid L_4 is revaporized (bp 53°C) to give vapor of composition V_4 (95% A, 5% B). This process continues to V_5, which condenses to give nearly pure liquid A. The fractionating process follows the stepped lines in the figure downward and to the left.

As this process continues, all of liquid A is removed from the distillation flask or vial, leaving nearly pure B behind. If the temperature is raised, liquid B may be distilled as a nearly pure fraction. Fractional distillation will have achieved a separation of A and B, a separation that would have been nearly impossible with simple distillation. Notice that the boiling point of the liquid becomes lower each time it vaporizes. Because the temperature at the bottom of a column is normally higher than the temperature at the top, successive vaporizations occur higher and higher in the column as the composition of the distillate approaches that of pure A. This process is illustrated in Figure 15.4, where the composition of the liquids, their boiling points, and the composition of the vapors present are shown alongside the fractionating column.

15.3 Raoult's Law

Two liquids (A and B) that are miscible and that do not interact form an **ideal solution** and follow Raoult's Law. The law states that the partial vapor pressure of component A in the solution (P_A) equals the vapor pressure of pure A (P_A°) times its mole fraction (N_A) (equation 1). A similar expression can be written for component B (equation 2). The mole fractions N_A and N_B were defined in Section 15.2.

$$\text{Partial vapor pressure of A in solution} = P_A = (P_A^\circ)(N_A) \tag{1}$$

$$\text{Partial vapor pressure of B in solution} = P_B = (P_B^\circ)(N_B) \tag{2}$$

P_A° is the vapor pressure of pure A, independent of B. P_B° is the vapor pressure of pure B, independent of A. In a mixture of A and B, the partial vapor pressures are added to give the total vapor pressure above the solution (equation 3). When the total pressure (sum of the partial pressures) equals the applied pressure, the solution boils.

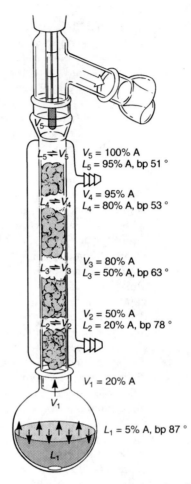

$V_5 = 100\%$ A
$L_5 = 95\%$ A, bp 51 °

$V_4 = 95\%$ A
$L_4 = 80\%$ A, bp 53 °

$V_3 = 80\%$ A
$L_3 = 50\%$ A, bp 63 °

$V_2 = 50\%$ A
$L_2 = 20\%$ A, bp 78 °

$V_1 = 20\%$ A

$L_1 = 5\%$ A, bp 87 °

Figure 15.4   Vaporization–condensation in a fractionation column.

$$P_{\text{total}} = P_A + P_B = P_A^{\circ}N_A + P_B^{\circ}N_B \tag{3}$$

The composition of A and B in the vapor produced is given by equations 4 and 5.

$$N_A \text{ (vapor)} = \frac{P_A}{P_{\text{total}}} \tag{4}$$

$$N_B \text{ (vapor)} = \frac{P_B}{P_{\text{total}}} \tag{5}$$

Several exercises involving applications of Raoult's Law are illustrated in Table 15.1. Note, particularly in the result from equation 4, that the vapor is richer ($N_A = 0.67$) in the lower-boiling (higher vapor pressure) component A than it was before vaporization ($N_A = 0.50$). This proves mathematically what was described in Section 15.2.

The consequences of Raoult's Law for distillations are shown schematically in Figure 15.5. In Part A the boiling points are identical (vapor pressures the same), and no separation is attained regardless of how the distillation is conducted. In Part B a fractional distillation is required, while in Part C a simple distillation provides an adequate separation.

TABLE 15.1   Sample Calculations with Raoult's Law

Consider a solution at 100 °C where $N_A = 0.5$ and $N_B = 0.5$.

1. What is the partial vapor pressure of A in the solution if the vapor pressure of pure A at 100 °C is 1020 mmHg?

    Answer: $P_A = P_A^o N_A = (1020)(0.5) = 510$ mmHg

2. What is the partial vapor pressure of B in the solution if the vapor pressure of pure B at 100 °C is 500 mmHg?

    Answer: $P_B = P_B^o N_B = (500)(0.5) = 250$ mmHg

3. Would the solution boil at 100 °C if the applied pressure were 760 mmHg?

    Answer: Yes. $P_{total} = P_A + P_B = (510 + 250) = 760$ mmHg

4. What is the composition of the vapor at the boiling point?

    Answer: The boiling point is 100 °C.

$$N_A(\text{vapor}) = \frac{P_A}{P_{total}} = 510/760 = 0.67$$

$$N_B(\text{vapor}) = \frac{P_B}{P_{total}} = 250/760 = 0.33$$

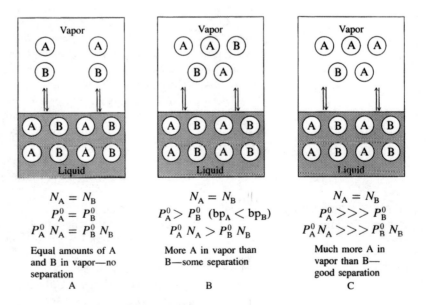

Figure 15.5 Consequences of Raoult's Law. (A) Boiling points (vapor pressures) are identical—no separation. (B) Boiling points somewhat less for A than for B—requires fractional distillation. (C) Boiling points much less for A than for B—simple distillation will suffice.

When a solid B (rather than another liquid) is dissolved in a liquid A, the boiling point is increased. In this extreme case, the vapor pressure of B is negligible, and the vapor will be pure A no matter how much solid B is added. Consider a solution of salt in water.

$$P_{total} = P^\circ_{water}N_{water} + P^\circ_{salt}N_{salt}$$

$$P^\circ_{salt} = 0$$

$$P_{total} = P^\circ_{water}N_{water}$$

A solution whose mole fraction of water is 0.7 will not boil at 100°C, because P_{total} = (760)(0.7) = 532 mmHg and is less than atmospheric pressure. If the solution is heated to 110°C, it will boil because P_{total} = (1085)(0.7) = 760 mmHg. Although the solution must be heated at 110°C to boil it, the vapor is pure water and has a boiling-point temperature of 100°C. (The vapor pressure of water at 110°C can be looked up in a handbook; it is 1085 mmHg.)

15.4 Column Efficiency

A common measure of the efficiency of a column is given by its number of **theoretical plates**. The number of theoretical plates in a column is related to the number of vaporization–condensation cycles that occur as a liquid mixture travels through it. Using the example mixture in Figure 15.3, if the first distillate (condensed vapor) had the composition at L_2 when starting with liquid of composition L_1, the column would be said to have *one theoretical plate*. This would correspond to a simple distillation, or one vaporization–condensation cycle. A column would have two theoretical plates if the first distillate had the composition at L_3. The two-theoretical-plate column essentially carries out "two simple distillations." According to Figure 15.3, *five theoretical plates* would be required to separate the mixture that started with composition L_1. Notice that this corresponds to the number of "steps" that need to be drawn in the figure to arrive at a composition of 100% A.

Most columns do not allow distillation in discrete steps, as indicated in Figure 15.3. Instead, the process is *continuous*, allowing the vapors to be continuously in contact with liquid of changing composition as they pass through the column. Any material can be used to pack the column as long as it can be wetted by the liquid and does not pack so tightly that vapor cannot pass.

The approximate relationship between the number of theoretical plates needed to separate an ideal two-component mixture and the difference in boiling points is given in Table 15.2. Notice that more theoretical plates are required as the boiling-point differences between the components decrease. For instance, a mixture of A (bp 130°C) and B (bp 166°C) with a boiling-point difference of 36°C would be expected to require a column with a minimum of five theoretical plates.

15.5 Types of Fractionating Columns and Packings

Several types of fractionating columns are shown in Figure 15.6. The Vigreux column (A) has indentations that incline downward at angles of 45° and are in pairs on opposite sides of the column. The projections into the column provide increased possibilities for condensation and for the vapor to equilibrate with the liquid. Vigreux columns are popular in cases where only a small number of theoretical plates are required. They are not very efficient (a 20-cm column might have only 2.5 theoretical plates), but they allow for rapid distillation and have a small **holdup** (the amount of liquid retained by the column). A column packed with a stainless-steel sponge is a

TABLE 15.2   Theoretical Plates Required to Separate Mixtures, Based on Boiling-Point Differences of Components

Boiling-Point Difference	Number of Theoretical Plates
108	1
72	2
54	3
43	4
36	5
20	10
10	20
7	30
4	50
2	100

more effective fractionating column than a Vigreux column, but not by a large margin. Glass beads or glass helices can also be used as a packing material, and they have even a slightly greater efficiency. The air condenser or the water condenser can be used as an improvised column if an actual fractionating column is unavailable. If a condenser is packed with glass beads, glass helices, or sections of glass tubing, the packing must be held in place by inserting a small plug of stainless steel sponge into the bottom of the condenser.

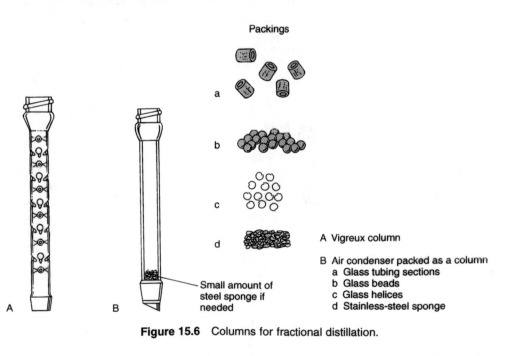

Figure 15.6   Columns for fractional distillation.

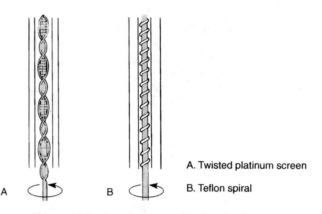

A. Twisted platinum screen

B. Teflon spiral

Figure 15.7   Bands for spinning-band columns.

The most effective type of column is the **spinning-band column**. In the most elegant form of this device, a tightly fitting, twisted platinum screen or a Teflon rod with helical threads is rotated rapidly inside the bore of the column (see Figure 15.7). A spinning-band column that is available for microscale work is shown in Figure 15.8. This spinning-band column has a band about 2–3 cm in length and provides four or five theoretical plates. It can separate 1–2 mL of a mixture with a 30°C boiling-point difference. Larger research models of this spinning-band column can provide as many as 20 or 30 theoretical plates and can separate mixtures with a boiling-point difference of as little as 5–10°C.

Manufacturers of fractionating columns often offer them in a variety of lengths. Because the efficiency of a column is a function of its length, longer columns have more theoretical plates than shorter ones do. It is common to express efficiency of a column in a unit called **HETP**, the **H**eight of a column that is **E**quivalent to one **T**heoretical **P**late. HETP is usually expressed in units of cm/plate. When the height of the column (in centimeters) is divided by this value, the total number of theoretical plates is specified.

Fractionating columns must be insulated so that temperature equilibrium is maintained at all times. External temperature fluctuations will interfere with a good separation. Many fractionating columns are jacketed as a condenser is, but instead of water passing through the outer jacket, the jacket is evacuated and sealed. A vacuum jacket provides very good insulation of the inner column from the outside air temperature. In most student macroscale kits, the fractionating column is not evacuated but does have a jacket for insulation. This jacket, even though not evacuated, is usually sufficient for the demands of the introductory laboratory. The fractionating column looks very much like a water condenser; however, it has a larger diameter both for the inner tube and for the jacket. Be sure to take care to distinguish the larger-diameter fractionating column from the smaller-diameter water condenser.

15.6 Fractional Distillation: Methods and Practice

Many fractionating columns must be insulated so that temperature equilibrium is maintained at all times. Additional insulation will not be required for columns that have an outer jacket, but those that do not can benefit from being wrapped in insulation.

Figure 15.8 A commercially available microscale spinning-band column.

Cotton and aluminum foil (shiny side in) are often used for insulation. You can wrap the column with cotton and then use a wrapping of the aluminum foil to keep it in place. Another version of this method, which is especially effective, is to make an insulation blanket by placing a layer of cotton between two rectangles of aluminum foil, placed shiny side in. The sandwich is bound together with duct tape. This blanket, which is reusable, can be wrapped around the column and held in place with twist ties or tape.

The **reflux ratio** is defined as the ratio of the number of drops of distillate that return to the distillation flask compared to the number of drops of distillate collected. In an efficient column, the reflux ratio should equal or exceed the number of theoretical plates. A high reflux ratio ensures that the column will achieve temperature equilibrium and achieve its maximum efficiency. This ratio is not easy to determine; in fact, it is impossible to determine when using a Hickman head, and it should not concern a beginning student. In some cases, the **throughput**, or **rate of takeoff**, of a column may be specified. This is expressed as the number of milliliters of distillate that can be collected per unit of time, usually as mL/min.

Macroscale Apparatus. Figure 15.2 illustrates a fractional distillation assembly that can be used for larger-scale distillations. It has a glass-jacketed column that is packed with a stainless-steel sponge. This apparatus would be common in situations where quantities of liquid in excess of 10 mL were to be distilled.

In a fractional distillation, the column should be clamped in a vertical position. The distilling flask would normally be heated by a heating mantle, which allows a precise adjustment of the temperature. A proper rate of distillation is extremely important. The distillation should be conducted as slowly as possible to allow as many vaporization–condensation cycles as possible to occur as the vapor passes through the column. However, the rate of distillation must be steady enough to produce a constant temperature reading at the thermometer. A rate that is too fast will cause the column to "flood" or "choke." In this instance, there is so much condensing liquid flowing downward in the column that the vapor cannot rise upward, and the column fills with liquid. Flooding can also occur if the column is not well insulated and has a large temperature difference from bottom to top. This situation can be remedied by employing one of the insulation methods that uses cotton or aluminum foil, as described in Section 15.5. It may also be necessary to insulate the distilling head at the top of the column. If the distilling head is cold, it will stop the progress of the distilling vapor. The distillation temperature can be monitored most accurately by using a partial immersion mercury thermometer (see Technique 13, Section 13.4).

Microscale Apparatus. The apparatus shown in Figure 15.9 is the one you are most likely to use in the microscale laboratory. If your laboratory is one of the better equipped ones, you may have access to spinning-band columns like the one shown in Figure 15.8.

PART B. AZEOTROPES

15.7 Nonideal Solutions: Azeotropes

Some mixtures of liquids, because of attractions or repulsions between the molecules, do not behave ideally; they do not follow Raoult's Law. There are two types of vapor–liquid composition diagrams that result from this nonideal behavior: **minimum-boiling-point** and **maximum-boiling-point** diagrams. The minimum or maximum points in these diagrams correspond to a constant-boiling mixture called an **azeotrope**. An azeotrope is a mixture with a fixed composition that cannot be altered by either simple or fractional distillation. An azeotrope behaves as if it were a pure compound, and it distills from the beginning to the end of its distillation at a constant temperature, giving a distillate of constant (azeotropic) composition. The vapor in equilibrium with an azeotropic liquid has the same composition as the azeotrope. Because of this, an azeotrope is represented as a *point* on a vapor–liquid composition diagram.

A. Minimum-Boiling-Point Diagrams

A minimum-boiling-point azeotrope results from a slight incompatibility (repulsion) between the liquids being mixed. This incompatibility leads to a higher-than-expected combined vapor pressure from the solution. This higher combined vapor pressure brings about a lower boiling point for the mixture than is observed for the pure components. The most common two-component mixture that gives a minimum-boiling-point azeotrope is the ethanol–water system shown in Figure 15.10.

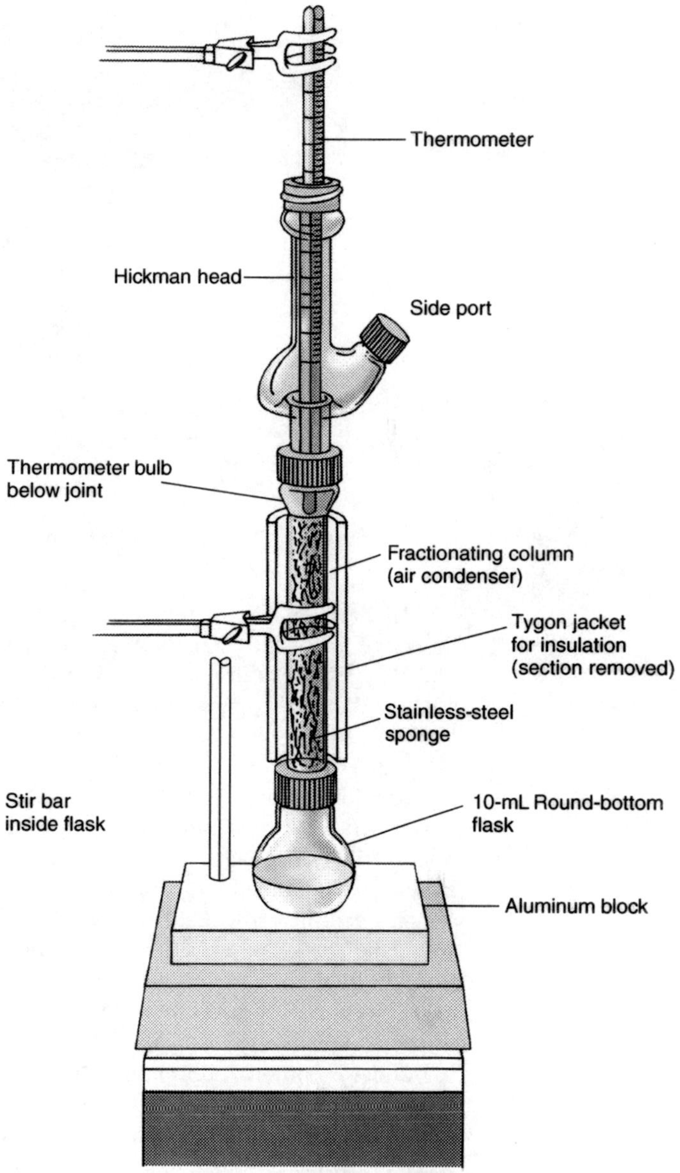

Figure 15.9   Microscale apparatus for fractional distillation.

The azeotrope at V_3 has a composition of 96% ethanol–4% water and a boiling point of 78.1°C. This boiling point is not much lower than that of pure ethanol (78.3°C), but it means that it is impossible to obtain pure ethanol from the distillation of any ethanol–water mixture that contains more than 4% water. Even with the best fractionating column, you cannot obtain 100% ethanol. The remaining 4% of water can be removed by adding benzene and removing a different azeotrope, the ternary benzene–water–ethanol azeotrope (bp 65°C). Once the water is removed, the excess benzene is removed as an ethanol–benzene azeotrope (bp 68°C). The resulting material is free of water and is called "absolute" ethanol.

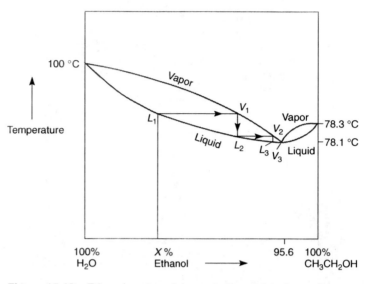

Figure 15.10   Ethanol–water minimum-boiling-point phase diagram.

The fractional distillation of an ethanol–water mixture of composition X can be described as follows. The mixture is heated (follow line XL_1) until it is observed to boil at L_1. The resulting vapor at V_1 will be richer in the lower-boiling component, ethanol, than the original mixture was.[1] The condensate at L_2 is vaporized to give V_2. The process continues, following the lines to the right, until the azeotrope is obtained at V_3. The liquid that distills is not pure ethanol, but it has the azeotropic composition of 96% ethanol and 4% water, and it distills at 78.1°C. The azeotrope, which is richer in ethanol than the original mixture was, continues to distill. As it distills, the percentage of water left behind in the distillation flask continues to increase. When all the ethanol has been distilled (as the azeotrope), pure water remains behind in the distillation flask, and it distills at 100°C.

If the azeotrope obtained by the preceding procedure is redistilled, it distills from the beginning to the end of the distillation at a constant temperature of 78.1°C as if it were a pure substance. There is no change in the composition of the vapor during the distillation.

Some common minimum-boiling-point azeotropes are given in Table 15.3. Numerous other azeotropes are formed in two- and three-component systems; such azeotropes are common. Water forms azeotropes with many substances; therefore, water must be carefully removed with **drying agents** whenever possible before compounds are distilled. Extensive azeotropic data are available in references such as the *CRC Handbook of Chemistry and Physics*.[2]

B. Maximum-Boiling-Point Diagrams

A maximum-boiling-point azeotrope results from a slight attraction between the component molecules. This attraction leads to lower combined vapor pressure

---

[1] Keep in mind that this distillate is not pure ethanol, but is an ethanol–water mixture.
[2] More examples of azeotropes, with their compositions and boiling points, can be found in the *CRC Handbook of Chemistry and Physics*; also in L. H. Horsley, ed., *Advances in Chemistry Series*, No. 116, Azeotropic Data, III (Washington, DC: American Chemical Society, 1973).

TABLE 15.3   Common Minimum-Boiling-Point Azeotropes

Azeotrope	Composition (Weight Percentage)	Boiling Point (°C)
Ethanol–water	95.6% C_2H_5OH, 4.4% H_2O	78.17
Benzene–water	91.1% C_6H_6, 8.9% H_2O	69.4
Benzene–water–ethanol	74.1% C_6H_6, 7.4% H_2O, 18.5% C_2H_5OH	64.9
Methanol–carbon tetrachloride	20.6% CH_3OH, 79.4% CCl_4	55.7
Ethanol–benzene	32.4% C_2H_5OH, 67.6% C_6H_6	67.8
Methanol–toluene	72.4% CH_3OH, 27.6% $C_6H_5CH_3$	63.7
Methanol–benzene	39.5% CH_3OH, 60.5% C_6H_6	58.3
Cyclohexane–ethanol	69.5% C_6H_{12}, 30.5% C_2H_5OH	64.9
2-Propanol–water	87.8% $(CH_3)_2CHOH$, 12.2% H_2O	80.4
Butyl acetate–water	72.9% $CH_3COOC_4H_9$, 27.1% H_2O	90.7
Phenol–water	9.2% C_6H_5OH, 90.8% H_2O	99.5

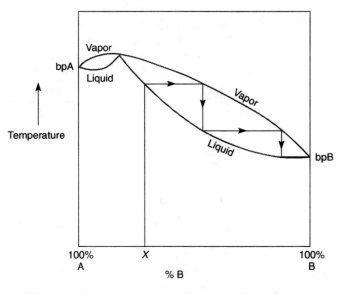

Figure 15.11   A maximum-boiling-point phase diagram.

than expected in the solution. The lower combined vapor pressures cause a higher boiling point than what would be characteristic for the components. A two-component maximum-boiling-point azeotrope is illustrated in Figure 15.11. Because the azeotrope has a higher boiling point than any of the components, it will be concentrated in the distillation flask as the distillate (pure B) is removed. The distillation of a solution of composition X would follow to the right along the lines in Figure 15.11. Once the composition of the material remaining in the flask has reached that of the azeotrope, the temperature will rise, and the azeotrope will begin to distill. The azeotrope will continue to distill until all of the material in the distillation flask has been exhausted.

TABLE 15.4   Maximum-Boiling-Point Azeotropes

Azeotrope	Composition (Weight Percentage)	Boiling Point (°C)
Acetone–chloroform	20.0% CH_3COCH_3, 80.0% $CHCl_3$	64.7
Chloroform–methyl ethyl ketone	17.0% $CHCl_3$, 83.0% $CH_3COCH_2CH_3$	79.9
Hydrochloric acid	20.2% HCl, 79.8% H_2O	108.6
Acetic acid–dioxane	77.0% CH_3COCH, 23.0% $C_4H_8O_2$	119.5
Benzaldehyde–phenol	49.0% C_6H_5CHO, 51.0% C_6H_5OH	185.6

Some maximum-boiling-point azeotropes are listed in Table 15.4. They are not nearly as common as minimum-boiling-point azeotropes.[3]

C. Generalizations

There are some generalizations that can be made about azeotropic behavior. They are presented here without explanation, but you should be able to verify them by thinking through each case using the phase diagrams given. (Note that pure A is always to the left of the azeotrope in these diagrams, and pure B is to the right of the azeotrope.)

Minimum-Boiling-Point Azeotropes

Initial Composition	Experimental Result
To left of azeotrope	Azeotrope distills first, pure A second
Azeotrope	Inseparable
To right of azeotrope	Azeotrope distills first, pure B second

Maximum-Boiling-Point Azeotropes

Initial Composition	Experimental Result
To left of azeotrope	Pure A distills first, azeotrope second
Azeotrope	Inseparable
To right of azeotrope	Pure B distills first, azeotrope second

15.8 Azeotropic Distillation: Applications

There are numerous examples of chemical reactions in which the amount of product is low because of an unfavorable equilibrium. An example is the direct acid-catalyzed esterification of a carboxylic acid with an alcohol:

$$R-\overset{\overset{\displaystyle O}{\|}}{C}-OH + R-O-H \overset{H^+}{\rightleftharpoons} R-\overset{\overset{\displaystyle O}{\|}}{C}-OR + H_2O$$

---

[3] See footnote 2.

Because the equilibrium does not favor formation of the ester, it must be shifted to the right, in favor of the product, by using an excess of one of the starting materials. In most cases, the alcohol is the least expensive reagent and is the material used in excess. Isopentyl acetate (Experiment 12) is an example of an ester prepared by using one of the starting materials in excess.

Another way of shifting the equilibrium to the right is to remove one of the products from the reaction mixture as it is formed. In the previous example, water can be removed as it is formed by **azeotropic distillation**. A common large-scale method is to use the Dean–Stark water separator shown in Figure 15.12A. In this technique, an inert solvent, commonly benzene or toluene, is added to the reaction mixture contained in the round-bottom flask. The sidearm of the water separator is also filled with this solvent. If benzene is used, as the mixture is heated under reflux, the benzene–water azeotrope (bp 69.4°C, Table 15.3) distills out of the flask.[4] When the vapor condenses, it enters the sidearm directly below the condenser, and water separates from the benzene–water condensate; benzene and water mix as vapors, but they are not miscible as cooled liquids. Once the water (lower phase) separates from the benzene (upper phase), liquid benzene overflows from the sidearm back into the flask. The cycle is repeated continuously until no more water forms in the sidearm. You may calculate the weight of water that should theoretically be produced and compare this value with the amount of water collected in the sidearm. Because the density of water is 1.0, the volume of water collected can be compared directly with the calculated amount, assuming 100% yield.

An improvised water separator, constructed from the components found in the traditional organic kit, is shown in Figure 15.12B. Although this requires the condenser to be placed in a nonvertical position, it works quite well.

At the microscale level, water separation can be achieved using a standard distillation assembly with a water condenser and a Hickman head (see Figure 15.13). The side-ported variation of the Hickman head is the most convenient one to use for this purpose, but it is not essential. In this variation, you simply remove all of the distillate (both solvent and water) several times during the course of the reaction. Use a Pasteur pipet to remove the distillate, as shown in Technique 14 (see Figure 14.7). Because both the solvent and water are removed in this procedure, it may be desirable to add more solvent from time to time, adding it through the condenser with a Pasteur pipet.

The most important consideration in using azeotropic distillation to prepare an ester (described on the previous page) is that the azeotrope containing water must have a **lower boiling point** than the alcohol used. With ethanol, the benzene–water azeotrope boils at a much lower temperature (69.4°C) than ethanol (78.3°C), and the technique previously described works well. With higher-boiling-point alcohols, azeotropic distillation works well because of the large boiling-point difference between the azeotrope and the alcohol.

With methanol (bp 65°C), however, the boiling point of the benzene–water azeotrope is actually *higher* by about 5°C, and methanol distills first. Thus, in esterifications involving methanol, a totally different approach must be taken.

---

[4] Actually, with ethanol, a lower-boiling-point, three-component azeotrope distills at 64.9°C (see Table 15.3). It consists of benzene–water–ethanol. Because some ethanol is lost in the azeotropic distillation, a large excess of ethanol is used in esterification reactions. The excess also helps to shift the equilibrium to the right.

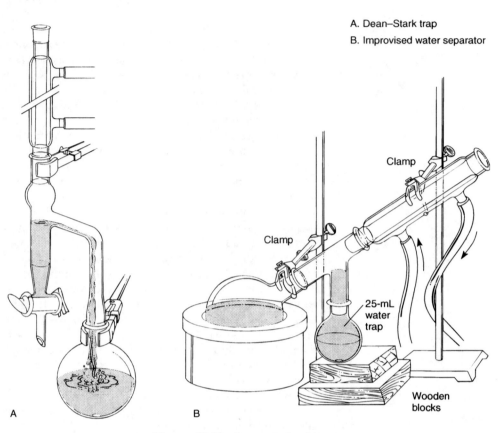

A. Dean–Stark trap

B. Improvised water separator

Clamp

Clamp

25-mL
water
trap

Wooden
blocks

A   B

Figure 15.12   Large-scale water separators.

For example, you can mix the carboxylic acid, methanol, the acid catalyst, and *1,2-dichloroethane* in a conventional reflux apparatus (see Technique 7, Figure 7.6) without a water separator. During the reaction, water separates from the 1,2-dichlo-roethane because it is not miscible; however, the remainder of the components are soluble, so the reaction can continue. The equilibrium is shifted to the right by the "removal" of water from the reaction mixture.

Azeotropic distillation is also used in other types of reactions, such as ketal or acetal formation, and in enamine formation.

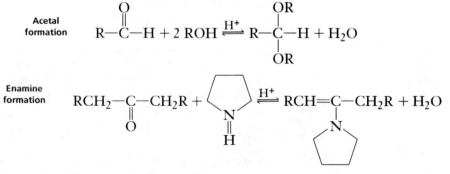

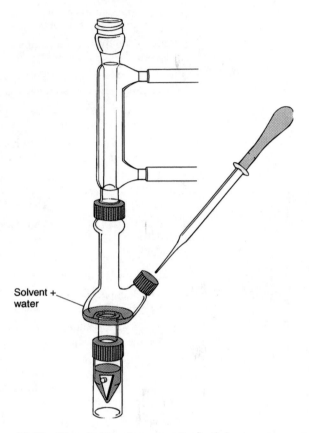

Figure 15.13 Microscale water separator (both layers are removed).

PROBLEMS

1. In the accompanying chart are approximate vapor pressures for benzene and toluene at various temperatures.

Temp (°C)	mmHg	Temp (°C)	mmHg
Benzene 30	120	Toluene 30	37
40	180	40	60
50	270	50	95
60	390	60	140
70	550	70	200
80	760	80	290
90	1010	90	405
100	1340	100	560
		110	760

a. What is the mole fraction of each component if 3.9 g of benzene (C_6H_6) is dissolved in 4.6 g of toluene (C_7H_8)?

b. Assuming that this mixture is ideal, that is, it follows Raoult's Law, what is the partial vapor pressure of benzene in this mixture at 50 °C?

c. Estimate to the nearest degree the temperature at which the vapor pressure of the solution equals 1 atm (bp of the solution).

d. Calculate the composition of the vapor (mole fraction of each component) that is in equilibrium in the solution at the boiling point of this solution.

e. Calculate the composition in weight percentage of the vapor that is in equilibrium with the solution.

2. Estimate how many theoretical plates are needed to separate a mixture that has a mole fraction of B equal to 0.70 (70% B) in Figure 15.3.

3. Two moles of sucrose are dissolved in 8 moles of water. Assume that the solution follows Raoult's Law and that the vapor pressure of sucrose is negligible. The boiling point of water is 100 °C. The distillation is carried out at 1 atm (760 mmHg).

a. Calculate the vapor pressure of the solution when the temperature reaches 100 °C.

b. What temperature would be observed during the entire distillation?

c. What would be the composition of the distillate?

d. If a thermometer were immersed below the surface of the liquid of the boiling flask, what temperature would be observed?

4. Explain why the boiling point of a two-component mixture rises slowly throughout a simple distillation when the boiling-point differences are not large.

5. Given the boiling points of several known mixtures of A and B (mole fractions are known) and the vapor pressures of A and B in the pure state (P_A° and P_B°) at these same temperatures, how would you construct a boiling-point-composition phase diagram for A and B? Give a stepwise explanation.

6. Describe the behavior upon distillation of a 98% ethanol solution through an efficient column. Refer to Figure 15.10.

7. Construct an approximate boiling-point-composition diagram for a benzene-methanol system. The mixture shows azeotropic behavior (see Table 15.3). Include on the graph the boiling points of pure benzene and pure methanol and the boiling point of the azeotrope. Describe the behavior for a mixture that is initially rich in benzene (90%) and then for a mixture that is initially rich in methanol (90%).

8. Construct an approximate boiling-point-composition diagram for an acetone–chloroform system, which forms a maximum-boiling-point azeotrope (see Table 15.4). Describe the behavior upon distillation of a mixture that is initially rich in acetone (90%), and then describe the behavior of a mixture that is initially rich in chloroform (90%).

9. Two components have boiling points of 130 °C and 150 °C. Estimate the number of theoretical plates needed to separate these substances in a fractional distillation.

10. A spinning-band column has an HETP of 0.25 in./plate. If the column has 12 theoretical plates, how long is it?

22   **TECHNIQUE 22**

Gas Chromatography

Gas chromatography is one of the most useful instrumental tools for separating and analyzing organic compounds that can be vaporized without decomposition. Common uses include testing the purity of a substance and separating the components of a mixture. The relative amounts of the components in a mixture may also be determined. In some cases, gas chromatography can be used to identify a compound. In microscale work, it can also be used as a preparative method to isolate pure compounds from a small amount of a mixture.

Gas chromatography resembles column chromatography in principle, but it differs in three respects. First, the partitioning processes for the compounds to be separated are carried out between a **moving gas phase** and a **stationary liquid phase**. (Recall that in column chromatography, the moving phase is a liquid, and the stationary phase is a solid adsorbent.) Second, the temperature of the gas system can be controlled, because the column is contained in an insulated oven. And third, the concentration of any given compound in the gas phase is a function of its vapor pressure only. Because gas chromatography separates the components of a mixture primarily on the basis of their vapor pressures (or boiling points), this technique is also similar in principle to fractional distillation. In microscale work, it is sometimes used to separate and isolate compounds from a mixture; fractional distillation would normally be used with larger amounts of material.

Gas chromatography (GC) is also known as vapor-phase chromatography (VPC) and as gas–liquid partition chromatography (GLPC). All three names, as well as their indicated abbreviations, are often found in the literature of organic chemistry. In reference to the technique, the last term, GLPC, is the most strictly correct and is preferred by most authors.

22.1 The Gas Chromatograph

The apparatus used to carry out a gas–liquid chromatographic separation is generally called a **gas chromatograph**. A typical student-model gas chromatograph, the GOW-MAC model 69-350, is illustrated in Figure 22.1. A schematic block diagram of a basic gas chromatograph is shown in Figure 22.2. The basic elements of the apparatus are apparent. The sample is injected into the chromatograph, and it is immediately vaporized in a heated injection chamber and introduced into a moving stream of gas, called the **carrier gas**. The vaporized sample is then swept into a column filled with particles coated with a liquid adsorbent. The column is contained in a

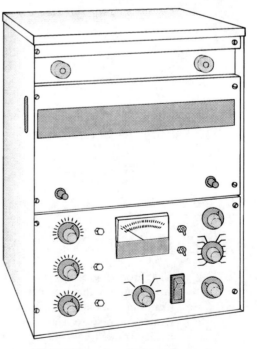

Figure 22.1   A gas chromatograph.

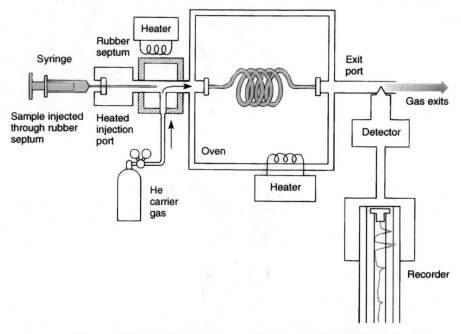

Figure 22.2   A schematic diagram of a gas chromatograph.

temperature-controlled oven. As the sample passes through the column, it is subjected to many gas–liquid partitioning processes, and the components are separated. As each component leaves the column, its presence is detected by an electrical detector that generates a signal that is recorded on a strip chart recorder.

Many modern instruments are also equipped with a microprocessor, which can be programmed to change parameters, such as the temperature of the oven, while a mixture is being separated on a column. With this capability, it is possible to optimize the separation of components and to complete a run in a relatively short time.

22.2 The Column

The heart of the gas chromatograph is the packed column. This column is usually made of copper or stainless steel tubing, but sometimes glass is used. The most common diameters of tubing are $\frac{1}{8}$ inch (3 mm) and $\frac{1}{4}$ inch (6 mm). To construct a column, cut a piece of tubing to the desired length and attach the proper fittings on each of the two ends to connect to the apparatus. The most common length is 4–12 feet, but some columns may be up to 50 feet in length.

The tubing (column) is then packed with the **stationary phase**. The material chosen for the stationary phase is usually a liquid, a wax, or a low-melting solid. This material should be relatively nonvolatile; that is, it should have a low vapor pressure and a high boiling point. Liquids commonly used are high-boiling hydrocarbons, silicone oils, waxes, and polymeric esters, ethers, and amides. Some typical substances are listed in Table 22.1.

The liquid phase is usually coated onto a **support material**. A common support material is crushed firebrick. Many methods exist for coating the high-boiling liquid phase onto the support particles. The easiest is to dissolve the liquid (or low-melting wax or solid) in a volatile solvent such as methylene chloride (bp 40°C). The firebrick (or other support) is added to this solution, which is then slowly evaporated (rotary evaporator) so as to leave each particle of support material evenly coated. Other support materials are listed in Table 22.2.

TABLE 22.1   Typical Liquid Phases

		Type	Composition	Maximum Temperature (°C)	Typical Use
Increasing polarity	Apiezons (L, M, N, etc.)	Hydrocarbon greases (varying MW)	Hydrocarbon mixtures	250–300	Hydrocarbons
	SE-30	Methyl silicone rubber	Like silicone oil, but cross-linked	350	General applications
	DC-200	Silicone oil (R = CH$_3$)	$R_3Si-O-\left[\begin{array}{c}R\\|\\Si-O\\|\\R\end{array}\right]_n-SiR_3$	225	Aldehydes, ketones, halocarbons
	DC-710	Silicone oil (R = CH$_3$) (R′ = C$_6$H$_5$)	$\left[\begin{array}{c}R'\\|\\Si-O\\|\\R\end{array}\right]_n$	300	General applications
	Carbowaxes (400–20M)	Polyethylene glycols (varying chain lengths)	Polyether $HO-(CH_2CH_2-O)n-CH_2CH_2OH$	Up to 250	Alcohols, ethers, halocarbons
	DEGS	Diethylene glycol succinate	Polyester $\left(CH_2CH_2-O-\underset{\underset{O}{\|}}{C}-(CH_2)_2-\underset{\underset{C}{\|}}{C}-O\right)_n$	200	General applications

TABLE 22.2   Typical Solid Supports

Crushed firebrick	Chromosorb T
Nylon beads	(Teflon beads)
Glass beads	Chromosorb P
Silica	(pink diatomaceous earth,
Alumina	high absorptivity, pH 6–7)
Charcoal	Chromosorb W
Molecular sieves	(white diatomaceous earth,
	medium absorptivity, pH 8–10)
	Chromosorb G
	(like the above,
	low absorptivity, pH 8.5)

In the final step, the liquid-phase-coated support material is packed into the tubing as evenly as possible. The tubing is bent or coiled so that it fits into the oven of the gas chromatograph with its two ends connected to the gas entrance and exit ports.

Selection of a liquid phase usually revolves around two factors. First, most liquid phases have an upper temperature limit above which they cannot be used. Above the specified limit of temperature, the liquid phase itself will begin to "bleed" off the column. Second, the materials to be separated must be considered. For polar samples, it is usually best to use a polar liquid phase; for nonpolar samples, a nonpolar liquid phase is indicated. The liquid phase performs best when the substances to be separated *dissolve* in it.

Most researchers today buy packed columns from commercial sources rather than pack their own. A wide variety of types and lengths is available.

Alternatives to packed columns are Golay or glass capillary columns of diameters 0.1–0.2 mm. With these columns, no solid support is required, and the liquid is coated directly on the inner walls of the tubing. Liquid phases commonly used in glass capillary columns are similar in composition to those used in packed columns. They include DB-1 (similar to SE-30), DB-17 (similar to DC-710), and DB-WAX (similar to Carbowax 20M). The length of a capillary column is usually very long, typically 50–100 feet. Because of the length and small diameter, there is increased interaction between the sample and the stationary phase. Gas chromatographs equipped with these small-diameter columns are able to separate components more effectively than instruments using larger packed columns.

22.3 Principles of Separation

After a column is selected, packed, and installed, the **carrier gas** (usually helium, argon, or nitrogen) is allowed to flow through the column supporting the liquid phase. The mixture of compounds to be separated is introduced into the carrier gas stream, where its components are equilibrated (or partitioned) between the moving gas phase and the stationary liquid phase (see Figure 22.3). The latter is held stationary because it is adsorbed onto the surfaces of the support material.

The sample is introduced into the gas chromatograph by a microliter syringe. It is injected as a liquid or as a solution through a rubber septum into a heated chamber, called the **injection port**, where it is vaporized and mixed with the carrier gas.

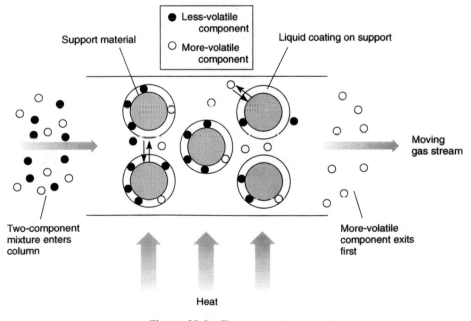

Figure 22.3 The separation process.

As this mixture reaches the column, which is heated in a controlled oven, it begins to equilibrate between the liquid and gas phases. The length of time required for a sample to move through the column is a function of how much time the sample spends in the vapor phase and how much time it spends in the liquid phase. The more time the sample spends in the vapor phase, the faster it gets to the end of the column. In most separations, the components of a sample have similar solubilities in the liquid phase. Therefore, the time the different compounds spend in the vapor phase is primarily a function of the vapor pressure of the compounds, and the more-volatile component arrives at the end of the column first, as illustrated in Figure 22.3. When the correct temperature of the oven and the correct liquid phase have been selected, the compounds in the injected mixture travel through the column at different rates and are separated.

22.4 Factors Affecting Separation

Several factors determine the rate at which a given compound travels through a gas chromatograph. First, compounds with low boiling points will generally travel through the gas chromatograph faster than compounds with higher boiling points. The reason is that the column is heated, and low-boiling compounds always have higher vapor pressures than higher-boiling compounds. In general, therefore, for compounds with the same functional group, the higher the molecular weight, the longer the retention time. For most molecules, the boiling point increases as the molecular weight increases. If the column is heated to a temperature that is too high, however, the entire mixture to be separated is flushed through the column at the same rate as the carrier gas, and no equilibration takes place with the liquid phase. On the other hand, at too low a temperature, the mixture dissolves in the liquid phase and never revaporizes. Thus, it is retained on the column.

The second factor is the rate of flow of the carrier gas. The carrier gas must not move so rapidly that molecules of the sample in the vapor phase cannot equilibrate with those dissolved in the liquid phase. This may result in poor separation between components in the injected mixture. If the rate of flow is too slow, however, the bands broaden significantly, leading to poor resolution (see Section 22.8).

The third factor is the choice of liquid phase used in the column. The molecular weights, functional groups, and polarities of the component molecules in the mixture to be separated must be considered when a liquid phase is being chosen. A different type of material is generally used for hydrocarbons, for instance, than for esters. The materials to be separated should dissolve in the liquid. The useful temperature limit of the liquid phase selected must also be considered.

The fourth factor is the length of the column. Compounds that resemble one another closely, in general, require longer columns than dissimilar compounds. Many kinds of isomeric mixtures fit into the "difficult" category. The components of isomeric mixtures are so much alike that they travel through the column at very similar rates. You need a longer column, therefore, to take advantage of any differences that may exist.

22.5 Advantages of Gas Chromatography

All factors that have been mentioned must be adjusted by the chemist for any mixture to be separated. Considerable preliminary investigation is often required before a mixture can be separated successfully into its components by gas chromatography. Nevertheless, the advantages of the technique are many.

First, many mixtures can be separated by this technique when no other method is adequate. Second, as little as 1–10 μL (1 μL = 10^{-6} L) of a mixture can be separated by this technique. This advantage is particularly important when working at the microscale level. Third, when gas chromatography is coupled with an electronic recording device (see the following discussion), the amount of each component present in the separated mixture can be estimated quantitatively.

The range of compounds that can be separated by gas chromatography extends from gases, such as oxygen (bp −183°C) and nitrogen (bp −196°C), to organic compounds with boiling points over 400°C. The only requirement for the compounds to be separated is that they have an appreciable vapor pressure at a temperature at which they can be separated and that they be thermally stable at this temperature.

22.6 Monitoring The Column (The Detector)

To follow the separation of the mixture injected into the gas chromatograph, it is necessary to use an electrical device called a **detector**. Two types of detectors in common use are the **thermal conductivity detector (TCD)** and the **flame-ionization detector (FID)**.

The thermal conductivity detector is simply a hot wire placed in the gas stream at the column exit. The wire is heated by constant electrical voltage. When a steady stream of carrier gas passes over this wire, the rate at which it loses heat and its electrical conductance have constant values. When the composition of the vapor stream changes, the rate of heat flow from the wire, and hence its resistance, changes. Helium, which has a thermal conductivity higher than that of most organic substances, is a common carrier gas. Thus, when a substance elutes in the vapor stream, the thermal conductivity of the moving gases will be lower than with helium alone. The wire then heats up, and its resistance decreases.

A typical TCD operates by difference. Two detectors are used: one exposed to the actual effluent gas and the other exposed to a reference flow of carrier gas only. To achieve this situation, a portion of the carrier gas stream is diverted before it enters the injection port. The diverted gas is routed through a reference column into which no sample has been admitted. The detectors mounted in the sample and reference columns are arranged to form the arms of a Wheatstone bridge circuit, as shown in Figure 22.4. As long as the carrier gas alone flows over both detectors, the circuit is in balance. However, when a sample elutes from the sample column, the bridge circuit becomes unbalanced, creating an electrical signal. This signal can be amplified and used to activate a strip chart recorder. The recorder is an instrument that plots, by means of a moving pen, the unbalanced bridge current versus time on a

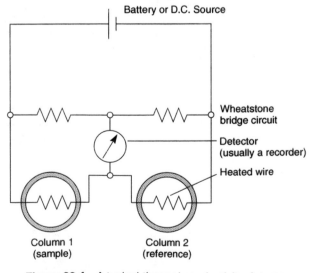

Figure 22.4   A typical thermal conductivity detector.

continuously moving roll of chart paper. This record of detector response (current) versus time is called a **chromatogram**. A typical gas chromatogram is illustrated in Figure 22.5. Deflections of the pen are called **peaks**.

When a sample is injected, some air (CO_2, H_2O, N_2, and O_2) is introduced along with the sample. The air travels through the column almost as rapidly as the carrier gas; as air passes the detector, it causes a small pen response, thereby giving a peak, called the **air peak**. At later times (t_1, t_2, t_3), the components also give rise to peaks on the chromatogram as they pass out of the column and past the detector.

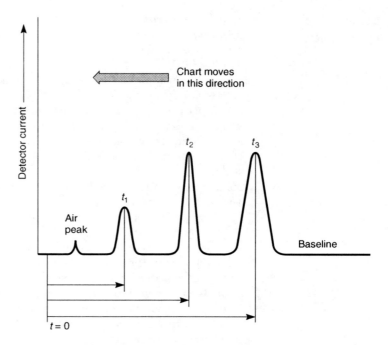

Figure 22.5   A typical gas chromatograph.

In a flame-ionization detector, the effluent from the column is directed into a flame produced by the combustion of hydrogen, as illustrated in Figure 22.6. As organic compounds burn in the flame, ion fragments are produced and collect on the ring above the flame. The resulting electrical signal is amplified and sent to a recorder in a manner similar to that for a TCD, except that an FID does not produce an air peak. The main advantage of the FID is that it is more sensitive and can be used to analyze smaller quantities of sample. Also, because an FID does not respond to water, a gas chromatograph with this detector can be used to analyze aqueous solutions. Two disadvantages are that it is more difficult to operate and the detection process destroys the sample. Therefore, an FID gas chromatograph cannot be used to do preparative work.

22.7 Retention Time

The period following injection that is required for a compound to pass through the column is called the **retention time** of that compound. For a given set of constant conditions (flow rate of carrier gas, column temperature, column length, liquid phase, injection port temperature, carrier), the retention time of any compound is always constant (much like the R_f value in thin-layer chromatography, as described in Technique 20, Section 20.9). The retention time is measured from the time of injection to the time of maximum pen deflection (detector current) for the component being

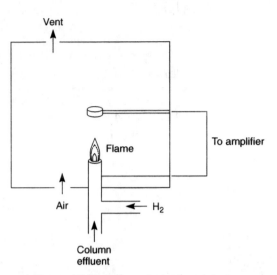

Figure 22.6   A flame-ionization detector.

observed. This value, when obtained under controlled conditions, can identify a compound by a direct comparison of it with values for known compounds determined under the same conditions. For easier measurement of retention times, most strip chart recorders are adjusted to move the paper at a rate that corresponds to time divisions calibrated on the chart paper. The retention times (t_1, t_2, t_3) are indicated in Figure 22.5 for the three peaks illustrated.

Most modern gas chromatographs are attached to a "data station," which uses a computer or a microprocessor to process the data. With these instruments, the chart often does not have divisions. Instead, the computer prints the retention time, usually to the nearest 0.01 minute, above each peak. A more complete discussion of the results obtained from a modern data station and how these data are treated may be found in Section 22.13.

22.8 Chiral Stationary Phases

A recent innovation in gas chromatography is to use chiral adsorbent materials to achieve separations of stereoisomers. The interaction between a particular stereoisomers and the chiral adsorbent may be different from the interaction between the opposite stereoisomer and the same chiral adsorbent. As a result, retention times for the two stereoisomers are likely to be sufficiently different to allow for a clean separation. The interactions between a chiral substance and the chiral adsorbent will include hydrogen-bonding and dipole-dipole attraction forces, although other properties may also be involved. One enantiomer should interact more strongly with the adsorbent than its opposite form. Thus, one enantiomer should pass through the gas chromatography column more slowly than its opposite form.

The ability of chiral adsorbents to separate stereoisomers is rapidly finding many useful applications, particularly in the synthesis of pharmaceutical agents. The biological activity of chiral substances often depends upon their stereochemistry because the living body is a highly chiral environment. A large number of pharmaceutical compounds have two enantiomeric forms that in many cases show significant differences in their behavior and activity. The ability to prepare enantiomerically pure drugs is very important because these pure substances are much more potent (and often have fewer side effects) than their racemic analogues.

Another type of stationary phase in gas chromatography is based on molecules such as the **cyclodextrins**. With these materials, the discrimination between enantiomers depends on the interactions between the stereoisomers and the chiral cavity that is formed within these materials. Because enantiomers differ in shape, they will fit differently within the chiral cavity. The result will be that the enantiomers will pass through the cyclodextrin stationary phase at different rates, thus leading to a separation.

The cyclodextrins owe their specificity to their structure, which is based on polymers of D-(+)- glucose. The hydroxyl groups of the glucose have been alkylated, so that the cavity is relatively nonpolar. The exterior hydroxyl groups of the cyclodextrins have also been substituted with *tert*-butyldimethylsilyl groups. The result is a material that can also utilize differences in hydrogen-bonding and dipole-dipole interactions to separate stereoisomers.

The structure of one important cyclodextrin-based chiral adsorbent is shown in Figure 22.7. Gas chromatography using this chiral adsorbent as a stationary phase has been used to separate a wide variety of stereoisomers. In one recent publication, this method was used to isolate a pure sample of (S)-(+)-2-methyl-4-octanol, a male-specific compound released by the sugarcane weevil, *Sphenophorus levis*.[1]

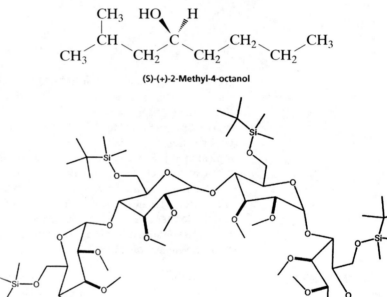

Figure 22.7 Cyclodextrin derivative used as a chiral adsorbent in gas chromatography.

[1]Zarbin, P. H. G., Princival, J. L., dos Santos, A. A., and de Oliveira, A. R. M. "Synthesis of (S)-()-2-Methyl-4-octanol: Male-Specific Compound Released by Sugarcane Weevil *Sphenophorus levis*." *Journal of the Brazilian Chemical Society*, 15 (2004): 331–334.

22.9 Poor Resolution and Tailing

The peaks in Figure 22.5 are well **resolved**. That is, the peaks are separated from one another, and between each pair of adjacent peaks the tracing returns to the baseline. In Figure 22.8, the peaks overlap and the resolution is not good. Poor resolution is often caused by using too much sample; by a column that is too short, has too high a temperature, or has too large a diameter; by a liquid phase that does not discriminate well between the two components; or, in short, by almost any wrongly adjusted parameter. When peaks are poorly resolved, it is more difficult to determine the relative amount of each component. Methods for determining the relative percentages of each component are given in Section 22.12.

Another desirable feature illustrated by the chromatogram in Figure 22.5 is that each peak is symmetrical. A common example of an unsymmetrical peak is one in which **tailing** has occurred, as shown in Figure 22.9. Tailing usually results from injecting too much sample into the gas chromatograph. Another cause of tailing occurs with polar compounds, such as alcohols and aldehydes. These compounds may be temporarily adsorbed on column walls or areas of the support material that are not adequately coated by the liquid phase. Therefore, they do not leave in a band, and tailing results.

22.10 Qualitative Analysis

A disadvantage of the gas chromatograph is that it gives no information about the identities of the substances it has separated. The little information it does provide is given by the retention time. It is hard to reproduce this quantity from day to day, however, and exact duplications of separations performed last month may be difficult to make this month. It is usually necessary to **calibrate** the column each time it is used. That is, you must run pure samples of all known and suspected components of a mixture individually, just before chromatographing the mixture, to obtain the retention time of each known compound. As an alternative, each suspected

Figure 22.8   Poor resolution, or peaks overlap.

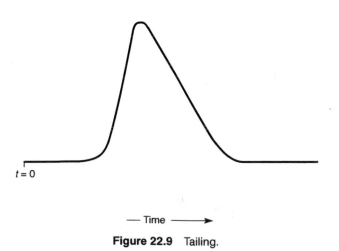

$t = 0$

— Time ⟶

Figure 22.9   Tailing.

component can be added, one by one, to the unknown mixture while the operator looks to see which peak has its intensity increased relative to the unmodified mixture. Another solution is to collect the components individually as they emerge from the gas chromatograph. Each component can then be identified by other means, such as by infrared or nuclear magnetic resonance spectroscopy or by mass spectrometry.

22.11 Collecting the Sample

For gas chromatographs with a thermal conductivity detector, it is possible to collect samples that have passed through the column. One method uses a gas collection tube (see Figure 22.10), which is included in most microscale glassware kits. A collection tube is joined to the exit port of the column by inserting the ⊤ 5/5 inner joint into a metal adapter, which is connected to the exit port. When a sample is eluted from the column in the vapor state, it is cooled by the connecting adapter and the gas collection tube and condenses in the collection tube. The gas collection tube is removed from the adapter when the recorder indicates that the desired sample has completely passed through the column. After the first sample has been collected, the process can be repeated with another gas collection tube.

To isolate the liquid, insert the tapered joint of the collection tube into a 0.1-mL conical vial, which has a ⊤ 5/5 outer joint. Place the assembly into a test tube, as illustrated in Figure 22.11. During centrifugation, the sample is forced into the bottom of the conical vial. After disassembling the apparatus, the liquid can be removed from the vial with a syringe for a boiling-point determination or analysis by infrared spectroscopy. If a determination of the sample weight is desired, the empty conical vial and cap should be tared and reweighed after the liquid has been collected. It is advisable to dry the gas collection tube and the conical vial in an oven before use to prevent contamination by water or other solvents used in cleaning this glassware.

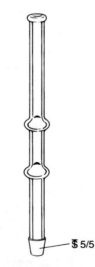

⊤ 5/5

Figure 22.10   A gas chromatography collection tube.

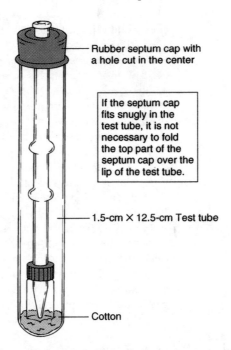

Figure 22.11   A gas chromatography collection tube and a 0.1-mL conical vial.

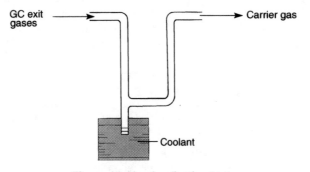

Figure 22.12   A collection trap.

Another method for collecting samples is to connect a cooled trap to the exit port of the column. A simple trap, suitable for microscale work, is illustrated in Figure 22.12. Suitable coolants include ice water, liquid nitrogen, or dry ice–acetone. For instance, if the coolant is liquid nitrogen (bp –196°C) and the carrier gas is helium (bp –269°C), compounds boiling above the temperature of liquid nitrogen generally are condensed or trapped in the small tube at the bottom of the U-shaped tube. The small tube is scored with a file just below the point at which it is connected to the larger tube, the tube is broken off, and the sample is removed for analysis. To collect each component of the mixture, you must change the trap after each sample is collected.

22.12 Quantitative Analysis

The area under a gas chromatograph peak is proportional to the amount (moles) of compound eluted. Hence, the molar percentage composition of a mixture can be approximated by comparing relative peak areas. This method of analysis assumes that the detector is equally sensitive to all compounds eluted and that it gives a linear response with respect to amount. Nevertheless, it gives reasonably accurate results.

The simplest method of measuring the area of a peak is by geometric approximation, or triangulation. In this method, you multiply the height h of the peak above the baseline of the chromatogram by the width of the peak at half of its height $w_{1/2}$. This is illustrated in Figure 22.13. The baseline is approximated by drawing a line between the two sidearms of the peak. This method works well only if the peak is symmetrical. If the peak has tailed or is unsymmetrical, it is best to cut out the peaks with scissors and weigh the pieces of paper on an **analytical balance**. Because the weight per area of a piece of good chart paper is reasonably constant from place to place, the ratio of the areas is the same as the ratio of the weights. To obtain a percentage composition for the mixture, first add all the peak areas (weights). Then, to calculate the percentage of any component in the mixture, divide its individual area by the total area and multiply the result by 100. A sample calculation is illustrated in Figure 22.14. If peaks overlap (see Figure 22.8), either the gas chromatographic conditions must be readjusted to achieve better resolution of the peaks or the peak shape must be estimated.

There are various instrumental means, which are built into recorders, of detecting the amounts of each sample automatically. One method uses a separate pen that produces a trace that integrates the area under each peak. Another method employs an electronic device that automatically prints out the area under each peak and the percentage composition of the sample.

Most modern data stations (see Section 22.13) label the top of each peak with its retention time in minutes. When the trace is completed, the computer prints a table of all the peaks with their retention times, areas, and the percentage of the total area (sum of all the peaks) that each peak represents. Some caution should be used with these results because the computer often does not include smaller peaks and occasionally does not resolve narrow peaks that are so close together that they overlap. If the trace has several peaks and you would like the ratio of only two of them, you will have to determine their percentages yourself using only their two areas or instruct the instrument to integrate only these two peaks.

For many applications, one assumes that the detector is equally sensitive to all compounds eluted. Compounds with different functional groups or with widely varying molecular weights, however, produce different responses with both TCD

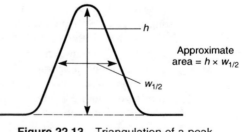

Figure 22.13   Triangulation of a peak.

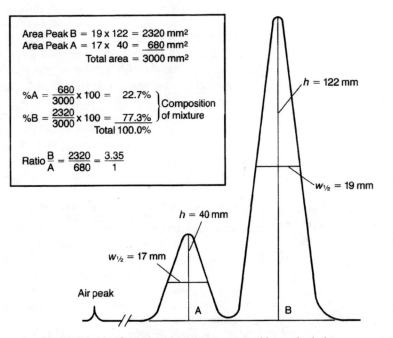

Area Peak B = 19 x 122 = 2320 mm²
Area Peak A = 17 x 40 = __680__ mm²
            Total area = 3000 mm²

$\%A = \dfrac{680}{3000} \times 100 = 22.7\%$ } Composition
$\%B = \dfrac{2320}{3000} \times 100 = \underline{77.3\%}$ } of mixture
                    Total 100.0%

Ratio $\dfrac{B}{A} = \dfrac{2320}{680} = \dfrac{3.35}{1}$

h = 122 mm

$w_{1/2}$ = 19 mm

h = 40 mm

$w_{1/2}$ = 17 mm

Air peak

A   B

Figure 22.14 Sample percentage composition calculation.

and FID gas chromatographs. With a TCD, the responses are different because not all compounds have the same thermal conductivity. Different compounds analyzed with an FID gas chromatograph also give different responses because the detector response varies with the type of ions produced. For both types of detectors, it is possible to calculate a **response factor** for each compound in a mixture. Response factors are usually determined by making up an equimolar mixture of two compounds, one of which is considered to be the reference. The mixture is separated on a gas chromatograph, and the relative percentages are calculated using one of the methods described previously. From these percentages, you can determine a response factor for the compound being compared to the reference. If you do this for all the components in a mixture, you can then use these correction factors to make more accurate calculations of the relative percentages for the compounds in the mixture.

To illustrate how response factors are determined, consider the following example. An equimolar mixture of benzene, hexane, and ethyl acetate is prepared and analyzed using a flame-ionization gas chromatograph. The peak areas obtained are

Hexane	831158
Ethyl acetate	1449695
Benzene	966463

In most cases, benzene is taken as the standard, and its response factor is defined to be equal to 1.00. Calculation of the response factors for the other components of the test mixture proceeds as follows:

Hexane	831158/966463 = 0.86
Ethyl acetate	1449695/966463 = 1.50
Benzene	966463/966463 = 1.00 (by definition)

Notice that the response factors calculated in this example are molar response factors. It is necessary to correct these values by the relative molecular weights of each substance to obtain weight response factors.

When you use a flame-ionization gas chromatograph for quantitative analysis, it is first necessary to determine the response factors for each component of the mixture being analyzed, as just shown. For a quantitative analysis, it is likely that you will have to convert molar response factors into weight response factors. Next, the chromatography experiment using the unknown samples is performed. The observed peak areas for each component are corrected using the response factors in order to arrive at the correct weight percentage of each component in the sample. The application of response factors to correct the original results of a quantitative analysis will be illustrated in the following section.

22.13 Treatment of Data: Chromatograms Produced by Modern Data Stations

A. Gas Chromatograms and Data Tables

Most modern gas chromatography instruments are equipped with computer-based data stations. Interfacing the instrument with a computer allows the operator to display and manipulate the results in whatever manner might be desired. The operator thus can view the output in a convenient form. The computer can both display the actual gas chromatogram and display the integration results. It can even display the result of two experiments simultaneously, making a comparison of parallel experiments convenient.

Figure 22.15 shows a gas chromatogram of a mixture of hexane, ethyl acetate, and benzene. The peaks corresponding to each peak can be seen; the peaks are labeled with their respective retention times:

	Retention Time (minutes)
Hexane	2.959
Ethyl acetate	3.160
Benzene	3.960

We can also see that there is a very small amount of an unspecified impurity, with a retention time of about 3.4 minutes.

Figure 22.16 shows part of the printed output that accompanies the gas chromatogram. It is this information that is used in the quantitative analysis of the mixture. According to the printout, the first peak has a retention time of 2.954 minutes (the difference between the retention times that appear as labels on the graph and those that appear in the data table are not significant). The computer has also determined the area under this peak (422373 counts). Finally, the computer has calculated the percentage of the first substance (hexane) by determining the total area of all the peaks in the chromatogram (1227054 counts) and dividing that into the area for the hexane peak. The result is displayed as 34.4217%. In a similar manner, the data table shows the retention times and peak areas for the other two peaks in the sample, along with a determination of the percentage of each substance in the mixture.

B. Application of Response Factors

If the detector responded with equal sensitivity to each of the components of the mixture, the data table shown in Figure 22.16 would contain the complete quantitative analysis of the sample. Unfortunately, as we have seen (see Section 22.12), gas

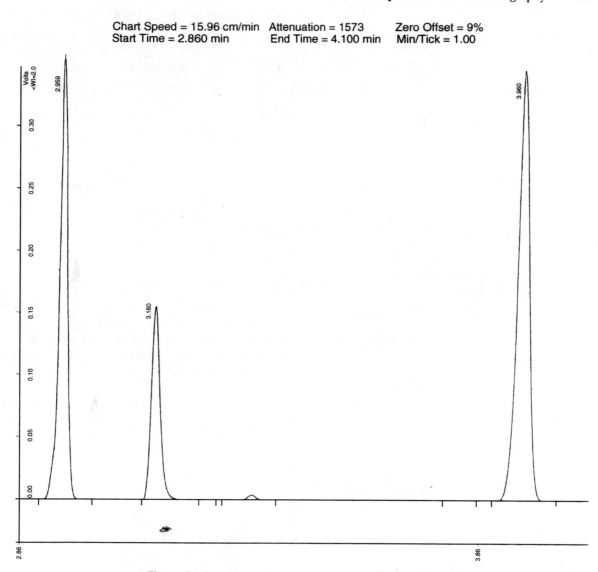

Chart Speed = 15.96 cm/min   Attenuation = 1573   Zero Offset = 9%
Start Time = 2.860 min   End Time = 4.100 min   Min/Tick = 1.00

Figure 22.15   A sample gas chromatogram obtained from a data station.

chromatography detectors respond more sensitively to some substances than they do to others. To correct for this discrepancy, it is necessary to apply corrections that are based on the **response factors** for each component of the mixture.

The method for determining the response factors was introduced in Section 22.12. In this section, we will see how this information is applied in order to obtain a correct analysis. This example should serve to demonstrate the procedure for correcting raw gas chromatography results when response factors are known. According to the data table, the reported peak area for the first (hexane) peak is 422373 counts. The response factor for hexane was previously determined to be 0.86. The area of the hexane peak is thus corrected as follows:

$$422373/0.86 = 491000$$

Notice that the calculated result has been adjusted to reflect a reasonable number of significant figures.

The areas for the other peaks in the gas chromatogram are corrected in a similar manner:

Hexane	422373/0.86 =	491000
Ethyl acetate	204426/1.50 =	136000
Benzene	600255/1.00 =	600000
Total peak area		1227000

Using these corrected areas, the true percentages of each component can be easily determined:

		Composition
Hexane	491000/1227000	40.0%
Ethyl acetate	136000/1227000	11.1%
Benzene	600000/1227000	48.9%
Total		100.0%

C. Determination of Relative Percentages of Components in a Complex Mixture

In some circumstances, one may wish to determine the relative percentages of two components when the mixture being analyzed may be more complex and may contain more than two components. Examples of this situation might include the analysis of a reaction product where the laboratory worker might be interested in the relative percentages of two isomeric products when the sample might also contain peaks arising from the solvent, unreacted starting material, or some other product or impurity.

The example provided in Figures 22.15 and 22.16 can be used to illustrate the method of determining the relative percentages of some, but not all, of the components

```
Run Mode         : Analysis
Peak Measurement: Peak Area
Calculation Type: Percent
```

Peak No.	Peak Name	Result ()	Ret. Time (min)	Time Offset (min)	Area (counts)	Sep. Code	Width 1/2 (sec)	Status Codes
1		34.4217	2.954	0.000	422373	BB	1.0	
2		16.6599	3.155	0.000	204426	BB	1.2	
3		48.9184	3.954	0.000	600255	BB	1.6	
	Totals:	100.0000		0.000	1227054			

```
Total Unidentified Counts:     1227054 counts

Detected Peaks: 8          Rejected Peaks: 5          Identified Peaks: 0

Multiplier: 1          Divisor: 1          Unidentified Peak Factor: 0

Baseline Offset: 1 microVolts

Noise (used): 28 microVolts — monitored before this run

Manual injection
```

Figure 22.16   A data table to accompany the gas chromatogram shown in Figure 22.14.

in the sample. Assume we are interested in the relative percentages of hexane and ethyl acetate in the sample but not in the percentage of benzene, which may be a solvent or an impurity. We know from the previous discussion that the *corrected* relative areas of the two peaks of interest are as follows:

	Relative Area
Hexane	491000
Ethyl acetate	136000
Total	627000

We can determine the relative percentages of the two components simply by dividing the area of each peak by the total area of the two peaks:

		Percentage
Hexane	491000/627000	78.3%
Ethyl acetate	136000/627000	21.7%
Total		100.0%

22.14 Gas Chromatography-Mass Spectrometry (GC-MS)

A recently developed variation on gas chromatography is **gas chromatography-mass spectrometry**, also known as **GC-MS**. In this technique, a gas chromatograph is coupled to a mass spectrometer (see Technique 28). In effect, the mass spectrometer acts as a detector. The gas stream emerging from the gas chromatograph is admitted through a valve into a tube, where it passes over the sample inlet system of the mass spectrometer. Some of the gas stream is thus admitted into the ionization chamber of the mass spectrometer.

The molecules in the gas stream are converted into ions in the ionization chamber, and thus the gas chromatogram is actually a plot of time versus **ion current**, a measure of the number of ions produced. At the same time that the molecules are converted into ions, they are also accelerated and passed through the **mass analyzer** of the instrument. The instrument, therefore, determines the mass spectrum of each fraction eluting from the gas chromatography column.

A drawback of this method involves the need for rapid scanning by the mass spectrometer. The instrument must determine the mass spectrum of each component in the mixture before the next component exits from the column so that the spectrum of one substance is not contaminated by the spectrum of the next fraction.

Because high-efficiency capillary columns are used in the gas chromatograph, in most cases compounds are completely separated before the gas stream is analyzed. The typical GC-MS instrument has the capability of obtaining at least one scan per second in the range of 10–300 amu. Even more scans are possible if a narrow range of masses is analyzed. Using capillary columns, however, requires the user to take particular care to ensure that the sample does not contain any particles that might obstruct the flow of gases through the column. For this reason, the sample is carefully filtered through a very fine filter before the sample is injected into the chromatograph.

With a GC-MS system, a mixture can be analyzed and results obtained that resemble very closely those shown in Figures 22.14 and 22.15. A library search on each component of the mixture can also be conducted. The data stations of most instruments contain a library of standard mass spectra in their computer memory. If the components are known compounds, they can be identified tentatively by a comparison of their mass spectrum with the spectra of compounds found in the computer library. In this way, a "hit list" can be generated that reports on the probability that the compound in the library matches the known substance. A typical printout from a GC-MS instrument will list probable compounds that fit the mass spectrum of the component, the names of the compounds, their CAS Nos. (see Technique 29, Section 29.11), and a "quality" or "confidence" number. This last number provides an estimate of how closely the mass spectrum of the component matches the mass spectrum of the substance in the computer library.

A variation on the GC-MS technique includes coupling a Fourier-transform infrared spectrometer (FT–IR) to a gas chromatograph. The substances that elute from the gas chromatograph are detected by determining their infrared spectra rather than their mass spectra. A new technique that also resembles GC-MS is **high-performance liquid chromatography–mass spectrometry (HPLC–MS)**. An HPLC instrument is coupled through a special interface to a mass spectrometer. The substances that elute from the HPLC column are detected by the mass spectrometer, and their mass spectra can be displayed, analyzed, and compared with standard spectra found in the computer library built into the instrument.

PROBLEMS

1. **a.** A sample consisting of 1-bromopropane and 1-chloropropane is injected into a gas chromatograph equipped with a nonpolar column. Which compound has the shorter retention time? Explain your answer.

   b. If the same sample were run several days later with the conditions as nearly the same as possible, would you expect the retention times to be identical to those obtained the first time? Explain.

2. Using triangulation, calculate the percentage of each component in a mixture composed of two substances, A and B. The chromatogram is shown in Figure 22.17.

3. Make a photocopy of the chromatogram in Figure 22.17. Cut out the peaks and weigh them on an analytical balance. Use the weights to calculate the percentage of each component in the mixture. Compare your answer to what you calculated in problem 2.

4. What would happen to the retention time of a compound if the following changes were made?

   a. Decrease the flow rate of the carrier gas

   b. Increase the temperature of the column

   c. Increase the length of the column

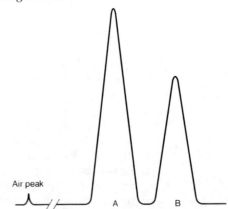

Figure 22.17   A chromatogram for problem 2.

TECHNIQUE 23

Polarimetry

23.1 Nature of Polarized Light

Light has a dual nature because it shows properties of both waves and particles. The wave nature of light can be demonstrated by two experiments: polarization and interference. Of the two, polarization is the more interesting to organic chemists, because they can take advantage of polarization experiments to learn something about the structure of an unknown molecule.

Ordinary white light consists of wave motion in which the waves have a variety of wavelengths and vibrate in all possible planes perpendicular to the direction of propagation. Light can be made to be **monochromatic** (of one wavelength or color) by using filters or special light sources. Frequently, a sodium lamp (sodium D line = 5893 Å) is used.[1] Although the light from this lamp consists of waves of essentially one wavelength, the individual light waves still vibrate in all possible planes perpendicular to the beam. If we imagine that the beam of light is aimed directly at the viewer, ordinary light can be represented by showing the edges of the planes oriented randomly around the path of the beam, as on the left side of Figure 23.1.

A Nicol prism, which consists of a specially prepared crystal of Iceland spar (or calcite), has the property of serving as a screen that can restrict the passage of light waves. Waves that are vibrating in one plane are transmitted; those in all other planes are rejected (either refracted in another direction or absorbed). The light that passes through the prism is called **plane-polarized light**, and it consists of waves that vibrate in only one plane. A beam of plane-polarized light aimed directly at the viewer can be represented by showing the edges of the plane oriented in one particular direction, as on the right side of Figure 23.1.

Iceland spar has the property of **double refraction**; that is, it can split, or doubly refract, an entering beam of ordinary light into two separate emerging beams of light. Each of the two emerging beams (labeled A and B in Figure 23.2) has only a single plane of vibration, and the plane of vibration in beam A is perpendicular to the plane of beam B. In other words, the crystal has separated the incident beam of ordinary light into two beams of plane-polarized light, with the plane of polarization of beam A perpendicular to the plane of beam B.

To generate a single beam of plane-polarized light, one can take advantage of the double-refracting property of Iceland spar. A Nicol prism, invented by the Scottish physicist William Nicol, consists of two crystals of Iceland spar cut to specified angles and cemented by Canada balsam. This prism transmits one of the two

Figure 23.1   Ordinary versus plane-polarized light.

---

[1]A sodium emission lamp actually emits *two* yellow lines near 5893Å, but they are closely spaced and only separated by high-resolution monochromaters.

beams of plane-polarized light while reflecting the other at a sharp angle so that it does not interfere with the transmitted beam. Plane-polarized light can also be generated by a Polaroid filter, a device invented by E. H. Land, an American physicist. Polaroid filters consist of certain types of crystals embedded in transparent plastic and capable of producing plane-polarized light.

After passing through a first Nicol prism, plane-polarized light can pass through a second Nicol prism, but only if the second prism has its axis oriented so that it is *parallel* to the incident light's plane of polarization. Plane-polarized light is *absorbed* by a Nicol prism that is oriented so that its axis is *perpendicular* to the incident light's plane of polarization. These situations can be illustrated by the picket-fence analogy, as shown in Figure 23.3. Plane-polarized light can pass through a fence whose slats are oriented in the proper direction, but is blocked out by a fence whose slats are oriented perpendicularly.

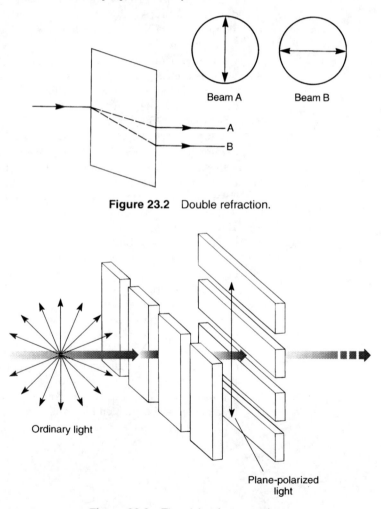

Beam A   Beam B

A
B

Figure 23.2   Double refraction.

Ordinary light

Plane-polarized
light

Figure 23.3   The picket-fence analogy.

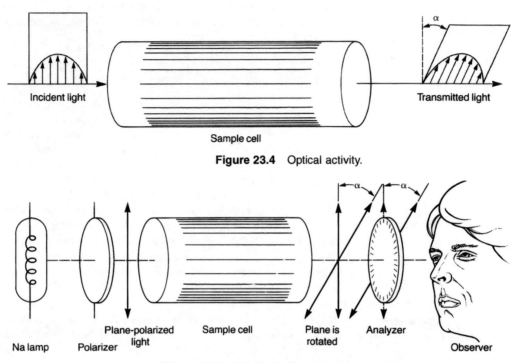

Figure 23.4   Optical activity.

Figure 23.5   Schematic diagram of a polarimeter.

An **optically active substance** is one that interacts with polarized light to rotate the plane of polarization through some angle α. Figure 23.4 illustrates this phenomenon.

23.2 The Polarimeter

An instrument called a **polarimeter** is used to measure the extent to which a substance interacts with polarized light. A schematic diagram of a polarimeter is shown in Figure 23.5. The light from the source lamp is polarized by being passed through a fixed Nicol prism, called a **polarizer**. This light passes through the sample with which it may or may not interact to have its plane of polarization rotated in one direction or the other. A second, rotatable Nicol prism, called the **analyzer**, is adjusted to allow the maximum amount of light to pass through. The number of degrees and the direction of rotation required for this adjustment are measured to give the **observed rotation** α.

So that data determined by several persons under different conditions can be compared, a standardized means of presenting optical rotation data is necessary. The most common way of presenting such data is by recording the **specific rotation** $[\alpha]_\lambda^t$, which has been corrected for differences in concentration, cell path length, temperature, solvent, and wavelength of the light source. The equation defining the specific rotation of a compound in solution is

$$[\alpha]_\lambda^t = \frac{\alpha}{cl}$$

where α = observed rotation in degrees, c = concentration in grams per milliliter of solution, l = length of sample tube in decimeters, λ = wavelength of light (usually indicated as "D," for the sodium D line), and t = temperature in degrees Celsius. For pure liquids, the density d of the liquid in grams per milliliter replaces c in the preceding formula. You may occasionally want to compare compounds of different molecular weights, so a **molecular rotation**, based on moles instead of grams, is more convenient than a specific rotation. The molecular rotation M_λ^t is derived from the specific rotation $[\alpha]_\lambda^t$, by

$$M_\lambda^t = \frac{[\alpha]_\lambda^t \times \text{Molecular weight}}{100}$$

Usually, measurements are made at 25°C with the sodium D line as a light source; consequently, specific rotations are reported as $[\alpha]_D^{25}$.

Polarimeters that are now available incorporate electronics to determine the angle of rotation of chiral molecules. These instruments are essentially automatic. The only real difference between an automatic polarimeter and a manual one is that a light detector replaces the eye. No visual observation of any kind is made with an automatic instrument. A microprocessor adjusts the analyzer until the light reaching the detector is at a minimum. The angle of rotation is displayed digitally in an LCD window, including the sign of rotation. The simplest instrument is equipped with a sodium lamp that gives rotations based on the sodium D line (589 nm). More expensive instruments use a tungsten lamp and filters so that wavelengths can be varied over a range of values. Using the latter instrument, a chemist can observe rotations at different wavelengths.

23.3 Sample Preparation, The Sample Cell

It is important that the solution whose optical rotation is to be determined contain no suspended particles of dust, dirt, or undissolved material that might disperse the incident polarized light. Therefore, you must clean the sample cell carefully, and your sample must be free of suspended particles. You must also prevent the presence of any air bubbles in the bore when you fill the cell. Most cells have a stem in the center or an area at one end of the cell where the diameter of the tube is increased. These features are designed to help you catch any bubbles in an area that is above the path that the light takes through the main bore.

Two modern **polarimetry cells** are shown in Figure 23.6. In the first case, the cell is filled until the liquid completely fills the bore and a small portion of the center stem. Then, if one gently rocks the cell back and forth along its axis, bubbles will rise and collect in the stem where they are above the light path. A stopper is placed in the stem when you are finished. In the second case, the cell is filled vertically, and the end is screwed on. Bubbles are trapped at the raised end when the cell is turned horizontally.

Sample cells are available in various lengths, with 0.5 dm and 1.0 dm being the most common. A typical 0.5-dm cell holds about 3–5 mL of solution, but many companies sell **microcells** that have a very narrow diameter bore and require much less solution. Polarimeter cells are quite expensive because the windows must be made out of quartz rather than ordinary glass. Be sure to handle them carefully and to avoid getting fingerprints on the end windows, as this will also disperse the polarized light.

Figure 23.6 Two modern polarimetry cells (Rudolph Research).

With liquid samples, it is often quite possible to use the **neat** (undiluted) liquid as your sample. In this case, the concentration of the sample is just the density of the liquid (g/mL). If you have a solid sample or if you have too little of a liquid to fill the cell, you will have to either dissolve or dilute the sample with a solvent. In this case, you must weigh (grams) the amount of material you use and divide by the total volume (mL) to obtain the concentration in g/mL. Water, methanol, and ethanol are the best solvents to use because they are unlikely to attack the cell you are using. Many cells have rubber parts or use a cement to attach the windows to the ends of the bore. Rubber and cements will often dissolve in stronger solvents such as acetone or methylene chloride, thereby damaging the cell. Check with your instructor before using any solvent stronger than water, methanol, or ethanol. These are also the preferred solvents to use for cleaning the cells.

23.4 Operation of the Polarimeter

A. The Zeiss Polarimeter, a Classic Instrument

The procedures given here are for the operation of the Zeiss polarimeter (see Figure 23.7), a classic analog instrument with a circular scale and a sodium lamp. Many other older polarimeters models are operated in a similar fashion.

Before taking any measurements, turn on the sodium lamp and wait 5–10 minutes for the lamp to warm up and stabilize. After the warm-up period is complete, you should make an initial check of the instrument by taking a zero reading with a sample cell filled only with solvent. If the zero reading does not correspond with the zero-degree (0°) calibration mark, then the difference in readings must be used to correct all subsequent readings.

To take the zero measurement, place the polarimeter cell with the sample in the sloped cradle or rack inside the instrument. If you are using a cell with an enlarged end, that end must be placed at the high end of the cradle, making sure that no bubbles are in the bore of the cell. After closing the cover and while watching through the eyepiece, turn the analyzer knob or ring until the proper angle of the analyzer is reached (the angle that allows no light to pass through the instrument). Most analog instruments, including the Zeiss polarimeter, are of the split-field type. When you look upward through the eyepiece, you see a circle split into three sectors (see Figure 23.8), with the center sector either lighter or darker than those on either side. The analyzer prism is rotated until all of the sectors are matched in intensity, usually the darker color (see Figure 23.8). This is called the **null** reading.

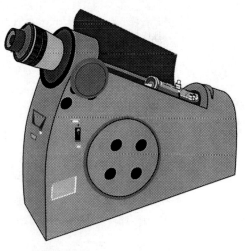

Figure 23.7   The Zeiss polarimeter.

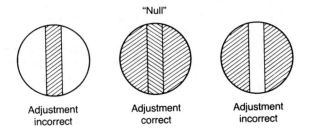

Figure 23.8   Image field sectiors in the polarimeter.

When you look downward in the eyepiece, you see the value of the angle through which the plane of the polarized light has been rotated (if any) indicated on a vernier degree scale (see Figure 23.9). Some polarimeters, such as the original Rudolph polarimeter, have instead a large circular scale, like a halo, attached directly to the knob you turn.

After determining the zero setting on the blank solution, place the polarimeter cell containing your sample into the polarimeter and measure the observed angle of rotation in the same way as described for the zero measurement. Be sure to record not only the numerical value of the reading but also the direction of rotation. Also record the solvent, temperature, and concentration, as these are also critical to the measurement. Rotations clockwise are due to dextrorotatory substances and are indicated by the "+" sign. Rotations counterclockwise are due to levorotatory substances and are indicated by the "−" sign. You should take several readings, including readings for which the value was approached from both sides. In other words, where the actual reading might be +75°, first approach this reading upward from somewhere between 0° and 75°; on the next measurement, approach the null from an angle greater than 75°. Duplicating readings, approaching the observed rotation from both sides, and averaging the readings reduce the error.

If you are not sure if you have a dextrorotatory or a levorotatory substance, you can make this determination by halving the concentration of your compound, reducing the length of the cell by half, or reducing the intensity of the light. The confusion between dextrorotatory and levorotatory arises because you are reading a circular scale. The null reading can be approached from either direction (clockwise or counterclockwise), starting from zero (see Figure 23.10). For instance, is your null at +120°, or is it at −240°? Both readings are at the same point on the scale. Figure 23.10 shows that by reducing the concentration, the cell length, or the light intensity in half (any one of these), the reading will change, and it will move in a different direction for levorotatory substances than for dextrorotatory substances. The direction of rotation is most often determined by making measurements at different dilutions.

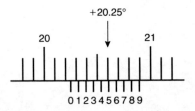

Figure 23.9   The vernier degree scale seen in the lower field of the Zeiss polarimeter.

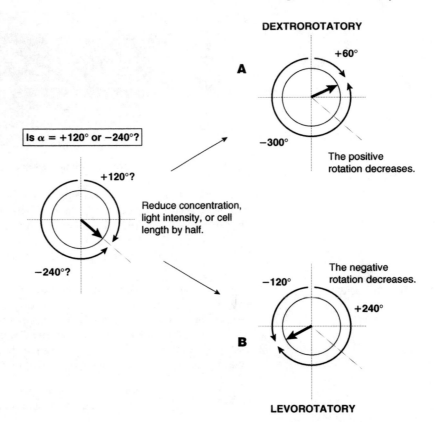

Figure 23.10   How to determine the direction of rotation. This diagram shows the effect on observed rotation if you reduce by half the concentration of the compound, the light intensity, or the length of the cell. By this method, it is easy to determine if the compound is dextrorotatory (A) or levorotatory (B).

Once you have determined the value and direction of the observed rotation α, you must correct it by the zero value and then use the formulas in Section 23.2 to convert it to the specific rotation $[\alpha]_D$. The specific rotation is always reported as a function of temperature, indicating the wavelength by "D" if a sodium lamp was used, and the solvent and concentration used are also reported. For example:

$$[\alpha]_D = +43.8 \ (c = 7.5 \ \text{g}/100 \ \text{mL, in absolute ethanol})$$

B. The Modern Digital Polarimeter

A modern digital polarimeter, such as the one shown in Figure 23.11, is much easier to operate than the older analog instruments. The modern instrument will store the zero reading for you, subtract it from every subsequent reading automatically, determine the direction of rotation, and calculate the specific rotation from the reading obtained on your sample. When finished, it can print everything out on a sheet of paper for you to take with you. In a typical instrument, you first determine the zero reading and then store it in electronic memory. Once the zero reading is determined, you place your sample in the instrument. The instrument automatically finds the null angle and the direction of rotation and displays it on an LED readout. The instrument approaches the null several times to be sure of its reading and determines the direction of rotation by reducing the intensity of the light. It can do

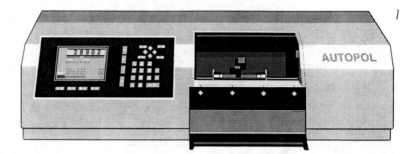

Figure 23.11   The Autopol IV (Rudolph Research), a modern digital polarimeter.

this in several different ways. One common method is to attenuate (reduce) the incident light intensity of the beam of polarized light and see what effect this has on the angle of rotation. Even a digital polarimeter, however, cannot extract a reading from a poor sample, such as one that is cloudy, has a bubble, or has suspended solid material. A good sample is still your responsibility.

23.5 Optical Purity

When you prepare a sample of an enantiomer by a resolution method, the sample is not always 100% of a single enantiomer. It frequently is contaminated by residual amounts of the opposite stereoisomer. If you know the amount of each enantiomer in a mixture, you can calculate the **optical purity**. Some chemists prefer to use the term **enantiomeric excess (ee)** rather than optical purity. The two terms can be used interchangeably. The percentage enantiomeric excess or optical purity is calculated as follows:

$$\% \text{ Optical purity } = \frac{\text{moles one enantiomer} - \text{moles of other enantiomer}}{\text{total moles of both enantiomers}} \times 100$$

$$\% \text{ Optical purity } = \% \text{ enantiomeric excess (ee)}$$

Often, it is difficult to apply the previous equation because you do not know the exact amount of each enantiomer present in a mixture. It is far easier to calculate the optical purity (ee) by using the observed specific rotation of the mixture and dividing it by the specific rotation of the pure enantiomer. Values for the pure enantiomers can sometimes be found in literature sources.

$$\% \text{ Optical purity } = \% \text{ enantiomeric excess } = \frac{\text{observed specific rotation}}{\text{specific rotation of pure enantiomer}} \times 100$$

This latter equation holds true only for mixtures of two chiral molecules that are mirror images of each other (enantiomers). If some other chiral substance is present in the mixture as an impurity, then the actual optical purity will deviate from the value calculated.

In a racemic (±) mixture, there is no excess enantiomer and the optical purity (enantiomeric excess) is zero; in a completely resolved material, the optical purity (enantiomeric excess) is 100%. A compound that is x% optically pure contains x% of one enantiomer and $(100 - x)$% of a racemic mixture.

Once the optical purity (enantiomeric excess) is known, the relative percentages of each of the enantiomers can be calculated easily. If the predominant form in the impure, optically active mixture is assumed to be the (+) enantiomer, the percentage of the (+) enantiomer is

$$\left[x + \left(\frac{100 - x}{2} \right) \right]\%$$

and the percentage of the $(-)$ enantiomer is $[(100 - x)/2]\%$. The relative percentages of $(+)$ and $(-)$ forms in a partially resolved mixture of enantiomers can be calculated as shown next. Consider a partially resolved mixture of camphor enantiomers. The specific rotation for pure $(+)$-camphor is $+43.8°$ in absolute ethanol, but the mixture shows a specific rotation of $+26.3°$.

$$\text{Optical purity} = \frac{+26.3°}{+43.8°} \times 100 = 60\% \text{ optically pure}$$

$$\% \; (+) \text{ enantiomer} = 60 + \left(\frac{100 - 60}{2}\right) = 80\%$$

$$\% \; (-) \text{ enantiomer} = \left(\frac{100 - 60}{2}\right) = 20\%$$

Notice that the difference between these two calculated values equals the optical purity or enantiomeric excess.

PROBLEMS

1. Calculate the specific rotation of a substance that is dissolved in a solvent (0.4 g/mL) and that has an observed rotation of $-10°$ as determined with a 0.5-dm cell.

2. Calculate the observed rotation for a solution of a substance (2.0 g/mL) that is 80% optically pure. A 2-dm cell is used. The specific rotation for the optically pure substance is $+20°$.

3. What is the optical purity of a partially racemized product if the calculated specific rotation is $-8°$ and the pure enantiomer has a specific rotation of $-10°$? Calculate the percentage of each of the enantiomers in the partially racemized product.

---

24   TECHNIQUE 24

Refractometry

The **refractive index** is a useful physical property of liquids. Often, a liquid can be identified from a measurement of its refractive index. The refractive index can also provide a measure of the purity of the sample being examined. This is accomplished by comparing the experimentally measured refractive index with the value reported in the literature for an ultrapure sample of the compound. The closer the measured sample's value to the literature value, the purer the sample.

24.1 The Refractive Index

The refractive index has as its basis the fact that light travels at a different velocity in condensed phases (liquids, solids) than in air. The refractive index n is defined as the ratio of the velocity of light in air to the velocity of light in the medium being measured:

$$n = \frac{V_{air}}{V_{liquid}} = \frac{\sin \theta}{\sin \phi}$$

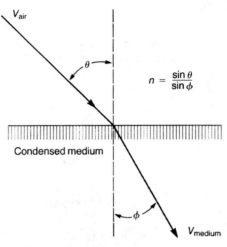

Figure 24.1   The refractive index.

It is not difficult to measure the ratio of the velocities experimentally. It corresponds to (sin θ/sin ϕ), where θ is the angle of incidence for a beam of light striking the surface of the medium and ϕ is the angle of refraction of the beam of light *within* the medium. This is illustrated in Figure 24.1.

The refractive index for a given medium depends on two variable factors. First, it is *temperature* dependent. The density of the medium changes with temperature; hence, the speed of light in the medium also changes. Second, the refractive index is *wavelength* dependent. Beams of light with different wavelengths are refracted to different extents in the same medium and give different refractive indices for that medium. It is usual to report refractive indices measured at 20°C, with a sodium discharge lamp as the source of illumination. The sodium lamp gives off yellow light of 589-nm wavelength, the so-called sodium D line. Under these conditions, the refractive index is reported in the following form:

$$n_{\mathrm{D}}^{20} = 1.4892$$

The superscript indicates the temperature, and the subscript indicates that the sodium D line was used for the measurement. If another wavelength is used for the determination, the D is replaced by the appropriate value, usually in nanometers (1 nm = 10^{-9} m).

Notice that the hypothetical value reported has four decimal places. It is easy to determine the refractive index to within several parts in 10,000. Therefore, n_{D} is a very accurate physical constant for a given substance and can be used for identification. However, it is sensitive to even small amounts of impurity in the substance measured. Unless the substance is purified *extensively*, you will not usually be able to reproduce the last two decimal places given in a handbook or other literature source. Typical organic liquids have refractive index values between 1.3400 and 1.5600.

24.2 The Abbé Refractometer

The instrument used to measure the refractive index is called a **refractometer**. Although many styles of refractometer are available, by far the most common instrument is the Abbé refractometer. This style of refractometer has the following advantages:

1. White light may be used for illumination; the instrument is compensated, however, so that the index of refraction obtained is actually that for the sodium D line.

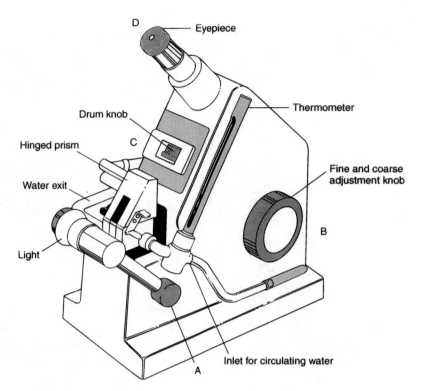

D —— Eyepiece

Drum knob

Hinged prism   C

Water exit

Light

Thermometer

Fine and coarse
adjustment knob

B

Inlet for circulating water
A

Figure 24.2 Abbé refractometer (Bausch and Lomb Abbé 3L).

2. The prisms can be temperature controlled.

3. Only a small sample is required (a few drops of liquid using the standard method, or about 5 μL using a modified technique).

A common type of Abbé refractometer is shown in Figure 24.2.

The optical arrangement of the refractometer is very complex; a simplified diagram of the internal workings is given in Figure 24.3. The letters A, B, C, and D label corresponding parts in both Figures 24.2 and 24.3. A complete description of refractometer optics is too difficult to attempt here, but Figure 24.3 gives a simplified diagram of the essential operating principles.

Using the standard method, introduce the sample to be measured between the two prisms. If it is a free-flowing liquid, it may be introduced into a channel along the side of the prisms, injected from a Pasteur pipet. If it is a viscous sample, the prisms must be opened (they are hinged) by lifting the upper one; a few drops of liquid are applied to the lower prism with a Pasteur pipet or a wooden applicator. If a Pasteur pipet is used, take care not to touch the prisms because they become scratched easily. When the prisms are closed, the liquid should spread evenly to make a thin film. With highly volatile samples, the remaining operations must be performed rapidly. Even when the prisms are closed, evaporation of volatile liquids can readily occur.

Next, turn on the light and look into the eyepiece (D). The hinged lamp is adjusted to give the maximum illumination to the visible field in the eyepiece. The light rotates at pivot (A).

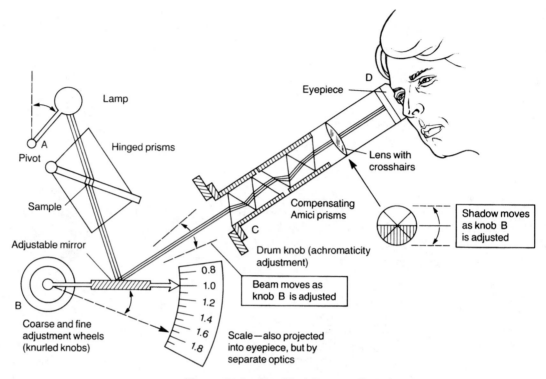

Figure 24.3 Simplified diagram of a refractometer.

Rotate the coarse and fine adjustment knobs at (B) until the dividing line between the light and dark halves of the visual field coincide with the center of the crosshairs (see Figure 24.4). If the crosshairs are not in sharp focus, adjust the eyepiece to focus them. If the horizontal line dividing the light and dark areas appears as a colored band, as in Figure 24.5, the refractometer shows **chromatic aberration** (color dispersion). This can be adjusted with the drum knob (C) (see Figure 24.3). This knurled knob rotates a series of prisms, called Amici prisms, that color-compensate the refractometer and cancel out dispersion. Adjust the drum knob to give a sharp, uncolored division between the light and dark segments. When you have adjusted everything correctly (as in Figure 24.4B), read the refractive index. In the instrument described here, press a small button on the left side of the housing to make the scale visible in the eyepiece. In other refractometers, the scale is visible at all times, frequently through a separate eyepiece.

Occasionally, the refractometer will be so far out of adjustment that it may be difficult to measure the refractive index of an unknown. When this happens, it is wise to place a pure sample of known refractive index in the instrument, set the scale to the correct value of refractive index, and adjust the controls for the sharpest line possible. Once this is done, it is easier to measure an unknown sample. It is especially helpful to perform this procedure prior to measuring the refractive index of a highly volatile sample.

NOTE: There are many styles of refractometer, but most have adjustments similar to those described here.

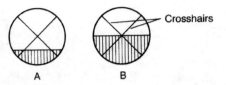

Figure 24.4   (A) Refractometer incorrectly adjusted. (B) Correct adjustment.

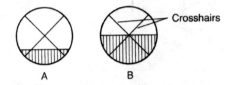

Figure 24.5   Refractometer showing chromatic aberration (color dispersion). The dispersion is incorrectly adjusted.

In the procedure just described, several drops of liquid are required to obtain the refractive index. In some experiments, you may not have enough sample to use this standard method. It is possible to modify the procedure so that a reasonably accurate refractive index can be obtained on about 5 μL of liquid. Instead of placing the sample directly onto the prism, you apply the sample to a small piece of lens paper. The lens paper can be conveniently cut with a hand-held paper punch,[1] and the paper disc (0.6-cm diameter) is placed in the center of the bottom prism of the refractometer. To avoid scratching the prism, use forceps or tweezers with plastic tips to handle the disc. About 5 μL of liquid is carefully placed on the lens paper using a microliter syringe. After closing the prisms, adjust the refractometer as described previously and read the refractive index. With this method, the horizontal line dividing the light and dark areas may not be as sharp as it is in the absence of the lens paper. It may also be impossible to eliminate color dispersion completely. Nonetheless, the refractive index values determined by this method are usually within 10 parts in 10,000 of the values determined by the standard procedure.

24.3 Cleaning the Refractometer

In using the refractometer, you should always remember that if the prisms are scratched, the instrument will be ruined.

NOTE: Do not touch the prisms with any hard object.

This admonition includes Pasteur pipets and glass rods.

When measurements are completed, the prisms should be cleaned with ethanol or petroleum ether. Moisten *soft* tissues with the solvent and wipe the prisms *gently*. When the solvent has evaporated from the prism surfaces, the prisms should be locked together. The refractometer should be left with the prisms closed to avoid collection of dust in the space between them. The instrument should also be turned off when it is no longer in use.

24.4 The Digital Refractometer

Today, there are modern digital refractometers available that determine the refractive index of a liquid electronically (see Figure 24.6). Once the instrument has been calibrated, it is only necessary to place a drop of your liquid between the prisms

---

[1] In order to cut the lens paper more easily, place several sheets between two pieces of heavier paper, such as that used for file folders.

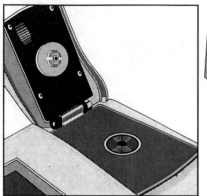

Figure 24.6 The Rudolph J-series, a modern digital refractometer. To make a measurement, place the sample on the lower prism (see the insert) and close the lid.

(see the inset in Figure 24.6), close the lid, and read the display. The instrument can make temperature corrections and store the values of your readings in its microprocessor memory. Once again, these instruments must be treated with respect, taking care not to scratch the prisms and to clean them after use.

24.5 Temperature Corrections

Most refractometers are designed so that circulating water at a constant temperature can maintain the prisms at 20°C. If this temperature-control system is not used or if the water is not at 20°C, a temperature correction must be made. Although the magnitude of the temperature correction may vary from one class of compound to another, a value of 0.00045 per degree Celsius is a useful approximation for most substances. The index of refraction of a substance *decreases* with *increasing* temperature. Therefore, add the correction to the observed n_D value for temperatures higher than 20°C and subtract it for temperatures lower than 20°C. For example, the reported n_D value for nitrobenzene is 1.5529. One would observe a value at 25°C of 1.5506. The temperature correction would be made as follows:

$$n_D^{20} = 1.5506 + 5(0.00045) = 1.5529$$

PROBLEMS

1. A solution consisting of isobutyl bromide and isobutyl chloride is found to have a refractive index of 1.3931 at 20°C. The refractive indices at 20°C of isobutyl bromide and isobutyl chloride are 1.4368 and 1.3785, respectively. Determine the molar composition (in percent) of the mixture by assuming a linear relation between the refractive index and the molar composition of the mixture.

2. The refractive index of a compound at 16°C is found to be 1.3982. Correct this refractive index to 20°C.

25 **TECHNIQUE 25**

Infrared Spectroscopy

Almost any compound having covalent bonds, whether organic or inorganic, will be found to absorb frequencies of electromagnetic radiation in the infrared region of the spectrum. The infrared region of the electromagnetic spectrum lies at wavelengths longer than those associated with visible light, which includes wavelengths from approximately 400 nm to 800 nm (1 nm = 10^{-9} m), but at wavelengths shorter than those associated with radio waves, which have wavelengths longer than 1 cm. For chemical purposes, we are interested in the *vibrational* portion of the infrared region. This portion includes radiations with wavelengths (λ) between 2.5 μm and 15 μm (1 μm = 10^{-6} m). The relation of the infrared region to other regions included in the electromagnetic spectrum is illustrated in Figure 25.1.

As with other types of energy absorption, molecules are excited to a higher energy state when they absorb infrared radiation. The absorption of the infrared radiation is, like other absorption processes, a quantized process. Only selected frequencies (energies) of infrared radiation are absorbed by a molecule. The absorption of infrared radiation corresponds to energy changes on the order of 8–40 kJ/mole (2–10 kcal/mole). Radiation in this energy range corresponds to the range encompassing the stretching and bending vibrational frequencies of the bonds in most covalent molecules. In the absorption process, those frequencies of infrared radiation that match the natural vibrational frequencies of the molecule in question are absorbed, and the energy absorbed increases the *amplitude* of the vibrational motions of the bonds in the molecule.

Most chemists refer to the radiation in the vibrational infrared region of the electromagnetic spectrum by units called **wavenumbers** ($\bar{\nu}$). Wavenumbers are expressed in reciprocal centimeters (cm^{-1}) and are easily computed by taking the reciprocal of the wavelength (λ) expressed in centimeters. This unit has the advantage, for those performing calculations, of being directly proportional to energy. Thus, the vibrational infrared region of the spectrum extends from about 4000 cm^{-1} to 650 cm^{-1} (or wavenumbers).

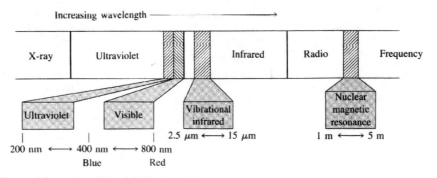
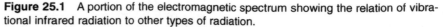

Figure 25.1 A portion of the electromagnetic spectrum showing the relation of vibrational infrared radiation to other types of radiation.

Wavelengths (μm) and wavenumbers (cm^{-1}) can be interconverted by the following relationships:

$$\text{cm}^{-1} = \frac{1}{(\mu\text{m})} \times 10{,}000$$

$$\mu\text{m} = \frac{1}{(\text{cm})^{-1}} \times 10{,}000$$

PART A. SAMPLE PREPARATION AND RECORDING THE SPECTRUM

25.1 Introduction

To determine the infrared spectrum of the compound, one must place the compound in a sample holder or cell. In infrared spectroscopy, this immediately poses a problem. Glass, quartz, and plastics absorb strongly throughout the infrared region of the spectrum (any compound with covalent bonds usually absorbs) and cannot be used to construct sample cells. Ionic substances must be used in cell construction. Metal halides (sodium chloride, potassium bromide, silver chloride) are commonly used for this purpose.

Sodium Chloride Cells. Single crystals of sodium chloride are cut and polished to give plates that are transparent throughout the infrared region. These plates are then used to fabricate cells that can be used to hold *liquid* samples. Because sodium chloride is water soluble, samples must be *dry* before a spectrum can be obtained. In general, sodium chloride plates are preferred for most applications involving liquid samples. Potassium bromide plates may also be used in place of sodium chloride.

Silver Chloride Cells. Cells may be constructed of silver chloride. These plates may be used for *liquid* samples that contain small amounts of water, because silver chloride is water insoluble. However, because water absorbs in the infrared region, as much water as possible should be removed, even when using silver chloride. Silver chloride plates must be stored in the dark. They darken when exposed to light, and they cannot be used with compounds that have an amino functional group. Amines react with silver chloride.

Solid Samples. The easiest way to hold a *solid* sample in place is to dissolve the sample in a volatile organic solvent, place several drops of this solution on a salt plate, and allow the solvent to evaporate. This dry film method can be used only with modern FT-IR spectrometers. The other methods described here can be used with both FT-IR and dispersion spectrometers. A solid sample can also be held in place by making a potassium bromide pellet that contains a small amount of dispersed compound. A solid sample may also be suspended in mineral oil, which absorbs only in specific regions of the infrared spectrum. Another method is to dissolve the solid compound in an appropriate solvent and place the solution between two sodium chloride or silver chloride plates.

25.2 Liquid Samples—NaCl Plates

The simplest method of preparing the sample, if it is a liquid, is to place a thin layer of the liquid between two sodium chloride plates that have been ground flat and polished. This is the method of choice when you need to determine the infrared

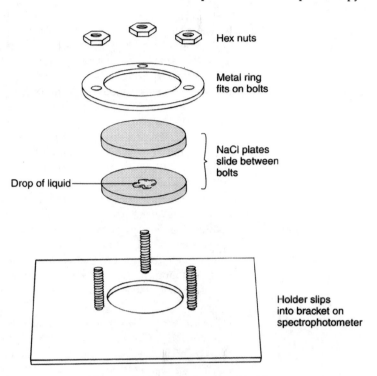

Figure 25.2   Salt plates and holder.

spectrum of a pure liquid. A spectrum determined by this method is referred to as a **neat** spectrum. No solvent is used. The polished plates are expensive because they are cut from a large, single crystal of sodium chloride. Salt plates break easily, and they are water soluble.

Preparing the Sample. Obtain two sodium chloride plates and a holder from the desiccator where they are stored. Moisture from fingers will mar and occlude the polished surfaces. Samples that contain water will destroy the plates.

NOTE: The plates should be touched only on their edges. Be certain to use a sample that is dry or free from water.

Add 1 or 2 drops of the liquid to the surface of one plate and then place the second plate on top.[1] The pressure of this second plate causes the liquid to spread out and form a thin capillary film between the two plates. As shown in Figure 25.2, set the plates between the bolts in a holder and place the metal ring carefully on the salt plates. Use the hex nuts to hold the salt plates in place.

NOTE: Do not overtighten the nuts or the salt plates will cleave or split.

---

[1] Use a Pasteur pipet or a short length of microcapillary tubing. If you use the microcapillary tubing, it can be filled by touching it into the liquid sample. When you touch it (lightly) to the salt plate, it will empty. Be careful not to scratch the plate.

Tighten the nuts firmly, but do not use any force to turn them. Spin them with the fingers until they stop; then turn them just another fraction of a full turn, and they will be tight enough. If the nuts have been tightened carefully, you should observe a *transparent film of sample* (a uniform wetting of the surface). If a thin film has not been obtained, either loosen one or more of the hex nuts and adjust them so that a uniform film is obtained or add more sample.

The thickness of the film obtained between the two plates is a function of two factors: (1) the amount of liquid placed on the first plate (1 drop, 2 drops, and so on), and (2) the pressure used to hold the plates together. If more than 1 or 2 drops of liquid have been used, the amount will probably be too much, and the resulting spectrum will show strong absorptions that are off the scale of the chart paper. Only enough liquid to wet both surfaces is needed.

If the sample has a very low viscosity, the capillary film may be too thin to produce a good spectrum. Another problem you may find is that the liquid is so volatile that the sample evaporates before the spectrum can be determined. In these cases, you may need to use the silver chloride plates discussed in Section 25.3 or a solution cell described in Section 25.6. Often, you can obtain a reasonable spectrum by assembling the cell quickly and running the spectrum before the sample runs out of the salt plates or evaporates.

Determining the Infrared Spectrum. Slide the holder into the slot in the sample beam of the spectrophotometer. Determine the spectrum according to the instructions provided by your instructor. In some cases, your instructor may ask you to calibrate your spectrum. If this is the case, refer to Section 25.8.

Cleaning and Storing the Salt Plates. Once the spectrum has been determined, demount the holder and rinse the salt plates with methylene chloride (or *dry* acetone). (Keep the plates away from water!) Use a soft tissue, moistened with the solvent, to wipe the plates. If some of your compound remains on the plates, you may observe a shiny surface. Continue to clean the plates with solvent until no more compound remains on the surfaces of the plates.

CAUTION   ⚠

Avoid direct contact with methylene chloride. Return the salt plates and holder to the desiccator for storage.

25.3 Liquid Samples— AgCl Plates

The minicell shown in Figure 25.3 may also be used with liquids.[2] The cell assembly consists of a two-piece threaded body, an O-ring, and two silver chloride plates. The plates are flat on one side, and there is a circular depression (0.025 mm or 0.10 mm deep) on the other side of the plate. An advantage of using silver chloride plates is that they may be used with wet samples or solutions. A disadvantage is that silver chloride darkens when exposed to light for extended periods. Silver chloride plates also scratch more easily than salt plates and react with amines.

---

[2] The Wilks Mini-Cell liquid sample holder is available from the Foxboro Company, 151 Woodward Avenue, South Norwalk, CT 06856. We recommend the AgCl cell windows with 0.10-mm depression rather than the 0.025-mm depression.

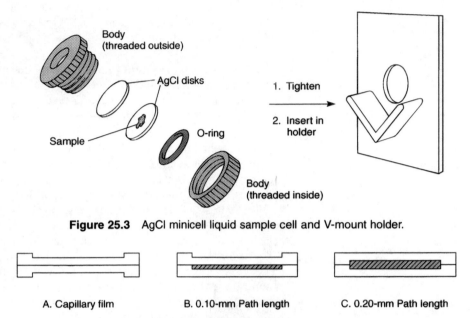

Figure 25.3   AgCl minicell liquid sample cell and V-mount holder.

A. Capillary film   B. 0.10-mm Path length   C. 0.20-mm Path length

Figure 25.4   Path-length variations for AgCl plates.

Preparing the Sample. Silver chloride plates should be handled in the same way as salt plates. Unfortunately, they are smaller and thinner (about like a contact lens) than salt plates, and care must be taken not to lose them! Remove them from the light-tight container with care. It is difficult to tell which side of the plate has the slight circular depression. Your instructor may have etched a letter on each plate to indicate which side is the flat one. To determine the infrared spectrum of a pure liquid (neat spectrum), select the flat side of each silver chloride plate. Insert the O-ring into the cell body as shown in Figure 25.3, place the plate into the cell body with the flat surface up, and add 1 drop or less of liquid to the plate.

NOTE: Do not use amines with AgCl plates.

Place the second plate on top of the first with the flat side down. The orientation of the silver chloride plates is shown in Figure 25.4A. This arrangement is used to obtain a capillary film of your sample. Screw the top of the minicell into the body of the cell so that the silver chloride plates are held firmly together. A tight seal forms because AgCl deforms under pressure.

Other combinations may be used with these plates. For example, you may vary the sample path length by using the orientations shown in Figures 25.4B and C. If you add your sample and the 0.10-mm depression of one plate and cover it with the flat side of the other one, you obtain a path length of 0.10 mm (see Figure 25.4B). This arrangement is useful for analyzing volatile or low-viscosity liquids. Placement of the two plates with their depressions toward each other gives a path length of 0.20 mm (see Figure 25.4C). This orientation may be used for a solution of a solid (or liquid) in carbon tetrachloride (see Section 25.6B).

Determining the Spectrum. Slide the V-mount holder shown in Figure 25.3 into the slot on the infrared spectrophotometer. Set the cell assembly in the V-mount holder, and determine the infrared spectrum of the liquid.

Cleaning and Storing the AgCl Plates. Once the spectrum has been determined, the cell assembly holder should be demounted and the AgCl plates rinsed with methylene chloride or acetone. Do not use tissue to wipe the plates, because they scratch easily. AgCl plates are light sensitive. Store the plates in a light-tight container.

25.4 Solid Samples— Dry Film

A simple method for determining the infrared spectrum of a solid sample is the **dry film** method. This method is easier than the other methods described here, it does not require any specialized equipment, and the spectra are excellent.[3] The disadvantage is that the dry film method can be used only with modern FT-IR spectrometers.

To use this method, place about 5 mg of your solid sample in a small, clean test tube. Add about 5 drops of methylene chloride (or diethyl ether, pentane, or dry acetone), and stir the mixture to dissolve the solid. Using a Pasteur pipet (not a capillary tube), place several drops of the solution on the face of a salt plate. Allow the solvent to evaporate; a uniform deposit of your product will remain as a dry film coating the salt plate. Mount the salt plate on a V-shaped holder in the infrared beam. Note that only one salt plate is used; the second salt plate is not used to cover the first. Once the salt plate is positioned properly, you may determine the spectrum in the normal manner. With this method, it is *very important* that you clean your material off the salt plate. When you are finished, use methylene chloride or dry acetone to clean the salt plate.

25.5 Solid Samples—KBr Pellets and Nujol Mulls

The methods described in this section can be used with both FT-IR and dispersion spectrometers.

A. KBr Pellets

One method of preparing a solid sample is to make a **potassium bromide (KBr) pellet**. When KBr is placed under pressure, it melts, flows, and seals the sample into a solid solution, or matrix. Because potassium bromide does not absorb in the infrared spectrum, a spectrum can be obtained on a sample without interference.

Preparing the Sample. Remove the agate mortar and pestle from the desiccator for use in preparing the sample. (Take care of them; they are expensive.) Grind 1 mg (0.001 g) of the solid sample for 1 minute in the agate mortar. At this point, the particle size will become so small that the surface of the solid appears shiny. Add 80 mg (0.080 g) of *powdered* KBr and grind the mixture for about 30 seconds with the pestle. Scrape the mixture into the middle with a spatula and grind the mixture again for about 15 seconds. This grinding operation helps to mix the sample thoroughly with the KBr. You should work as rapidly as possible because KBr absorbs water. The sample and KBr must be finely ground, or the mixture will scatter the infrared radiation excessively. Using your spatula, heap the mixture in the center of the mortar. Return the bottle of potassium bromide to the desiccator where it is stored when it is not in use.

---

[3] Feist, P. L. "Sampling Techniques for Organic Solids in IR Spectroscopy: Thin Solid Films as the Method of Choice in Teaching Laboratories." *Journal of Chemical Education,* 78 (2001): 351.

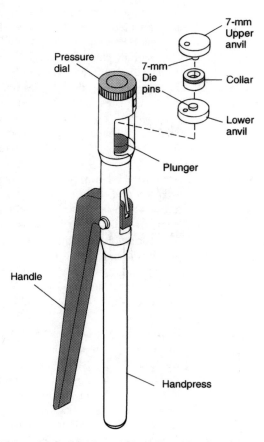

Figure 25.5   Making a KBr pellet with a handpress.

The sample and potassium bromide should be weighed on an analytical balance the first few times that a pellet is prepared. After some experience, you can estimate these quantities quite accurately by eye.

Making a Pellet Using a KBr Handpress. Two methods are commonly used to prepare KBr pellets. The first method uses the handpress apparatus shown in Figure 25.5.[4] Remove the die set from the storage container. Take extreme care to avoid scratching the polished surfaces of the die set. Place the anvil with the shorter die pin (lower anvil in Figure 25.5) on a bench. Slip the collar over the pin. Remove about one fourth of your KBr mixture with a spatula and transfer it into the collar. The powder may not cover the head of the pin completely, but do not be concerned about this. Place the anvil with the longer die pin into the collar so that the die pin comes into contact with the sample. Never press the die set unless it contains a sample.

Lift the die set carefully by holding onto the lower anvil so that the collar stays in place. If you are careless with this operation, the collar may move enough to allow the powder to escape. Open the handle of the handpress slightly, tilt the press back a bit, and insert the die set into the press. Make sure that the die set is seated

---

[4] KBr Quick Press unit is available from Wilmad Glass Company, Inc., Route 40 and Oak Road, Buena, NJ 08310.

against the side wall of the chamber. Close the handle. It is imperative that the die set be seated against the side wall of the chamber so that the die is centered in the chamber. Pressing the die in an off-centered position can bend the anvil pins.

With the handle in the closed position, rotate the pressure dial so that the upper ram of the handpress just touches the upper anvil of the die assembly. Tilt the unit back so that the die set does not fall out of the handpress. Open the handle and rotate the pressure dial clockwise about one-half turn. Slowly compress the KBr mixture by closing the handle. The pressure should be no greater than that exerted by a very firm handshake. Do not apply excessive pressure or the dies may be damaged. If in doubt, rotate the pressure dial counterclockwise to lower the pressure. If the handle closes too easily, open the handle, rotate the pressure dial clockwise, and compress the sample again. Compress the sample for about 60 seconds.

After this time, tilt the unit back so that the die set does not fall out of the handpress. Open the handle and carefully remove the die set from the unit. Turn the pressure dial counterclockwise about one full turn. Pull the die set apart and inspect the KBr pellet. Ideally, the pellet should appear clear like a piece of glass, but usually it will be translucent or somewhat opaque. There may be some cracks or holes in the pellet. The pellet will produce a good spectrum, even with imperfections, as long as light can travel through the pellet. Clean the dies using the procedure outlined below, in "Cleaning and Storing the Equipment."

Making a Pellet with a KBr Minipress. The second method of preparing a pellet uses the minipress apparatus shown in Figure 25.6. Obtain a ground KBr mixture as described in "Preparing the Sample" and transfer a portion of the finely ground powder (usually not more than half) into a die that compresses it into a translucent pellet. As shown in Figure 25.6, the die consists of two stainless steel bolts and a threaded barrel. The bolts have their ends ground flat. To use this die, screw one of the bolts into the barrel, but not all the way; leave one or two turns. Carefully add the powder with a spatula into the open end of the partly assembled die and tap it lightly on the benchtop to give an even layer on the face of the bolt. While keeping the barrel upright, carefully screw the second bolt into the barrel until it is finger tight. Insert the head of the bottom bolt into the hexagonal hole in a plate bolted to the benchtop. This plate keeps the head of one bolt from turning. The top bolt is tightened with a torque wrench to compress the KBr mixture. Continue to turn the torque wrench until you hear a loud click (the ratchet mechanism makes softer clicks) or until you reach the appropriate torque value (20 ft-lb). If you tighten the bolt beyond this point, you may twist the head off one of the bolts. Leave the die under pressure for about 60 seconds; then reverse the ratchet on the torque wrench or pull the torque wrench in the opposite

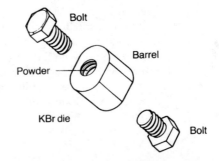

Figure 25.6   Making a KBr pellet with a minipress.

direction to open the assembly. When the two bolts are loose, hold the barrel horizontally and carefully remove the two bolts. You should observe a clear or translucent KBr pellet in the center of the barrel. Even if the pellet is not totally transparent, you should be able to obtain a satisfactory spectrum as long as light passes through the pellet.

Determining the Infrared Spectrum. To obtain the spectrum, slide the holder appropriate for the type of die that you are using into the slot on the infrared spectrophotometer. Set the die containing the pellet in the holder so that the sample is centered in the optical path. Obtain the infrared spectrum. If you are using a double-beam instrument, you may be able to compensate (at least partially) for a marginal pellet by placing a wire screen or attenuator in the reference beam, thereby balancing the lowered transmittance of the pellet. An FT-IR instrument will automatically deal with the low intensity if you select the "autoscale" option.

Problems with an Unsatisfactory Pellet. If the pellet is unsatisfactory (too cloudy to pass light), one of several things may have been wrong:

1. The KBr mixture may not have been ground finely enough, and the particle size may be too big. The large particle size creates too much light scattering.
2. The sample may not be dry.
3. Too much sample may have been used for the amount of KBr taken.
4. The pellet may be too thick; that is, too much of the powdered mixture was put into the die.
5. The KBr may have been "wet" or have acquired moisture from the air while the mixture was being ground in the mortar.
6. The sample may have a low melting point. Low-melting solids not only are difficult to dry, but also melt under pressure. You may need to dissolve the compound in a solvent and run the spectrum in solution (see Section 25.6).

Cleaning and Storing the Equipment. After you have determined the spectrum, punch the pellet out of the die with a wooden applicator stick (a spatula should not be used as it may scratch the dies). Remember that the polished faces of the die set must not be scratched, or they become useless. After the pellet has been punched out, wash all parts of the die set or minipress with warm water. Then rinse the parts with acetone and dry them using a Kimwipe. Check with your instructor to see if there are additional instructions for cleaning the die set. Return the dies to the storage container. Wash the mortar and pestle with water, dry them carefully with paper towels, and return them to the desiccator. Return the KBr powder to its desiccator.

B. Nujol Mulls

If an adequate KBr pellet cannot be obtained or if the solid is insoluble in a suitable solvent, the spectrum of a solid may be determined as a **Nujol mull**. In this method, finely grind about 5 mg of the solid sample in an agate mortar with a pestle. Then add 1 or 2 drops of Nujol mineral oil (white) and grind the mixture to a very fine dispersion. The solid is not dissolved in the Nujol; it is actually a suspension. This mull is then placed between two salt plates using a rubber policeman. Mount the salt plates in the holder in the same way as for liquid samples (see Section 25.2).

Nujol is a mixture of high-molecular-weight hydrocarbons. Hence, it has absorptions in the C—H stretch and CH_2 and CH_3 bending regions of the spectrum (see Figure 25.7). Clearly, if Nujol is used, no information can be obtained in these portions of the spectrum. In interpreting the spectrum, you must ignore these Nujol peaks. It is important to label the spectrum immediately after it was determined, noting that it was determined as a Nujol mull. Otherwise, you might forget that the C—H peaks belong to Nujol and not to the dispersed solid.

A. Method A—Solution Between Salt (NaCl) Plates

**25.6 Solid Samples—
Solution Spectra**

For substances that are soluble in carbon tetrachloride, a quick and easy method for determining the spectra of solids is available. Dissolve as much solid as possible in 0.1 mL of carbon tetrachloride. Place 1 or 2 drops of the solution between sodium chloride plates in precisely the same manner as used for pure liquids (see Section 25.2). The spectrum is determined as described for pure liquids using salt plates (see Section 25.2). You should work as quickly as possible. If there is a delay, the solvent will evaporate from between the plates before the spectrum is recorded. Because the spectrum contains the absorptions of the solute superimposed on the absorptions of carbon tetrachloride, it is important to remember that any absorption that appears near 800 cm^{-1} may be due to the stretching of the C—Cl bond of the solvent. Information contained to the right of about 900 cm^{-1} is not usable in this method. There are no other interfering bands for this solvent (see Figure 25.8), and any other absorptions can be attributed to your sample. Chloroform solutions should not be studied by this method because the solvent has too many interfering absorptions (see Figure 25.9).

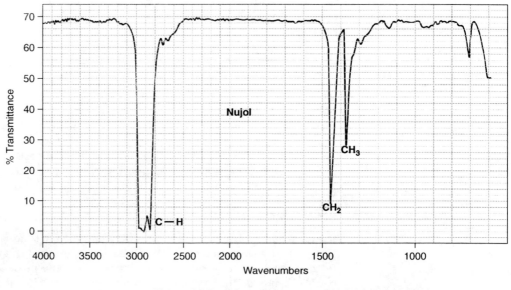

Figure 25.7   Infrared spectrum of Nujol (mineral oil).

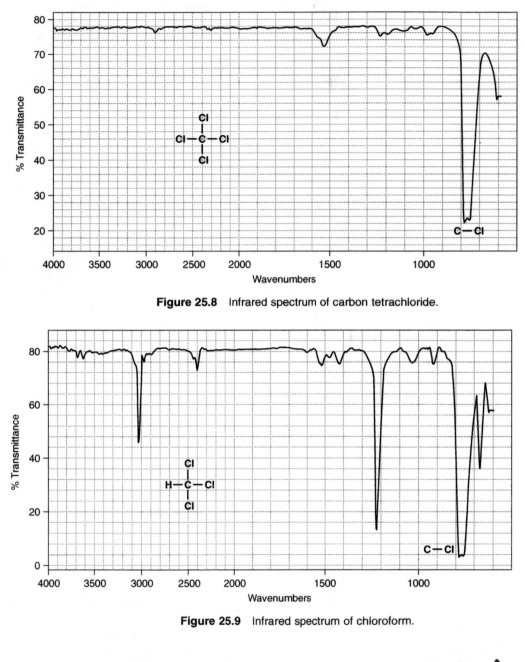

Figure 25.8 Infrared spectrum of carbon tetrachloride.

Figure 25.9 Infrared spectrum of chloroform.

CAUTION

Carbon tetrachloride is a hazardous solvent. Work under the hood!

Carbon tetrachloride, besides being toxic, is suspected of being a carcinogen. Despite the health problems associated with its use, there is no suitable alternative solvent for infrared spectroscopy. Other solvents have too many interfering infrared absorption bands. Handle carbon tetrachloride carefully to minimize the adverse health effects. The spectroscopic-grade carbon tetrachloride should be stored in a glass-stoppered bottle in a hood. A Pasteur pipet should be attached to the bottle, possibly by storing it in a test tube taped to the side of the bottle. All sample preparation should be conducted in a hood. Rubber or plastic gloves should be worn. The cells should also be cleaned in the hood. All carbon tetrachloride used in preparing samples should be disposed of in an appropriately marked waste container.

B. Method B—AgCl Minicell

The AgCl minicell described in Section 25.3 may be used to determine the infrared spectrum of a solid dissolved in carbon tetrachloride. Prepare a 5–10% solution (5–10 mg in 0.1 mL) in carbon tetrachloride. If it is not possible to prepare a solution of this concentration because of low solubility, dissolve as much solid as possible in the solvent. Following the instructions given in Section 25.3, position the AgCl plates as shown in Figure 25.4C to obtain the maximum possible path length of 0.20 mm. When the cell is tightened firmly, the cell will not leak.

As indicated in method A, the spectrum will contain the absorptions of the dissolved solid superimposed on the absorptions of carbon tetrachloride. A strong absorption appears near 800 cm^{-1} for the C—Cl stretch in the solvent. No useful information may be obtained for the sample to the right of about 900 cm^{-1}, but other bands that appear in the spectrum will belong to your sample. Read the safety material provided in method A. Carbon tetrachloride is toxic, and it should be used under a hood.

NOTE: Care should be taken in cleaning the AgCl plates. Because AgCl plates scratch easily, they should not be wiped with tissue. Rinse them with methylene chloride and keep them in a dark place. Amines will destroy the plates.

C. Method C—Solution Cells (NaCl)

The spectra of solids may also be determined in a type of permanent sample cell called a **solution cell**. (The infrared spectra of liquids may also be determined in this cell.) The solution cell, shown in Figure 25.10, is made from two salt plates, mounted with a Teflon spacer between them to control the thickness of the sample. The top sodium chloride plate has two holes drilled in it so that the sample can be introduced into the cavity between the two plates. These holes are extended through the face plate by two tubular extensions designed to hold Teflon plugs, which seal the internal chamber and prevent evaporation. The tubular extensions are tapered so that a syringe body (Luer lock without a needle) will fit snugly into them from the outside. The cells are thus filled from a syringe; usually, they are held upright and filled from the bottom entrance port.

These cells are expensive, and you should try either method A or B before using solution cells. If you do need them, obtain your instructor's permission and receive instruction before using the cells. The cells are purchased in matched pairs, with identical path lengths. Dissolve a solid in a suitable solvent, usually carbon tetrachloride, and add the solution to one of the cells (**sample cell**) as described in the previous paragraph. The pure solvent, identical to that used to dissolve the solid, is placed in the other cell (**reference cell**). The spectrum of the solvent is subtracted from the spectrum of the solution (not always completely), and a spectrum of the solute is thus provided. For the solvent compensation to be as exact as possible and to avoid contamination of the reference cell, it is essential that one cell be used as

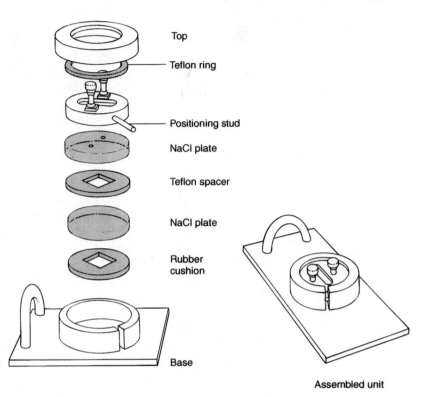

Top

Teflon ring

Positioning stud

NaCl plate

Teflon spacer

NaCl plate

Rubber cushion

Base

Assembled unit

Figure 25.10   A solution cell.

a reference and that the other cell be used as a sample cell without ever being inter-changed. After the spectrum is determined, it is important to clean the cells by flushing them with clean solvent. They should be dried by passing dry air through the cell.

Solvents most often used in determining infrared spectra are carbon tetra-chloride (see Figure 25.8), chloroform (see Figure 25.9), and carbon disulfide (see Figure 25.11). A 5–10% solution of solid in one of these solvents usually gives a good spectrum. Carbon tetrachloride and chloroform are suspected carcinogens; however, because there are no suitable alternative solvents, these compounds must be used in infrared spectroscopy. The procedure outlined above for carbon tetrachloride should be followed. This procedure serves equally well for chloroform.

NOTE: Before you use the solution cells, you must obtain the instructor's permission and instruc-tion on how to fill and clean the cells.

25.7 Recording the Spectrum

The instructor will describe how to operate the infrared spectrophotometer, because the controls vary considerably, depending on the manufacturer, model of the instru-ment, and type. For example, some instruments involve pushing only a few but-tons, whereas others use a more complicated computer interface system.

In all cases, it is important that the sample, the solvent, the type of cell or method used, and any other pertinent information be written on the spectrum immediately after the determination. This information may be important, and it is easily forgotten if not recorded. You may also need to calibrate the instrument (see Section 25.8).

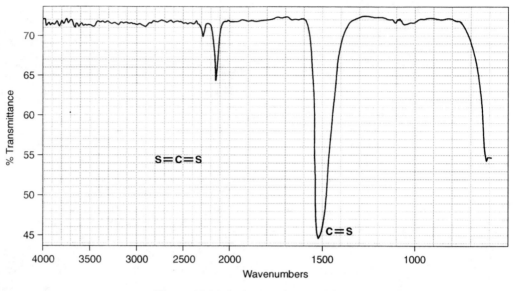

Figure 25.11   Infrared spectrum of carbon disulfide.

25.8 Calibration

For some instruments, the frequency scale of the spectrum must be calibrated so that you know the position of each absorption peak precisely. You can recalibrate by recording a very small portion of the spectrum of polystyrene over the spectrum of your sample. The complete spectrum of polystyrene is shown in Figure 25.12. The most important of these peaks is at 1603 cm^{-1}; other useful peaks are at

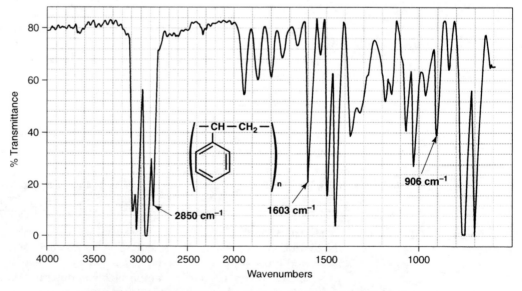

Figure 25.12   Infrared spectrum of polystyrene (thin film).

2850 cm^{-1} and 906 cm^{-1}. After you record the spectrum of your sample, substitute a thin film of polystyrene for the sample cell and record the tips (not the entire spectrum) of the most important peaks over the sample spectrum.

It is always a good idea to calibrate a spectrum when the instrument uses chart paper with a preprinted scale. It is difficult to align the paper properly so that the scale matches the absorption lines precisely. You often need to know the precise values for certain functional groups (for example, the carbonyl group). Calibration is essential in these cases.

With computer-interfaced instruments, the instrument does not need to be calibrated. With this type of instrument, the spectrum and scale are printed on blank paper at the same time. The instrument has an internal calibration that ensures that the positions of the absorptions are known precisely and that they are placed at the proper positions on the scale. With this type of instrument, it is often possible to print a list of the locations of the major peaks as well as to obtain the complete spectrum of your compound.

PART B. INFRARED SPECTROSCOPY

25.9 Uses of the Infrared Spectrum

Because every type of bond has a different natural frequency of vibration and because the same type of bond in two different compounds is in a slightly different environment, no two molecules of different structure have exactly the same infrared absorption pattern, or **infrared spectrum**. Although some of the frequencies absorbed in the two cases might be the same, in no case of two different molecules will their infrared spectra (the patterns of absorption) be identical. Thus, the infrared spectrum can be used to identify molecules much as a fingerprint can be used to identify people. Comparing the infrared spectra of two substances thought to be identical will establish whether or not they are in fact identical. If the infrared spectra of two substances coincide peak for peak (absorption for absorption), in most cases, the substances are identical.

A second and more important use of the infrared spectrum is that it gives structural information about a molecule. The absorptions of each type of bond (N—H, C—H, O—H, C—X, C=O, C—O, C—C, C=C, C≡C, C≡N, and so on) are regularly found only in certain small portions of the vibrational infrared region. A small range of absorption can be defined for each type of bond. Outside this range, absorptions will normally be due to some other type of bond. Thus, for instance, any absorption in the range $3000 \pm 150 \text{ cm}^{-1}$ will almost always be due to the presence of a CH bond in the molecule; an absorption in the range $1700 \pm 100 \text{ cm}^{-1}$ will normally be due to the presence of a C=O bond (carbonyl group) in the molecule. The same type of range applies to each type of bond. The way these are spread out over the vibrational infrared is illustrated schematically in Figure 25.13. It is a good idea to remember this general scheme for future convenience.

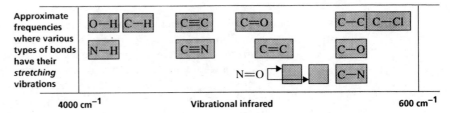

Figure 25.13 Approximate regions in which various common types of bonds absorb. (Bending, twisting, and other types of bond vibration have been omitted for clarity.)

25.10 Modes of Vibration

The simplest types, or **modes**, of vibrational motion in a molecule that are **infrared active**, that is, give rise to absorptions, are the stretching and bending modes.

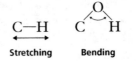

Other, more complex types of stretching and bending are also active, however. To introduce several words of terminology, the normal modes of vibration for a methylene group are shown below.

In any group of three or more atoms—at least two of which are identical—there are *two* modes of stretching or bending: the symmetric mode and asymmetric mode. Examples of such groupings are $-CH_3$, $-CH_2-$, $-NO_2$, $-NH_2$, and anhydrides $(CO)_2O$. For the anhydride, owing to asymmetric and symmetric modes of stretch, this functional group gives *two* absorptions in the $C=O$ region. A similar phenomenon is seen for amino groups, where primary amines usually have *two* absorptions in the NH stretch region, whereas secondary amines R_2NH have only one absorption peak. Amides show similar bands. There are two strong $N=O$ stretch peaks for a nitro group, which are caused by asymmetric and symmetric stretching modes.

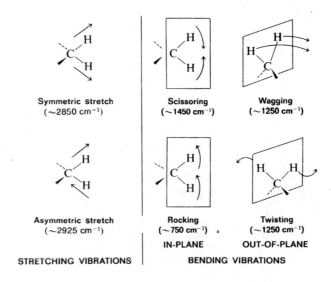

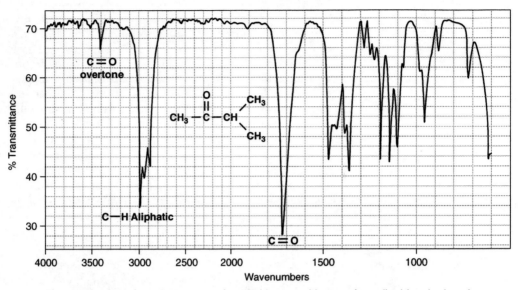

Figure 25.14   Infrared spectrum of methyl isopropyl ketone (neat liquid, salt plates).

25.11 What to Look for in Examining Infrared Spectra

The instrument that determines the absorption spectrum for a compound is called an **infrared spectrophotometer**. The spectrophotometer determines the relative strengths and positions of all the absorptions in the infrared region and plots this information on a piece of paper. This plot of absorption intensity versus wavenumber or wavelength is referred to as the **infrared spectrum** of the compound. A typical infrared spectrum, that of methyl isopropyl ketone, is shown in Figure 25.14.

The strong absorption in the middle of the spectrum corresponds to C=O, the carbonyl group. Note that the C=O peak is quite intense. In addition to the characteristic position of absorption, the **shape** and **intensity** of this peak are also unique to the C=O bond. This is true for almost every type of absorption peak; both shape and intensity characteristics can be described, and these characteristics often make it possible to distinguish the peak in a confusing situation. For instance, to some extent both C=O and C=C bonds absorb in the same region of the infrared spectrum:

$$C=O \quad 1850–1630 \text{ cm}^{-1}$$

$$C=C \quad 1680–1620 \text{ cm}^{-1}$$

However, the C=O bond is a strong absorber, whereas the C=C bond generally absorbs only weakly. Hence, a trained observer would not normally interpret a strong peak at 1670 cm^{-1} to be a carbon–carbon double bond or a weak absorption at this frequency to be due to a carbonyl group.

The shape of a peak often gives a clue to its identity as well. Thus, although the NH and OH regions of the infrared overlap,

$$OH \quad 3650–3200 \text{ cm}^{-1}$$

$$NH \quad 3500–3300 \text{ cm}^{-1}$$

NH usually gives a **sharp** absorption peak (absorbs a very narrow range of frequencies), and OH, when it is in the NH region, usually gives a **broad** absorption peak. Primary amines give *two* absorptions in this region, whereas alcohols give only one.

Therefore, while you are studying the sample spectra in the pages that follow, you should also notice shapes and intensities. They are as important as the frequency at which an absorption occurs, and you must train your eye to recognize these features. In the literature of organic chemistry, you will often find absorptions referred to as strong (s), medium (m), weak (w), broad, or sharp. The author is trying to convey some idea of what the peak looks like without actually drawing the spectrum. Although the intensity of an absorption often provides useful information about the identity of a peak, be aware that the relative intensities of all of the peaks in the spectrum are dependent on the amount of sample that is used and the sensitivity setting of the instrument. Therefore, the *actual* intensity of a particular peak may vary from spectrum to spectrum, and you must pay attention to *relative* intensities.

25.12 Correlation Charts and Tables

To extract structural information from infrared spectra, you must know the frequencies or wavelengths at which various functional groups absorb. Infrared **correlation tables** present as much information as is known about where the various functional groups absorb. The books listed at the end of this chapter present extensive lists of correlation tables. Sometimes, the absorption information is given in a chart, called a **correlation chart**. A simplified correlation table is given in Table 25.1.

Although you may think assimilating the mass of data in Table 25.1 will be difficult, it is not if you make a modest start and then gradually increase your familiarity with the data. An ability to interpret the fine details of an infrared spectrum will follow. This is most easily accomplished by first establishing the broad visual patterns of Figure 25.13 firmly in mind. Then, as a second step, a "typical absorption value" can be memorized for each of the functional groups in this pattern. This value will be a single number that can be used as a pivot value for the memory. For instance, start with a simple aliphatic ketone as a model for all typical carbonyl compounds. The typical aliphatic ketone has a carbonyl absorption of 1715 ± 10 cm^{-1}. Without worrying about the variation, memorize 1715 cm^{-1} as the base value for carbonyl absorption. Then learn the extent of the carbonyl range and the visual pattern of how the different kinds of carbonyl groups are arranged throughout this region. See, for instance, Figure 25.27, which gives typical values for carbonyl compounds. Also learn how factors such as ring size (when the functional group is contained in a ring) and conjugation affect the base values (that is, in which direction the values are shifted). Learn the trends—always remembering the base value (1715 cm^{-1}). It might prove useful as a beginning to memorize the base values in Table 25.2 for this approach. Notice that there are only eight values.

25.13 Analyzing a Spectrum (Or What You Can Tell at a Glance)

In analyzing the spectrum of an unknown, concentrate first on establishing the presence (or absence) of a few major functional groups. The most conspicuous peaks are C=O, O—H, N—H, C—O, C=C, C≡C, C≡N, and NO$_2$. If they are present, they give immediate structural information. Do not try to analyze in detail the CH absorptions near 3000 cm^{-1}; almost all compounds have these absorptions.

TABLE 25.1 A Simplified Correlation Table

	Type of Vibration		Frequency (cm^{-1})	Intensity[a]
C—H	Alkanes	(stretch)	3000–2850	s
	—CH$_3$	(bend)	1450 and 1375	m
	—CH$_2$—	(bend)	1465	m
	Alkenes	(stretch)	3100–3000	m
		(bend)	1700–1000	s
	Aromatics	(stretch)	3150–3050	s
		(out-of-plane bend)	1000–700	s
	Alkyne	(stretch)	ca. 3300	s
	Aldehyde		2900–2800	w
			2800–2700	w
C—C	Alkane	Not interpretatively useful		
C=C	Alkene		1680–1600	m–w
	Aromatic		1600–1400	m–w
C≡C	Alkyne		2250–2100	m–w
C=O	Aldehyde		1740–1720	s
	Ketone (acyclic)		1725–1705	s
	Carboxylic acid		1725–1700	s
	Ester		1750–1730	s
	Amide		1700–1640	s
	Anhydride		ca. 1810	s
			ca. 1760	s
C—O	Alcohols, ethers, esters, carboxylic acids		1300–1000	s
O—H	Alcohol, phenols			
	Free		3650–3600	m
	H-Bonded		3400–3200	m
	Carboxylic acids		3300–2500	m
N—H	Primary and secondary amines		ca. 3500	m
C≡N	Nitriles		2260–2240	m
N=O	Nitro (R—NO$_2$)		1600–1500	s
			1400–1300	s
C—X	Fluoride		1400–1000	s
	Chloride		800–600	s
	Bromide, iodide		<600	s

[a] s, strong; m, medium; w, weak.

TABLE 25.2 Base Values for Absorptions of Bonds

O—H	3400 cm^{-1}	C≡C	2150 cm^{-1}
N—H	3500 cm^{-1}	C=O	1715 cm^{-1}
C—H	3000 cm^{-1}	C=C	1650 cm^{-1}
C≡N	2250 cm^{-1}	C—O	1100 cm^{-1}

Do not worry about subtleties of the exact type of environment in which the functional group is found. A checklist of the important gross features follows:

1. Is a carbonyl group present?
   The C=O group gives rise to a strong absorption in the region 1820–1600 cm^{-1}. The peak is often the strongest in the spectrum and of medium width. You can't miss it.

2. If C=O is present, check the following types. (If it is absent, go to item 3.)

Acids	Is O—H also present?
	Broad absorption near 3300–2500 cm^{-1} (usually overlaps C—H).
Amides	Is N—H also present?
	Medium absorption near 3500 cm^{-1}, sometimes a double peak, equivalent halves.
Esters	Is C—O also present?
	Medium intensity absorptions near 1300–1000 cm^{-1}.
Anhydrides	Have *two* C=O absorptions near 1810 and 1760 cm^{-1}.
Aldehydes	Is aldehyde C—H present?
	Two weak absorptions near 2850 cm^{-1} and 2750 cm^{-1} on the right side of C—H absorptions.
Ketones	The preceding five choices have been eliminated.

3. If C=O is absent

Alcohols or Phenols	Check for O—H.
	Broad absorption near 3600–3300 cm^{-1}.
	Confirm this by finding C—O near 1300–1000 cm^{-1}.
Amines	Check for N—H.
	Medium absorption(s) near 3500 cm^{-1}.
Ethers	Check for C—O (and absence of O—H) near 1300–1000 cm^{-1}.

4. Double bonds or aromatic rings or both
   C=C is a **weak** absorption near 1650 cm^{-1}.
   Medium to strong absorptions in the region 1650–1450 cm^{-1} often imply an aromatic ring.
   Confirm the above by consulting the C—H region.
   Aromatic and vinyl C—H occur to the left of 3000 cm^{-1} (aliphatic C—H occurs to the right of this value).

5. Triple bonds   C≡N is a medium, sharp absorption near 2250 cm^{-1}.
   C≡C is a weak but sharp absorption near 2150 cm^{-1}.
   Check also for acetylenic C—H near 3300 cm^{-1}.

6. Nitro groups   *Two* strong absorptions near 1600–1500 cm^{-1} and 1390–1300 cm^{-1}.

7. Hydrocarbons   None of the above is found.
   Main absorptions are in the C—H region near 3000 cm^{-1}.
   Very simple spectrum, only other absorptions are near 1450 cm^{-1} and 1375 cm^{-1}.

The beginning student should resist the idea of trying to assign or interpret *every* peak in the spectrum. You simply will not be able to do this. Concentrate first on learning the principal peaks and recognizing their presence or absence. This is best done by carefully studying the illustrative spectra in the section that follows.

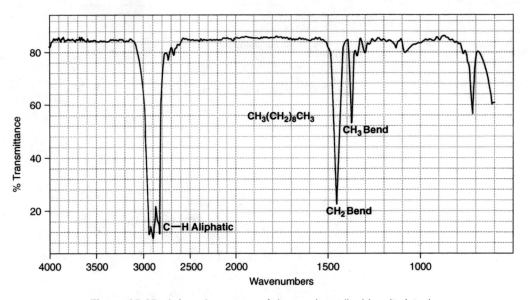

Figure 25.15   Infrared spectrum of decane (neat liquid, salt plates).

NOTE: In describing the shifts of absorption peaks or their relative positions, we have used the phrases "to the left" and "to the right." This was done to simplify descriptions of peak positions. The meaning is clear because all spectra are conventionally presented left to right from 4000–600 cm^{-1}.

25.14 Survey of the Important Functional Groups

A. Alkanes

The spectrum is usually simple, with a few peaks.

C—H   Stretch occurs around 3000 cm^{-1}.
      1. In alkanes (except strained ring compounds), absorption always occurs to the right of 3000 cm^{-1}.
      2. If a compound has vinylic, aromatic, acetylenic, or cyclopropyl hydrogens, the CH absorption is to the left of 3000 cm^{-1}.

CH$_2$ Methylene groups have a characteristic absorption at approximately 1450 cm^{-1}.

CH$_3$ Methyl groups have a characteristic absorption at approximately 1375 cm^{-1}.

C—C   Stretch—not interpretatively useful—has many peaks.

The spectrum of decane is shown in Figure 25.15.

B. Alkenes

=C—H   Stretch occurs to the left of 3000 cm^{-1}.
=C—H   Out-of-plane (oop) bending occurs at 1000–650 cm^{-1}.
      The C—H oop absorptions often allow you to determine the type of substitution pattern on the double bond, according to the number of absorptions and their positions. The correlation chart in Figure 25.16 shows the positions of these bands.

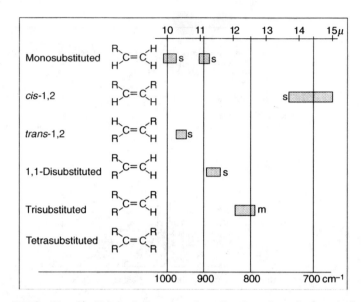

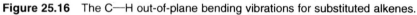

Figure 25.16   The C—H out-of-plane bending vibrations for substituted alkenes.

C═C   Stretch 1675–1600cm^{-1}, often weak.
         Conjugation moves C═C stretch to the right.
         Symmetrically substituted bonds, as in 2,3-dimethyl-2-butene, do
            not absorb in the infrared region (no dipole change). Highly substi-
            tuted double bonds are often vanishingly weak in absorption.

The spectra of 4-methylcyclohexene and styrene are shown in Figures 25.17 and
25.18.

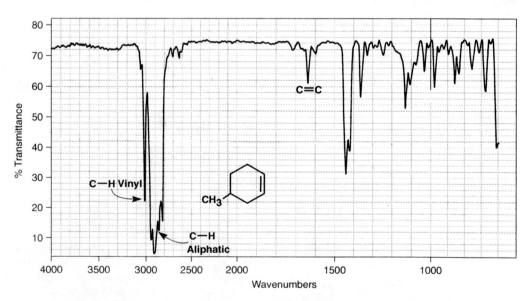

Figure 25.17   Infrared spectrum of 4-methylcyclohexene (neat liquid, salt plates).

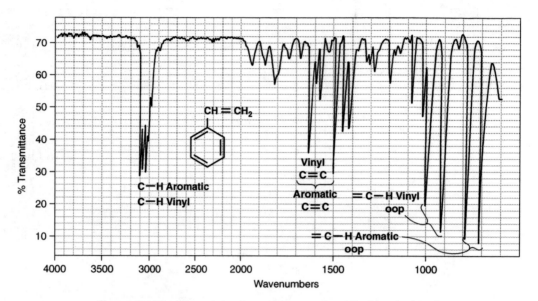

Figure 25.18   Infrared spectrum of styrene (neat liquid, salt plates).

C. Aromatic Rings

=C—H   Stretch is always to the left of 3000 cm^{-1}.

=C—H   Out-of-plane oop bending occurs at 900 to 690 cm^{-1}.

The C—H oop absorptions often allow you to determine the type of ring substitution by their numbers, intensities, and positions. The correlation chart in Figure 25.19A indicates the positions of these bands.

The patterns are generally reliable—they are most reliable for rings with alkyl substituents and least reliable for polar substituents.

Ring Absorptions (C=C). There are often four sharp absorptions that occur in pairs at 1600 cm^{-1} and 1450 cm^{-1} and are characteristic of an aromatic ring. See, for example, the spectra of anisole (Figure 25.23), benzonitrile (Figure 25.26), and methyl benzoate (Figure 25.35).

There are many weak combination and overtone absorptions that appear between 2000 cm^{-1} and 1667 cm^{-1}. The relative shapes and numbers of these peaks can be used to determine whether an aromatic ring is monosubstituted or di-, tri-, tetra-, penta-, or hexa-substituted. Positional isomers can also be distinguished. Because the absorptions are weak, these bands are best observed by using neat liquids or concentrated solutions. If the compound has a high-frequency carbonyl group, this absorption overlaps the weak overtone bands, so no useful information can be obtained from analyzing this region. The various patterns that are obtained in this region are shown in Figure 25.19B.

The spectra of styrene and *o*-dichlorobenzene are shown in Figures 25.18 and 25.20.

D. Alkynes

≡C—H   Stretch is usually near 3300 cm^{-1}, sharp peak.

C≡C   Stretch is near 2150 cm^{-1}, sharp peak.

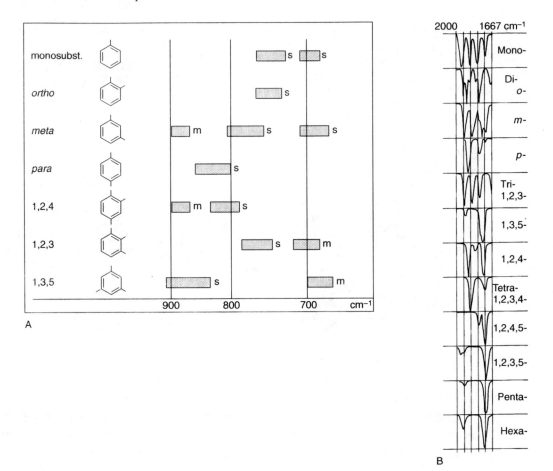

Figure 25.19 (**A**) The C—H out-of-plane bending vibrations for substituted benzenoid compounds. (**B**) The 2000–1667 cm^{-1} region for substituted benzenoid compounds. (From Dyer, J.R., *Applications of Absorption Spectroscopy of Organic Compounds,* Englewood Cliffs, NJ: Prentice Hall, 1965.)

Conjugation moves C≡C stretch to the right.
Disubstituted or symmetrically substituted triple bonds give either no absorption or weak absorption.

E. Alcohols and Phenols

O—H Stretch is a sharp peak at 3650–3600 cm^{-1} if no hydrogen bonding takes place. (This is usually observed only in dilute solutions.)

If there is hydrogen bonding (usual in neat or concentrated solutions), the absorption is *broad* and occurs more to the right at 3500–3200 cm^{-1}, sometimes overlapping C—H stretch absorptions.

C—O Stretch is usually in the range of 1300–1000 cm^{-1}.

Phenols are like alcohols. The 2-naphthol shown in Figure 25.21 has some molecules hydrogen bonded and some free. The spectrum of 4-methylcyclohexanol is shown in Figure 25.22. This alcohol, which was determined neat, would also have had a free OH spike to the left of this hydrogen-bonded band if it had been determined in dilute solution.

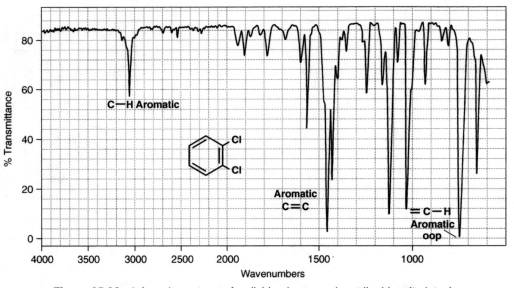

Figure 25.20   Infrared spectrum of o-dichlorobenzene (neat liquid, salt plates).

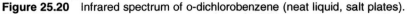

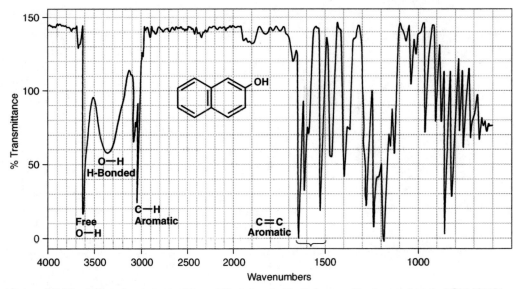

Figure 25.21   Infrared spectrum of 2-naphthol showing both free and hydrogen-bonded OH (CHCl$_3$ solution).

F. Ethers

C—O   The most prominent band is due to C—O stretch at 1300–1000 cm^{-1}. Absence of C=O and O—H bands is required to be sure the C—O stretch is not due to an alcohol or ester. Phenyl and vinyl ethers are found in the left portion of the range, aliphatic ethers in the right. (Conjugation with the oxygen moves the absorption to the left.)

The spectrum of anisole is shown in Figure 25.23.

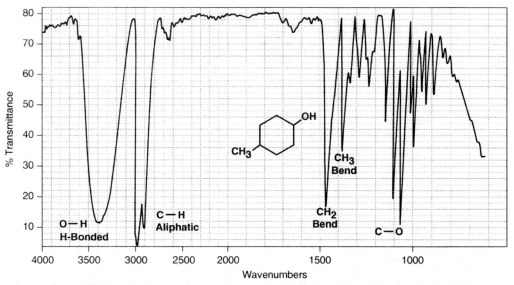

Figure 25.22   Infrared spectrum of 4-methylcyclohexanol (neat liquid, salt plates).

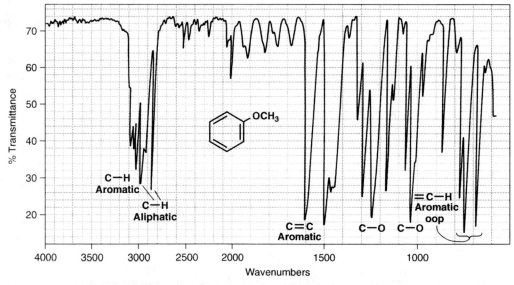

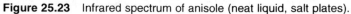

Figure 25.23   Infrared spectrum of anisole (neat liquid, salt plates).

G. Amines

N—H   Stretch occurs in the range of 3500–3300 cm^{-1}.
Primary amines have *two* bands typically 30 cm^{-1} apart.
Secondary amines have one band, often vanishingly weak.
Tertiary amines have no NH stretch.

C—N   Stretch is weak and occurs in the range of 1350–1000 cm^{-1}.

N—H   Scissoring bending mode occurs in the range of 1640–1560 cm^{-1} (broad).
An oop bending absorption can sometimes be observed at about 800 cm^{-1}.

The spectrum of *n*-butylamine is shown in Figure 25.24.

H. Nitro Compounds

N=O   Stretch is usually two strong bands at 1600–1500 cm^{-1} and 1390–1300 cm^{-1}.

The spectrum of nitrobenzene is shown in Figure 25.25.

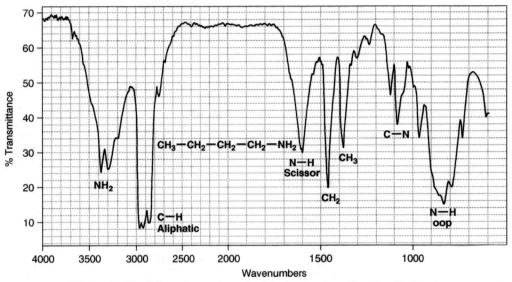

Figure 25.24 Infrared spectrum of *n*-butylamine (neat liquid, salt plates).

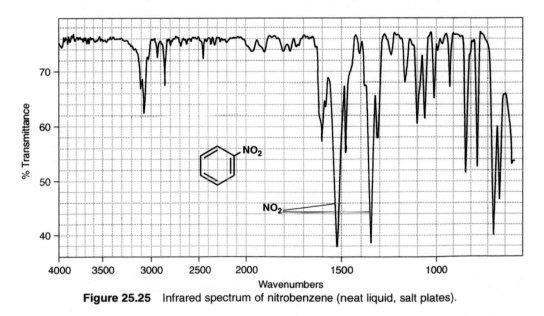

Figure 25.25 Infrared spectrum of nitrobenzene (neat liquid, salt plates).

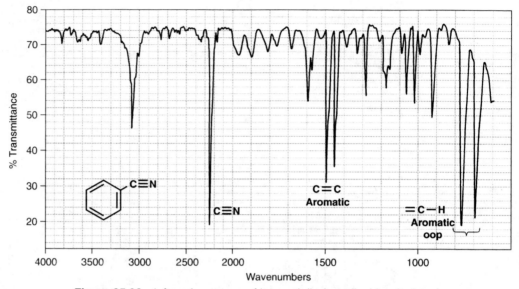

Figure 25.26   Infrared spectrum of benzonitrile (neat liquid, salt plates).

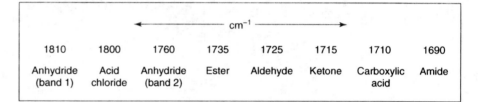

1810	1800	1760	1735	1725	1715	1710	1690
Anhydride (band 1)	Acid chloride	Anhydride (band 2)	Ester	Aldehyde	Ketone	Carboxylic acid	Amide

Figure 25.27   Normal base values for the C=O stretching vibrations for carbonyl groups.

I. Nitriles

C≡N   Stretch is a sharp absorption near 2250 cm^{-1}.
Conjugation with double bonds or aromatic rings moves the absorption to the right.

The spectrum of benzonitrile is shown in Figure 25.26.

J. Carbonyl Compounds

The carbonyl group is one of the most strongly absorbing groups in the infrared region of the spectrum. This is mainly due to its large dipole moment. It absorbs in a variety of compounds (aldehydes, ketones, acids, esters, amides, anhydrides, and acid chlorides) in the range of 1850–1650 cm^{-1}. In Figure 25.27, the normal values for the various types of carbonyl groups are compared. In the sections that follow, each type is examined separately.

K. Aldehydes

C=O   Stretch at approximately 1725 cm^{-1} is normal.
Aldehydes *seldom* absorb to the left of this value.
Conjugation moves the absorption to the right.

C—H   Stretch, aldehyde hydrogen (—CHO), consists of *weak* bands at
about 2750 cm^{-1} and 2850 cm^{-1}. Note that the CH stretch in alkyl
chains does not usually extend this far to the right.

The spectrum of an unconjugated aldehyde, nonanal, is shown in Figure 25.28, and
the conjugated aldehyde, benzaldehyde, is shown in Figure 25.29.

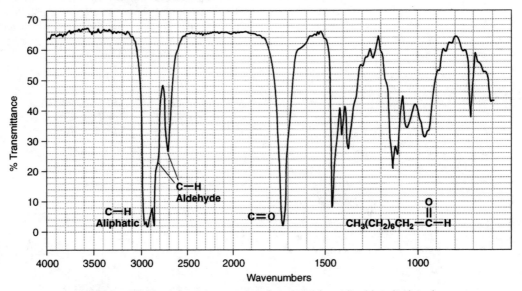

Figure 25.28   Infrared spectrum of nonanal (neat liquid, salt plates).

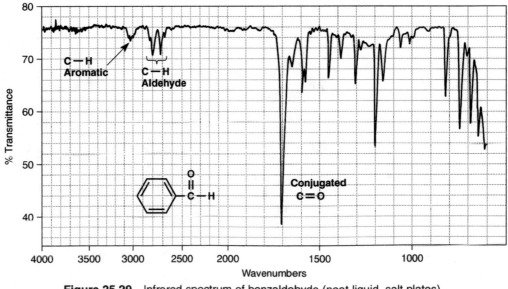

Figure 25.29   Infrared spectrum of benzaldehyde (neat liquid, salt plates).

L. Ketones

C=O   Stretch at approximately 1715 cm^{-1} is normal.
Conjugation moves the absorption to the right.
Ring strain moves the absorption to the left in cyclic ketones
(see Figure 25.30).

The spectra of methyl isopropyl ketone and mesityl oxide are shown in Figures 25.14
and 25.31. The spectrum of camphor, shown in Figure 25.32, has a carbonyl group
that has been shifted to a higher frequency because of ring strain (1745 cm^{-1}).

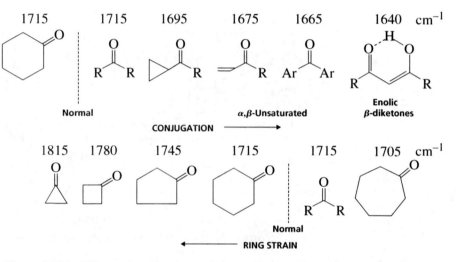

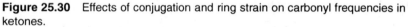

Figure 25.30   Effects of conjugation and ring strain on carbonyl frequencies in
ketones.

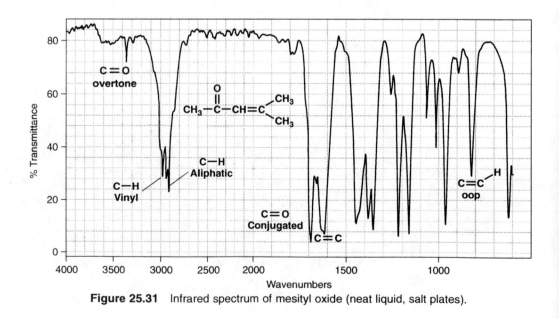

Figure 25.31   Infrared spectrum of mesityl oxide (neat liquid, salt plates).

M. Acids

O—H	Stretch, usually *very broad* (strongly hydrogen-bonded) at 3300–2500 cm^{-1}, often interferes with C—H absorptions.
C═O	Stretch, broad, 1730–1700 cm^{-1}. Conjugation moves the absorption to the right.
C—O	Stretch, in the range of 1320–1210 cm^{-1}, is strong.

The spectrum of benzoic acid is shown in Figure 25.33.

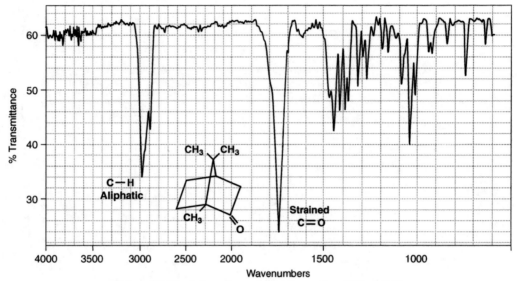

Figure 25.32 Infrared spectrum of camphor (KBr pellet).

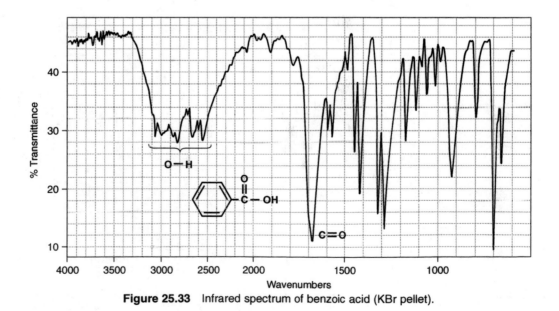

Figure 25.33 Infrared spectrum of benzoic acid (KBr pellet).

$$\text{N. Esters} \left(R-\overset{\overset{\textstyle O}{\|}}{C}-OR' \right)$$

C=O   Stretch occurs at about 1735 cm^{-1} in normal esters.
1. Conjugation in the R part moves the absorption to the right.
2. Conjugation with the O in the R' part moves the absorption to the left.
3. Ring strain (lactones) moves the absorption to the left.

C—O   Stretch, two bands or more, one stronger than the others, is in the range of 1300–1000 cm^{-1}.

The spectrum of an unconjugated ester, isopentyl acetate, is shown in Figure 25.34 (C=O appears at 1740 cm^{-1}). A conjugated ester, methyl benzoate, is shown in Figure 25.35 (C=O appears at 1720 cm^{-1}).

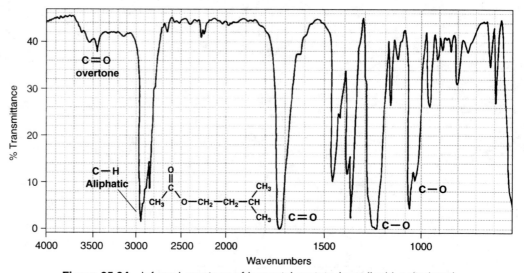

Figure 25.34   Infrared spectrum of isopentyl acetate (neat liquid, salt plates).

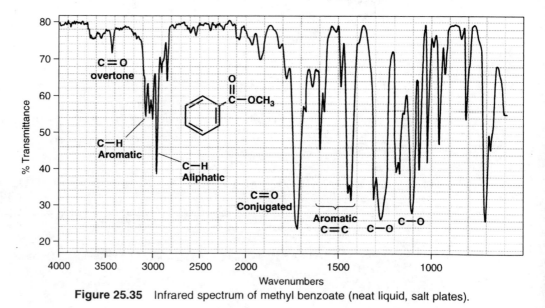

Figure 25.35   Infrared spectrum of methyl benzoate (neat liquid, salt plates).

O. Amides

C═O   Stretch is at approximately 1670–1640 cm^{-1}.
      Conjugation and ring size (lactams) have the usual effects.

N—H   Stretch (if monosubstituted or unsubstituted) is at 3500–3100 cm^{-1}.
      Unsubstituted amides have two bands (—NH$_2$) in this region.

N—H   Bending around 1640–1550 cm^{-1}.

The spectrum of benzamide is shown in Figure 25.36.

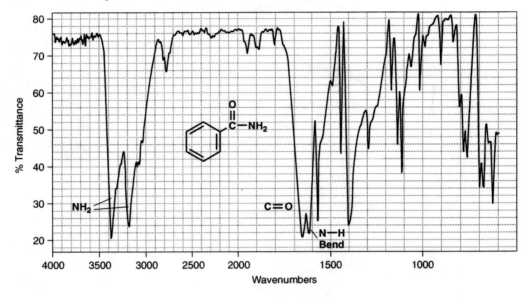

Figure 25.36   Infrared spectrum of benzamide (solid phase, KBr).

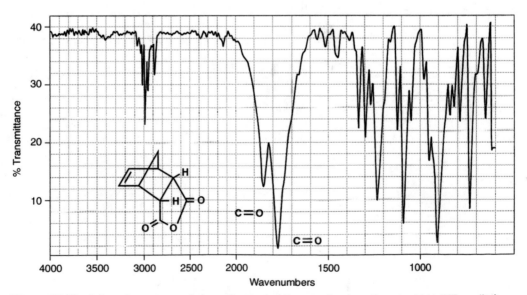

Figure 25.37   Infrared spectrum of cis-norbornene-5,6-endo-dicarboxylic anhydride (KBr pellet).

P. Anhydrides

C=O   Stretch always has *two* bands: 1830–1800 cm^{-1} and 1775–1740 cm^{-1}.
Unsaturation moves the absorptions to the right.
Ring strain (cyclic anhydrides) moves the absorptions to the left.

C—O   Stretch is at 1300–900 cm^{-1}. The spectrum of *cis*-norbornene-5,6-*endo*-dicarboxylic anhydride is shown in Figure 25.37.

Q. Acid Chlorides

C=O   Stretch occurs in the range 1810–1775 cm^{-1} in unconjugated chlorides. Conjugation lowers the frequency to 1780–1760 cm^{-1}.

C—O   Stretch occurs in the range 730–550 cm^{-1}.

R. Halides

It is often difficult to determine either the presence or the absence of a halide in a compound by infrared spectroscopy. The absorption bands cannot be relied on, especially if the spectrum is being determined with the compound dissolved in CCl_4 or $CHCl_3$ solution.

C—F   Stretch, 1350–960 cm^{-1}.
C—Cl   Stretch, 850–500 cm^{-1}.
C—Br   Stretch, to the right of 667 cm^{-1}.
C—I   Stretch, to the right of 667 cm^{-1}.

The spectra of the solvents, carbon tetrachloride and chloroform, are shown in Figures 25.8 and 25.9, respectively.

REFERENCES

Bellamy, L. J. *The Infra-Red Spectra of Complex Molecules*, 3rd ed.; New York: Methuen, 1975.

Colthup, N. B.; Daly, L. H.; Wiberly, S. E. *Introduction to Infrared and Raman Spectroscopy*, 3rd ed.; San Diego, CA: Academic Press, 1990.

Dyer, J. R. *Applications of Absorption Spectroscopy of Organic Compounds*; Englewood Cliffs, NJ: Prentice Hall, 1965.

Lin-Vien, D.; Colthup, N. B.; Fateley, W. G.; Grasselli, J. G. *Infrared and Raman Characteristic Frequencies of Organic Molecules*; San Diego, CA: Academic Press, 1991.

Nakanishi, K.; Soloman, P. H. *Infrared Absorption Spectroscopy*, 2nd ed.; San Francisco: Holden-Day, 1977.

Pavia, D. L.; Lampman, G. M.; Kriz, G. S.; Vyvyan, J. R. *Introduction to Spectroscopy: A Guide for Students of Organic Chemistry*, 4th ed. Brooks/Cole, 2008.

Silverstein, R. M.; Webster, F. X.; Kiemle, D. J. *Spectrometric Identification of Organic Compounds*, 7th ed.; New York: Wiley & Sons, 2005.

PROBLEMS

1. Comment on the suitability of running the infrared spectrum under each of the following conditions. If there is a problem with the conditions given, provide a suitable alternative method.

   a. A neat spectrum of liquid with a boiling point of 150 °C is determined using salt plates.

   b. A neat spectrum of a liquid with a boiling point of 35 °C is determined using salt plates.

   c. A KBr pellet is prepared with a compound that melts at 200 °C.

   d. A KBr pellet is prepared with a compound that melts at 30 °C.

   e. A solid aliphatic hydrocarbon compound is determined as a Nujol mull.

   f. Silver chloride plates are used to determine the spectrum of aniline.

   g. Sodium chloride plates are selected to run the spectrum of a compound that contains some water.

2. Indicate how you could distinguish between the following pairs of compounds by using infrared spectroscopy.

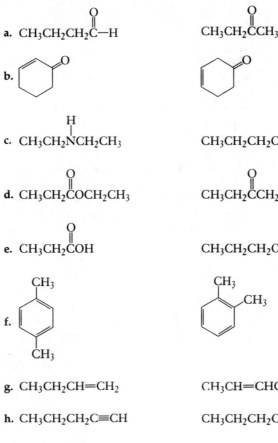

$$\text{a. } CH_3CH_2CH_2\overset{\displaystyle O}{\overset{\|}{C}}\text{—H} \qquad\qquad CH_3CH_2\overset{\displaystyle O}{\overset{\|}{C}}CH_3$$

b.

$$\text{c. } CH_3CH_2\overset{\displaystyle H}{\overset{|}{N}}CH_2CH_3 \qquad\qquad CH_3CH_2CH_2CH_2NH_2$$

$$\text{d. } CH_3CH_2\overset{\displaystyle O}{\overset{\|}{C}}OCH_2CH_3 \qquad\qquad CH_3CH_2\overset{\displaystyle O}{\overset{\|}{C}}CH_2OCH_3$$

$$\text{e. } CH_3CH_2\overset{\displaystyle O}{\overset{\|}{C}}OH \qquad\qquad CH_3CH_2CH_2OH$$

f.

g. $CH_3CH_2CH=CH_2$ \qquad\qquad $CH_3CH=CHCH_3$ (trans)

h. $CH_3CH_2CH_2C\equiv CH$ \qquad\qquad $CH_3CH_2CH_2CH=CH_2$

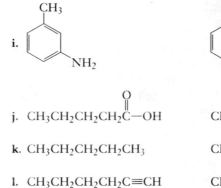

i.

j. $CH_3CH_2CH_2CH_2\overset{O}{\overset{\|}{C}}-OH$ $CH_3CH_2CH_2\overset{O}{\overset{\|}{C}}OCH_3$

k. $CH_3CH_2CH_2CH_2CH_3$ $CH_2{=}CHCH_2CH_2CH_2CH_3$

l. $CH_3CH_2CH_2CH_2C{\equiv}CH$ $CH_3CH_2CH_2C{\equiv}CCH_3$

---

26   TECHNIQUE 26

Nuclear Magnetic Resonance Spectroscopy (Proton NMR)

Nuclear magnetic resonance (NMR) spectroscopy is an instrumental technique that allows the number, type, and relative positions of certain atoms in a molecule to be determined. This type of spectroscopy applies only to those atoms that have nuclear magnetic moments because of their nuclear spin properties. Although many atoms meet this requirement, hydrogen atoms (^1_1H) are of the greatest interest to the organic chemist. Atoms of the ordinary isotopes of carbon ($^{12}_6C$) and oxygen ($^{16}_8O$) do not have nuclear magnetic moments, and ordinary nitrogen atoms ($^{14}_7N$), although they do have magnetic moments, generally fail to show typical NMR behavior for other reasons. The same is true of the halogen atoms, except for fluorine ($^{19}_9F$), which does show active NMR behavior. Of the atoms mentioned here, the hydrogen nucleus (^1_1H) and carbon-13 nucles ($^{13}_6C$) are the most important to organic chemists. Proton (^1H) NMR is discussed here and carbon (^{13}C) NMR is described in Technique 27.

Nuclei of NMR-active atoms placed in a magnetic field can be thought of as tiny bar magnets. In hydrogen, which has two allowed nuclear spin states ($+\frac{1}{2}$ and $-\frac{1}{2}$), either the nuclear magnets of individual atoms can be aligned with the magnetic field (spin $+\frac{1}{2}$) or they can be opposed to it (spin $-\frac{1}{2}$). A slight majority of the nuclei are aligned with the field, because this spin orientation constitutes a slightly lower-energy spin state. If radiofrequency waves of the appropriate energy are supplied, nuclei aligned with the field can absorb this radiation and reverse their direction of spin or become reoriented so that the nuclear magnet opposes the applied magnetic field (see Figure 26.1).

The frequency of radiation required to induce spin conversion is a direct function of the strength of the applied magnetic field. When a spinning hydrogen nucleus is placed in a magnetic field, the nucleus begins to precess with angular frequency ω, much like a child's toy top. This precessional motion is depicted in Figure 26.2. The angular frequency of nuclear precession ω increases as the strength of the applied magnetic field is increased. The radiation that must be supplied to

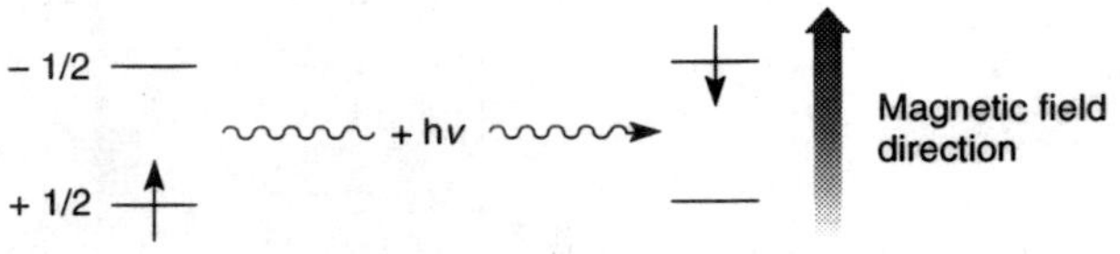

Figure 26.1   The NMR absorption process.

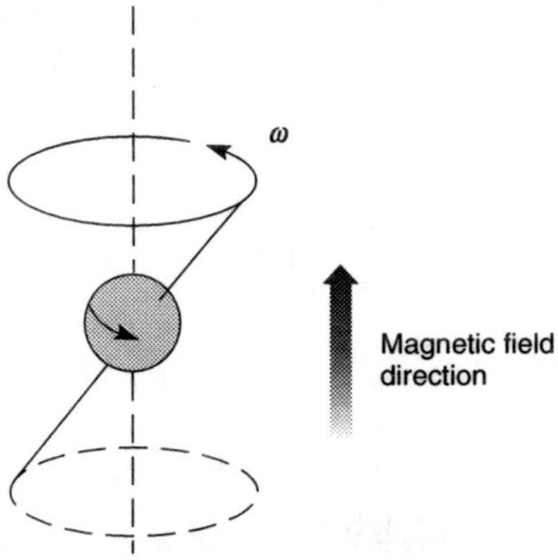

Figure 26.2   Precessional motion of a spinning nucleus in an applied magnetic field.

induce spin conversion in a hydrogen nucleus of spin $+\frac{1}{2}$ must have a frequency that just matches the angular precessional frequency ω. This is called the resonance condition, and spin conversion is said to be a resonance process.

For the average proton (hydrogen atom), if a magnetic field of approximately 1.4 tesla is applied, radio-frequency radiation of 60 MHz is required to induce a spin transition.[1] Fortunately, the magnetic field strength required to induce the various protons in a molecule to absorb 60-MHz radiation varies from proton to proton within the molecule and is a sensitive function of the immediate *electronic* environment of each proton. The proton nuclear magnetic resonance spectrometer supplies a basic radio-frequency radiation of 60 MHz to the sample being measured and *increases* the strength of the applied magnetic field over a range of several parts per million from the basic field strength. As the field increases, various protons come into resonance (absorb 60-MHz energy), and a resonance signal is generated for each proton. An NMR spectrum is a plot of the strength of the magnetic field versus the intensity of the absorptions. A typical 60-MHz NMR spectrum is shown in Figure 26.3.

Modern FT–NMR instruments produce the same type of NMR spectrum just described, even though they do it by a different method. See your lecture textbook for a discussion of the differences between classic CW instruments and modern FT–NMR instruments. Fourier transform spectrometers operating at magnetic field strengths of at least 7.1 tesla and at spectrometer frequencies of 300 MHz and above allow chemists to obtain both the proton and carbon NMR spectra on the same sample.

---

[1] Most modern instruments (FT-NMR instruments) use higher fields than described here and operate differently. The classical 60-MHz continous wave (CW) instrument is used here as a simple example.

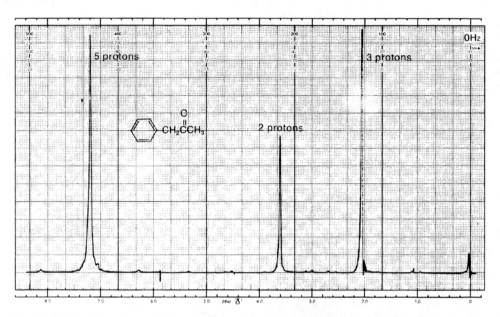

Figure 26.3 Nuclear magnetic resonance spectrum of phenylacetone (the absorption peak at the far right is caused by the added reference substance tetramethylsilane).

PART A. PREPARING A SAMPLE FOR NMR SPECTROSCOPY

The NMR sample tubes used in most instruments are approximately 0.5 cm × 18 cm in overall dimension and are fabricated of uniformly thin glass tubing. These tubes are very fragile and expensive, so care must be taken to avoid breaking the tubes.

CAUTION

NMR tubes are made out of very thin glass and break easily. Never place the cap on tightly, and take special care when removing it.

To prepare the solution, you must first choose the appropriate solvent. The solvent should not have NMR absorption peaks of its own, that is, it should contain no protons. Carbon tetrachloride (CCl_4) fits this requirement and can be used in some instruments. However, because FT–NMR spectrometers require deuterium to stabilize (lock) the field, organic chemists usually use deuterated chloroform ($CDCl_3$) as a solvent. This solvent dissolves most organic compounds and is relatively inexpensive. You can use this solvent with any NMR instrument. You should not use normal chloroform $CHCl_3$, because the solvent contains a proton. Deuterium ^2H does not absorb in the proton region and is thus "invisible," or not seen, in the proton NMR spectrum. Use deuterated chloroform to dissolve your sample, unless you are instructed to use another solvent, such as deuterated derivatives of water, acetone, or dimethylsulfoxide.

26.1 Routine Sample Preparation Using Deuterated Chloroform

1. Most organic liquids and low-melting solids will dissolve in deuterated chloroform. However, you should first determine whether your sample will dissolve in ordinary $CHCl_3$ before using the deuterated solvent. If your sample does not dissolve in chloroform, consult your instructor about a possible alternative solvent, or consult Section 26.2.

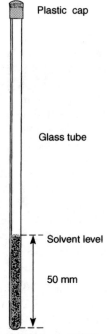

Plastic cap

Glass tube

Solvent level

50 mm

Figure 26.4 An NMR sample tube.

CAUTION

Chloroform, deuterated chloroform, and carbon tetrachloride are all toxic solvents. In addition, they may be carcinogenic substances.

---

2. If you are using an FT–NMR spectrometer, add 30 mg (0.030 g) of your liquid or solid sample to a tared conical vial or test tube. Use a Pasteur pipet to transfer a liquid or a spatula to transfer a solid. Non-FT instruments usually require a more concentrated solution in order to obtain an adequate spectrum. Typically, a 10–30% sample concentration (weight/weight) is used.

3. Transfer about 0.5 mL of the deuterated chloroform with a clean, dry Pasteur pipet to your sample. Swirl the test tube or conical vial to help dissolve the sample. At this point, the sample should have completely dissolved. Add a little more solvent, if necessary, to dissolve the sample fully.

4. Transfer the solution to the NMR tube using a clean, dry Pasteur pipet. Be careful when transferring the solution to avoid breaking the edge of the fragile NMR tube. It is best to hold the NMR tube and the container with the solution in the same hand when making the transfer.

5. Once the solution has been transferred to the NMR tube, use a clean pipet to add enough deuterated chloroform to bring the total solution height to about 50 mm (see Figure 26.4). In some cases, you will need to add a small amount of tetramethylsilane (TMS) as a reference substance (see Section 26.3). Check with your instructor to see if you need to add TMS to your sample. Deuterated chloroform has a small amount of $CHCl_3$ impurity, which gives rise to a low-intensity peak in the NMR spectrum at 7.27 parts per million (ppm). This impurity may also help you to "reference" your spectrum.

6. Cap the NMR tube. Do this firmly but not too tightly. If you jam the cap on, you may have trouble removing it later without breaking the end off of the very thin glass tube. Make sure that the cap is on straight. Invert the NMR tube several times to mix the contents.

7. You are now ready to record the NMR spectrum of your sample. Insert the NMR tube into its holder and adjust its depth by using the gauge provided to you.

Cleaning the NMR Tube

1. Carefully uncap the tube so that you do not break it. Turn the tube upside down and hold it vertically over a beaker. Shake the tube up and down gently so that its contents empty into the beaker.

2. Partially refill the NMR tube with acetone using a Pasteur pipet. Carefully replace the cap and invert the tube several times to rinse it.

3. Remove the cap and drain the tube as before. Place the open tube upside down in a beaker with a Kimwipe or paper towel placed in the bottom of the beaker.

Leave the tube standing in this position for at least one laboratory period so that the acetone completely evaporates. Alternatively, you may place the beaker and NMR tube in an oven for at least 2 hours. If you need to use the NMR tube before the acetone has fully evaporated, attach a piece of pressure tubing to the tube and pull a vacuum with an aspirator. After several minutes, the acetone should have fully evaporated. Because acetone contains protons, you must not use the NMR tube until the acetone has evaporated completely[2].

4. Once the acetone is evaporated, place the clean tube and its cap (do not cap the tube) in its storage container and place it in your desk. The storage container will prevent the tube from being crushed.

Health Hazards Associated With NMR Solvents

Carbon tetrachloride, chloroform (and chloroform-d), and benzene (and benzene-d$_6$) are hazardous solvents. Besides being highly toxic, they are suspected carcinogens. In spite of these health problems, these solvents are commonly used in NMR spectroscopy. Deuterated acetone may be a safer alternative. These solvents are used because they contain no protons and are excellent solvents for most organic compounds. Therefore, you must learn to handle these solvents with great care to minimize the hazard. These solvents should be stored either under a hood or in septum-capped bottles. If the bottles have screw caps, a pipet should be attached to each bottle. A recommended way of attaching the pipet is to store it in a test tube taped to the side of the bottle. Septum-capped bottles can be used only by withdrawing the solvent with a hypodermic syringe that has been designated solely for this use. All samples should be prepared under a hood, and solutions should be disposed of in an appropriately designated waste container that is stored under the hood. Wear rubber or plastic gloves when preparing or discarding samples.

26.2 Nonroutine Sample Preparation

Some compounds do not dissolve readily in CDCl$_3$. A commercial solvent called Unisol will often dissolve the difficult cases. Unisol is a mixture of CDCl$_3$ and DMSO-d$_6$. Deuterated acetone may also dissolve more polar substances.

With highly polar substances, you may find that your sample will not dissolve in deuterated chloroform or Unisol. If this is the case, you may be able to dissolve the sample in deuterium oxide D$_2$O. Spectra determined in D$_2$O often show a small peak at about 5 ppm because of OH impurity. If the sample compound has acidic hydrogens, they may *exchange* with D$_2$O, leading to the appearance of an OH peak in the spectrum and the *loss* of the original absorption from the acidic proton, owing to the exchanged hydrogen. In many cases, this will also alter the splitting patterns of a compound.

Many solid carboxylic acids do not dissolve in CDCl$_3$ or even D$_2$O. In such cases, add a small piece of sodium metal to about 1 mL of D$_2$O. The acid is then dissolved in this solution. The resulting basic solution enhances the solubility of the carboxylic acid. In such a case, the hydroxyl proton of the carboxylic acid cannot be observed in the NMR spectrum because it exchanges with the solvent. A large DOH peak is observed, however, due to the exchange and the H$_2$O impurity in the D$_2$O solvent.

---

[2] If you can't wait to be sure all of the acetone has evaporated, you may rinse the tube once or twice with a *very small* amount of CDCl$_3$ before using it.

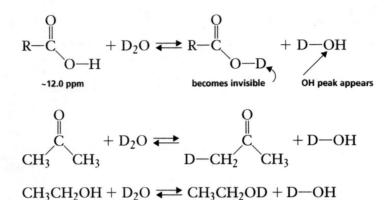

$$CH_3CH_2OH + D_2O \rightleftharpoons CH_3CH_2OD + D{-}OH$$

When the above solvents fail, other special solvents can be used. Acetone, acetonitrile, dimethylsulfoxide, pyridine, benzene, and dimethylformamide can be used if you are not interested in the region or regions of the NMR spectrum in which they give rise to absorption. The deuterated (but expensive) analogs of these compounds are also used in special instances (for example, acetone-d_6, dimethylsulfoxide-d_6, dimethylformamide-d_7, and benzene-d_6). If the sample is not sensitive to acid, trifluoroacetic acid (which has no protons with $\delta < 12$) can be used. You must be aware that these solvents often lead to chemical shift values different from those determined in CCl_4 or $CDCl_3$. Variations of as much as 0.5–1.0 ppm have been observed. In fact, it is sometimes possible, by switching to pyridine, benzene, acetone, or dimethylsulfoxide as solvents, to separate peaks that overlap when CCl_4 or $CDCl_3$ solutions are used.

26.3 Reference Substances

To provide the internal reference standard, TMS must be added to the sample solution. This substance has the formula $(CH_3)_4Si$. By universal convention, the chemical shifts of the protons in this substance are defined as 0.00 ppm. The spectrum should be shifted so that the TMS signal appears at this position on precalibrated paper.

The concentration of TMS in the sample should range from 1%–3%. Some people prefer to add 1 to 2 drops of TMS to the sample just before determining the spectrum. Because TMS has 12 equivalent protons, not much of it needs to be added. A Pasteur pipet or a syringe may be used for the addition. It is far easier to have available in the laboratory a prepared solvent that already contains TMS. Deuterated chloroform and carbon tetrachloride often have TMS added to them. Because TMS is highly volatile (bp 26.5°C), such solutions should be stored, tightly stoppered, in a refrigerator. Tetramethylsilane itself is best stored in a refrigerator as well.

Tetramethylsilane does not dissolve in D_2O. For spectra determined in D_2O, a different internal standard, sodium 2,2-dimethyl-2-silapentane-5-sulfonate, must be used. This standard is water soluble and gives a resonance peak at 0.00 ppm.

$$CH_3{-}\underset{\underset{CH_3}{|}}{\overset{\overset{CH_3}{|}}{Si}}{-}CH_2{-}CH_2{-}CH_2{-}SO_3^-Na^+$$

Sodium 2,2-dimethyl-2-silapentane-5-sulfonate (DSS)

PART B. NUCLEAR MAGNETIC RESONANCE (^{1}H NMR)

26.4 The Chemical Shift

The differences in the applied field strengths at which the various protons in a molecule absorb 60-MHz radiation are extremely small. The different absorption positions amount to a difference of only a few parts per million (ppm) in the magnetic field strength. Because it is experimentally difficult to measure the precise field strength at which each proton absorbs to less than one part in a million, a technique has been developed whereby the *difference* between two absorption positions is measured directly. A standard reference substance is used to achieve this measurement, and the positions of the absorptions of all other protons are measured relative to the values for the reference substance. The reference substance that has been universally accepted is **tetramethylsilane** $(CH_3)_4Si$, which is also called **TMS**. the proton resonances in this molecule appear at a higher field strength than the proton resonances in most other molecules, and all the protons of TMS have resonance at the same field strength.

To give the position of absorption of a proton, a quantitative measurement, a parameter called the **chemical shift** (δ), has been defined. One δ unit corresponds to a one-ppm change in the magnetic field strength. To determine the chemical shift value for the various protons in a molecule, the operator determines an NMR spectrum of the molecule with a small quantity of TMS added directly to the sample. That is, both spectra are determined *simultaneously*. The TMS absorption is adjusted to correspond to the δ=0 ppm position on the recording chart, which is calibrated in δ units, and the δ values of the absorption peaks for all other protons can be read directly from the chart.

Because the NMR spectrometer increases the magnetic field as the pen moves from left to right on the chart, the TMS absorption appears at the extreme right edge of the spectrum (δ= 0 ppm) or at the *upfield* end of the spectrum. The chart is calibrated in δ units (or ppm), and most other protons absorb at a lower field strength (or *downfield*) from TMS.

The shift from TMS for a given proton depends on the strength of the applied magnetic field. In an applied field of 1.41 tesla, the resonance of a proton is approximately 60 MHz, whereas in an applied field of 2.35 tesla, (23,500 gauss), the resonance appears at approximately 100 MHz. The ratio of the resonance frequencies is the same as the ratio of the two field strengths:

$$\frac{100 \text{ MHz}}{60 \text{ MHz}} = \frac{2.35 \text{ Tesla}}{1.41 \text{ Tesla}} = \frac{23,500 \text{ Gauss}}{14,100 \text{ Gauss}} = \frac{5}{3}$$

Hence, for a given proton, the shift (in hertz) from TMS is five-thirds larger in the 100-MHz range than in the 60-MHz range. This can be confusing for workers trying to compare data if they have spectrometers that differ in the strength of the applied magnetic field. The confusion is easily overcome by defining a new parameter that is independent of field strength—for instance, by dividing the shift in hertz of a given proton by the frequency in megahertz of the spectrometer with which the shift value was obtained. In this manner, a field-independent measure called the **chemical shift** (δ) is obtained:

$$\delta = \frac{(\text{shift in Hz})}{(\text{spectrometer frequency in MHz})} \tag{1}$$

The chemical shift in δ units expresses the amount by which a proton resonance is shifted from TMS, in parts per million (ppm), of the spectrometer's basic operating frequency. Values of δ for a given proton are always the same, irrespective of whether the measurement was made at 60 MHz, 100 MHz, or 300 MHz. For instance, at 60 MHz, the shift of the protons in CH_3Br is 162 Hz from TMS; at 100 MHz, the shift is 270 Hz; and at 300 MHz, the shift is 810 Hz. However, all three correspond to the same value of δ = 2.70 ppm:

$$\delta = \frac{162 \text{ Hz}}{60 \text{ MHz}} = \frac{270 \text{ Hz}}{100 \text{ MHz}} = \frac{810 \text{ Hz}}{300 \text{ MHz}} = 2.70 \text{ ppm}$$

26.5 Chemical Equivalence—Integrals

All of the protons in a molecule that are in chemically identical environments often exhibit the same chemical shift. Thus, all of the protons in TMS or all of the protons in benzene, cyclopentane, or acetone have their own respective resonance values all at the same δ value. Each compound gives rise to a single absorption peak in its NMR spectrum. The protons are said to be **chemically equivalent**. On the other hand, molecules that have sets of protons that are chemically distinct from one another may give rise to an absorption peak from each set.

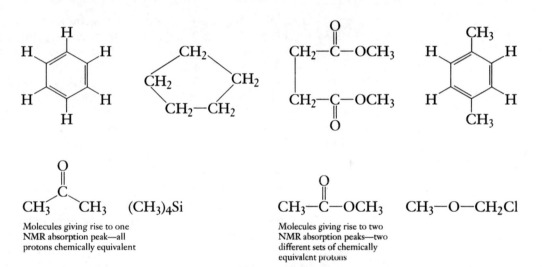

Molecules giving rise to one NMR absorption peak—all protons chemically equivalent

Molecules giving rise to two NMR absorption peaks—two different sets of chemically equivalent protons

The NMR spectrum given in Figure 26.3 is that of phenylacetone, a compound having *three* chemically distinct types of protons:

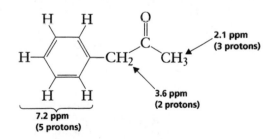

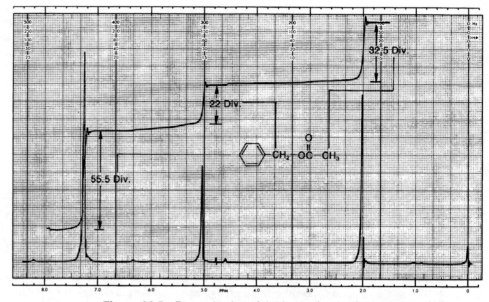

Figure 26.5   Determination of the integral ratios for benzyl acetate.

You can immediately see that the NMR spectrum furnishes valuable information on this basis alone. In fact, the NMR spectrum not only can distinguish how
many types of protons a molecule has, but also can reveal *how many* of each type are
contained within the molecule.

In the NMR spectrum, the area under each peak is proportional to the number
of hydrogens generating that peak. Hence, in the case of phenylacetone, the area
ratio of the three peaks is 5:2:3, the same as the ratio of the numbers of each type of
hydrogen. The NMR spectrometer can electronically "integrate" the area under each
peak. It does this by tracing over each peak a vertically rising line, which rises in
height by an amount proportional to the area under the peak. Shown in Figure 26.5
is an NMR spectrum of benzyl acetate, with each of the peaks integrated in this way.

It is important to note that the height of the integral line does not give the
absolute number of hydrogens; it gives the *relative* numbers of each type of hydrogen. For a given integral to be of any use, there must be a second integral to which
it is referred. The benzyl acetate case provides a good example of this. The first integral rises for 55.5 divisions on the chart paper, the second for 22.0 divisions, and the
third for 32.5 divisions. These numbers are relative and give the *ratios* of the various types of protons. You can find these ratios by dividing each of the larger numbers by the smallest number:

$$\frac{55.5 \text{ div}}{22.0 \text{ div}} = 2.52 \qquad \frac{22.0 \text{ div}}{22.0 \text{ div}} = 1.00 \qquad \frac{32.5 \text{ div}}{22.0 \text{ div}} = 1.48$$

Thus, the number ratio of the protons of each type is 2.52:1.00:1.48. If you assume
that the peak at 5.1 ppm is really caused by two hydrogens and that the integrals
are slightly in error (this can be as much as 10%), then you can arrive at the true
ratios by multiplying each figure by 2 and rounding off; we then get 5:2:3. Clearly,
the peak at 7.3 ppm, which integrates for 5, arises from the resonance of the aromatic ring protons, and the peak at 2.0 ppm, which integrates for 3, is caused by the
methyl protons. The two-proton resonance at 5.1 ppm arises from the benzyl

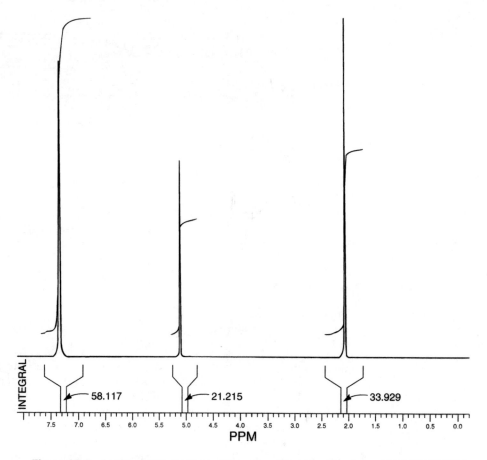

Figure 26.6   An integrated spectrum of benzyl acetate determined on a 300-MHzFT-NMR.

protons. Notice then that the integrals give the simplest ratios, but not necessarily the true ratios, of the number of protons in each type.

In addition to the rising integral line, modern instruments usually give digitized numerical values for the integrals. Like the heights of the integral lines, these digitized integral values are not absolute but relative, and they should be treated as explained in the preceding paragraph. These digital values are also not exact; like the integral lines, they have the potential for a small degree of error (up to 10%). Figure 26.6 is an example of an integrated spectrum of benzyl acetate determined on a 300-MHz pulsed FT–NMR instrument. The digitized values of the integrals appear under the peaks.

26.6 Chemical Environment and Chemical Shift

If the resonance frequencies of all protons in a molecule were the same, NMR would be of little use to the organic chemist. However, not only do different types of protons have different chemical shifts but they also have a value of chemical shift that characterizes the type of proton they represent. Every type of proton has only a limited range of δ values over which it gives resonance. Hence, the numerical value of the chemical shift for a proton indicates the *type of proton* originating the signal, just as the infrared frequency suggests the type of bond or functional group.

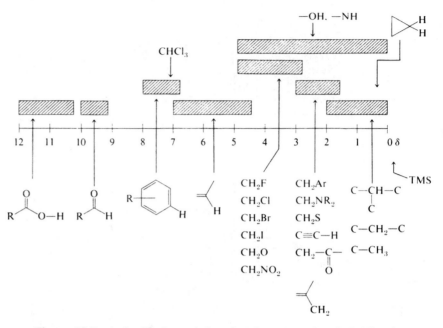

Figure 26.7   A simplified correlation chart for proton chemical shift values.

Notice, for instance, that the aromatic protons of both phenylacetone (See Figure 26.3) and benzyl acetate (See Figure 26.5) have resonance near 7.3 ppm and that both methyl groups attached directly to a carbonyl group have a resonance of approximately 2.1 ppm. Aromatic protons characteristically have resonance near 7–8 ppm, and acetyl groups (the methyl protons) have their resonance near 2 ppm. These values of chemical shift are diagnostic. Notice also how the resonance of the benzyl (—CH_2—) protons comes at a higher value of chemical shift (5.1 ppm) in benzyl acetate than in phenylacetone (3.6 ppm). Being attached to the electronega-tive element, oxygen, these protons are more deshielded (see Section 26.7) than the protons in phenylacetone. A trained chemist would have readily recognized the probable presence of the oxygen by the chemical shift shown by these protons.

It is important to learn the ranges of chemical shifts over which the most com-mon types of protons have resonance. Figure 26.7 is a correlation chart that contains the most essential and frequently encountered types of protons. Table 26.1 lists the chemical shift ranges for selected types of protons. For the beginner, it is often dif-ficult to memorize a large body of numbers relating to chemical shifts and proton types. However, this needs to be done only crudely. It is more important to "get a feel" for the regions and the types of protons than to know a string of actual num-bers. To do this, study Figure 26.7 carefully.

The values of chemical shift given in Figure 26.7 and in Table 26.1 can be easi-ly understood in terms of two factors: local diamagnetic shielding and anisotropy. These two factors are discussed in Sections 26.7 and 26.8.

26.7 Local Diamagnetic Shielding

The trend of chemical shifts that is easiest to explain is that involving electronegative elements substituted on the same carbon to which the protons of interest are attached. The chemical shift simply increases as the electronegativity of the attached element increases. This is illustrated in Table 26.2 for several compounds of the type CH_3X.

TABLE 26.1   Approximate Chemical Shift Ranges (ppm) for Selected Types of Protons

Left group		Shift	Right group	Shift
$R-CH_3$		0.7–1.3	$R-N-\overset{\vert}{\underset{\vert}{C}}-H$	2.2–2.9
$R-CH_2-R$		1.2–1.4		
R_3CH		1.4–1.7	$R-S-\overset{\vert}{\underset{\vert}{C}}-H$	2.0–3.0
$R-\overset{\vert}{C}=\overset{\vert}{C}-\overset{\vert}{\underset{\vert}{C}}-H$		1.6 – 2.6	$I-\overset{\vert}{\underset{\vert}{C}}-H$	2.0–4.0
$R-\overset{O}{\overset{\Vert}{C}}-\overset{\vert}{\underset{\vert}{C}}-H$, $H-\overset{O}{\overset{\Vert}{C}}-\overset{\vert}{\underset{\vert}{C}}-H$		2.1 – 2.4	$Br-\overset{\vert}{\underset{\vert}{C}}-H$	2.7–4.1
			$Cl-\overset{\vert}{\underset{\vert}{C}}-H$	3.1–4.1
$RO-\overset{O}{\overset{\Vert}{C}}-\overset{\vert}{\underset{\vert}{C}}-H$, $HO-\overset{O}{\overset{\Vert}{C}}-\overset{\vert}{\underset{\vert}{C}}-H$		2.1 – 2.5	$R-\overset{O}{\underset{O}{\overset{\Vert}{\underset{\Vert}{S}}}}-O-\overset{\vert}{\underset{\vert}{C}}-H$	ca. 3.0
$N\equiv C-\overset{\vert}{\underset{\vert}{C}}-H$		2.1 – 3.0	$RO-\overset{\vert}{\underset{\vert}{C}}-H$, $HO-\overset{\vert}{\underset{\vert}{C}}-H$	3.2–3.8
⬡$-\overset{\vert}{\underset{\vert}{C}}-H$		2.3 – 2.7	$R-\overset{O}{\overset{\Vert}{C}}-O-\overset{\vert}{\underset{\vert}{C}}-H$	3.5–4.8
$R-C\equiv C-H$		1.7 – 2.7	$O_2N-\overset{\vert}{\underset{\vert}{C}}-H$	4.1–4.3
$R-S-H$	var	1.0 – 4.0[a]	$F-\overset{\vert}{\underset{\vert}{C}}-H$	4.2–4.8
$R-\overset{\vert}{N}-H$	var	0.5 – 4.0[a]		
$R-O-H$	var	0.5 – 5.0[a]	$R-\overset{\vert}{C}=\overset{\vert}{C}-H$	4.5–6.5
⬡$-O-H$	var	4.0 – 7.0[a]	⬡$-H$	6.5–8.0
⬡$-\overset{\vert}{N}-H$	var	3.0 – 5.0[a]	$R-\overset{O}{\overset{\Vert}{C}}-H$	9.0–10.0
$R-\overset{O}{\overset{\Vert}{C}}-\overset{\vert}{N}-H$	var	5.0 – 9.0[a]	$R-\overset{O}{\overset{\Vert}{C}}-OH$	11.0–12.0

Note: For those hydrogens shown as $-\overset{\vert}{\underset{\vert}{C}}-H$, if that hydrogen is part of a methyl group (CH_3), the shift is generally at the low end of the range given; if the hydrogen is in a methylene group ($-CH_2-$), the shift is intermediate; and if the hydrogen is in a methine group ($-CH-$), the shift is typically at the high end of the range given.

[a]The chemical shift of these groups is variable, depending on the chemical environment in the molecule and on concentration, temperature, and solvent.

TABLE 26.2   Dependence of Chemical Shift of CH_3X on the Element X

Compound CH_3X	CH_3F	CH_3OH	CH_3Cl	CH_3Br	CH_3I	CH_4	$(CH_3)_4Si$
Element X	F	O	Cl	Br	I	H	Si
Electronegativity of X	4.0	3.5	3.1	2.8	2.5	2.1	1.8
Chemical shift (ppm)	4.26	3.40	3.05	2.68	2.16	0.23	0

TABLE 26.3   Substitution Effects

	$C\underline{H}Cl_3$	$C\underline{H}_2Cl_2$	$C\underline{H}_3Cl$	$-C\underline{H}_2Br$	$-C\underline{H}_2-CH_2Br$	$-C\underline{H}_2-CH_2CH_2Br$
δ (ppm)	7.27	5.30	3.05	3.3	1.69	1.25

Note: Values apply to underlined hydrogens.

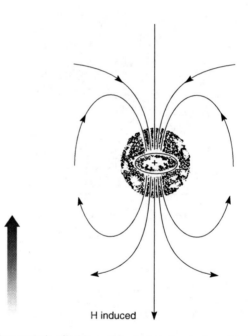

H_0 applied   H induced

Figure 26.8   Local diamagnetic shielding of a photon due to its valence electrons.

Multiple substituents have a stronger effect than a single substituent. The influence of the substituent drops off rapidly with distance. An electronegative element has little effect on protons that are more than three carbons away from it. These effects are illustrated in Table 26.3.

Electronegative substituents attached to a carbon atom, because of their electron withdrawing effects, reduce the valence electron density around the protons attached to that carbon. These electrons *shield* the proton from the applied magnetic field. This effect, called **local diamagnetic shielding**, occurs because the applied magnetic field induces the valence electrons to circulate. This circulation generates an induced magnetic field, which *opposes* the applied field. This is illustrated in Figure 26.8. Electronegative substituents on carbon reduce the local diamagnetic shielding in the vicinity of the attached protons because they reduce the electron density around those protons. Substituents that produce this effect are said to *deshield* the proton. The greater the electronegativity of the substituent, the more the deshielding of the protons and, hence, the greater the chemical shift of those protons.

26.8 Anisotropy

Figure 26.7 clearly shows that several types of protons have chemical shifts not easily explained by a simple consideration of the electronegativity of the attached groups. Consider, for instance, the protons of benzene or other aromatic systems. Aryl protons generally have a chemical shift that is as large as that for the proton of chloroform. Alkenes, alkynes, and aldehydes also have protons whose resonance values are not in line with the expected magnitude of any electron-withdrawing effects. In each of these cases, the effect is due to the presence of an unsaturated system (π electrons) in the vicinity of the proton in question. In benzene, for example, when the π electrons in the aromatic ring system are placed in a magnetic field, they are induced to circulate around the ring. This circulation is called a **ring current**. Moving electrons (the ring current) generate a magnetic field much like that generated in a loop of wire through which a current is induced to flow. The magnetic field covers a spatial volume large enough to influence the shielding of the benzene hydrogens. This is illustrated in Figure 26.9. The benzene hydrogens are deshielded by the **diamagnetic anisotropy** of the ring. An applied magnetic field is nonuniform (anisotropic) in the vicinity of a benzene molecule because of the labile

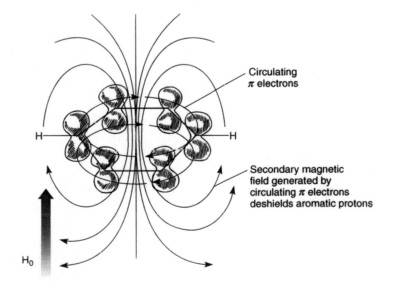

Figure 26.9　Diamagnetic anisotropy in benzene.

electrons in the ring that interact with the applied field. Thus, a proton attached to a benzene ring is influenced by *three* magnetic fields: the strong magnetic field applied by the magnets of the NMR spectrometer and two weaker fields, one due to the usual shielding by the valence electrons around the proton and the other due to the anisotropy generated by the ring system electrons. It is this anisotropic effect that gives the benzene protons a greater chemical shift than is expected. These protons just happen to lie in a **deshielding** region of this anisotropic field. If a proton were placed in the center of the ring rather than on its periphery, the proton would be shielded because the field lines would have the opposite direction.

All groups in a molecule that have π electrons generate secondary anisotropic fields. In acetylene, the magnetic field generated by induced circulation of π electrons has a geometry such that the acetylene hydrogens are **shielded**. Hence, acetylenic hydrogens come at a higher field than expected. The shielding and deshielding regions due to the various π electron functional groups have characteristic shapes and directions; they are illustrated in Figure 26.10. Protons falling within the cones are shielded, and those falling outside the conical areas are deshielded. Because the magnitude of the anisotropic field diminishes with distance, beyond a certain distance anisotropy has essentially no effect.

26.9 Spin–Spin Splitting (*n* + 1 Rule)

We have already considered how the chemical shift and the integral (peak area) can give information about the numbers and types of hydrogens contained in a molecule. A third type of information available from the NMR spectrum is derived from spin-spin splitting. Even in simple molecules, each type of proton rarely gives a single resonance peak. For instance, in 1,1,2-trichloroethane there are two chemically distinct types of hydrogen:

$$Cl-\overset{\overset{\textstyle H}{|}}{\underset{\underset{\textstyle Cl}{|}}{C}}-CH_2-Cl$$

From information given thus far, you would predict *two* resonance peaks in the NMR spectrum of 1,1,2-trichloroethane with an area ratio (integral ratio) of 2:1. In fact, the NMR spectrum of this compound has *five* peaks. A group of three peaks (called a *triplet*) exists at 5.77 ppm, and a group of two peaks (called a *doublet*) is found at 3.95 ppm. The spectrum is shown in Figure 26.11. The methine (CH) resonance (5.77 ppm) is split into a triplet, and the methylene resonance (3.95 ppm) is

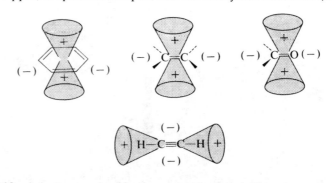

Figure 26.10   Anisotropy caused by the presence of π electrons in some common multiple-bond systems.

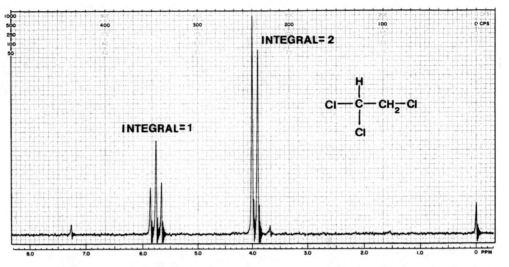

Figure 26.11 NMR spectrum of 1,1,2-trichloroethane. (Courtesy of Varian Associates.)

split into a doublet. The area under the three triplet peaks is *one*, relative to an area of *two* under the two doublet peaks.

This phenomenon is called **spin–spin splitting**. Empirically, spin–spin splitting can be explained by the "$n + 1$ rule." Each type of proton "senses" the number of equivalent protons (n) on the carbon atom or atoms next to the one to which it is bonded, and its resonance peak is split into $n + 1$ components.

Let's examine the case at hand, 1,1,2-trichloroethane, using the $n + 1$ rule. First, the lone methine hydrogen is situated next to a carbon bearing two methylene protons. According to the rule, it has two equivalent neighbors ($n = 2$) and is split into $n + 1 = 3$ peaks (a triplet). The methylene protons are situated next to a carbon bearing only one methine hydrogen. According to the rule, they have one neighbor ($n = 1$) and are split into $n + 1 = 2$ peaks (a doublet).

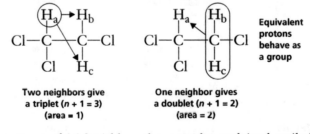

The spectrum of 1,1,2-trichloroethane can be explained easily by the interaction, or coupling, of the spins of protons on adjacent carbon atoms. The position of absorption of proton H_a is affected by the spins of protons H_b and H_c attached to the neighboring (adjacent) carbon atom. If the spins of these protons are aligned with the applied magnetic field, the small magnetic field generated by their nuclear spin properties will augment the strength of the field experienced by the first-mentioned proton H_a. The proton H_a will thus be *deshielded*. If the spins of H_b and H_c are opposed to the applied field, they will decrease the field experienced by proton H_a. It will then be *shielded*. In each of these situations, the absorption position of H_a will be altered. Among the many molecules in the solution, you will find all the various possible spin combinations for H_b and H_c; hence, the NMR spectrum of the

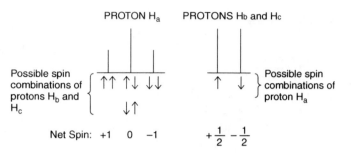

PROTON H_a PROTONS H_b and H_c

Possible spin combinations of protons H_b and H_c
↑↑   ↑↓   ↓↓
↓↑

Possible spin combinations of proton H_a
↑   ↓

Net Spin: +1   0   −1 $+\frac{1}{2}$ $-\frac{1}{2}$

Figure 26.12   Analysis of spin–spin splitting pattern for 1,1,2-trichloroethane.

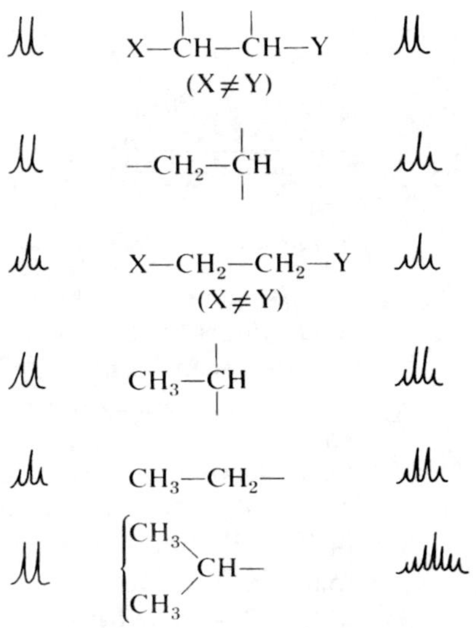

$$X-\overset{|}{C}H-\overset{|}{C}H-Y$$
$$(X \neq Y)$$

$$-CH_2-\overset{|}{C}H$$

$$X-CH_2-CH_2-Y$$
$$(X \neq Y)$$

$$CH_3-\overset{|}{C}H$$

$$CH_3-CH_2-$$

$$\begin{Bmatrix} CH_3 \\ CH_3 \end{Bmatrix} CH-$$

Figure 26.13   Some common splitting patterns.

molecular solution will give *three* absorption peaks (a triplet) for H_a because H_b and H_c have three different possible spin combinations (Figure 26.12). By a similar analysis, it can be seen that protons H_b and H_c should appear as a doublet.

Some common splitting patterns that can be predicted by the n + 1 rule and that are frequently observed in a number of molecules are shown in Figure 26.13. Notice particularly the last entry, where *both* methyl groups (six protons in all) function as a unit and split the methine proton into a septet (6 + 1 = 7).

26.10 The Coupling Constant

The quantitative amount of spin–spin interaction between two protons can be defined by the **coupling constant**. The spacing between the component peaks in a single multiplet is called the coupling constant *J*. This distance is measured on the same scale as the chemical shift and is expressed in hertz (Hz).

Coupling constants for protons on adjacent carbon atoms have magnitudes of from about 6 Hz to 8 Hz (see Table 26.4). You should expect to see a coupling constant in this range for compounds where there is free rotation about a single bond. Because three bonds separate protons from each other on adjacent carbon atoms, we label these coupling constants as ^3J. For example, the coupling constant for the compound shown in Figure 26.11 would be written as $^3J = 6$ Hz. The boldfaced lines in the following diagram show how the protons on adjacent carbon atoms are three bonds away from each other.

TABLE 26.4 Representative Coupling Constants and Approximate Values (Hz)

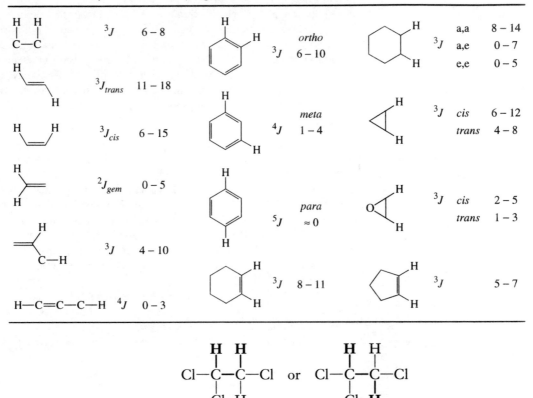

In compounds where there is a C=C double bond, free rotation is restricted. In compounds of this kind, we often find two types of ^3J coupling constants; $^3J_{trans}$ and $^3J_{cis}$. These coupling constants vary in value as shown in Table 26.4, but $^3J_{trans}$ is almost always larger than $^3J_{cis}$. The magnitudes of these ^3J_s often provide important structural clues. You can distinguish, for example, between a *cis* alkene and a *trans* alkene on the basis of the observed coupling constants for the two vinyl protons on disubstituted alkenes. Most of the coupling constants shown in the first column of Table 26.4 are three bond couplings, but you will notice that there is a two-bond (^2J) coupling constant listed. These protons that are bonded to a common carbon atom are often referred to as *geminal* protons and can be labeled as $^2J_{gem}$. Notice that the coupling constants for *geminal* protons are quite small for alkenes. The ^2J couplings are observed only when the protons on a methylene group are in a different environment (see Section 26.11). The following structure shows the various types of couplings that you observe for protons on a C=C double bond in a typical alkene, vinyl acetate. The spectrum for this compound is described in detail in Section 26.11.

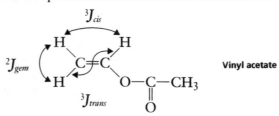

Vinyl acetate

Longer-range couplings that occur over four or more bonds are observed in some alkenes and also in aromatic compounds. Thus, in Table 26.4, we see that it is possible to observe a small H—H coupling (^4J = 0–3 Hz) occurring over four bonds in an alkene. In an aromatic compound, you often observe a small but measurable coupling between *meta* protons that are four bonds away from each other (^4J = 1–4 Hz). Couplings over five bonds are usually quite small, with values close to 0 Hz. The long-range couplings are usually observed only in *unsaturated* compounds. The spectra of saturated compounds are often more easily interpreted because they usually have only three bond couplings. Aromatic compounds are discussed in detail in Section 26.13.

26.11 Magnetic Equivalence

In the example of spin–spin splitting in 1,1,2-trichloroethane (see Figure 26.11), notice that the two protons H_b and H_c, which are attached to the same carbon atom, do not split one another. They behave as an integral group. Actually, the two protons H_b and H_c *are* coupled to one another; however, for reasons we cannot explain fully here, protons that are attached to the same carbon and both of which have the same chemical shift do not show spin–spin splitting. Another way of stating this is that protons coupled to the same extent to *all* other protons in a molecule do not show spin–spin splitting. Protons that have the same chemical shift and are coupled equivalently to all other protons are magnetically equivalent and do not show spin–spin splitting. Thus, in 1,1,2-trichloroethane in (see Figure 26.11), protons H_b and H_c have the same value of δ and are coupled by the same value of J to proton H_a. They are magnetically equivalent, and $^2J_{gem}$ = 0.

It is important to differentiate magnetic equivalence and chemical equivalence. Note the following two compounds.

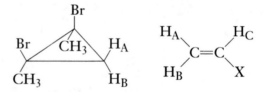

In the cyclopropane compound, the two geminal hydrogens H_A and H_B are chemically equivalent; however, they are not magnetically equivalent. Proton H_A is on the same side of the ring as the two halogens. Proton H_B is on the same side of the ring as the two methyl groups. Protons H_A and H_B will have different chemical shifts, will couple to one another, and will show spin–spin splitting. Two doublets will be seen for H_A and H_B. For cyclopropane rings, $^2J_{gem}$ is usually around 5 Hz.

The general vinyl structure (alkene) shown in the previous figure and the specific example of vinyl acetate shown in Figure 26.14 are examples of cases in which the methylene protons H_A and H_B are nonequivalent. They appear at different chemical shift values and will split each other. This coupling constant, $^2J_{gem}$, is usually small with vinyl compounds (about 2 Hz).

The spectrum of vinyl acetate is shown in Figure 26.14. H_C appears downfield at about 7.3 ppm because of the electronegativity of the attached oxygen atom. This proton is split by H_B into a doublet ($^3J_{trans}$ = $^3J_{BC}$ = 15 Hz), and then each leg of the doublet is split by H_A into a doublet ($^3J_{cis}$ = $^3J_{AC}$ = 7 Hz). Notice that then $n + 1$ rule is applied individually to each adjacent proton. The pattern that results is usually referred to as a doublet of doublets (dd). The graphic analysis shown in Figure 26.15 should help you understand the pattern obtained for proton H_C.

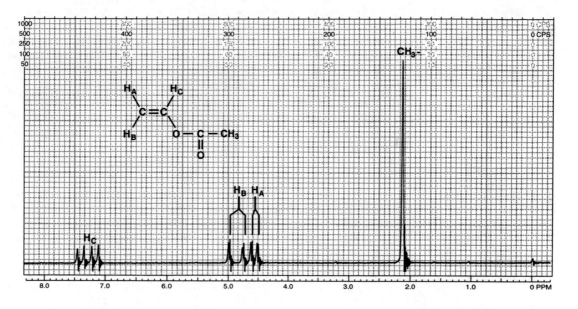

Figure 26.14   NMR spectrum of vinyl acetate. (Courtesy of Varian Associates.)

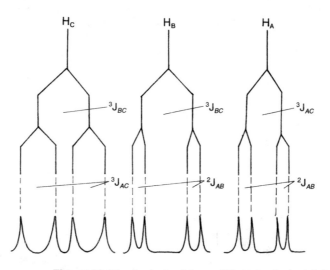

Figure 26.15   Analysis of the splittings in vinyl acetate.

Now look at the pattern shown in Figure 26.14 for proton H_B at 4.85 ppm. It is also a doublet of doublets. Proton H_B is split by proton H_C into a doublet $(^3J_{trans} = {}^3J_{BC} = 15$ Hz), and then each leg of the doublet is split by the geminal proton H_A into doublets $(^2J_{gem} = {}^2J_{AB} = 2$ Hz).

Proton H_A shown in Figure 26.14 appears at 4.55 ppm. This pattern is also a doublet of doublets. Proton H_A is split by proton H_C into a doublet $(^3J_{cis} = 3J_{AB} = 7$ Hz), and then each leg of the doublet is split by the geminal proton H_B into doublets $(^2J_{gem} = {}^2J_{AB} = 2$ Hz). For each proton shown in Figure 26.14, the NMR spectrum must be analyzed graphically, splitting by splitting. This complete graphic analysis is shown in Figure 26.15.

26.12 Spectra at Higher Field Strength

Occasionally, the 60-MHz spectrum of an organic compound, or a portion of it, is almost undecipherable because the chemical shifts of several groups of protons are all very similar. In these cases, all the proton resonances occur in the same area of the spectrum, and peaks often overlap so extensively that individual peaks and splittings cannot be extracted. One way to simplify such a situation is to use a spectrometer that operates at a higher frequency. Although both 60-MHz and 100-MHz instruments are still in use, it is becoming increasingly common to find instruments operating at much higher fields and with spectrometer frequencies 300, 400, or 500 MHz.

Although NMR coupling constants do not depend on the frequency or the field strength of operation of the NMR spectrometer, chemical shifts in hertz depend on these parameters. This circumstance can often be used to simplify an otherwise undecipherable spectrum. Suppose, for instance, that a compound contained three multiplets derived from groups of protons with very similar chemical shifts. At 60 MHz, these peaks might overlap, as illustrated in Figure 26.16, and simply give an unresolved envelope of absorption. It turns out that the $n + 1$ rule fails to make the proper predictions when chemical shifts are similar for the protons in a molecule. The spectral patterns that result are said to be **second order**, and what you end up seeing is an amorphous blob of unrecognizable patterns!

Figure 26.16 also shows the spectrum of the same compound at two higher frequencies (100 MHz and 300 MHz). When the spectrum is redetermined at a higher frequency, the coupling constants (J) do not change, but the chemical shifts in *hertz* (not ppm) of the proton groups (H_A, H_B, H_C) responsible for the multiplets do increase. It is important to realize, however, that the chemical shift in *ppm* is a constant, and it will not change when the frequency of the spectrometer is increased (see equation 1 in Section 26.4).

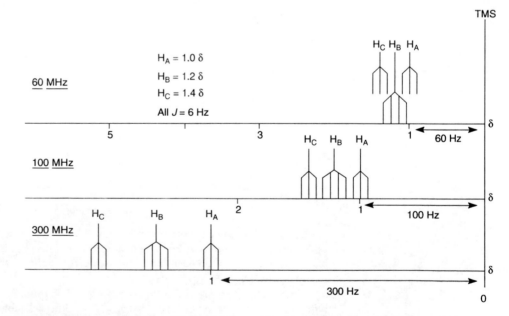

Figure 26.16   A comparison of the spectrum of a compound with overlapping multiplets at 60 MHz, with spectra of the same compound also determined at 100 MHz and 300 MHz.

Notice that at 300 MHz, the individual multiplets are cleanly separated and resolved. At high frequency, the chemical shift differences of each proton increase, resulting in more clearly recognizable patterns (that is, triplets, quartets, and so on) and less overlap of proton patterns in the spectrum. At high frequency, the chemical shift differences are large, and the $n + 1$ rule will more likely correctly predict the patterns. Thus, it is a clear advantage to use NMR spectrometers operating at high frequency (300 MHz or above) because the resulting spectra are more likely to provide nonoverlapped and well-resolved peaks. When the protons in a spectrum follow the $n + 1$ rule, the spectrum is said to be **first order**. The result is that you will obtain a spectrum with much more recognizable patterns, as shown in Figure 26.16.

26.13 Aromatic Compounds—Substituted Benzene Rings

Phenyl rings are so common in organic compounds that it is important to know a few facts about NMR absorptions in compounds that contain them. In general, the ring protons of a benzenoid system have resonance near 7.3 ppm; however, electron-withdrawing ring substituents (for example, nitro, cyano, carboxyl, or carbonyl) move the resonance of these protons downfield (larger ppm values), and electron-donating ring substituents (for example, methoxy or amino) move the resonance of these protons upfield (smaller ppm values). Table 26.5 shows these trends for a series of symmetrically p-disubstituted benzene compounds. The p-disubstituted compounds were chosen because their two planes of symmetry render all of the hydrogens equivalent. Each compound gives only one aromatic peak (a singlet) in the proton NMR spectrum. Later, you will see that some positions are affected more strongly than others in systems with substitution patterns different from this one.

In the sections that follow, we will attempt to cover some of the most important types of benzene ring substitution. In some cases, it will be necessary to examine sample spectra taken at both 60 MHz and 300 MHz. Many benzenoid rings show second-order splittings at 60 MHz, but are essentially first order at 300 MHz.

A. Monosubstituted Rings

Alkylbenzenes. In monosubstituted benzenes in which the substituent is neither a strongly electron-withdrawing nor a strongly electron-donating group, all the ring protons give rise to what appears to be a *single resonance* when the spectrum is determined at 60 MHz. This is a particularly common occurrence in alkyl-substituted benzenes. Although the protons *ortho, meta,* and *para* to the substituent are

TABLE 26.5 Proton Chemical Shifts in p-disubstituted Benzene Compounds

Substituent X		δ (ppm)	
	—OCH$_3$	6.80	Electron donating
X	—OH	6.60	(shielding)
	—NH$_2$	6.36	
	—CH$_3$	7.05	
	—H	7.32	
X	—COOH	8.20	Electron withdrawing
	—NO$_2$	8.48	(deshielding)

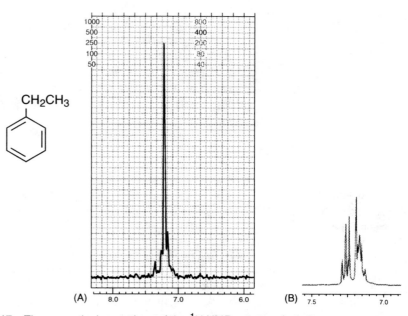

(A)   8.0   7.0   6.0   (B)   7.5   7.0

Figure 26.17 The aromatic ring portions of the ^{1}H NMR spectra of ethylbenzene at (A) 60 MHz and (B) 300 MHz.

not chemically equivalent, they generally give rise to a single unresolved absorption peak. A possible explanation is that the chemical shift differences, which should be small in any event, are somehow eliminated by the presence of the ring current, which tends to equalize them. All of the protons are nearly equivalent under these conditions. The NMR spectra of the aromatic portions of alkylbenzene compounds are good examples of this type of circumstance. Figure 26.17A is the 60-MHz ^{1}H spectrum of ethylbenzene.

The 300-MHz spectrum of ethylbenzene, shown in Figure 26.17B, presents quite a different picture. With the increased frequency shifts at 300 MHz, the nearly equivalent (at 60 MHz) protons are neatly separated into two groups. The *ortho* and *para* protons appear upfield from the *meta* protons. The splitting pattern is clearly second order.

Electron-Donating Groups. When electron-donating groups are attached to the ring, the ring protons are not equivalent, even at 60 MHz. A highly activating substituent such as methoxy clearly increases the electron density at the *ortho* and *para* positions of the ring (by resonance) and helps to give these protons greater shielding than those in the *meta* positions and, thus, a substantially different chemical shift.

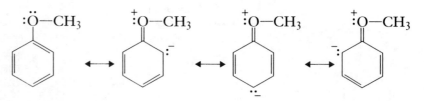

At 60 MHz, this chemical shift difference results in a complicated second-order splitting pattern for anisole (methoxybenzene), but the protons do fall clearly into two groups, the *ortho/para* protons and the *meta* protons. The 60-MHz NMR spectrum of the aromatic portion of anisole (see Figure 26.18A) has a complex multiplet

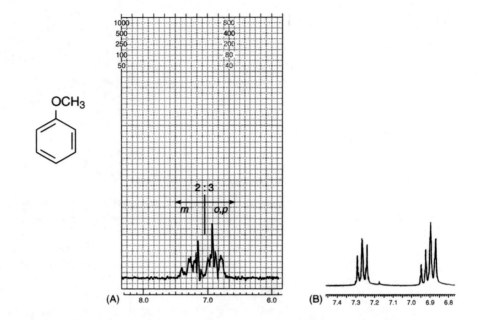

Figure 26.18 The aromatic ring portions of the 1H NMR spectra of anisole at (A) 60 MHz and (B) 300 MHz.

for the *o,p,* protons (integrating for three protons) that is upfield from the *meta* protons (integrating for two protons), with a clear distinction (gap) between the two types. Aniline (aminobenzene) provides a similar spectrum, also with a 3:2 split, owing to the electron-releasing effect of the amino group.

The 300-MHz spectrum of anisole (see Figure 26.18B) shows the same separation between the *ortho/para* hydrogens (upfield) and the *meta* hydrogens (downfield). However, because the actual shift in Hertz between the two types of hydrogens is greater, there is less second-order interaction and the lines in the pattern are sharper at 300 MHz. In fact, it might be tempting to try to interpret the observed pattern as if it were first order, a triplet at 7.25 ppm (*meta*, 2 H) and an overlapping triplet (*para*, 1 H) with a doublet (*ortho*, 2 H) at about 6.9 ppm.

Anisotropy—Electron-Withdrawing Groups. A carbonyl or a nitro group would be expected to show (aside from anisotropy effects) a reverse effect, because these groups are electron withdrawing. It would be expected that the group would act to decrease the electron density around the *ortho* and *para* positions, thus deshielding the *ortho* and *para* hydrogens and providing a pattern exactly the reverse of the one shown for anisole (3:2 ratio, downfield:upfield). Convince yourself of this by drawing resonance structures. Nevertheless, the actual NMR spectra of nitrobenzene and benzaldehyde do not have the appearances that would be predicted on the basis of resonance structures. Instead, the *ortho* protons are much more deshielded than the *meta* and *para* protons, due to the magnetic anisotropy of the π bonds in these groups.

Anisotropy is observed when a substituent group bonds a carbonyl group directly to the benzene ring (see Figure 26.19). Once again, the ring protons fall into two groups, with the *ortho* protons downfield from the *meta/para* protons. Benzaldehyde (see Figure 26.20) and acetophenone both show this effect in their NMR spectra. A similar effect is sometimes observed when a carbon–carbon double bond is attached to the ring. The 300-MHz spectrum of benzaldehyde (see Figure 26.20B) is a nearly first-order spectrum and shows a doublet (H_C, 2 H), a triplet (H_B, 1 H), and a triplet (H_A, 2 H). It can be analyzed by the n + 1 rule.

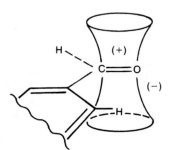

Figure 26.19 Anisotropic deshielding of the ortho protons of benzaldehyde.

B. *para*-Disubstituted Rings

Of the possible substitution patterns of a benzene ring, some are easily recognized. One of these is the para-disubstituted benzene ring. Examine anethole (see Figure 26.21) as a first example.

On one side of the anethole ring shown in Figure 26.21, proton H_a is coupled to H_b, $^3J = 8$ Hz resulting in a doublet at about 6.80 ppm in the spectrum. Proton H_a appears upfield (smaller ppm value) relative to H_b because of shielding by the electron-releasing effect of the methoxy group. Likewise, H_b is coupled to H_a, $^3J = 8$ Hz, producing another doublet at 7.25 ppm for this proton. Because of the plane of symmetry, both halves of the ring are equivalent. Thus, H_a and H_b on the other side of the ring also appear at 6.80 ppm and 7.25 ppm, respectively. Each doublet, therefore, integrates for two protons each. A *para*-disubstituted ring, with two different substituents attached, is easily recognized by the appearance of two doublets, each integrating for two protons each.

As the chemical shifts of H_a and H_b approach each other in value, the *para*-disubstituted pattern becomes similar to that of 4-allyloxyanisole (see Figure 26.22). The inner peaks move closer together, and the outer ones become smaller or even disappear. Ultimately, when H_a and H_b approach each other closely enough in chemical shift, the outer peaks disappear, and the two inner peaks merge into a *singlet*; 1,4-dimethylbenzene (*para*-xylene), for instance, gives a singlet at 7.05 ppm.

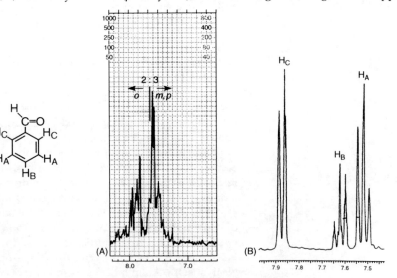

Figure 26.20 The aromatic ring portions of the ^{1}H NMR spectra of benzaldehyde at (A) 60 MHZ and (B) 300 MHZ.

Technique 26 ■ Nuclear Magnetic Resonance Spectroscopy (Proton NMR)   **911**

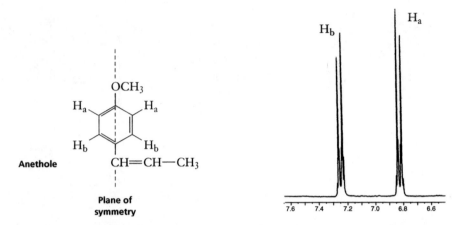

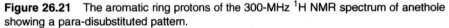

Figure 26.21   The aromatic ring protons of the 300-MHz ^{1}H NMR spectrum of anethole showing a para-disubstituted pattern.

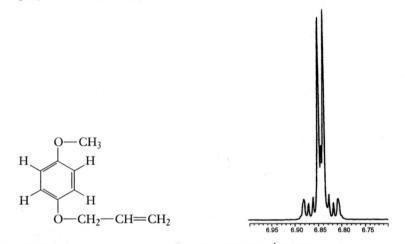

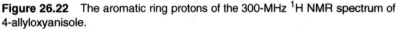

Figure 26.22   The aromatic ring protons of the 300-MHz ^{1}H NMR spectrum of 4-allyloxyanisole.

Hence, a single aromatic resonance integrating for four protons could easily represent a *para*-disubstituted ring, but the substituents would obviously be either identical or very similar.

C. Other Substitution

Figure 26.23 shows the 300-MHz ^{1}H spectra of the aromatic ring portions of 2-, 3-, and 4-nitroaniline (the *ortho*, *meta*, and *para* isomers). The characteristic pattern of a *para*-disubstituted ring, with its pair of doublets, makes it easy to recognize 4-nitroaniline. The splitting patterns for 2- and 3-nitroaniline are first order, and they can be analyzed by the $n + 1$ rule. As an exercise, see if you can analyze these patterns, assigning the multiplets to specific protons on the ring. Use the indicated multiplicities (s, d, t) and expected chemical shifts to help your assignments. Remember that the amino group releases electrons by resonance, and the nitro group shows a significant anisotropy toward ortho protons. You may ignore any *meta* and *para* couplings, remembering that these long-range couplings will be too small in magnitude to be observed on the scale on which these figures are presented. If the spectra were expanded, you would be able to observe ^4J couplings.

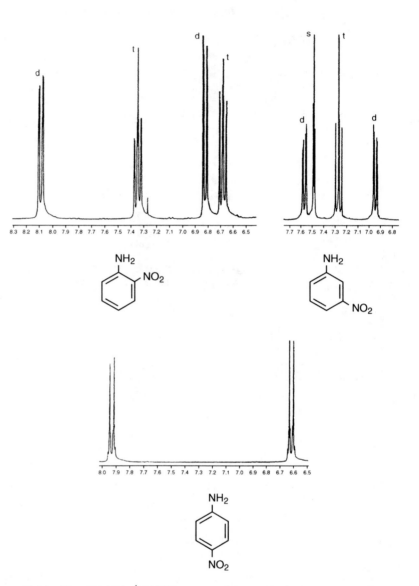

Figure 26.23 The 300-MHz ^{1}H NMR spectra of the aromatic ring portions of 2-, 3-, and 4-nitroaniline (s, singlet; d, doublet; t, triplet).The NH$_2$ group is not shown.

The spectrum shown in Figure 26.24 is of 2-nitrophenol. It is helpful to look also at the coupling constants for the benzene ring found in Table 26.4. Because the spectrum is expanded, it is now possible to see ^3J couplings (about 8 Hz) as well as ^4J couplings (about 1.5 Hz). ^5J couplings are not observed ($^5J \approx 0$). Each of the protons on this compound is assigned on the spectrum. Proton H$_d$ appears downfield at 8.11 ppm as a doublet of doublets ($^3J_{ad}$ = 8 Hz and $^4J_{cd}$ = 1.5 Hz); H$_c$ appears at 7.6 ppm as a triplet of doublets ($^3J_{ac} = ^3J_{bc}$ = 8 Hz and $^4J_{cd}$ = 1.5 Hz); H$_b$ appears at 7.17 ppm as a doublet of doublets ($^3J_{bc}$ = 8 Hz and $^4J_{ab}$ = 1.5 Hz); and H$_a$ appears at 7.0 ppm as a triplet of doublets ($^3J_{ac} = ^3J_{ad}$ = 8 Hz and $^4J_{ab}$ = 1.5 Hz). H$_d$ appears the furthest downfield because of the anisotropy of the nitro group. H$_a$ and H$_b$ are relatively shielded because of the resonance-releasing effect of the hydroxyl group, which shields these two protons. H$_c$ is assigned by a process of elimination in the absence of these two effects.

26.14 Protons Attached to Atoms Other Than Carbon

Protons attached to atoms other than carbon often have a widely variable range of absorptions. Several of these groups are tabulated in Table 26.6. In addition, under the usual conditions of determining an NMR spectrum, protons on heteroelements normally do not couple with protons on adjacent carbon atoms to give spin–spin splitting. The primary reason is that such protons often exchange rapidly with those of the solvent medium. The absorption position is variable because these groups also undergo various degrees of hydrogen bonding in solutions of different

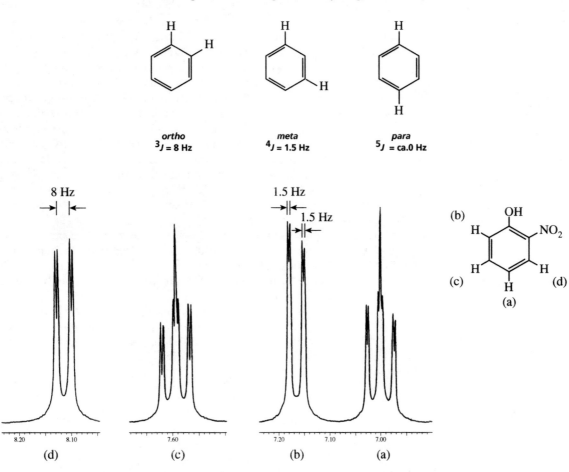

Figure 26.24 Expansions of the aromatic ring proton multiplets from the 300-MHz ^{1}H spectrum of 2-nitrophenol. The accompanying hydroxyl absorption (OH) is not shown. Coupling constants are indicated on some of the peaks of the spectrum to give an idea of scale.

TABLE 26.6 Typical Ranges for Groups with Variable Chemical Shift

Acids	RCOOH	10.5–12.0 ppm
Phenols	ArOH	4.0–7.0
Alcohols	ROH	0.5–5.0
Amines	RNH$_2$	0.5–5.0
Amides	RCONH$_2$	5.0–8.0
Enols	CH=CH—OH	≥15

concentrations. The amount of hydrogen bonding that occurs with a proton radically affects the valence electron density around that proton and produces correspondingly large changes in the chemical shift. The absorption peaks for protons that have hydrogen bonding or are undergoing exchange are frequently broad relative to other singlets and can often be recognized on that basis. For a different reason, called **quadrupole broadening**, protons attached to nitrogen atoms often show an extremely broad resonance peak, often almost indistinguishable from the baseline.

26.15 Chemical Shift Reagents

Researchers have known for some time that interactions between molecules and solvents, such as those due to hydrogen bonding, can cause large changes in the resonance positions of certain types of protons (for example, hydroxyl and amino). They have also known that the resonance positions of some groups of protons can be greatly affected by changing from the usual NMR solvents such as CCl_4 and $CDCl_3$ to solvents such as benzene, which impose local anisotropic effects on surrounding molecules. In many cases, it is possible to resolve partially overlapping multiplets by such a solvent change. The use of **chemical shift reagents** for this purpose dates from about 1969. Most of these chemical shift reagents are organic complexes of paramagnetic rare earth metals from the lanthanide series of elements. When these metal complexes are added to the compound whose spectrum is being determined, profound shifts in the resonance positions of the various groups of protons are observed. The direction of the shift (upfield or downfield) depends primarily on which metal is being used. Complexes of europium, erbium, thulium, and ytterbium shift resonances to lower field; complexes of cerium, praseodymium, neodymium, samarium, terbium, and holmium generally shift resonances to higher field. The advantage of using such reagents is that shifts similar to those observed at higher field can be induced without the purchase of an expensive higher-field instrument.

Of the lanthanides, europium is probably the most commonly used metal. Two of its widely used complexes are *tris*-(dipivalomethanato)europium and *tris*-(6,6,7,7,8,8,8-heptafluoro-2,2-dimethyl-3,5-octanedionato)europium. These are frequently abbreviated Eu(dpm)$_3$ and Eu(fod)$_3$, respectively.

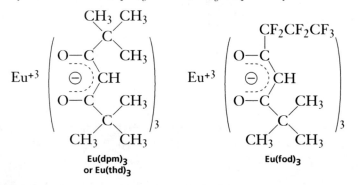

These lanthanide complexes produce spectral simplifications in the NMR spectrum of any compound that has a relatively basic pair of electrons (unshared pair) that can coordinate with Eu^{3+}. Typically, aldehydes, ketones, alcohols, thiols, ethers, and amines will all interact:

$$2B: + Eu(dpm)_3 \longrightarrow \begin{array}{c} B: \\ \\ B: \end{array} Eu \begin{array}{c} dpm \\ dpm \\ dpm \end{array}$$

The amount of shift that a given group of protons will experience depends (1) on the distance separating the metal (Eu^{3+}) and that group of protons, and (2) on the concentration of the shift reagent in the solution. Because of the latter dependence, it is necessary when reporting a lanthanide-shifted spectrum to report the number of mole equivalents of shift reagent used or its molar concentration.

The distance factor is illustrated in the spectra of hexanol, which are given in Figures 26.25 and 26.26. In the absence of shift reagent, the normal spectrum is obtained (see Figure 26.25). Only the triplet of the terminal methyl group and the triplet of the methylene group next to the hydroxyl are resolved in the spectrum. The other protons (aside from OH) are found together in a broad unresolved group. With shift reagent added (see Figure 26.26), each of the methylene groups is clearly separated and resolved into the proper multiplet structure. The spectrum is first-order and simplified; all the splittings are explained by the $n + 1$ rule.

One final consequence of using a shift reagent should be noted. Notice in Figure 26.26 that the multiplets are not as nicely resolved into sharp peaks as you might expect. This is due to the fact that shift reagents cause a small amount of peak broadening. At high-shift reagent concentrations, this problem becomes serious, but at most useful concentrations the amount of broadening experienced is tolerable.

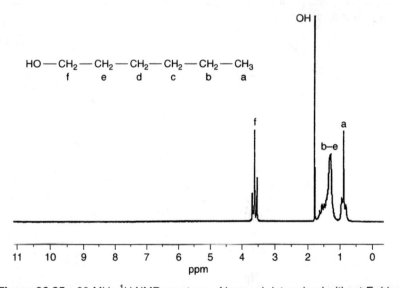

Figure 26.25   90-MHz ^{1}H NMR spectrum of hexanol determined without Eu(dpm)$_3$
© National Institute of Advanced Industrial Science and Technology.

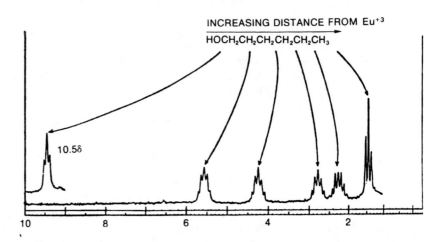

Figure 26.26 The 100-MHz^{1}H NMR spectrum of hexanol with 0.29 mole equivalents of Eu(dpm)$_3$ added. From Sanders J. K. M. and Williams, D. H. Chemical Communications, (1970): 422. Reproduced by permission of The Royal Society of Chemistry.

REFERENCES

Textbooks

Friebolin, H. *Basic One- and Two-Dimensional NMR Spectroscopy*, 3rd ed. New York: VCH Publishers, 1998.

Gunther, H. *NMR Spectroscopy*, 2nd ed. New York: John Wiley & Sons, 1995.

Jackman, L. M., and Sternhell, S. *Nuclear Magnetic Resonance Spectroscopy* in *Organic Chemistry*, 2nd ed. New York: Pergamon Press, 1969.

Macomber, R. S. *A Complete Introduction to Modern NMR Spectroscopy*. NewYork: John Wiley & Sons, 1997.

Macomber, R. S. *NMR Spectroscopy: Essential Theory and Practice*. New York: College Outline Series, Harcourt Brace Jovanovich, 1988.

Pavia, D. L., Lampman, G. M., and vyvyan, J. R. Kriz, G. S. Brooks Cole 2008. *Introduction to Spectroscopy*, 4th ed.

Sanders, J. K. M., and Hunter, B. K. *Modern NMR Spectroscopy—A Guide for Chemists*, 2nd ed. Oxford: Oxford University Press, 1993.

Silverstein, R. M., and Webster, F. X. and Kiemle, D. *Spectrometric Identification of Organic Compounds*, 7th ed. New York: John Wiley & Sons, 2005.

Compilations of Spectra

Pouchert, C. J. *The Aldrich Library of NMR Spectra, 60 MHz*, 2nd ed. Milwaukee, WI: Aldrich Chemical Company, 1983.

Pouchert, C. J., and Behnke, J. *The Aldrich Library of ^{13}C and ^{1}H FT–NMR Spectra, 300 MHz*. Milwaukee, WI: Aldrich Chemical Company, 1993.

Pretsch, E., Clerc, T., Seibl, J., and Simon, W. *Tables of Spectral Data for Structure Determination of Organic Compounds*, 2nd ed. Berlin and New York: Springer-Verlag, 1989. Translated from the German by K. Biemann.

Web Sites

http://www.aist.go.jp/RIODB/SDBS/menu-e.html
Integrated Spectral DataBase System for Organic Compounds, National Institute of Materials and Chemical Research, Tsukuba, Ibaraki 305-8565, Japan. This database includes infrared, mass spectra, and NMR data (proton and carbon-13) for a large number of compounds.

http://www.chem.ucla.edu/~webspectra/
UCLA Department of Chemistry and Biochemistry in connection with Cambridge University Isotope Laboratories maintains a Web site, WebSpectra, that provides NMR and IR spectroscopy problems for students to interpret. They provide links to other sites with problems for students to solve.

PROBLEMS

1. Describe the method that you should use to determine the proton NMR spectrum of a carboxylic acid, which is insoluble in *all* the common organic solvents that your instructor is likely to make available.

2. To save money, a student uses chloroform instead of deuterated chloroform to run a proton NMR spectrum. Is this a good idea?

3. Look up the solubilities for the following compounds and decide whether you would select deuterated chloroform or deuterated water to dissolve the substances for NMR spectroscopy.

   a. Glycerol (1,2,3-propanetriol)

   b. 1,4-Diethoxybenzene

   c. Propyl pentanoate (propyl ester of pentanoic acid)

4. Assign each of the proton patterns in the spectra of 2-, 3-, and 4-nitroaniline as shown in Figure 26.23.

5. The following two compounds are isomeric esters derived from acetic acid, each with formula $C_5H_{10}O_2$. These expanded spectra clearly show the splitting patterns: singlet, doublet, triplet, quartet, etc. Integral curves are drawn on the spectra, along with relative integration values provided just above the scale and under each set of peaks. These numbers indicate the number of protons assigned to each pattern. Remember that these integral values are approximate. You will need to round the values off to the nearest whole number. Draw the structure of each compound.

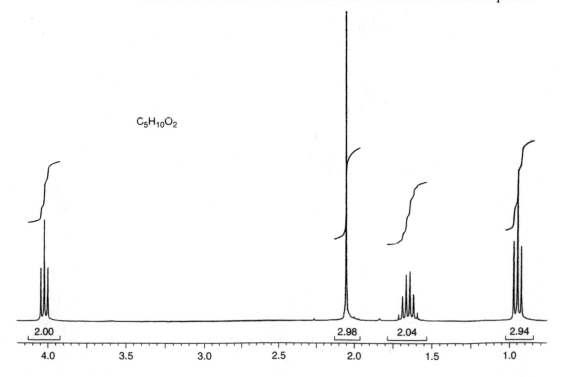

$C_5H_{10}O_2$

2.00   2.98   2.04   2.94

4.0   3.5   3.0   2.5   2.0   1.5   1.0

b. The set of peaks centering on 5 ppm is expanded in both the x and y directions in order to show the pattern more clearly. This expanded pattern is shown as an inset on the full spectrum.

6. The compound that gives the following NMR spectrum has the formula $C_3H_6Br_2$. Draw the structure.

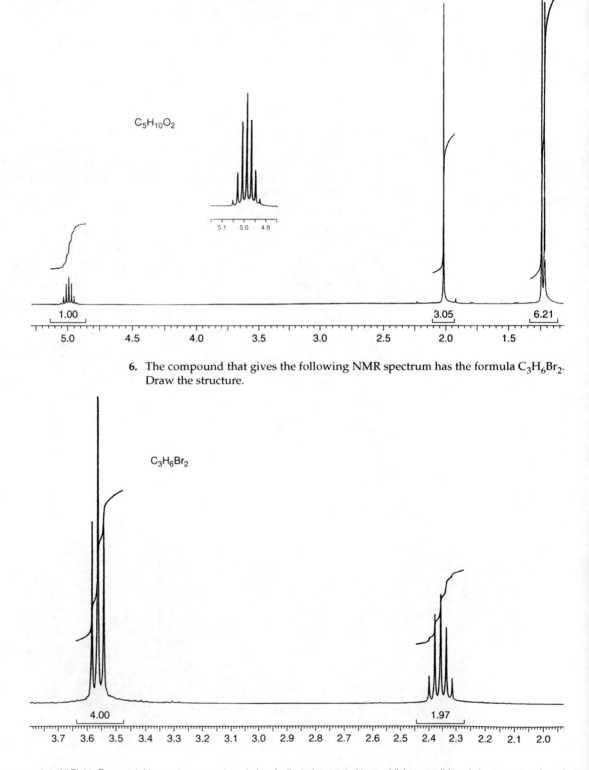

7. Draw the structure of an ether with formula $C_5H_{12}O_2$ that fits the following NMR spectrum.

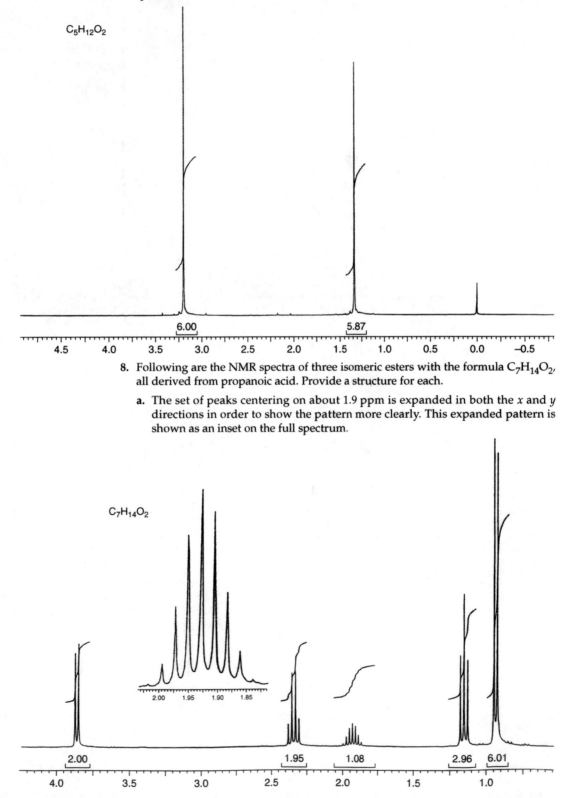

8. Following are the NMR spectra of three isomeric esters with the formula $C_7H_{14}O_2$, all derived from propanoic acid. Provide a structure for each.

a. The set of peaks centering on about 1.9 ppm is expanded in both the x and y directions in order to show the pattern more clearly. This expanded pattern is shown as an inset on the full spectrum.

b.

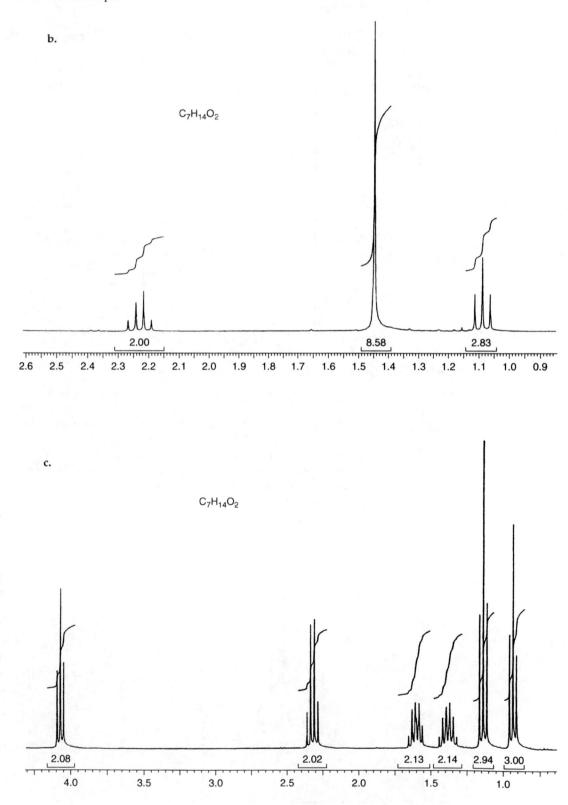

9. The two isomeric carboxylic acids that give the following NMR spectra both have the formula $C_3H_5ClO_2$. Draw their structures.

a. The broad singlet integrating for one proton that is shown as an inset on the spectrum appears downfield at 11.5 ppm.

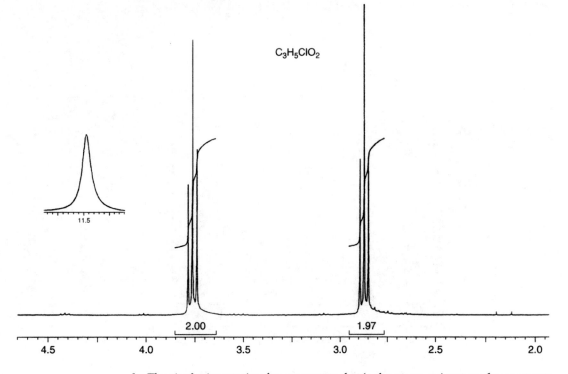

$C_3H_5ClO_2$

11.5

2.00   1.97

4.5   4.0   3.5   3.0   2.5   2.0

b. The singlet integrating for one proton that is shown as an inset on the spectrum appears downfield at 12.0 ppm.

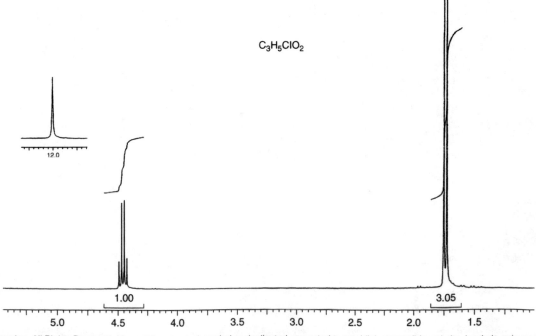

$C_3H_5ClO_2$

12.0

1.00   3.05

5.0   4.5   4.0   3.5   3.0   2.5   2.0   1.5

10. The following compounds are isomers with formula $C_{10}H_{12}O$. Their infrared spectra show strong bands near 1715 cm^{-1} and in the range from 1600 cm^{-1} to 1450 cm^{-1}. Draw their structures.

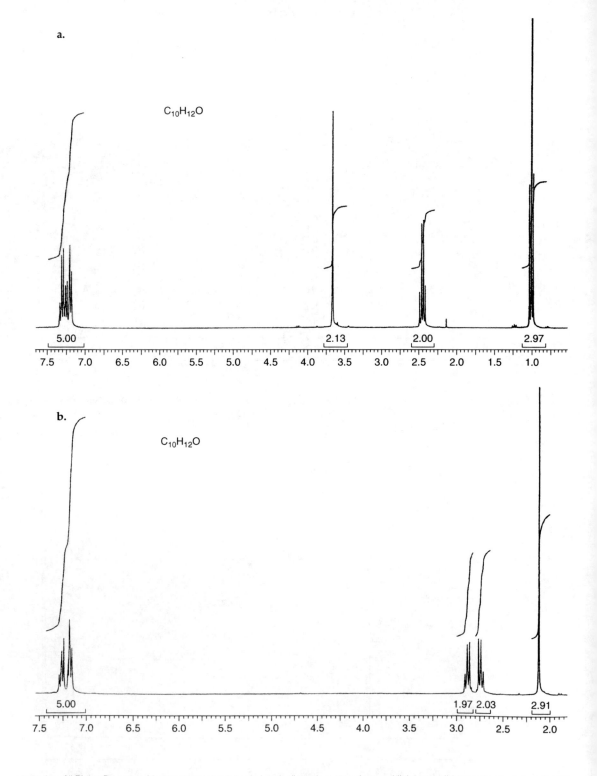

27 **TECHNIQUE 27**

Carbon-13 Nuclear Magnetic Resonance Spectroscopy

Carbon-12, the most abundant isotope of carbon, does not possess spin ($I = 0$); it has both an even atomic number and an even atomic weight. The second principal isotope of carbon, ^{13}C, however, does have the nuclear spin property ($I = \frac{1}{2}$). ^{13}C atom resonances are not easy to observe, due to a combination of two factors. First, the natural abundance of ^{13}C is low; only 1.08% of all carbon atoms are ^{13}C. Second, the magnetic moment μ of ^{13}C is low. For these two reasons, the resonances of ^{13}C are about 6000 times weaker than those of hydrogen. With special Fourier transform (FT) instrumental techniques, which are not discussed here, it is possible to observe ^{13}C nuclear magnetic resonance (carbon-13) spectra on samples that contain only the natural abundance of ^{13}C.

The most useful parameter derived from carbon-13 spectra is the chemical shift. Integrals are unreliable and are not necessarily related to the relative numbers of ^{13}C atoms present in the sample. Hydrogens that are attached to ^{13}C atoms cause spin–spin splitting, but spin–spin interaction between adjacent carbon atoms is rare. With the low natural abundance carbon-13 (0.0108), the probability of finding two ^{13}C atoms adjacent to one another is extremely low.

Carbon spectra can be used to determine the number of nonequivalent carbons and to identify the types of carbon atoms (methyl, methylene, aromatic, carbonyl, and so on) that may be present in a compound. Thus, carbon NMR provides direct information about the carbon skeleton of a molecule. Because of the low natural abundance of carbon-13 in a sample, it is often necessary to acquire multiple scans over what is needed for proton NMR.

For a given magnetic field strength, the resonance frequency of a ^{13}C nucleus is about one-fourth the frequency required to observe proton resonances. For example, in a 7.05-tesla applied magnetic field, protons are observed at 300 MHz, and ^{13}C nuclei are observed at about 75 MHz.

27.1 Preparing a Sample for Carbon-13 NMR

Technique 26, Section 26.1, describes the technique for preparing samples for proton NMR. Much of what is described there also applies to carbon NMR. There are some differences, however, in determining a carbon spectrum. Fourier transform instruments require a deuterium signal to stabilize (lock) the field. Therefore, the solvents must contain deuterium. Deuterated chloroform, $CDCl_3$, is used most commonly for this purpose because of its relatively low cost. Other deuterated solvents may also be used.

Modern FT–NMR spectrometers allow chemists to obtain both the proton and carbon NMR spectra of the same sample in the same NMR tube. After changing several parameters in the program operating the spectrometer, you can obtain both spectra without removing the sample from the probe. The only real difference is that a proton spectrum may be obtained after a few scans, whereas the carbon spectrum may require 10–100 times more scans.

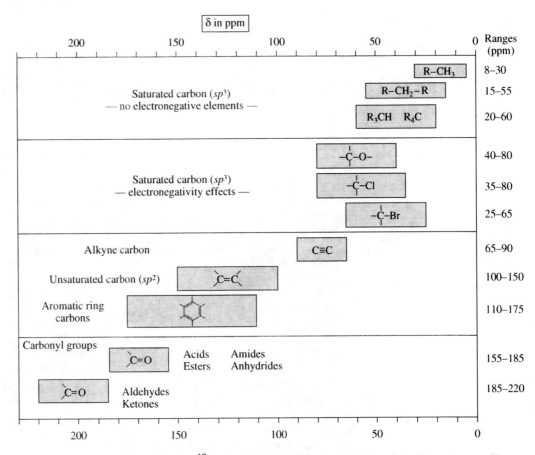

Figure 27.1   A correlation chart for ^{13}C chemical shifts (chemical shifts are listed in parts per million from tetramethylsilane).

Tetramethylsilane (TMS) may be added as an internal reference standard, where the chemical shift of the methyl carbon is defined as 0.00 ppm. Alternatively, you may use the center peak of the CDCl$_3$ pattern, which is found at 77.0 ppm. This pattern can be observed as a small "triplet" near 77.0 ppm in a number of the spectra given in this chapter.

27.2 Carbon-13 Chemical Shifts

An important parameter derived from carbon-13 spectra is the chemical shift. The correlation chart in Figure 27.1 shows typical ^{13}C chemical shifts, listed in parts per million (ppm) from TMS, where the carbons of the methyl groups of TMS (not the hydrogens) are used for reference. Notice that the chemical shifts appear over a range (0–220 ppm) much larger than that observed for protons (0–12 ppm). Because of the very large range of values, nearly every nonequivalent carbon atom in an organic molecule gives rise to a peak with a different chemical shift. Peaks rarely overlap as they often do in proton NMR.

The correlation chart is divided into four sections. Saturated carbon atoms appear at the highest field, nearest to TMS (8–60 ppm). The next section of the chart demonstrates the effect of electronegative atoms (40–80 ppm). The third section includes alkene and aromatic-ring carbon atoms (100–175 ppm). Finally, the fourth section contains carbonyl carbons, which appear at the lowest field values (155–220 ppm).

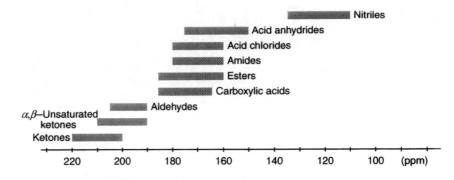

Figure 27.2   A ^{13}C correlation chart for carbonyl and nitrile functional groups.

Electronegativity, hybridization, and anisotropy all affect ^{13}C chemical shifts in nearly the same fashion as they affect ^{1}H chemical shifts; however ^{13}C chemical shifts are about 20 times larger. Electronegativity (see Section 26.7) produces the same deshielding effect in carbon NMR as in proton NMR—the electronegative element produces a large downfield shift. The shift is greater for a ^{13}C atom than for a proton because the electronegative atom is directly attached to the ^{13}C atom and the effect occurs through only a single bond, C—X. With protons, the electronegative atoms are attached to carbon, not hydrogen; the effect occurs through two bonds, H—C—X, rather than one.

Analogous with ^{1}H shifts, changes in hybridization also produce larger shifts for the carbon-13 that is *directly involved* (no bonds) than they do for the hydrogens attached to that carbon (one bond). In ^{13}C NMR, the carbons of carbonyl groups have the largest chemical shifts, due both to sp^2 hybridization and to the fact that an electronegative oxygen is directly attached to the carbonyl carbon, deshielding it even further. Anisotropy (see Section 26.8) is responsible for the large chemical shifts of the carbons in aromatic rings and alkenes.

Notice that the range of chemical shifts is larger for carbon atoms than for hydrogen atoms. Because the factors affecting carbon shifts operate either through one bond or directly on carbon, they are greater than those for hydrogen, which operate through more bonds. As a result, the entire range of chemical shifts becomes larger for ^{13}C (0–220 ppm) than for ^{1}H (0–12 ppm).

Many of the important functional groups of organic chemistry contain a carbonyl group. In determining the structure of a compound containing a carbonyl group, it is frequently helpful to have some idea of the type of carbonyl group in the unknown. Figure 27.2 illustrates the typical ranges of ^{13}C chemical shifts for some carbonyl-containing functional groups. Although there is some overlap in the ranges, ketones and aldehydes are easy to distinguish from the other types. Chemical shift data for carbonyl carbons are particularly powerful when combined with data from an infrared spectrum.

27.3 Proton-Coupled ^{13}C Spectra—Spin–Spin Splitting of Carbon-13 Signals

Unless a molecule is artificially enriched by synthesis, the probability of finding two ^{13}C atoms in the same molecule is low. The probability of finding two ^{13}C atoms adjacent to each other in the same molecule is even lower. Therefore, we rarely observe **homonuclear** (carbon–carbon) spin–spin splitting patterns where the interaction occurs between two ^{13}C atoms. However, the spins of protons attached directly to ^{13}C atoms do interact with the spin of carbon and cause the

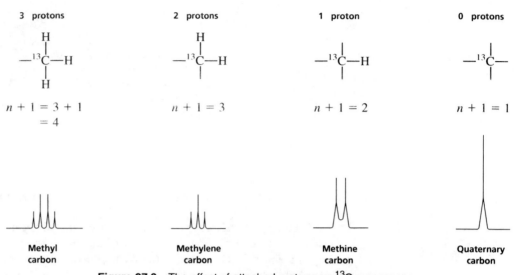

Figure 27.3   The effect of attached protons on ^{13}C resonances.

carbon signal to be split according to the $n + 1$ rule. This is **heteronuclear** (carbon–hydrogen) coupling involving two different types of atoms. With ^{13}C NMR, we generally examine splitting that arises from the protons *directly attached* to the carbon atom being studied. This is a one-bond coupling. In proton NMR, the most common splittings are *homonuclear* (hydrogen–hydrogen), which occur between protons attached to *adjacent* carbon atoms. In these cases, the interaction is a three-bond coupling, H—C—C—H.

Figure 27.3 illustrates the effect of protons directly attached to a ^{13}C atom. The $n + 1$ rule predicts the degree of splitting in each case. The resonance of a ^{13}C atom with three attached protons, for instance, is split into a quartet ($n + 1 = 3 + 1 = 4$). Because the hydrogens are directly attached to the carbon-13 (one-bond couplings), the coupling constants for this interaction are quite large, with J values of about 100 Hz to 250 Hz. Compare the typical three-bond H—C—C—H couplings that are common in NMR spectra, which have J values of about 4 Hz to 18 Hz.

It is important to note while examining Figure 27.3 that you are not "seeing" protons directly when looking at a ^{13}C spectrum (proton resonances occur at frequencies outside the range used to obtain ^{13}C spectra); you are observing only the effect of the protons on ^{13}C atoms. Also remember that we cannot observe ^{12}C, because it is NMR inactive.

Spectra that show the spin–spin splitting, or coupling, between carbon-13 and the protons directly attached to it are called **proton-coupled spectra**. Figure 27.4 A is the proton-coupled ^{13}C NMR spectrum of ethyl phenylacetate. In this spectrum, the first quartet downfield from TMS (14.2 ppm) corresponds to the carbon of the methyl group. It is split into a quartet ($J = 127$ Hz) by the three attached hydrogen atoms (^{13}C—H, one-bond couplings). In addition, although it cannot be seen on the scale of this spectrum (an expansion must be used), each of the quartet lines is split into a closely spaced triplet ($J = $ ca. 1 Hz). This additional fine splitting is caused by the two protons on the adjacent —CH_2— group. These are two-bond couplings (H—C—^{13}C) of a type that occurs commonly in ^{13}C spectra, with coupling constants that are generally quite small ($J = 0$–2 Hz) for systems with carbon atoms in

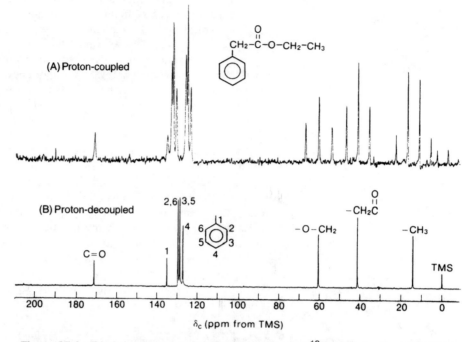

Figure 27.4   Ethyl phenylacetate. (A) The proton-coupled ^{13}C NMR spectrum (20 MHz). (B) The proton-decoupled ^{13}C spectrum (20 MHz). (From Moore, J. A., Dalrymple, D. L., and Rodig, O. R. Experimental Methods in Organic Chemistry, 3rd ed. [Philadelphia: W. B. Saunders, 1982].)

an aliphatic chain. Because of their small size, these couplings are frequently ignored in the routine analysis of spectra, with greater attention being given to the larger one-bond splittings seen in the quartet itself.

 There are two —CH$_2$— groups in ethyl phenylacetate. The one corresponding to the ethyl —CH$_2$— group is found farther downfield (60.6 ppm), as this carbon is deshielded by the attached oxygen. It is a triplet because of the two attached hydrogens (one-bond couplings). Again, although it is not seen in this unexpanded spectrum, the three hydrogens on the adjacent methyl group finely split each of the triplet peaks into a quartet. The benzyl —CH$_2$— carbon is the intermediate triplet (41.4 ppm). Farthest downfield is the carbonyl-group carbon (171.1 ppm). On the scale of this presentation, it is a singlet (no directly attached hydrogens), but because of the adjacent benzyl —CH$_2$— group, it is actually split finely into a triplet. The aromatic ring carbons also appear in the spectrum, and they have resonances in the range from 127 ppm to 136 ppm. Section 27.7 will discuss aromatic ring ^{13}C resonances.

 Proton-coupled spectra for large molecules are often difficult to interpret. The multiplets from different carbons commonly overlap because the ^{13}C—H coupling constants are frequently larger than the chemical shift differences of the carbons in the spectrum. Sometimes, even simple molecules such as ethyl phenylacetate (see Figure 27.4A) are difficult to interpret. Proton decoupling, which is discussed in the next section, avoids this problem.

27.4 Proton-Decoupled ^{13}C Spectra

By far, the great majority of ^{13}C NMR spectra are obtained as **proton-decoupled spectra**. The decoupling technique obliterates all interactions between protons and ^{13}C nuclei; therefore, only **singlets** are observed in a decoupled ^{13}C NMR spectrum.

Although this technique simplifies the spectrum and avoids overlapping multiplets, it has the disadvantage that the information on attached hydrogens is lost.

Proton **decoupling** is accomplished in the process of determining a ^{13}C NMR spectrum by simultaneously irradiating all of the protons in the molecule with a broad spectrum of frequencies in the proper range for protons. Modern NMR spectrometers provide a second, tunable radio-frequency generator, the **decoupler**, for this purpose. Irradiation causes the protons to become saturated, and they undergo rapid upward and downward transitions, among all their possible spin states. These rapid transitions decouple any spin–spin interactions between the hydrogens and the ^{13}C nuclei being observed. In effect, all spin interactions are averaged to zero by the rapid changes. The carbon nucleus "senses" only one average spin state for the attached hydrogens rather than two or more distinct spin states.

Figure 27.4B is a proton-decoupled spectrum of ethyl phenylacetate. The proton coupled spectrum (see Figure 27.4A) was discussed in Section 27.3. It is interesting to compare the two spectra to see how the proton-decoupling technique simplifies the spectrum. Every chemically and magnetically distinct carbon gives only a single peak. Notice, however, that the two *ortho* ring carbons (carbons 2 and 6) and the two *meta* ring carbons (carbons 3 and 5) are equivalent by symmetry and that each pair gives only a single peak.

Figure 27.5 is a second example of a proton-decoupled spectrum. Notice that the spectrum shows three peaks corresponding to the exact number of

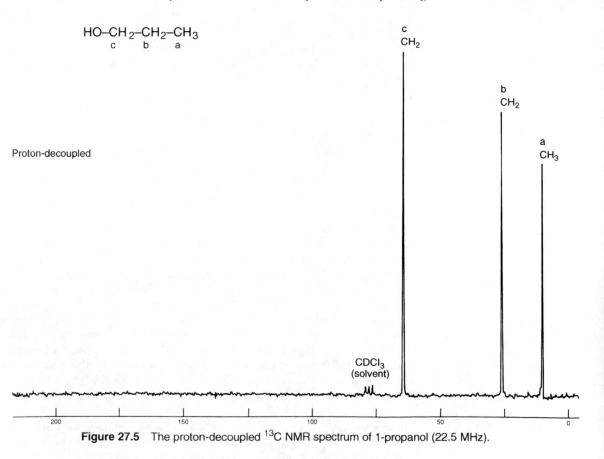

Figure 27.5   The proton-decoupled ^{13}C NMR spectrum of 1-propanol (22.5 MHz).

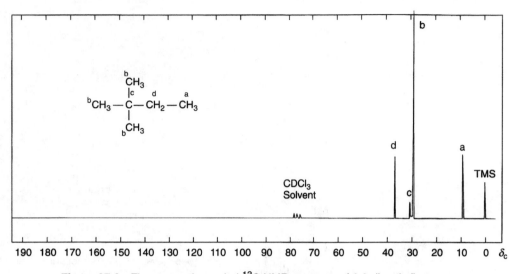

Figure 27.6 The proton-decoupled ^{13}C NMR spectrum of 2,2-dimethylbutane.

carbon atoms in 1-propanol. If there are no equivalent carbon atoms in a molecule, a ^{13}C peak will be observed for *each* carbon. Notice also that the assignments given in Figure 27.5 are consistent with the values in the chemical shift chart (see Figure 27.1). The carbon atom closest to the electronegative oxygen is farthest downfield, and the methyl carbon is at highest field.

The three-peak pattern centered at $\delta = 77$ ppm is due to the solvent CDCl$_3$. This pattern results from the coupling of a deuterium (^{2}H) nucleus to the ^{13}C nucleus. Often, the CDCl$_3$ pattern is used as an internal reference in place of TMS.

27.5 Some Sample Spectra—Equivalent Carbons

Equivalent ^{13}C atoms appear at the same chemical shift value. Figure 27.6 shows the proton-decoupled carbon spectrum for 2,2-dimethylbutane. The three methyl groups at the left side of the molecule are equivalent by symmetry.

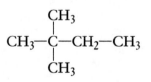

Although this compound has a total of six carbons, there are only four peaks in the ^{13}C NMR spectrum. The ^{13}C atoms that are equivalent appear at the same chemical shift. The single methyl carbon, a, appears at highest field (9 ppm), and the three equivalent methyl carbons, b, appear at 29 ppm. The quaternary carbon, c, gives rise to the small peak at 30 ppm, and the methylene carbon, d, appears at 37 ppm. The relative sizes of the peaks are related, in part, to the number of each type of carbon atom present in the molecule. For example, notice in Figure 27.6 that the peak at 29 ppm (b) is much larger than the others. This peak is generated by three carbons. The quaternary carbon at 30 ppm (c) is very weak. Because no hydrogens are attached to this carbon, there is very little nuclear Overhauser enhancement (NOE) (see Section 27.6). Without attached hydrogen atoms, relaxation times are also

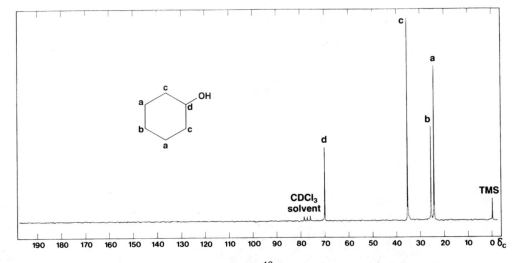

Figure 27.7   The proton-decoupled ^{13}C NMR spectrum of cyclohexanol.

longer than for other carbon atoms. Quaternary carbons, those with no hydrogens attached, frequently appear as weak peaks in proton-decoupled ^{13}C NMR spectra (see Section 27.6).

Figure 27.7 is a proton-decoupled ^{13}C spectrum of cyclohexanol. This compound has a plane of symmetry passing through its hydroxyl group, and it shows only four carbon resonances. Carbons a and c are doubled due to symmetry and give rise to larger peaks than carbons b and d. Carbon d, bearing the hydroxyl group, is deshielded by oxygen and has its peak at 70.0 ppm. Notice that this peak has the lowest intensity of all of the peaks. Its intensity is lower than that of carbon b in part because the carbon d peak receives the least amount of NOE; there is only one hydrogen attached to the hydroxyl carbon, whereas each of the other carbons has two hydrogens.

A carbon attached to a double bond is deshielded due to its sp^2 hybridization and some diamagnetic anisotropy. This effect can be seen in the ^{13}C NMR spectrum of cyclohexene (see Figure 27.8). Cyclohexene has a plane of symmetry that runs perpendicular to the double bond. As a result, we observe only three absorption peaks. There are two of each type of sp^3 carbon. Each of the double-bond carbons c has only one hydrogen, whereas each of the remaining carbons has two. As a result of a reduced NOE, the double-bond carbons (127 ppm) have a lower-intensity peak in the spectrum.

In Figure 27.9, the spectrum of cyclohexanone, the carbonyl carbon has the lowest intensity. This is due not only to reduced NOE (no hydrogen attached) but also to the long relaxation time of the carbonyl carbon (see Section 27.6). Notice also that Figure 27.2 predicts the large chemical shift for this carbonyl carbon (211 ppm).

27.6 Nuclear Overhauser Enhancement (NOE)

When we obtain a proton-decoupled ^{13}C spectrum, the intensities of many of the carbon resonances increase significantly above those observed in a proton-coupled experiment. Carbon atoms with hydrogen atoms directly attached are enhanced the most, and the enhancement increases (but not always linearly) as more hydrogens are attached. This effect is known as the nuclear Overhauser effect, and the degree of increase in the signal is called the **nuclear Overhauser enhancement (NOE)**. Thus,

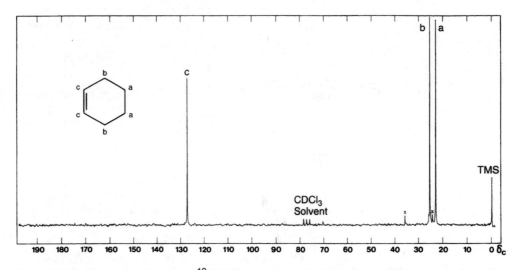

Figure 27.8 The proton-decoupled ^{13}C NMR spectrum of cyclohexanone. (The peak marked with an x are impurities.)

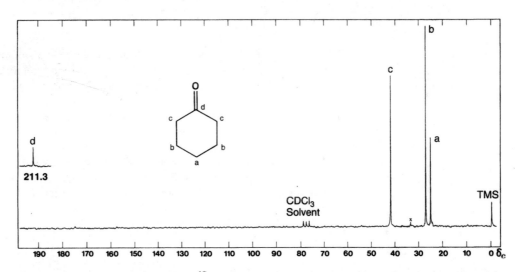

Figure 27.9 The proton-decoupled ^{13}C NMR spectrum of cyclohexanone. (The peak marked with an x is an impurity.)

we expect that the intensity of the carbon peaks should increase in the following order in a typical carbon-13 NMR spectrum:

$$CH_3 > CH_2 > CH > C$$

Carbon atom relaxation times influence the intensity of peaks in a spectrum. When more protons are attached to a carbon atom, relaxation times become shorter, resulting in more intense peaks. Thus, we expect methyl and methylene groups to be relatively more intense than the intensity observed for quaternary carbon atoms where there are no attached protons. Thus, a weak-intensity peak is observed for the quaternary carbon atom at 30 ppm in 2,2-dimethylbutane (see Figure 27.6).

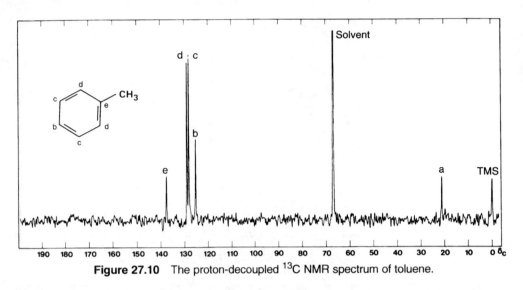

Figure 27.10   The proton-decoupled ^{13}C NMR spectrum of toluene.

In addition, weak carbonyl carbon peaks are observed at 171 ppm in ethyl phenyl-acetate (see Figure 27.4) and at 211 ppm in cyclohexanone (see Figure 27.9).

27.7 Compounds with Aromatic Rings

Compounds with carbon–carbon double bonds or aromatic rings give rise to chemical shifts from 100 ppm to 175 ppm. Because relatively few other peaks appear in this range, a great deal of useful information is available when peaks appear here.

A **monosubstituted** benzene ring shows *four* peaks in the aromatic carbon area of a proton-decoupled ^{13}C spectrum, because the *ortho* and *meta* carbons are doubled by symmetry. Often the carbon with no protons attached, the *ipso* carbon, has a very weak peak due to a long relaxation time and a weak NOE. In addition, there are two larger peaks for the doubled *ortho* and *meta* carbons and a medium-sized peak for the *para* carbon. In many cases, it is not important to be able to assign all of the peaks precisely. In the example of toluene, shown in Figure 27.10, notice that carbons c and d are not easy to assign by inspection of the spectrum.

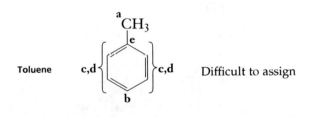

In a proton-coupled ^{13}C spectrum, a monosubstituted benzene ring shows three doublets and one singlet. The singlet arises from the *ipso* carbon, which has no attached hydrogen. Each of the other carbons in the ring (*ortho*, *meta*, and *para*) has one attached hydrogen and yields a doublet.

Figure 27.4B is the proton-decoupled spectrum of ethyl phenylacetate, with the assignments noted next to the peaks. Notice that the aromatic ring region shows

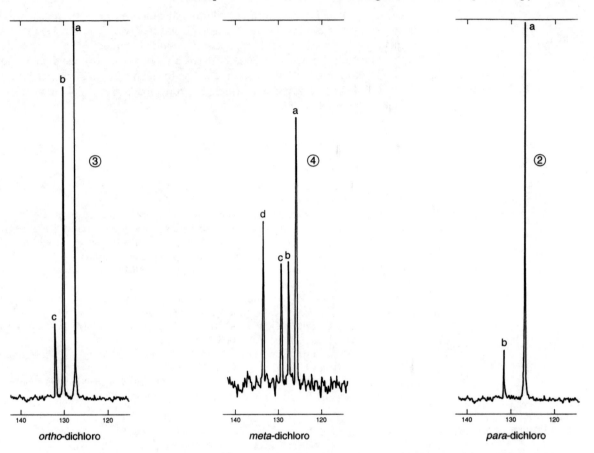

Figure 27.11 The proton-decoupled ^{13}C NMR spectra of the three isomers of dichlorobenzene (25 MHz).

four peaks between 125 ppm and 135 ppm, consistent with a monosubstituted ring. There is one peak for the methyl carbon (13 ppm), and there are two peaks for the methylene carbons. One of the methylene carbons is directly attached to an electronegative oxygen atom and appears at 61 ppm, and the other is more shielded (41 ppm). The carbonyl carbon (an ester) has resonance at 171 ppm. All of the carbon chemical shifts agree with the values in the correlation chart (see Figure 27.1).

Depending on the mode of substitution, a symmetrically **disubstituted** benzene ring can show two, three, or four peaks in the proton-decoupled ^{13}C spectrum. The following drawings illustrate this for the isomers of dichlorobenzene.

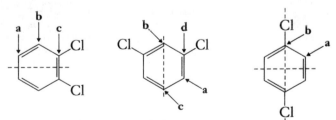

Three unique carbon atoms   Four unique carbon atoms   Two unique carbon atoms

Figure 27.11 shows the spectra of all three dichlorobenzenes, each of which has the number of peaks consistent with the analysis just given. You can see that ^{13}C NMR spectroscopy is very useful in the identification of isomers.

Most other polysubstitution patterns on a benzene ring yield six peaks in the proton-decoupled ^{13}C NMR spectrum, one for each carbon. However, when identical substituents are present, watch carefully for planes of symmetry that may reduce the number of peaks.

REFERENCES

Textbooks

Friebolin, H. *Basic One- and Two-Dimensional NMR Spectroscopy,* 3rd ed. New York: VCH Publishers, 1998.

Gunther, H. *NMR Spectroscopy,* 2nd ed. New York: John Wiley & Sons, 1995.

Levy, G. C. *Topics in Carbon-13 Spectroscopy.* New York: John Wiley & Sons, 1984.

Levy, G. C., Lichter, R. L., and Nelson, G. L. *Carbon-13 Nuclear Magnetic Resonance Spectroscopy,* 2nd ed. NewYork: John Wiley & Sons, 1980.

Macomber, R. S. *A Complete Introduction to Modern NMR Spectroscopy.* New York: John Wiley & Sons, 1997.

Macomber, R. S. *NMR Spectroscopy—Essential Theory and Practice.* New York: College Outline Series, Harcourt Brace Jovanovich, 1988.

Pavia, D. L., Lampman, G. M., and Kriz, G. S. *Introduction to Spectroscopy,* 4th ed. and vyvyan, J. R. Brooks/Cole 2008.

Sander, J. K. M., and Hunter, B. K. *Modern NMR Spectroscopy—A Guide for Chemists,* 2d ed. Oxford, England: Oxford University Press, 1993.

Silverstein, R. M., Webster, F. X., and Kiemle, D. *Spectrometric Identification of Organic Compounds,* 7th ed. New York: John Wiley & Sons, 2005.

Compilations of Spectra

Johnson, L. F., and Jankowski, W. C. *Carbon-13 NMR Spectra: A Collection of Assigned, Coded, and Indexed Spectra, 25 MHz.* New York: Wiley-Interscience, 1972.

Pouchert, C. J., and Behnke, J. *The Aldrich Library of ^{13}C and ^1H FT–NMR Spectra, 75 and 300 MHz.* Milwaukee, WI: Aldrich Chemical Company, 1993.

Pretsch, E., Clerc, T., Seibl, J., and Simon, W. *Tables of Spectral Data for Structure Determination of Organic Compounds,* 2nd ed. Berlin and New York: Springer-Verlag, 1989. Translated from the German by K. Biemann.

Web Sites

http://www.aist.go.jp/RIODB/SDBS/menu-e.html

Integrated Spectral DataBase System for Organic Compounds, National Institute of Materials and Chemical Research, Tsukuba, Ibaraki 305-8565, Japan. This database includes infrared, mass spectra, and NMR data (proton and carbon-13) for a number of compounds.

http://www.chem.ucla.edu/~webspectra

UCLA Department of Chemistry and Biochemistry in connection with Cambridge University Isotope Laboratories maintains a Web site, WebSpectra, that provides NMR and IR spectroscopy problems for students to interpret. They provide links to other sites with problems for students to solve.

PROBLEMS

1. Predict the number of peaks that you would expect in the proton-decoupled ^{13}C spectrum of each of the following compounds. Problems 1a and 1b are provided as examples. Dots are used to show the nonequivalent carbon atoms in these two examples.

a.

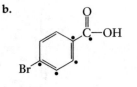

Four peaks

b.

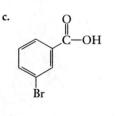

Five peaks

c.

d.

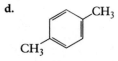

e.

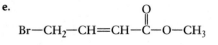

f.

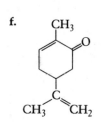

g.

h.

i.

j.

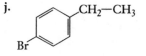

k.

2. Following are the ^{1}H and ^{13}C spectra for two isomeric bromoalkanes (**A** and **B**) with formula C_4H_9Br. Integral curves are drawn on the spectra, along with relative integral values provided just above the scale and under each set of peaks. These numbers indicate the relative number of protons assigned to each pattern. Remember that these integral values are approximate. You will need to round the values off to the nearest whole number. Also, in some cases, the lowest whole-number ratios are given. In such cases, the values provided may need to be multiplied by two or three in order to obtain the actual number of protons in each pattern.

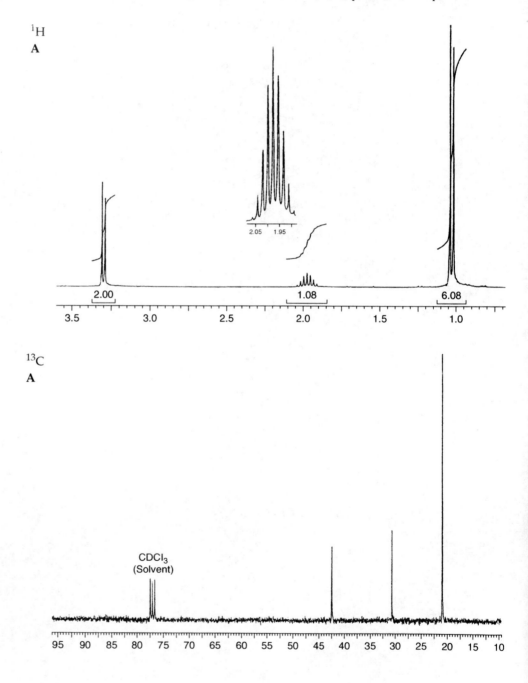

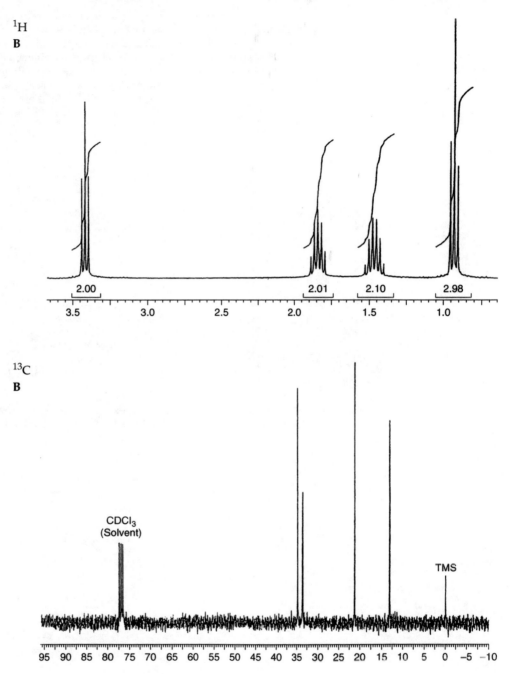

3. Following are the ^{1}H and ^{13}C spectra for each of three isomeric ketones (**A**, **B**, and **C**) with formula $C_7H_{14}O$. Integral curves are drawn on the spectra, along with relative integral values provided just above the scale and under each set of peaks. These numbers indicate the relative number of protons assigned to each pattern. Remember that these integral values are approximate. You will need to round the values off to the nearest whole number. Also, in some cases, the lowest whole-number ratios are given. In such cases, the values provided may need to be multiplied by two or three in order to obtain the actual number of protons in each pattern.

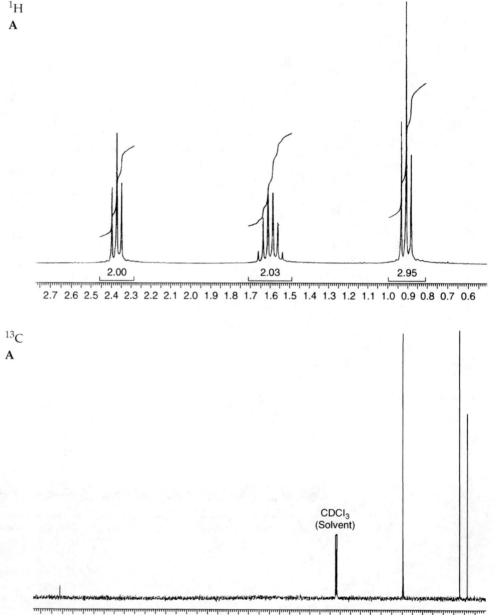

^{1}H

A

2.00   2.03   2.95

2.7 2.6 2.5 2.4 2.3 2.2 2.1 2.0 1.9 1.8 1.7 1.6 1.5 1.4 1.3 1.2 1.1 1.0 0.9 0.8 0.7 0.6

^{13}C

A

CDCl$_3$
(Solvent)

220 210 200 190 180 170 160 150 140 130 120 110 100 90 80 70 60 50 40 30 20 10

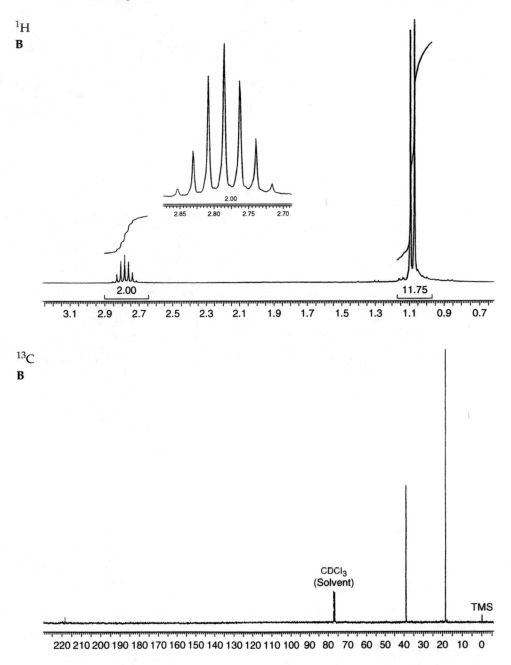

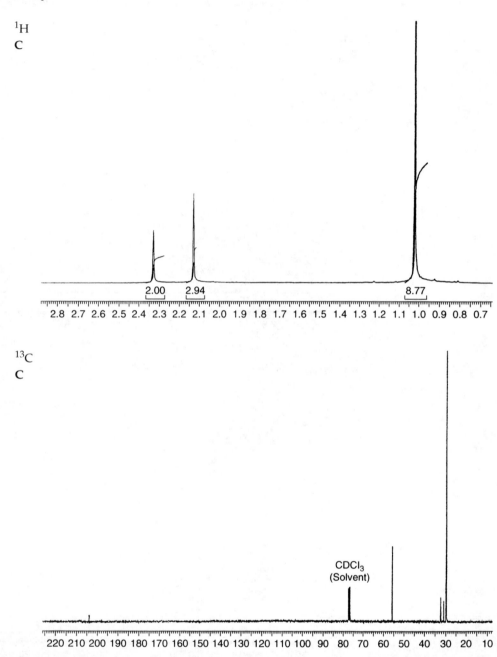

28

TECHNIQUE 28

Mass Spectrometry

In its simplest form, the mass spectrometer performs three essential functions. First, molecules are bombarded by a stream of high-energy electrons, converting some of the molecules to positive ions. Because of their high energy, some of these ions **fragment**, or break apart into smaller ions. All of these ions are accelerated in an electric field. Second, the accelerated ions are separated according to their mass-to-charge ratio in a magnetic or electric field. Finally, the ions with a particular mass-to-charge ratio are detected by a device that is able to count the number of ions that strike it. The output of the detector is amplified and fed to a recorder. The trace from the recorder is a **mass spectrum**—a graph of the number of particles detected as a function of mass-to-charge ratio.

Ions are formed in an **ionization chamber**. The sample is introduced into the ionization chamber using a sample inlet system. In the ionization chamber, a heated **filament** emits a beam of high-energy electrons. The filament is heated to several thousand degrees Celsius. In normal operation, the electrons have an energy of about 70 electron-volts. These high-energy electrons strike a stream of molecules that has been admitted from the sample system and ionize the molecules in the sample stream by removing electrons from them. The molecules are thus converted into **radical-cations**.

$$e^- + M \longrightarrow 2e^- + M^{+\bullet}$$

The energy required to remove an electron from an atom or molecule is its **ionization potential**. The ionized molecules are accelerated and focused into a beam of rapidly moving ions by means of charged plates.

From the ionization chamber, the beam of ions passes through a short field-free region. From there, the beam enters the **mass analyzer**, where the ions are separated according to their mass-to-charge ratio.

The detector of most instruments consists of a counter that produces a current proportional to the number of ions that strike it. Electron multiplier circuits allow accurate measurement of the current from even a single ion striking the detector. The signal from the detector is fed to **a recorder**, which produces the actual mass spectrum.

28.1 The Mass Spectrum

The **mass spectrum** is a plot of ion abundance versus mass-to-charge (*m/e*) ratio. A typical mass spectrum is shown in Figure 28.1. The spectrum shown is that of dopamine, a substance that acts as a neurotransmitter in the central nervous system. The spectrum is displayed as a bar graph of percentage ion abundance (relative abundance) plotted against *m/e*.

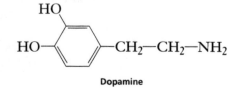

Dopamine

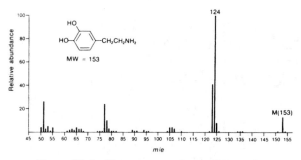

Figure 28.1 The mass spectrum of dopamine.

The most abundant ion formed in the ionization chamber gives rise to the tallest peak in the mass spectrum, called the **base peak**. For dopamine, the base peak appears at $m/e = 124$. The relative abundances of all the other peaks in the spectrum are reported as percentages of the abundance of the base peak.

The beam of electrons in the ionization chamber converts some of the sample molecules into positive ions. Removal of a single electron from a molecule yields an ion whose weight is the actual molecular weight of the original molecule. This ion is the **molecular ion**, frequently symbolized as M^+. The value of m/e at which the molecular ion appears on the mass spectrum, assuming that the ion has only one electron removed, gives the molecular weight of the original molecule. In the mass spectrum of dopamine, the molecular ion appears at $m/e = 153$, the molecular weight of dopamine. If you can identify the molecular ion peak in the mass spectrum, you can use the spectrum to determine the molecular weight of an unknown substance. If the presence of heavy isotopes is ignored for the moment, the molecular ion peak corresponds to the heaviest particle observed in the mass spectrum.

Molecules do not occur in nature as isotopically pure species. Virtually all atoms have heavier isotopes that occur in varying natural abundances. Hydrogen occurs largely as ^1H, but a small percent of hydrogen atoms occur as the isotope ^2H. Further, carbon normally occurs as ^{12}C, but a small percent of carbon atoms are the heavier isotope, ^{13}C. With the exception of fluorine, most other elements have a certain percentage of heavier isotopes that occur naturally. Peaks caused by ions bearing these heavier isotopes are also found in the mass spectrum. The relative abundances of these isotopic peaks are proportional to the abundances of the isotopes in nature. Most often, the isotopes occur at one or two mass units above the mass of the "normal" atom. Therefore, besides looking for the molecular ion (M^+) peak, you should also attempt to locate the M + 1 and M + 2 peaks. As will be demonstrated later, you can use the relative abundances of these M + 1 and M + 2 peaks to determine the molecular formula of the substance being studied.

The beam of electrons in the ionization chamber can produce the molecular ion. This beam also has sufficient energy to break some of the bonds in the molecule, producing a series of molecular fragments. Fragments that are positively charged are also accelerated in the ionization chamber, sent through the analyzer, detected, and recorded on the mass spectrum. These **fragment ion peaks** appear at m/e values corresponding to their individual masses. Very often, a fragment ion rather than the molecular ion will be the most abundant ion produced in the mass spectrum (the base peak). A second means of producing fragment ions occurs with the molecular ion, which, once it is formed, is so unstable that it disintegrates before it can pass into the accelerating region of the ionization chamber. Lifetimes shorter than 10^{-5} seconds are typical in this type of fragmentation. Those fragments that are charged then appear as fragment ions in the mass spectrum. As a result of these fragmentation processes, the typical mass spectrum can be quite complex, containing many more peaks than the molecular ion and M+1 and M+2 peaks. Structural information about a substance can be determined by examining the fragmentation pattern in the mass spectrum. Fragmentation patterns are discussed further in Section 28.3.

28.2 Molecular Formula Determination

Mass spectrometry can be used to determine the molecular formulas of molecules that provide reasonably abundant molecular ions. Although there are at least two principal techniques for determining a molecular formula, only one will be described here.

The molecular formula of a substance can be determined through the use of **precise atomic masses**. High-resolution mass spectrometers are required for this method. Atoms are normally thought of as having integral atomic masses; for example, H = 1, C = 12, and O = 16. If you can determine atomic masses with sufficient precision, however, you find that the masses do not have values that are exactly integral. The mass of each atom actually differs from a whole mass number by a small fraction of a mass unit. The actual masses of some atoms are given in Table 28.1.

TABLE 28.1   Precise Masses of Some Common Elements

Element	Atomic Weight	Nuclide	Precise Mass
Hydrogen	1.00797	^{1}H	1.00783
		^{2}H	2.01410
Carbon	12.01115	^{12}C	12.0000
		^{13}C	13.00336
Nitrogen	14.0067	^{14}N	14.0031
		^{15}N	15.0001
Oxygen	15.9994	^{16}O	15.9949
		^{17}O	16.9991
		^{18}O	17.9992
Fluorine	18.9984	^{19}F	18.9984
Silicon	28.086	^{28}Si	27.9769
		^{29}Si	28.9765
		^{30}Si	29.9738
Phosphorus	30.974	^{31}P	30.9738
Sulfur	32.064	^{32}S	31.9721
		^{33}S	32.9715
		^{34}S	33.9679
Chlorine	35.453	^{35}Cl	34.9689
		^{37}Cl	36.9659
Bromine	79.909	^{79}Br	78.9183
		^{81}Br	80.9163
Iodine	126.904	^{127}I	126.9045

Depending on the atoms that are contained within a molecule, it is possible for particles of the same nominal mass to have slightly different measured masses when precise mass determinations can be made. To illustrate, a molecule whose molecular weight is 60 could be C_3H_8O, $C_2H_8N_2$, $C_2H_4O_2$, or CH_4N_2O. The species have the following precise masses:

C_3H_8O	60.05754
$C_2H_8N_2$	60.06884
$C_2H_4O_2$	60.02112
CH_4N_2O	60.03242

Observing a molecular ion with a mass of 60.058 would establish that the unknown molecule was C_3H_8O. Distinguishing among these possibilities is well within the capability of a modern high-resolution instrument.

In another method, these four compounds may also be distinguished by differences in the relative intensities of their M, M+1, and M+2 peaks. The predicted intensities are either calculated by formula or looked up in tables. Details of this method may be found in the References at the end of this Technique Chapter.

28.3 Detecting Halogens

When chlorine or bromine is present in a molecule, the isotope peak that is two mass units heavier than the molecular ion (the M+2 peak) becomes very significant. The heavy isotope of each of these elements is two mass units heavier than the lighter isotope. The natural abundance of ^{37}Cl is 32.5% that of ^{35}Cl; the natural abundance of ^{81}Br is 98.0% that of ^{79}Br. When these elements are present, the M+2 peak becomes quite intense, and the pattern is characteristic of the particular halogen present. If a compound contains two chlorine or bromine atoms, a quite distinct M+4 peak should be observed, as well as an intense M+2 peak. In these cases, you should exercise caution in identifying the molecular ion peak in a mass spectrum, but the pattern of peaks is characteristic of the nature of the halogen substitution in the molecule. Table 28.2 gives the relative intensities of isotope peaks for various combinations of bromine and chlorine atoms. The patterns of molecular ion and isotopic peaks observed with halogen substitution are shown in Figure 28.2. Examples of these patterns can be seen in the mass spectra of chloroethane (see Figure 28.3) and bromoethane (see Figure 28.4).

TABLE 28.2 Relative Intensities of Isotope Peaks for Various Combinations of Bromine and Chlorine

Halogen	M	M+2	M+4	M+6
Br	100	97.7	—	—
Br_2	100	195.0	95.4	—
Br_3	100	293.0	286.0	93.4
Cl	100	32.6	—	—
Cl_2	100	65.3	10.6	—
Cl_3	100	97.8	31.9	3.47
BrCl	100	130.0	31.9	—
Br_2Cl	100	228.0	159.0	31.2
$BrCl_2$	100	163.0	74.4	10.4

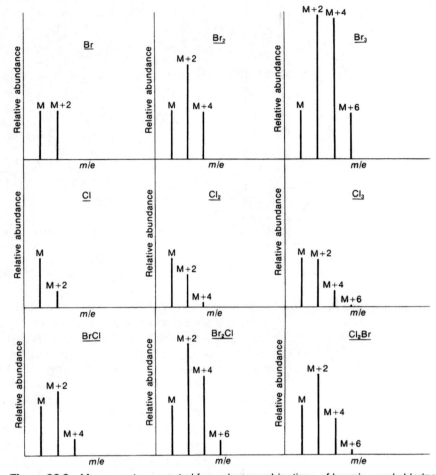

Figure 28.2   Mass spectra expected for various combinations of bromine and chlorine.

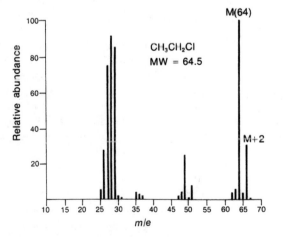

Figure 28.3   The mass spectrum of chloroethane.

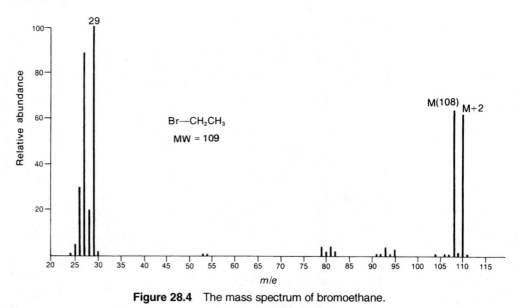

Figure 28.4   The mass spectrum of bromoethane.

28.4 Fragmentation Patterns

When the molecule has been bombarded by high-energy electrons in the ionization chamber of a mass spectrometer, besides losing one electron to form an ion, the molecule also absorbs some of the energy transferred in the collision between the molecule and the incident electrons. This extra energy puts the molecular ion in an excited vibrational state. The vibrationally excited molecular ion is often unstable and may lose some of this extra energy by breaking apart into fragments. If the lifetime of an individual molecular ion is longer than 10^{-5} seconds, a peak corresponding to the molecular ion will be observed in the mass spectrum. Those molecular ions with lifetimes shorter than 10^{-5} seconds will break apart into fragments before they are accelerated within the ionization chamber. In such cases, peaks corresponding to the mass-to-charge ratios for these fragments will also appear in the mass spectrum. For a given compound, not all the molecular ions formed by ionization have precisely the same lifetime. The ions have a range of lifetimes; some individual ions may have shorter lifetimes than others. As a result, peaks are usually observed arising from both the molecular ion and the fragment ions in a typical mass spectrum.

For most classes of compounds, the mode of fragmentation is somewhat characteristic. In many cases, it is possible to predict how a molecule will fragment. Remember that the ionization of the sample molecule forms a molecular ion that not only carries a positive charge but also has an unpaired electron. The molecular ion, then, is actually a **radical–cation**, and it contains an odd number of electrons. In the structural formulas that follow, the radical–cation is indicated by enclosing the structure in square brackets. The positive charge and the unshared electron are shown as superscripts.

$$[\text{R}-\text{CH}_3]^{+}$$

When fragment ions form in the mass spectrometer, they almost always form by means of unimolecular processes. The pressure of the sample in the ionization chamber is too low to permit a significant number of bimolecular collisions. Those unimolecular processes that require the least energy will give rise to the most abundant fragment ions.

Fragment ions are cations. Much of the chemistry of these fragment ions can be explained in terms of what is known about carbocations in solution. For example, alkyl substitution stabilizes fragment ions (and promotes their formation) in much the same way that it stabilizes carbocations. Those fragmentation processes that lead to more stable ions will be favored over processes that lead to the formation of less-stable ions.

Fragmentation often involves the loss of an electrically neutral fragment. The neutral fragment does not appear in the mass spectrum, but you can deduce its existence by noting the difference in masses of the fragment ion and the original molecular ion. Again, processes that lead to the formation of a more stable neutral fragment will be favored over those that lead to the formation of a less-stable neutral fragment. The loss of a stable neutral molecule, such as water, is commonly observed in the mass spectrometer.

A. Cleavage of One Bond

The most common mode of fragmentation involves the cleavage of one bond. In this process, the odd-electron molecular ion yields an odd-electron neutral fragment and an even-electron fragment. The neutral fragment that is lost is a **free radical**, whereas the ionic fragment is of the carbocation type. Cleavages that lead to the formation of more stable carbocations will be favored. Thus, the ease of fragmentation to form ions increases in the following order:

$$CH_3^+ < RCH_2^+ < R_2CH^+ < R_3C^+ < CH_2{=}CH{-}CH_2^+ < C_6H_5{-}CH_2^+$$

Increasing ease of formation →

The following reactions show examples of fragmentation that take place with the cleavage of one bond:

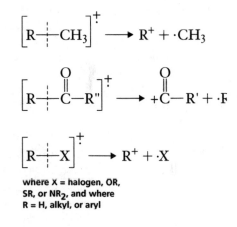

where X = halogen, OR,
SR, or NR₂, and where
R = H, alkyl, or aryl

B. Cleavage of Two Bonds

The next most important type of fragmentation involves the cleavage of two bonds. In this type of process, the odd-electron molecular ion yields an odd-electron fragment ion and an even-electron neutral fragment, usually a small, stable molecule. Examples of this type of cleavage are shown next:

$$\left[\begin{matrix} H & OH \\ | & | \\ RCH\!-\!\!-\!\!CHR' \end{matrix}\right]^{+\cdot} \longrightarrow \left[RCH\!=\!CHR'\right]^{+\cdot} + H_2O$$

$$\left[\begin{matrix} CH_2\!-\!CH_2 \\ | \qquad | \\ RCH\!-\!\!-\!\!CH_2 \end{matrix}\right]^{+\cdot} \longrightarrow \left[RCH\!=\!CH_2\right]^{+\cdot} + CH_2\!=\!CH_2$$

$$\left[\begin{matrix} & & & O \\ & & & \| \\ RCH\!-\!\!-\!CH_2\!+\!O\!-\!C\!-\!CH_3 \\ | \\ H \end{matrix}\right]^{+\cdot} \longrightarrow \left[RCH\!=\!CH_2\right]^{+\cdot} + HO\!-\!\overset{\displaystyle O}{\overset{\|}{C}}\!-\!CH_3$$

C. Other Cleavage Processes

In addition to the processes just mentioned, fragmentation reactions involving rearrangements, migrations of groups, and secondary fragmentations of fragment ions are also possible. These processes occur less often than the types of processes just described. Nevertheless, the pattern of molecular ion and fragment ion peaks observed in the typical mass spectrum is quite complex and unique for each particular molecule. As a result, the mass spectral pattern observed for a given substance can be compared with the mass spectra of known compounds as a means of identification. The mass spectrum is like a fingerprint. For a treatment of the specific modes of fragmentation characteristic of particular classes of compounds, refer to more advanced textbooks (see References at the end of this chapter). The unique appearance of the mass spectrum for a given compound is the basis for identifying the components of a mixture in the **gas chromatography–mass spectrometry** (GC–MS) technique (see Technique 22, Section 22.14). The mass spectrum of every component in a mixture is compared with standard spectra stored in the computer memory of the instrument. The printed output produced by a GC–MS instrument includes an identification based on the results of the computer matching of mass spectra.

28.5 Interpreted Mass Spectra

In this section, the mass spectra of some representative organic compounds are presented. The important fragment ion peaks in each mass spectrum are identified. In some of the examples, identification of the fragments is presented without explanation, although some interpretation is provided where an unusual or interesting process takes place. In the first example, that of butane, a more complete explanation of the symbolism used is offered.

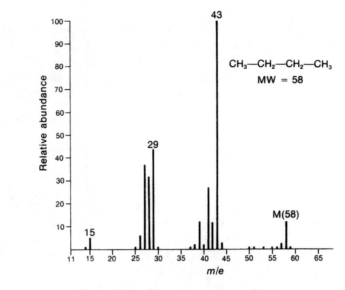

Figure 28.5   The mass spectrum of butane.

Butane; C_4H_{10}, MW = 58 (see Figure 28.5)

$$CH_3\!\!\underset{15}{\overset{\dashv}{|}}\!\!CH_2\!\!\underset{29}{\overset{\dashv}{|}}\!\!CH_2\!\!\underset{43}{\overset{\dashv}{|}}\!\!CH_3$$

In the structural formula of butane, the dashed lines represent the location of bond-breaking processes that occur during fragmentation. In each case, the fragmentation process involves the breaking of one bond to yield a neutral radical and a cation. The arrows point toward the fragment that bears the positive charge. This positive fragment is the ion that appears in the mass spectrum. The mass of the fragment ion is indicated beneath the arrow.

The mass spectrum shows the molecular ion at m/e = 58. Breaking of the C1—C2 bond yields a three-carbon fragment with a mass of 43.

$$CH_3\!\!-\!\!CH_2\!\!-\!\!CH_2\!\!\overset{|}{|}\!\!CH_3 \longrightarrow CH_3\!\!-\!\!CH_2\!\!-\!\!CH_2^+ + \cdot CH_3$$
$$m/e = 43$$

Cleavage of the central bond yields an ethyl cation, with a mass of 29.

$$CH_3\!\!-\!\!CH_2\!\!\overset{|}{|}\!\!CH_2\!\!-\!\!CH_3 \longrightarrow CH_3\!\!-\!\!CH_2^+ + \cdot CH_2\!\!-\!\!CH_3$$
$$m/e = 29$$

The terminal bond can also break to yield a methyl cation, which has a mass of 15.

$$CH_3\!\!\overset{|}{|}\!\!CH_2\!\!-\!\!CH_2\!\!-\!\!CH_3 \longrightarrow CH_3^+ + \cdot CH_2\!\!-\!\!CH_2\!\!-\!\!CH_3$$
$$m/e = 15$$

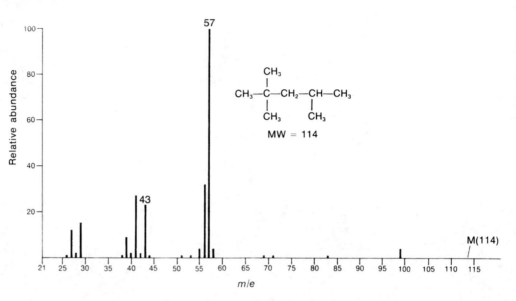

Figure 28.6   The mass spectrum of 2,2,4-trimethylpentane ("isooctane").

Each of these fragments appears in the mass spectrum of butane and has been identified.

2,2,4-Trimethylpentane; C_8H_{18}, MW = 114 (see Figure 28.6)

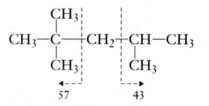

Notice that in the case of 2,2,4-trimethylpentane, by far the most abundant fragment is the *tert*-butyl cation (m/e = 57). This result is not surprising when one considers that the *tert*-butyl cation is a particularly stable carbocation.

Cyclopentane; C_5H_{10}, MW = 70 (see Figure 28.7)

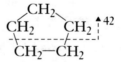

In the case of cyclopentane, the most abundant fragment results from the simultaneous cleavage of two bonds. This mode of fragmentation eliminates a neutral molecule of ethene (MW = 28), and results in the formation of a cation at m/e = 42.

1-Butene; C_4H_8, MW = 56 (see Figure 28.8)

$$CH_2\!\!=\!\!CH-CH_2\dashv CH_3$$
$$41$$

An important fragment in the mass spectra of alkenes is the allyl cation (m/e = 41). This cation is particularly stable due to resonance.

$$[^+CH_2\!-\!CH\!=\!CH_2 \longleftrightarrow CH_2\!=\!CH\!-\!CH_2{}^+]$$

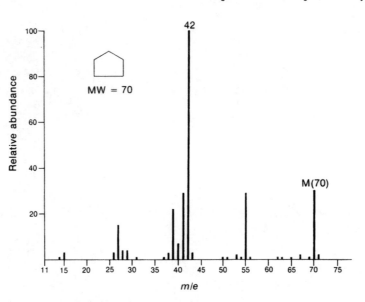

Figure 28.7   The mass spectrum of cyclopentane.

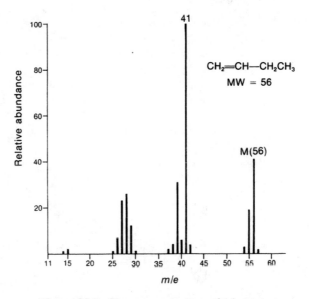

Figure 28.8   The mass spectrum of 1-butene.

Toluene; C_7H_8, MW = 92 (see Figure 28.9)

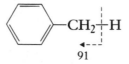

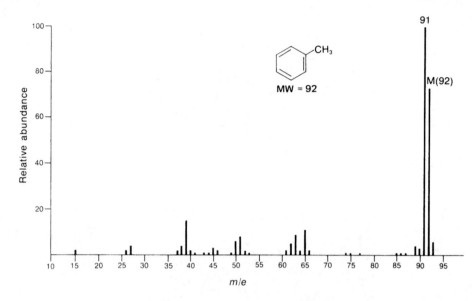

Figure 28.9   The mass spectrum of toluene.

When an alkyl group is attached to a benzene ring, preferential fragmentation occurs at a benzylic position to form a fragment ion of the formula $C_7H_7^+$ ($m/e = 91$). In the mass spectrum of toluene, loss of hydrogen from the molecule ion gives a strong peak at $m/e = 91$. Although it may be expected that this fragment ion peak is due to the benzyl carbocation, evidence suggests the benzyl carbocation actually rearranges to form the **tropylium ion.** Isotope-labeling experiments tend to confirm the formation of the tropylium ion. The tropylium ion is a seven-carbon ring system that contains six electrons in π-molecular orbitals and hence is resonance-stabilized in a manner similar to that observed in benzene.

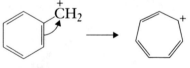

Benzyl cation   **Tropylium ion**

1-Butanol; $C_4H_{10}O$, MW = 74 (see Figure 28.10)

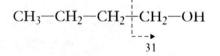

The most important fragmentation reaction for alcohols is loss of an alkyl group:

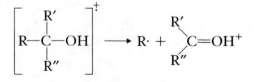

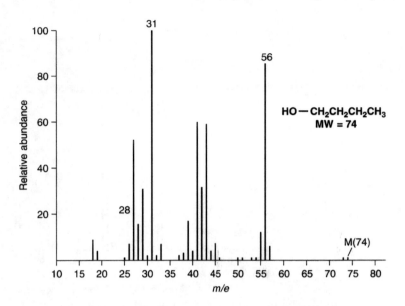

Figure 28.10   The mass spectrum of 1-butanol.

The largest alkyl group is the one that is lost most readily. In the spectrum of 1-butanol, the intense peak at $m/e = 31$ is due to the loss of a propyl group to form

A second common mode of fragmentation involves dehydration. Loss of a molecule of water from 1-butanol leaves a cation of mass 56.

$$CH_3-CH_2-\underset{H}{\overset{|}{C}}H-\underset{OH}{\overset{|}{C}}H_2 \;\overset{\blacktriangle 56}{}$$

Benzaldehyde; C_7H_6O, MW = 106 (see Figure 28.11)

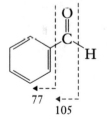

The loss of a hydrogen atom from an aldehyde is a favorable process. The resulting fragment ion is a benzoyl cation, a particularly stable type of carbocation.

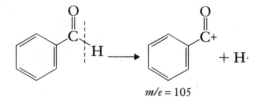

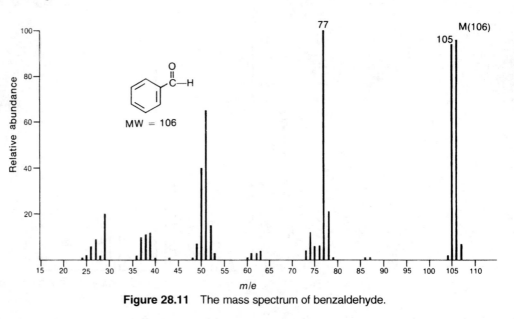

Figure 28.11   The mass spectrum of benzaldehyde.

Loss of the entire aldehyde functional group leaves a phenyl cation. This ion can be seen in the spectrum of an m/e value of 77.

2-Butanone; C_4H_8O, MW = 72 (see Figure 28.12)

$$CH_3\!-\!CH_2\!\!\underset{}{+}\!\!\overset{\overset{\textstyle O}{\|}}{C}\!\!\underset{\substack{\blacktriangleleft\text{-}\\ 57\\ \text{-}\!\blacktriangleright\\ 43}}{+}\!\!CH_3$$

If the methyl group is lost as a neutral fragment, the resulting cation, an **acylium ion**, has an m/e value of 57. If the ethyl group is lost, the resulting acylium ion appears at an m/e value of 43.

$$CH_3\!-\!CH_2\!-\!\overset{\overset{\textstyle O}{\|}}{C}\!+\!CH_3 \longrightarrow CH_3\!-\!CH_2\!-\!\overset{\overset{\textstyle O}{\|}}{C^+} + \cdot CH_3$$
$$m/e = 57$$

$$CH_3\!-\!CH_2\!+\!\overset{\overset{\textstyle O}{\|}}{C}\!-\!CH_3 \longrightarrow CH_3\!-\!\overset{\overset{\textstyle O}{\|}}{C^+} + \cdot CH_2CH_3$$
$$m/e = 43$$

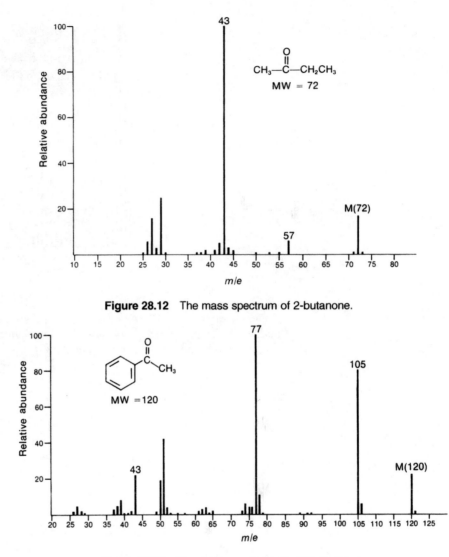

Figure 28.12   The mass spectrum of 2-butanone.

Figure 28.13   The mass spectrum of acetophenone.

Acetophenone; C_8H_8O, MW = 120 (see Figure 28.13)

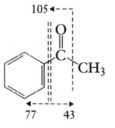

Aromatic ketones undergo α-cleavage to lose the alkyl group and form the benzoyl cation (*m/e* = 105). This ion subsequently loses carbon monoxide to form the

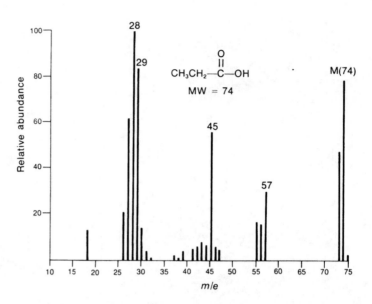

Figure 28.14 The mass spectrum of propanoic acid.

phenyl cation ($m/e = 77$). Aromatic ketones also undergo α-cleavage on the other side of the carbonyl group, forming an alkyl acylium ion. In the case of acetophenone, this ion appears at an m/e value of 43.

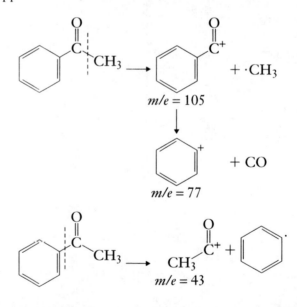

Propanoic acid; $C_3H_6O_2$, MW = 74 (see Figure 28.14)

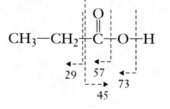

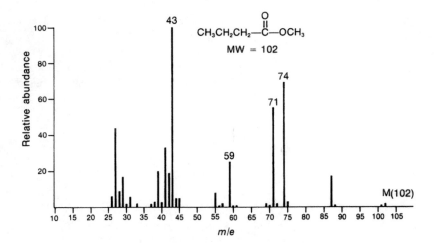

Figure 28.15   The mass spectrum of methyl butanoate.

With short-chain carboxylic acids, the loss of OH and COOH through α-cleavage on either side of the C=O group may be observed. In the mass spectrum of propanoic acid, loss of OH gives rise to a peak at $m/e = 57$. Loss of COOH gives rise to a peak at $m/e = 29$. Loss of the alkyl group as a free radical, leaving the COOH$^+$ ion ($m/e = 45$), also occurs. The intense peak at $m/e = 28$ is due to additional fragmentation of the ethyl portion of the acid molecule.

Methyl butanoate; $C_5H_{10}O_2$, MW = 102 (see Figure 28.15)

$$CH_3-CH_2-CH_2\!\!\mid\!\!\overset{\overset{O}{\|}}{C}\!\!\mid\!\!O-CH_3$$

43   59

71

The most important of the α-cleavage reactions involves the loss of the alkoxy group from the ester to form the corresponding acylium ion, RCO$^+$. The acylium ion peak appears at $m/e = 71$ in the mass spectrum of methyl butanoate. A second important peak results from the loss of the alkyl group from the acyl portion of the ester molecule, leaving a fragment CH$_3$—O—C=O$^+$ that appears at $m/e = 59$. Loss of the carboxylate function group to leave the alkyl group as a cation gives rise to a peak at $m/e = 43$. The intense peak at $m/e = 74$ results from a rearrangement process (see Section 28.6).

1-Bromohexane; $C_6H_{13}Br$, MW = 165 (see Figure 28.16)

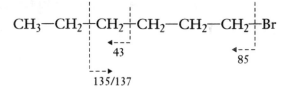

43   85

135/137

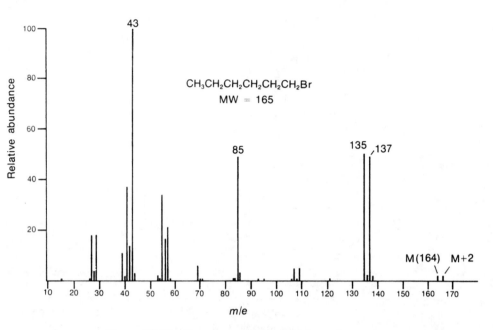

Figure 28.16   The mass spectrum of 1-bromohexane.

The most interesting characteristic of the mass spectrum of 1-bromohexane is the presence of the doublet in the molecular ion. These two peaks, of equal height and separated by two mass units, are strong evidence that bromine is present in the substance. Notice also that loss of the terminal ethyl group yields a fragment ion that still contains bromine (m/e = 135 and 137). The presence of the doublet demonstrates that this fragment contains bromine.

28.6 Rearrangement Reactions

Because the fragment ions that are detected in a mass spectrum are cations, we can expect that these ions will exhibit behavior we are accustomed to associate with carbocations. It is well known that carbocations are prone to rearrangement reactions, converting a less-stable carbocation into a more stable one. These types of rearrangements are also observed in the mass spectrum. If the abundance of a cation is especially high, it is assumed that a rearrangement to yield a longer-lived cation must have occurred.

Other types of rearrangements are also known. An example of a rearrangement that is not normally observed in solution chemistry is the rearrangement of a benzyl cation to a tropylium ion. This rearrangement is seen in the mass spectrum of toluene (see Figure 28.9).

A particular type of rearrangement process that is unique to mass spectrometry is the **McLafferty rearrangement**. This type of rearrangement occurs when an alkyl chain of at least three carbons in length is attached to an energy-absorbing structure such as a phenyl or carbonyl group that can accept the transfer of a hydrogen ion. The mass spectrum of methyl butanoate (see Figure 28.15) contains a prominent peak at m/e = 74. This peak arises from a McLafferty rearrangement of the molecular ion.

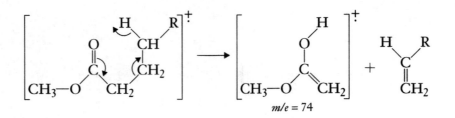

$m/e = 74$

REFERENCES

Beynon, J. H. Mass *Spectrometry and Its Applications to Organic Chemistry. Elsevier*: Amsterdam, 1960.

Biemann, K. *Mass Spectrometry: Organic Chemical Applications*. McGraw-Hill: New York, 1962.

Budzikiewicz, H.; Djerassi, C; Williams, D. H. *Mass Spectrometry of Organic Compounds*. Holden-Day: San Francisco, 1967.

McLafferty, F. W.; Tureccek, F. *Interpretation of Mass Spectra*, 4th ed. University Science Books: Mill Valley, CA, 1993.

Pavia, D. L.; Lampman, G. M.; Kriz, G. S., *Introduction to Spectroscopy, A Guide for Students of Organic Chemistry*, 4th ed., and vyvya., J.R. Brooks/Cole 2008.

Silverstein, R. M.; Webster, F. X. and Kiemele, D, J. *Spectrometric Identification of Organic Compounds*, 7th ed. John Wiley & Sons: New York, 2005.

Appendices

1   APPENDIX 1

Tables of Unknowns and Derivatives

More extensive tables of unknowns may be found in Z. Rappoport, ed. *Handbook of Tables for Organic Compound Identification*, 3rd ed. CRC Press: Boca Raton FL, 1967.

ALDEHYDES

Compound	BP	MP	Semi-carbazone*	2,4-Dinitro-phenyl-hydrazone*
Ethanal (acetaldehyde)	21	—	162	168
Propanal (propionaldehyde)	48	—	89	148
Propenal (acrolein)	52	—	171	165
2-Methylpropanal (isobutyraldehyde)	64	—	125	187
Butanal (butyraldehyde)	75	—	95	123
3-Methylbutanal (isovaleraldehyde)	92	—	107	123
Pentanal (valeraldehyde)	102	—	—	106
2-Butenal (crotonaldehyde)	104	—	199	190
2-Ethylbutanal (diethylacetaldehyde)	117	—	99	95
Hexanal (caproaldehyde)	130	—	106	104
Heptanal (heptaldehyde)	153	—	109	108
2-Furaldehyde (furfural)	162	—	202	212
2-Ethylhexanal	163	—	254	114
Octanal (caprylaldehyde)	171	—	101	106
Benzaldehyde	179	—	222	237
Nonanal (nonyl aldehyde)	185	—	100	100
Phenylethanal (phenylacetaldehyde)	195	33	153	121
2-Hydroxybenzaldehyde (salicylaldehyde)	197	—	231	248
4-Methylbenzaldehyde (*p*-tolualdehyde)	204	—	234	234
3,7-Dimethyl-6-octenal (citronellal)	207	—	82	77
Decanal (decyl aldehyde)	207	—	102	104
2-Chlorobenzaldehyde	213	11	229	213
3 Chlorobenzaldehyde	214	18	228	248
3-Methoxybenzaldehyde (*m*-anisaldehyde)	230	—	233 d.	—
3-Bromobenzaldehyde	235	—	205	—
4-Methoxybenzaldehyde (*p*-anisaldehyde)	248	2.5	210	253
trans-Cinnamaldehyde	250 d.	—	215	255
3,4-Methylenedioxybenzaldehyde (piperonal)	263	37	230	266 d.
2-Methoxybenzaldehyde (*o*-anisaldehyde)	245	38	215 d.	254
3,4-Dimethoxybenzaldehyde	—	44	177	261
2-Nitrobenzaldehyde	—	44	256	265
4-Chlorobenzaldehyde	—	48	230	254
4-Bromobenzaldehyde	—	57	228	257
3-Nitrobenzaldehyde	—	58	246	293

ALDEHYDES *(Cont.)*

Compound	BP	MP	Semi-carbazone*	2,4-Dinitro-phenyl-hydrazone*
2,4-Dimethoxybenzaldehyde	—	71	—	—
2,4-Dichlorobenzaldehyde	—	72	—	—
4-Dimethylaminobenzaldehyde	—	74	222	325
4-Hydroxy-3-methoxybenzaldehyde (vanillin)	—	82	230	271
3-Hydroxybenzaldehyde	—	104	198	259
5-Bromo-2-hydroxybenzaldehyde (5-bromosalicylaldehyde)	—	106	297 d.	—
4-Nitrobenzaldehyde	—	106	221	320 d.
4-Hydroxybenzaldehyde	—	116	224	280 d.
(±)-Glyceraldehyde	—	142	160 d.	167

Note:"d" indicates "decomposition."
*See Appendix 2, "Procedures for Preparing Derivatives."

KETONES

Compound	BP	MP	Semi-carbazone*	2,4-Dinitro-phenyl-hydrazone*
2-Propanone (acetone)	56	—	187	126
2-Butanone (methyl ethyl ketone)	80	—	146	117
3-Buten-2-one (methyl vinyl ketone)	81	—	140	—
3-Methyl-2-butanone (isopropyl methyl ketone)	94	—	112	120
2-Pentanone (methyl propyl ketone)	102	—	112	143
3-Pentanone (diethyl ketone)	102	—	138	156
3,3-Dimethyl-2-butanone (pinacolone)	106	—	157	125
4-Methyl-2-pentanone (isobutyl methyl ketone)	117	—	132	95
2,4-Dimethyl-3-pentanone (diisopropyl ketone)	124	—	160	86
3-Hexanone	125	—	113	130
2-Hexanone (methyl butyl ketone)	128	—	121	106
4-Methyl-3-penten-2-one (mesityl oxide)	130	—	164	200
Cyclopentanone	131	—	210	146
5-Hexen-2-one	131	—	102	108
2,3-Pentanedione	134	—	122 (mono) 209 (di)	209
5-Methyl-3-hexanone	136	—	—	—
2,4-Pentanedione (acetylacetone)	139	—	122 (mono)	209

KETONES (Cont.)

Compound	BP	MP	Semi-carbazone*	2,4-Dinitro-phenyl-hydrazone*
			209 (di)	
4-Heptanone (dipropyl ketone)	144	—	132	75
5-Methyl-2-hexanone	145	—	—	—
1-Hydroxy-2-propanone (hydroxyacetone, acetol)	146	—	196	129
3-Heptanone	148	—	101	—
2-Heptanone (methyl amyl ketone)	151	—	123	89
Cyclohexanone	156	—	166	162
2-Methylcyclohexanone	165	—	191	136
3-Octanone	167	—	—	—
2,6-Dimethyl-4-heptanone (diisobutyl ketone)	168	—	122	66
2-Octanone	173	—	122	92
Cycloheptanone	181	—	163	148
Ethyl acetoacetate	181	—	129 d.	93
5-Nonanone	186	—	90	—
3-Nonanone	187	—	112	—
2,5-Hexanedione (acetonylacetone)	191	−9	185 (mono) 224 (di)	257 (di)
2-Nonanone	195	-8	118	—
Acetophenone (methyl phenyl ketone)	202	20	198	238
2-Hydroxyacetophenone	215	28	210	212
1-Phenyl-2-propanone (phenylacetone)	216	27	198	156
Propiophenone (1-phenyl-1-propanone)	218	21	173	191
Isobutyrophenone (2-methyl-1-phenyl-1-propanone)	222	—	181	163
1-Phenyl-2-butanone	226	—	135	—
4-Methylacetophenone	226	28	205	258
3-Chloroacetophenone	228	—	232	—
2-Chloroacetophenone	229	—	160	—
Butyrophenone (1-phenyl-1-butanone)	230	12	187	190
2-Undecanone	231	12	122	63
4-Chloroacetophenone	232	12	204	231
4-Phenyl-2-butanone (benzylacetone)	235	—	142	127
2-Methoxyacetophenone	239	—	183	—
3-Methoxyacetophenone	240	—	196	—
Valerophenone (1-phenyl-1-pentanone)	248	—	160	166
4-Chloropropiophenone	—	36	176	—
4-Phenyl-3-buten-2-one (benzalacetone)	—	37	187	227
4-Methoxyacetophenone	—	38	198	220
3-Bromopropiophenone	—	40	183	—
1-Indanone	—	41	233	258

KETONES *(Cont.)*

Compound	BP	MP	Semi-carbazone*	2,4-Dinitro-phenyl-hydrazone*
Benzophenone	—	48	164	238
4-Bromoacetophenone	—	51	208	230
3,4-Dimethoxyacetophenone	—	51	218	207
2-Acetonaphthone (methyl 2-naphthyl ketone)	—	53	234	262 d.
Desoxybenzoin (benzyl phenyl ketone)	—	60	148	204
1,1-Diphenylacetone	—	61	170	—
4-Chlorobenzophenone	—	76	—	185
3-Nitroacetophenone	—	80	257	228
4-Nitroacetophenone	—	80	—	—
4-Bromobenzophenone	—	82	350	230
Fluorenone	—	83	—	283
4-Hydroxyacetophenone	—	109	199	210
Benzoin	—	136	206	245
4-Hydroxypropiophenone	—	148	—	229
(±)-Camphor	—	179	237	164

Note: "d" indicates "decomposition."
*See Appendix 2, "Procedures for Preparing Derivatives."

CARBOXYLIC ACIDS

Compound	BP	MP	p-Toluidide*	Anilide*	Amide*
Methanoic acid (formic acid)	101	8	53	47	43
Ethanoic acid (acetic acid)	118	17	148	114	82
Propenoic acid (acrylic acid)	139	13	141	104	85
Propanoic acid (propionic acid)	141	—	124	103	81
2-Methylpropanoic acid (isobutyric acid)	154		104	105	128
Butanoic acid (butyric acid)	162	—	72	95	115
3-Butenoic acid (vinylacetic acid)	163	—	—	58	73
2-Methylpropenoic acid (methacrylic acid)	163	16	—	87	102
Pyruvic acid	165 d.	14	109	104	124
3-Methylbutanoic acid (isovaleric acid)	176	—	106	109	135
3,3-Dimethylbutanoic acid	185	—	134	132	132
Pentanoic acid (valeric acid)	186	—	74	63	106
2-Chloropropanoic acid	186	—	124	92	80

CARBOXYLIC ACIDS *(Cont.)*

Compound	BP	MP	*p*-Toluidide*	Anilide*	Amide*
Dichloroacetic acid	194	6	153	118	98
2-Methylpentanoic acid	195	—	80	95	79
Hexanoic acid (caproic acid)	205	—	75	95	101
2-Bromopropanoic acid	205 d.	24	125	99	123
Heptanoic acid	223	—	81	70	96
2-Ethylhexanoic acid	228	—	—	—	102
Cyclohexanecarboxylic acid	233	31	—	146	186
Octanoic acid (caprylic acid)	237	16	70	57	107
Nonanoic acid	254	12	84	57	99
Decanoic acid (capric acid)	—	32	78	70	108
4-Oxopentanoic acid (levulinic acid)	—	33	108	102	108 d.
Trimethylacetic acid (pivalic acid)	—	35	120	130	155
3-Chloropropanoic acid	—	40	—	—	101
Dodecanoic acid (lauric acid)	—	43	87	78	100
3-Phenylpropanoic acid (hydrocinnamic acid)	—	48	135	98	105
Bromoacetic acid	—	50	—	131	91
4-Phenylbutanoic acid	—	52	—	—	84
Tetradecanoic acid (myristic acid)	—	54	93	84	103
Trichloroacetic acid	—	57	113	97	141
3-Bromopropanoic acid	—	61	—	—	111
Hexadecanoic acid (palmitic acid)	—	62	98	90	106
Chloroacetic acid	—	63	162	137	121
Cyanoacetic acid	—	66	—	198	120
Octadecanoic acid (stearic acid)	—	69	102	95	109
trans-2-Butenoic acid (crotonic acid)	—	72	132	118	158
Phenylacetic acid	—	77	136	118	156
α-Methyl-*trans*-cinnamic acid	—	81	—	—	128
4-Methoxyphenylacetic acid	—	87	—	—	189
3,4-Dimethoxyphenyl acetic acid	—	97	—	—	147
Pentanedioic acid (glutaric acid)	—	98	218 (di)	224 (di)	176 (di)
Phenoxyacetic acid	—	99	—	99	102
2-Methoxybenzoic acid (*o*-anisic acid)	—	100	—	131	129
2-Methylbenzoic acid (*o*-toluic acid)	—	104	144	125	142
Nonanedioic acid (azelaic acid)	—	106	201 (di)	107 (mono) 186 (di)	93 (mono) 175 (di)
3-Methoxybenzoic acid (*m*-anisic acid)	—	107	—	—	136
3-Methylbenzoic acid (*m*-toluic acid)	—	111	118	126	94
4-Bromophenylacetic acid	—	117	—	—	194
(±)-Phenylhydroxyacetic acid (mandelic acid)	—	118	172	151	133
Benzoic acid	—	122	158	163	130
2,4-Dimethylbenzoic acid	—	126	—	141	180
2-Benzoylbenzoic acid	—	127	—	195	165

CARBOXYLIC ACIDS *(Cont.)*

Compound	BP	MP	*p*-Toluidide*	Anilide*	Amide*
Maleic acid	—	130	142 (di)	198 (mono) 187 (di)	172 (mono) 260 (di)
Decanedioic acid (sebacic acid)	—	133	201 (di)	122 (mono) 200 (di)	170 (mono) 210 (di)
3-Chlorocinnamic acid	—	133	142	135	76
2-Furoic acid	—	133	170	124	143
trans-Cinnamic acid	—	133	168	153	147
2-Acetylsalicylic acid (aspirin)	—	138	—	136	138
5-Chloro-2-nitrobenzoic acid	—	139	—	164	154
2-Chlorobenzoic acid	—	140	131	118	139
3-Nitrobenzoic acid	—	140	162	155	143
4-Chloro-2-nitrobenzoic acid	—	142	—	—	172
2-Nitrobenzoic acid	—	146	—	155	176
2-Aminobenzoic acid (anthranilic acid)	—	146	151	131	109
Diphenylacetic acid	—	148	172	180	167
2-Bromobenzoic acid	—	150	—	141	155
Benzilic acid	—	150	190	175	154
Hexanedioic acid (adipic acid)	—	152	239	151 (mono) 241 (di)	125 (mono) 220 (di)
Citric acid	—	153	189 (tri)	198 (tri)	210 (tri)
4-Nitrophenylacetic acid	—	153	—	198	198
2,5-Dichlorobenzoic acid	—	153	—	—	155
3-Chlorobenzoic acid	—	156	—	123	134
2,4-Dichlorobenzoic acid	—	158	—	—	194
4-Chlorophenoxyacetic acid	—	158	—	125	133
2-Hydroxybenzoic acid (salicylic acid)	—	158	156	136	142
5-Bromo-2-hydroxybenzoic acid (5-bromosalicylic acid)	—	165	—	222	232
3,4-Dimethylbenzoic acid	—	165	—	104	130
2-Chloro-5-nitrobenzoic acid	—	166	—	—	178
Methylenesuccinic acid (itaconic acid)	—	166 d.	—	152 (mono)	191 (di)
(+)-Tartaric acid	—	169	—	180 (mono) 264 (di)	171 (mono) 196 (di)
5-Chlorosalicylic acid	—	172	—	—	227
4-Methylbenzoic acid (*p*-toluic acid)	—	180	160	145	160
4-Chloro-3-nitrobenzoic acid	—	182	—	131	156
4-Methoxybenzoic acid (*p*-anisic acid)	—	184	186	169	167
Butanedioic acid (succinic acid)	—	188	180 (mono) 255 (di)	143 (mono) 230 (di)	157 (mono) 260 (di)
4-Ethoxybenzoic acid	—	198	—	170	202
Fumaric acid	—	200 s.	—	233 (mono) 314 (di)	270 (mono) 266 (di)

CARBOXYLIC ACIDS *(Cont.)*

Compound	BP	MP	*p*-Toluidide*	Anilide*	Amide*
3-Hydroxybenzoic acid	—	201 s.	163	157	170
3,5-Dinitrobenzoic acid	—	202	—	234	183
3,4-Dichlorobenzoic acid	—	209	—	—	133
Phthalic acid	—	210 d.	150 (mono)	169 (mono)	144 (mono)
			201 (di)	253 (di)	220 (di)
4-Hydroxybenzoic acid	—	214	204	197	162
3-Nitrophthalic acid	—	215	226 (di)	234 (di)	201 (di)
Pyridine-3-carboxylic acid (nicotinic acid)	—	236	150	132	128
4-Nitrobenzoic acid	—	240	204	211	201
4-Chlorobenzoic acid	—	242	—	194	179
4-Bromobenzoic acid	—	251	—	197	190

Note: "d" indicates "decomposition"; "s" indicates "sublimation."

*See Appendix 2, "Procedures for Preparing Derivatives."

PHENOLS†

Compound	BP	MP	α-Naphthyl-urethane*	Bromo Derivative*			
				Mono	Di	Tri	Tetra
2-Chlorophenol	176	7	120	48	76	—	—
3-Methylphenol (*m*-cresol)	203	12	128	—	—	84	—
2-Ethylphenol	207	—	—	—	—	—	—
2,4-Dimethylphenol	212	23	135	—	—	—	—
2-Methylphenol (*o*-cresol)	191	32	142	—	56	—	—
2-Methoxyphenol (guaiacol)	204	32	118	—	—	116	—
4-Methylphenol (*p*-cresol)	202	35	146	—	49	—	198
3-Chlorophenol	214	35	158	—	—	—	—
4-Methyl-2-nitrophenol	—	35	—	—	—	—	—
2,4-Dibromophenol	238	40	—	95	—	—	—
Phenol	181	42	133	—	—	95	—
4-Chlorophenol	217	43	166	33	90	—	—
4-Ethylphenol	219	45	128	—	—	—	—
2-Nitrophenol	216	45	113	—	117	—	—
2-Isopropyl-5-methylphenol (thymol)	234	51	160	55	—	—	—
4-Methoxyphenol	243	56	—	—	—	—	—
3,4-Dimethylphenol	225	64	141	—	—	171	—
4-Bromophenol	238	64	169	—	—	—	—
4-Chloro-3-methylphenol	235	66	153	—	—	—	—
3,5-Dimethylphenol	220	68	—	—	—	166	—
2,6-Di-*tert*-butyl-4-methylphenol	—	70	—	—	—	—	—

PHENOLS† (Cont.)

Compound	BP	MP	α-Naphthyl-urethane*	Bromo Derivative*			
				Mono	Di	Tri	Tetra
2,4,6-Trimethylphenol	232	72	—	—	—	—	—
2,5-Dimethylphenol	212	75	173	—	—	178	—
1-Naphthol (α-naphthol)	278	94	152	—	105	—	—
2-Methyl-4-nitrophenol	186	96	—	—	—	—	—
2-Hydroxyphenol (catechol)	245	104	175	—	—	—	192
2-Chloro-4-nitrophenol	—	106	—	—	—	—	—
3-Hydroxyphenol (resorcinol)	—	109	—	—	—	112	—
4-Nitrophenol	—	112	150	—	142	—	—
2-Naphthol (β-naphthol)	—	123	157	84	—	—	—
3-Methyl-4-nitrophenol	—	129	—	—	—	—	—
1,2,3-Trihydroxybenzene (pyrogallol)	—	133	—	—	158	—	—
4-Phenylphenol	—	164	—	—	—	—	—

*See Appendix 2, "Procedures for Preparing Derivatives."
†Also check:
  Salicylic acid (2-hydroxybenzoic acid)
  Esters of salicylic acid (salicylates)
  Salicylaldehyde (2-hydroxybenzaldehyde)
  4-Hydroxybenzaldehyde
  4-Hydroxypropiophenone
  3-Hydroxybenzoic acid
  4-Hydroxybenzoic acid
  4-Hydroxybenzophenone

PRIMARY AMINES†

Compound	BP	MP	Benzamide*	Picrate*	Acetamide*
t-Butylamine	46	—	134	198	101
Propylamine	48	—	84	135	—
Allylamine	56	—	—	140	—
sec-Butylamine	63	—	76	139	—
Isobutylamine	69	—	57	150	—
Butylamine	78	—	42	151	—
Isopentylamine (ioamylamine)	96	—	—	138	—
Pentylamine (amylamine)	104	—	—	139	—
Ethylenediamine	118	—	244 (di)	233 (di)	172 (di)
Hexylamine	132	—	40	126	—
Cyclohexylamine	135	—	149	—	101
1,3-Diaminopropane	140	—	148 (di)	250	126 (di)
Furfurylamine	145	—	—	150	—
Heptylamine	156	—	—	121	—

PRIMARY AMINES† *(Cont.)*

Compound	BP	MP	Benzamide*	Picrate*	Acetamide*
Octylamine	180	—	—	112	—
Benzylamine	184	—	105	194	65
Aniline	184	—	163	180	114
2-Methylaniline (*o*-toluidine)	200	—	144	213	110
3-Methylaniline (*m*-toluidine)	203	—	125	200	65
2-Chloroaniline	208	—	99	134	87
2,6-Dimethylaniline	216	11	168	180	177
2,5-Dimethylaniline	216	14	140	171	139
3,5-Dimethylaniline	220	—	144	225	—
4-Isopropylaniline	225	—	162	—	102
2-Methoxyaniline (*o*-anisidine)	225	6	60	200	85
3-Chloroaniline	230	—	120	177	74
2-Ethoxyaniline (*o*-phenetidine)	231	—	104	—	79
4-Chloro-2-methylaniline	241	29	142	—	140
4-Ethoxyaniline (*p*-phenetidine)	250	2	173	69	137
3-Bromoaniline	251	18	120	180	87
2-Bromoaniline	250	31	116	129	99
2,6-Dichloroaniline	—	39	—	—	—
4-Methylaniline (*p*-toluidine)	200	43	158	182	147
2-Ethylaniline	210	47	147	194	111
2,5-Dichloroaniline	251	50	120	86	132
4-Methoxyaniline (*p*-anisidine)	—	58	154	170	130
2,4-Dichloroaniline	245	62	117	106	145
4-Bromoaniline	245	64	204	180	168
4-Chloroaniline	—	72	192	178	179
2-Nitroaniline	—	72	110	73	92
2,4,6-Trichloroaniline	262	75	174	83	204
Ethyl *p*-aminobenzoate	—	89	148	—	110
o-Phenylenediamine	258	102	301 (di)	208	185 (di)
2-Methyl-5-nitroaniline	—	106	186	—	151
4-Aminoacetophenone	—	106	205	—	167
2-Chloro-4-nitroaniline	—	108	161	—	139
3-Nitroaniline	—	114	157	143	155
4-Methyl-2-nitroaniline	—	116	148	—	99
4-Chloro-2-nitroaniline	—	118	133	—	104
2,4,6-Tribromoaniline	—	120	200	—	232
2-Methyl-4-nitroaniline	—	130	—	—	202
2-Methoxy-4-nitroaniline	—	138	149	—	153
p-Phenylenediamine	—	140	128 (mono) 300 (di)	—	162 (mono) 304 (di)
4-Nitroaniline	—	148	199	100	215
4-Aminoacetanilide	—	162	—	—	304
2,4-Dinitroaniline	—	180	202	—	120

*See Appendix 2, "Procedures for Preparing Derivatives."

†Also check 4-aminobenzoic acid and its esters.

SECONDARY AMINES

Compound	BP	MP	Benzamide*	Picrate*	Acetamide*
Diethylamine	56	—	42	155	—
Diisopropylamine	84	—	—	140	—
Pyrrolidine	88	—	Oil	112	—
Piperidine	106	—	48	152	—
Dipropylamine	110	—	—	75	—
Morpholine	129	—	75	146	—
Diisobutylamine	139	—	—	121	86
N-Methylcyclohexylamine	148	—	85	170	—
Dibutylamine	159	—	—	59	—
Benzylmethylamine	184	—	—	117	—
N-Methylaniline	196	—	63	145	102
N-Ethylaniline	205	—	60	132	54
N-Ethyl-m-toluidine	221	—	72	—	—
Dicyclohexylamine	256	—	153	173	103
N-Benzylaniline	298	37	107	48	58
Indole	254	52	68	—	157
Diphenylamine	302	52	180	182	101
N-Phenyl-1-naphthylamine	335	62	152	—	115

*See Appendix 2, "Procedures for Preparing Derivatives."

TERTIARY AMINES†

Compound	BP	MP	Picrate*	Methiodide*
Triethylamine	89	—	173	280
Pyridine	115	—	167	117
2-Methylpyridine (α-picoline)	129	—	169	230
2,6-Dimethylpyridine (2,6-lutidine)	143	—	168	233
4-Methylpyridine (4-picoline)	143	—	167	—
3-Methylpyridine (β-picoline)	144	—	150	92
Tripropylamine	157	—	116	207
N,N-Dimethylbenzylamine	183	—	93	179
N,N-Dimethylaniline	193	—	163	228 d.
Tributylamine	216	—	105	186
N,N-Diethylaniline	217	—	142	102
Quinoline	237	—	203	72/133

Note: "d" indicates "decomposition."

*See Appendix 2, "Procedures for Preparing Derivatives."

†Also check nicotinic acid and its esters.

ALCOHOLS

Compound	BP	MP	3,5-Di-nitrobenzoate*	Phenyl-urethane*
Methanol	65	—	108	47
Ethanol	78	—	93	52
2-Propanol (isopropyl alcohol)	82	—	123	88
2-Methyl-2-propanol (t-butyl alcohol)	83	26	142	136
3-Buten-2-ol	96	—	54	—
2-Propen-1-ol (allyl alcohol)	97	—	49	70
1-Propanol	97	—	74	57
2-Butanol (sec-butyl alcohol)	99	—	76	65
2-Methyl-2-butanol (t-pentyl alcohol)	102	-8.5	116	42
2-Methyl-3-butyn-2-ol	104	—	112	—
2-Methyl-1-propanol (isobutyl alcohol)	108	—	87	86
3-Buten-1-ol	113	—	59	25
3-Methyl-2-butanol	114	—	76	68
2-Propyn-1-ol (propargyl alcohol)	114	—	—	—
3-Pentanol	115	—	101	48
1-Butanol	118	—	64	61
2-Pentanol	119	—	62	—
3,3-Dimethyl-2-butanol	120	—	107	77
2,3-Dimethyl-2-butanol	121	—	111	65
2-Methyl-2-pentanol	123	—	72	—
3-Methyl-3-pentanol	123	—	96	43
2-Methoxyethanol	124	—	—	(113)[†]
2-Methyl-3-pentanol	128	—	85	50
2-Chloroethanol	129	—	95	51
3-Methyl-1-butanol (isoamyl alcohol)	132	—	61	56
4-Methyl-2-pentanol	132	—	65	143
2-Ethoxyethanol	135	—	75	(67)[†]
3-Hexanol	136	—	97	—
1-Pentanol	138	—	46	46
2-Hexanol	139	—	39	(61)[†]
2,4-Dimethyl-3-pentanol	140	—	—	95
Cyclopentanol	140	—	115	132
2-Ethyl-1-butanol	146	—	51	—
2,2,2-Trichloroethanol	151	—	142	87
1-Hexanol	157	—	58	42
2-Heptanol	159	—	49	(54)[†]
Cyclohexanol	160	—	113	82
3-Chloro-1-propanol	161	—	77	38
(2-Furyl)-methanol (furfuryl alcohol)	170	—	80	45
1-Heptanol	176	—	47	60
2-Octanol	179	—	32	114
2-Ethyl-1-hexanol	185	—	—	(61)[†]
1-Octanol	195	—	61	74

ALCOHOLS *(Cont.)*

Compound	BP	MP	3,5-Di-nitrobenzoate*	Phenyl-urethane*
3,7-Dimethyl-1,6-octadien-3-ol (linalool)	196	—	—	66
2-Nonanol	198	—	43	(56)†
Benzyl alcohol	204	—	113	77
1-Phenylethanol	204	20	92	95
1-Nonanol	214	—	52	62
1,3-Propanediol	215	—	178 (di)	137 (di)
2-Phenylethanol	219	—	108	78
1-Decanol	231	7	57	59
3-Phenylpropanol	236	—	45	92
1-Dodecanol (lauryl alcohol)	—	24	60	74
3-Phenyl-2-propen-1-ol (cinnamyl alcohol)	250	34	121	90
α-Terpineol	221	36	78	112
1-Tetradecanol (myristyl alcohol)	—	39	67	74
(–)-Menthol	212	41	158	111
1-Hexadecanol (cetyl alcohol)	—	49	66	73
2,2-Dimethyl-1-propanol (neopentyl alcohol)	113	56	—	144
4-Methylbenzyl alcohol	217	59	117	79
1-Octadecanol (stearyl alcohol)	—	59	77	79
Diphenylmethanol (benzhydrol)	—	68	141	139
4-Nitrobenzyl alcohol	—	93	157	—
Benzoin	—	136	—	165
Cholesterol	—	147	—	168
Triphenylmethanol	—	161	—	—
(+)-Borneol	—	208	154	138

*See Appendix 2, "Procedures for Preparing Derivatives."
†α-Naphthylurethane.

ESTERS

Compound	BP	MP	Compound	BP	MP
Methyl formate	32	—	Ethyl chloroformate	93	—
Ethyl formate	54	—	Methyl isobutyrate	93	—
Methyl acetate	57	—	(methyl 2-methylpropanoate)		
Isopropyl formate	71	—	2-Propenyl acetate (isopropenyl acetate)	94	—
Vinyl acetate	72	—	*tert*-Butyl acetate		
Ethyl acetate	77	—	(1,1-dimethylethyl acetate)	98	—
Methyl propionate			Ethyl propionate (ethyl propanoate)	99	—
(methyl propanoate)	80	—	Methyl methacrylate		
Methyl acrylate	80	—	(methyl 2-methylpropenoate)	100	—
Propyl formate	81	—	Methyl pivalate		
Isopropyl acetate	89	—	(methyl trimethyl acetate)	101	—

ESTERS *(Cont.)*

Compound	BP	MP	Compound	BP	MP
Ethyl acrylate (ethyl propenoate)	101	—	Ethyl heptanoate	187	—
Propyl acetate	102	—	Heptyl acetate	192	—
Methyl butyrate (methyl butanoate)	102	—	Dimethyl succinate	196	—
Ethyl isobutyrate			Phenyl acetate	197	—
(ethyl 2-methylpropanoate)	110	—	Diethyl malonate	199	—
Isopropyl propionate			Methyl benzoate	199	—
(isopropyl propanoate)	110	—	Dimethyl maleate	204	—
2-Butyl acetate (*sec*-butyl acetate)	111	—	Ethyl levulinate	206	—
Methyl isovalerate	117	—	Ethyl octanoate	208	—
(methyl 3-methylbutanoate)			Ethyl cyanoacetate	208	—
Isobutyl acetate			Ethyl benzoate	212	—
(2-methylpropyl acetate)	117	—	Benzyl acetate	217	—
Ethyl pivalate			Diethyl succinate	217	—
(ethyl 2,2-dimethylpropanoate)	118	—	Diethyl fumarate	219	—
Methyl crotonate (methyl 2-butenoate)	119	—	Methyl phenylacetate	220	—
Ethyl butyrate (ethyl butanoate)	121	—	Methyl salicylate	224	—
Propyl propionate (propyl propanoate)	123	—	Diethyl maleate	224	—
Butyl acetate	126	—	Ethyl phenylacetate	228	—
Methyl valerate (methyl pentanoate)	128	—	Propyl benzoate	231	—
Methyl methoxyacetate	130	—	Ethyl salicylate	234	—
Methyl chloroacetate	130	—	Dimethyl suberate	268	—
Ethyl isovalerate			Ethyl cinnamate	271	—
(ethyl 3-methylbutanoate)	134	—	Dimethyl phthalate	284	—
Ethyl crotonate (ethyl 2-butenoate)	138	—	Diethyl phthalate	298	—
Isopentyl acetate			Methyl cinnamate	—	36
(3-methylbutyl acetate)	142	—	Ethyl 2-furoate	—	36
2-Methoxyethyl acetate	145	—	Methyl stearate	—	39
Ethyl chloroacetate	145	—	Dimethyl itaconate	—	39
Ethyl valerate (ethyl pentanoate)	146	—	Phenyl salicylate	—	42
Ethyl α-chloropropanoate	146	—	Diethyl terephthalate	—	44
Pentyl acetate	147	—	Methyl 4-chlorobenzoate	—	44
Methyl hexanoate	151	—	Ethyl 3-nitrobenzoate	—	47
Ethyl lactate	154	—	Methyl mandelate	—	53
Butyl butyrate	167	—	Ethyl 4-nitrobenzoate	—	56
Ethyl hexanoate	168	—	Dimethyl isophthalate	—	68
Hexyl acetate	169	—	Phenyl benzoate	—	69
Methyl acetoacetate	170	—	Methyl 3-nitrobenzoate	—	78
Methyl heptanoate (methyl enanthlate)	172	—	Methyl 4-bromobenzoate	—	81
Furfuryl acetate	176	—	Ethyl 4-aminobenzoate	—	89
Methyl 2-furoate	181	—	Methyl 4-nitrobenzoate	—	96
Dimethyl malonate	181	—	Dimethyl fumarate	—	102
Ethyl acetoacetate	181	—	Cholesterol acetate	—	114
Diethyl oxalate	185	—	Ethyl 4-hydroxybenzoate	—	116

APPENDIX 2

Procedures for Preparing Derivatives

> **CAUTION**
>
> Some of the chemicals used in preparing derivatives are suspected carcinogens. Before beginning any of these procedures, consult the list of suspected carcinogens on pp. 561–562. Exercise care in handling these substances.

ALDEHYDES AND KETONES

Semicarbazones

Place 0.5 mL of a 2M stock solution of semicarbazide hydrochloride (or 0.5 mL of a solution prepared by dissolving 1.11 g of semicarbazide hydrochloride [$MW = 111.5$] in 5 mL of water) in a small test tube. Add 0.15 g of the unknown compound to the test tube. If the unknown does not dissolve in the solution or if the solution becomes cloudy, add enough methanol (maximum of 2 mL) to dissolve the solid and produce a clear solution. If a solid or cloudiness remains after adding 2 mL of methanol, do not add any more methanol and continue this procedure with the solid present. Using a Pasteur pipet, add 10 drops of pyridine and heat the mixture in a hotwater bath (about 60°C) for about 10–15 minutes. By that time, the product should have begun to crystallize. Collect the product by vacuum filtration. The product can be recrystallized from ethanol if necessary.

Semicarbazones (Alternative Method)

Dissolve 0.25 g of semicarbazide hydrochloride and 0.38 g of sodium acetate in 1.3 mL of water. Then dissolve 0.25 g of the unknown in 2.5 mL of ethanol. Mix the two solutions together in a 25-mL Erlenmeyer flask and heat the mixture to boiling for about 5 minutes. After heating the mixture, place the reaction flask in a beaker of ice and scratch the sides of the flask with a glass rod to induce crystallization of the derivative. Collect the derivative by vacuum filtration and recrystallize it from ethanol.

2, 4-Dinitrophenylhydrazones

Place 10 mL of a solution of 2, 4-dinitrophenylhydrazine (prepared as described for the classification test in Experiment 54D) in a test tube and add 0.15 g of the unknown compound. If the unknown is a solid, it should be dissolved in the minimum amount of 95% ethanol or 1,2-dimethoxyethane before it is added. If crystallization is not immediate, gently warm the solution for a minute in a hotwater bath (90°C) and then set it aside to crystallize. Collect the product by vacuum filtration.

CARBOXYLIC ACIDS

Working in a hood, place 0.50 g of the acid and 2 mL of thionyl chloride into a small round-bottom flask. Add a magnetic stir bar, and attach a water-jacketed condenser and a drying tube packed with calcium chloride to the flask. While stirring, heat the reaction mixture to boiling for 30 minutes on a hot plate. Allow the mixture to cool to room temperature. Use this mixture to prepare the amide, anilide, or *p*-toluidide derivatives by one of the following three procedures.

Amides

Working in a hood, add the thionyl chloride/carboxylic acid mixture dropwise from a Pasteur pipet into a beaker containing 5 mL of ice-cold concentrated ammonium hydroxide. The reaction is very exothermic. Stir the mixture vigorously after the addition for about 5 minutes. When the reaction is complete, collect the product by vacuum filtration and recrystallize it from water or from water–ethanol, using the mixed-solvents method (See Technique 11, Section 11.10).

Anilides

Dissolve 0.5 g of aniline in 13 mL of methylene chloride in a 50-mL Erlenmeyer flask. Using a Pasteur pipet, carefully add the mixture of thionyl chloride/carboxylic acid to this solution. Warm the mixture for an additional 5 minutes on a hot plate, unless a significant color change occurs. *If a color change occurs,* discontinue heating, add a magnetic stir bar, and stir the mixture for 20 minutes at room temperature. Then transfer the methylene chloride solution to a small separatory funnel and wash it sequentially with 2.5 mL of water, 2.5 mL of 5% hydrochloric acid, 2.5 mL of 5% sodium hydroxide, and a second 2.5-mL portion of water (the methylene chloride solution should be the bottom layer). Dry the methylene chloride layer over a small amount of anhydrous sodium sulfate. Decant the methylene chloride layer away from the drying agent into a small flask and evaporate the methylene chloride on a warm hot plate in the hood. Use a stream of air or nitrogen to speed up the evaporation. Recrystallize the product from water or from ethanol–water, using the mixed-solvents method (See Technique 11, Section 11.10).

p-Toluidides

Use the same procedure as that described in preparing anilides, but substitute *p*-toluidine for aniline.

PHENOLS

α-Naphthylurethanes

Follow the procedure given later for preparing phenylurethanes from alcohols, but substitute α-naphthylisocyanate for phenylisocyanate.

Bromo Derivatives

First, if a stock brominating solution is not available, prepare one by dissolving 0.75 g of potassium bromide in 5 mL of water and adding 0.5 g of bromine. Dissolve 0.1 g of the phenol in 1 mL of methanol or 1,2-dimethoxyethane; then add 1 mL of water. Add 1 mL of the brominating mixture to the phenol solution and swirl the mixture vigorously. Then continue adding the brominating solution dropwise while swirling, until the color of the bromine reagent persists. Finally, add 3–5 mL of water and shake the mixture vigorously. Collect the precipitated product by vacuum filtration and wash it well with water. Recrystallize the derivative from methanol–water, using the mixed-solvents method (See Technique 11, Section 11.10).

AMINES

Acetamides

Place 0.15 g of the amine and 0.5 mL of acetic anhydride in a small Erlenmeyer flask. Heat the mixture for about 5 minutes; then add 5 mL of water and stir the solution vigorously to precipitate the product and hydrolyze the excess acetic anhydride. If the product does not crystallize, it may be necessary to scratch the walls of the flask with a glass rod. Collect the crystals by vacuum filtration and wash them with several portions of cold 5% hydrochloric acid. Recrystallize the derivative from methanol–water, using the mixed-solvents method (See Technique 11, Section 11.10).

Aromatic amines, or those amines that are not very basic, may require pyridine (2 mL) as a solvent and a catalyst for the reaction. If pyridine is used, a longer period of heating is required (up to 1 hour), and the reaction should be carried out in an apparatus equipped with a reflux condenser. After reflux, the reaction mixture must be extracted with 5–10 mL of 5% sulfuric acid to remove the pyridine.

Benzamides

Using a centrifuge tube, suspend 0.15 g of the amine in 1 mL of 10% sodium hydroxide solution and add 0.5 g of benzoyl chloride. Cap the tube and shake the mixture vigorously for about 10 minutes. After shaking the mixture, add enough dilute hydrochloric acid to bring the pH of the solution to pH 7 or 8. Collect the precipitate by vacuum filtration, wash it thoroughly with cold water, and recrystallize it from ethanol–water, using the mixed-solvents method (See Technique 11, Section 11.10).

Benzamides (Alternative Method)

In a small round-bottom flask, dissolve 0.25 g of the amine in a solution of 1.2 mL of pyridine and 2.5 mL of toluene. Add 0.25 mL of benzoyl chloride to the solution, and heat the mixture under reflux for about 30 minutes. Pour the cooled reaction mixture into 25 mL of water, and stir the mixture vigorously to hydrolyze the excess benzoyl chloride. Separate the toluene layer and wash it, first with 1.5 mL of water, and then with 1.5 mL of 5% sodium carbonate. Dry the toluene over granular anhydrous sodium sulfate, decant the toluene into a small Erlenmeyer flask, and remove the toluene by evaporation on a hot plate in the hood. Use a stream of air or nitrogen to speed up the evaporation. Recrystallize the benzamide from ethanol or ethanol–water, using the mixed-solvents method (See Technique 11, Section 11.10).

Picrates

In an Erlenmeyer flask, dissolve 0.2 g of the unknown in about 5 mL of ethanol and add 5 mL of a saturated solution of picric acid in ethanol. Heat the solution to boiling and then allow it to cool slowly. Collect the product by vacuum filtration and rinse it with a small amount of cold ethanol.

CAUTION

Great care must be taken when working with saturated solutions of picric acid. Picric acid may detonate when heated above 300°C. It is also known to explode when hearted rapidly. For this reason, it is strongly recommended that you check with your instructor before preparing this derivation.

Methiodides

Mix equal-volume quantities of the amine and methyl iodide in a small round-bottom flask (about 0.25 mL is sufficient) and allow the mixture to stand for several minutes. Then heat the mixture gently under reflux for about 5 minutes. The methiodide should crystallize on cooling. If it does not, you can induce crystallization by scratching the walls of the flask with a glass rod. Collect the product by vacuum filtration and recrystallize it from ethanol or ethyl acetate.

ALCOHOLS

3,5-Dinitrobenzoates

Liquid Alcohols

Dissolve 0.25 g of 3,5-dinitrobenzoyl chloride in 0.25 mL of the alcohol and heat the mixture for about 5 minutes[1]. Allow the mixture to cool and add 1.5 mL of a 5% sodium carbonate solution and 1 mL of water. Stir the mixture vigorously and crush any solid that forms. Collect the product by vacuum filtration, and wash it with cold water. Recrystallize the derivative from ethanol–water, using the mixed-solvents method (See Technique 11, Section 11.10).

Solid Alcohols

Dissolve 0.25 g of the alcohol in 1.5 mL of dry pyridine and add 0.25 g of 3, 5-dinitrobenzoyl chloride. Heat the mixture under reflux for 15 minutes. Pour the cooled reaction mixture into a cold mixture of 2.5 mL of 5% sodium carbonate and 2.5 mL of water. Keep the solution cooled in an ice bath until the product crystallizes, and stir it vigorously during the entire period. Collect the product by vacuum filtration, wash it with cold water, and recrystallize it from ethanol–water, using the mixed-solvents method (See Technique 11, Section 11.10).

Phenylurethanes

Place 0.25 g of the *anhydrous* alcohol in a dry test tube and add 0.25 mL of phenyliso-cyanate (α-naphthylisocyanate for a phenol). If the compound is a phenol, add 1 drop of pyridine to catalyze the reaction. If the reaction is not spontaneous, heat the mixture in a hot-water bath (90°C) for 5–10 minutes. Cool the test tube in a beaker of ice, and scratch the tube with a glass rod to induce crystallization. Decant the liquid from the solid product or, if necessary, collect the product by vacuum fil-tration. Dissolve the product in 2.5–3 mL of hot ligroin or hexane, and filter the mix-ture by gravity (preheat funnel) to remove any unwanted and insoluble dipheny-lurea present. Cool the filtrate to induce crystallization of the urethane. Collect the product by vacuum filtration.

ESTERS

We recommend that esters be characterized by spectroscopic methods whenever possible. A derivative of the alcohol part of an ester can be prepared with the fol-lowing procedure. For other derivatives, consult a comprehensive textbook. Several are listed in Experiment 55I.

3,5-Dinitrobenzoates

Place 1.0 mL of the ester and 0.75 g of 3,5-dinitrobenzoic acid in a small round-bottom flask. Add 2 drops of concentrated sulfuric acid and a magnetic stir bar to the flask and attach a condenser. If the boiling point of the ester is above 150°C, heat at reflux while stirring for 30–45 minutes. If the boiling point of the ester is above 150°C, heat the mixture at about 150°C for 30–45 minutes. Cool the mixture, and transfer it to a small separatory funnel. Add 10 mL of ether. Extract the ether layer 2 times with 5 mL of 5% aqueous sodium carbonate (save the ether layer). Wash the organic layer with 5 mL of water, and dry the ether solution over magnesium sul-fate. Evaporate the ether in a hot-water bath in the hood. Use a stream of air or

---

[1] 3,5-Dinnitrobenzoyl chloride is an acid chloride and hydrolysis readily. The purity of this reagent should be checked before its use by determining its melting point (mp 69–71°C). When the car-boxylic acid is present, the melting point will be high.

nitrogen to speed the evaporation. Dissolve the residue, usually an oil, in 2 mL of boiling ethanol and add water dropwise until the mixture becomes cloudy. Cool the solution to induce crystallization of the derivative.

Preparation of a Solid Carboxylic Acid from an Ester.

An excellent derivative of an ester can be prepared by a basic hydrolysis of an ester when it yields a solid carboxylic acid. A procedure is provided in Experiment 55I. Melting points for solid carboxylic acids are included in the Carboxylic Acids Table in Appendix 1.

3 APPENDIX 3

Index of Spectra

INFRARED SPECTRA

^{1}H NMR SPECTRA

Benzocaine 352
Benzyl acetate (60-MHz NMR spectrum) 893
Benzyl acetate (300-MHz NMR spectrum) 894
Borneol 262
Camphor 262
Carvone 110
N,N-Diethyl-m-toluamide 364
6-Ethoxycarbonyl-3,5-diphenyl-2-cyclohexenone 326
Ethyl 3-hydroxybutanoate 233
1-Hexanol 914
(E)-4-(4-Hydroxy-3-methoxyphenyl)-2-buten-1-ol 309
(R)-4-Hydroxy-5-methyl-2-hexanone 320
Isoborneol 263
Limonene 110
Phenylacetone 887
1,1,2-Trichloroethane 900
Vegetable oil 217
Vinyl acetate 904

^{13}C NMR SPECTRA

Borneol 264
Camphor 263
Carvone 111
Cyclohexanol 929
Cyclohexanone 930
Cyclohexene 930
2,2-Dimethylbutane 928
Ethyl phenylacetate 926
Isoborneol 264
1-Propanol 927
Toluene 931

MASS SPECTRA

Acetophenone 954
Benzaldehyde 953
Bromoethane 945
1-Bromohexane 957
Butane 948
1-Butanol 952
2-Butanone 954
1-Butene 950
Chloroethane 944
Cyclopentane 950
Dopamine 941
Methyl butanoate 956

ULTRAVIOLET–VISIBLE SPECTRA

MIXTURES

Infrared Absorption Bands

		Type of Vibration	Frequency (cm^{21})	Intensity
C—H	Alkanes	(stretch)	3000–2850	s
	—CH$_3$	(bend)	1450 and 1375	m
	—CH$_2$—	(bend)	1465	m
	Alkenes	(stretch)	3100–3000	m
		(out-of-plane bend)	1000–650	s
	Aromatics	(stretch)	3150–3050	s
		(out-of-plane bend)	900–690	s
	Alkyne	(stretch)	ca. 3300	s
	Aldehyde		2900–2800	w
			2800–2700	w
O—H	Alcohol, phenols			
	Free		3650–3600	m
	H-bonded		3400–3200	m
	Carboxylic acids		3400–2400	m
N—H	Primary and secondary amines and amides			
	(stretch)		3500–3100	m
	(bend)		1640–1550	m–s
C≡C	Alkyne		2250–2100	m–w
C≡N	Nitriles		2260–2240	m
C=C	Alkene		1680–1600	m–w
	Aromatic		1600 and 1475	m–w
N=O	Nitro (R—NO$_2$)		1550 and 1350	s
C=O	Aldehyde		1740–1720	s
	Ketone		1725–1705	s
	Carboxylic acid		1725–1700	s
	Ester		1750–1730	s
	Amide		1680–1630	s
	Anhydride		1810 and 1760	s
	Acid chloride		1800	s
C—O	Alcohols, ethers, esters, carboxylic acids, anhydrides		1300–1000	s
C—N	Amines		1350–1000	m–s
C—X	Fluoride		1400–1000	s
	Chloride		785–540	s
	Bromide, iodide		< 667	s

NMR Chemical Shift Ranges (ppm) for Selected Protons

Group		Shift (ppm)	Group	Shift (ppm)
R–CH$_3$		0.7–1.3	R–N–C–H	2.2–2.9
R–CH$_2$–R		1.2–1.4		
R$_3$CH		1.4–1.7	R–S–C–H	2.0–3.0
R–C=C–C–H		1.6–2.6	I–C–H	2.0–4.0
R–C(=O)–C–H, H–C(=O)–C–H		2.1–2.4	Br–C–H	2.7–4.1
RO–C(=O)–C–H, HO–C(=O)–C–H		2.1–2.5	Cl–C–H	3.1–4.1
N≡C–C–H		2.1–3.0	R–S(=O)(=O)–O–C–H	ca. 3.0
(phenyl)–C–H		2.3–2.7	RO–C–H, HO–C–H	3.2–3.8
R–C≡C–H		1.7–2.7	R–C(=O)–O–C–H	3.5–4.8
R–S–H	var	1.0–4.0[a]	O$_2$N–C–H	4.1–4.3
R–N–H	var	0.5–4.0[a]	F–C–H	4.2–4.8
R–O–H	var	0.5–5.0[a]		
(phenyl)–O–H	var	4.0–7.0[a]	R–C=C–H	4.5–6.5
			(phenyl)–H	6.5–8.0
(phenyl)–N–H	var	3.0–5.0[a]	R–C(=O)–H	9.0–10.0
R–C(=O)–N–H	var	5.0–9.0[a]	R–C(=O)–OH	11.0–12.0

Note: For those hydrogens shown as —C—H, if that hydrogen is part of a methyl group (CH$_3$), the shift is generally at the low end of the range given; if the hydrogen is in a methylene group (—CH$_2$—), the shift is intermediate; and if the hydrogen is in a methine group (—CH—), the shift is typically at the high end of the range given.

[a] The chemical shift of these groups is variable, depending on the chemical environment in the molecule and on concentration, temperature, and solvent.